"Parke Wilde provides an indispensable introduction to U.S. food policy, and he helps shed much needed light on some of the complexities of the modern agriculture system and how it is affected by food and farm policy. Although I am less sanguine than Wilde about the ability of food policy to provide major fixes, he helps provide a solid foundation and framework for understanding the merits and demerits of food policy proposals."

– **Jayson Lusk**, Distinguished Professor and Head of the Department of Agricultural Economics, Purdue University, USA

"Parke Wilde's new second edition provides an excellent foundation for my course in Agricultural and Food Policy. I greatly appreciate the diverse viewpoints considered and the broad range of topics covered."

– **Larry Lev**, Professor and Extension Economist, Department of Applied Economics, Oregon State University, USA

Praise for the First Edition

"*Food Policy in the United States* is essential reading for anyone who wants to understand how our food system really works or to take action to change it. Professor Wilde provides a tough but balanced and decidedly nonpartisan overview of the facts behind the full range of policy areas – among them agricultural support, safety, dietary guidance – that affect food production and consumption. If you want to join the food movement to improve the system, here's how to find out where to start."

– **Marion Nestle**, Professor of Nutrition, Food Studies, and Public Health at New York University, USA, and author of Food Politics

"More than ever before, those of us who care about U.S. nutrition policy recognize that we need to pay attention to a whole wide world of policy and economic issues – including farm policy, food manufacturing, supermarkets, anti-hunger programs and more. For my students—and my colleagues—it can seem daunting! Without oversimplifying, *Food Policy in the United States* opens the doorway to these broader conversations and debates."

– **Miriam Nelson**, Ph.D., Nutrition Scientist, Professor and Best-selling Author of the Strong Women book series

"This is a very engaging book on the key issues of the food systems and policies today. The topics and material make an excellent foundation for classroom discussion and learning. Parke Wilde asks provocative questions throughout that help to engage the reader and reinforce the importance of trying to understand the economic factors and policy process. I look forward to having this book available for students!"

– **Helen H. Jensen**, Professor of Economics and Head of the Food and Nutrition Policy Division at the Centre for Agricultural and Rural Development, Iowa State University, USA

"Substance beyond many populist food politics-type books which have surged over the past decade distinguishes Dr. Wilde's contribution. His knowledgeable approach to underlying market (and government) failure which motivates the food policy topic of concern comes from his own background and experience in academia, government and working with NGOs. Occasional notes on advocacy come as a refreshing "so what" for the reader."

– Neal Hooker, Professor of Food Policy in the John Glenn
School of Public Affairs, Ohio State University, USA

Food Policy in the United States

This new edition offers a timely update to the leading textbook dedicated to all aspects of U.S. food policy. The update accounts for experience with policy changes in the 2014 Farm Bill and prospects for the next Farm Bill, the publication of the *2015–2020 Dietary Guidelines for Americans*, the removal of Generally Recognized as Safe (GRAS) status for *trans* fats, the collapse of the Trans Pacific Partnership (TPP) treaty, stalled child nutrition reauthorization legislation, reforms in food-labeling policy, the consequences of the 2016 presidential election and many other developments. The second edition offers greater attention both to food justice issues and to economic methods, including extensive economics appendices in a new online Companion Website.

As with the first edition, real-world controversies and debates motivate the book's attention to economic principles, policy analysis, nutrition science and contemporary data sources. The book assumes that the reader's concern is not just the economic interests of farmers and food producers but also includes nutrition, sustainable agriculture, food justice, the environment and food security. The goal is to make U.S. food policy more comprehensible to those inside and outside the agri-food sector whose interests and aspirations have been ignored.

The chapters cover U.S. agriculture, food production and the environment, international agricultural trade, food and beverage manufacturing, food retail and restaurants, food safety, dietary guidance, food labeling, advertising and federal food assistance programs for the poor.

The author is an agricultural economist with many years of experience in the nonprofit advocacy sector, the U.S. Department of Agriculture and as a professor at Tufts University. The author's blog on U.S. food policy provides a forum for discussion and debate of the issues set out in the book.

Parke Wilde is a food economist and professor at the Friedman School of Nutrition Science and Policy at Tufts University, Boston, USA. Previously, he worked for the Community Nutrition Institute and for USDA's Economic Research Service. He received his Ph.D. in agricultural economics from Cornell University, USA. At Tufts, Parke teaches graduate-level courses in statistics and U.S. food policy. His research addresses food security and hunger measurement, the economics of food assistance programs and federal dietary guidance policy. He is a director of the Tufts/University of Connecticut Research Innovation and Development Grants in Economics (RIDGE) Program. He has been a member of the Institute of Medicine's Food Forum and of the research committee advising AGree, a national food policy initiative. He is on the editorial board of *Applied Economics Perspectives and Policy* and keeps a blog at usfoodpolicy.com.

Other books in the Earthscan Food and Agriculture Series

For further details please visit the series page on the Routledge website:
http://www.routledge.com/books/series/ECEFA/

Environmental Justice and Farm Labor
Rebecca E. Berkey

Plantation Crops, Plunder and Power
Evolution and Exploitation
James F. Hancock

Food Security, Agricultural Policies and Economic Growth
Long-Term Dynamics in the Past, Present and Future
Niek Koning

Agriculture and Rural Development in a Globalizing World
Challenges and Opportunities
Edited by Prabhu Pingali and Gershon Feder

Food, Agriculture and Social Change
The Vitality of Everyday Food in Latin America
Edited by Stephen Sherwood, Alberto Arce and Myriam Paredes

Contract Farming and the Development of Smallholder Agricultural Businesses
Improving Markets and Value Chains in Tanzania
Edited by Joseph A. Kuzilwa, Niels Fold, Arne Henningsen and Marianne Nylandsted Larsen

Agribusiness and the Neoliberal Food System in Brazil
Frontiers and Fissures of Agro-neoliberalism
Antonio Augusto Rossotto Ioris

The Meat Crisis (2ed)
Developing more Sustainable and Ethical Production and Consumption
Edited by Joyce D'Silva and John Webster

Resistance to the Neoliberal Agri-Food Regime
A Critical Analysis
Edited by Alessandro Bonanno and Steven A. Wolf

Food Policy in the United States

An Introduction

Second Edition

Parke Wilde

Routledge
Taylor & Francis Group

NEW YORK AND LONDON

from Routledge

Second edition published 2018
by Routledge
711 Third Avenue, New York, NY 10017

and by Routledge
2 Park Square, Milton Park, Abingdon, Oxon, OX14 4RN

Routledge is an imprint of the Taylor & Francis Group, an informa business

© 2018 Parke Wilde

First edition published by Routledge 2013

British Library Cataloguing-in-Publication Data
A catalogue record for this book is available from the British Library

Library of Congress Cataloging-in-Publication Data
Names: Wilde, Parke, author.
Title: Food policy in the United States : an introduction / Parke Wilde.
Description: Second edition. | New York, NY : Routledge, 2018. | Includes
    bibliographical references and index.
Identifiers: LCCN 2017047011 | ISBN 9781138203983 (hardback) |
    ISBN 9781138204003 (pbk.) | ISBN 9781315470337 (ebook)
Subjects: LCSH: Nutrition policy—United States.
Classification: LCC TX360.U6 W55 2018 | DDC 363.8/5610973—dc23
LC record available at https://lccn.loc.gov/2017047011

ISBN: 978-1-138-20398-3 (hbk)
ISBN: 978-1-138-20400-3 (pbk)
ISBN: 978-1-315-47033-7 (ebk)

Typeset in Sabon
by Apex CoVantage, LLC

Visit the companion website: www.routledge.com/cw/wilde

Contents

Illustrations

Figures

Tables

Boxes

Acknowledgments

This book owes debts to more people than can possibly be acknowledged. My first mentors in food policy were Ray Hopkins at Swarthmore College and Rodney Leonard at the Community Nutrition Institute. That was a quarter of a century ago. This book carries echoes of the voices of dozens of people since that time who have shared their wisdom and insight. I am thankful for conversations with teachers, colleagues, teaching assistants and research collaborators who read early versions of the thoughts presented here. I am especially grateful to more than 400 students over 14 years who took the second-year graduate-level course in U.S. food policy at the Friedman School of Nutrition Science and Policy at Tufts University, on which this book is based.

Tufts University and the Friedman School contributed to this project in many ways, including support for a sabbatical year, during which half of the first edition was written. During that year, Dan Sumner and Julian Alston at the University of California, Davis, were generous hosts and fascinating teachers. Research support from USDA's Economic Research Service and Food and Nutrition Service, including two projects with terrific colleagues at Abt Associates, contributed indirectly to making that writing year possible.

Many colleagues and reviewers gave valuable comments on draft chapters, including Will Masters, Helen Jensen, Miriam Nelson, Marion Nestle, Tim Griffin, Mike Reed, Michael Carolan, Ben Senauer, Sara Folta, Dan Sumner, Margaret Wilde and Ted Wilde. Bea Rogers, who also has taught the U.S. food policy class at the Friedman School, offered great advice. My Ph.D. students Mehreen Ismail, Sara John, Joseph Llobrera and Natalie Valpiani enjoyed turning the tables and editing my writing for a change. I tried to recruit Friedman School Ph.D. student Dan Hatfield as a research assistant, but his skills and initiative so far surpassed expectations that he became a coauthor of Chapters 5 and 6, an editor of several other chapters and a valued adviser throughout. Tim Hardwick at Earthscan was an excellent editor, whose early interest, later patience and constant good advice were essential ingredients. All remaining errors and omissions are my own.

My children, Isaac and Keziah, and my wife, Sarah, invested their hearts in this project and also gave me time to write. And, perhaps more importantly, they reminded me at times to turn off the computer and go trekking with them.

Acronyms

ABA	American Beverage Association
ARC	Agricultural Risk Coverage program
AICR	American Institute of Cancer Research
AMS	Agricultural Marketing Service
ARMS	Agricultural Resource Management Survey
ARRA	American Recovery and Reinvestment Act
BBB	Council of Better Business Bureaus
BLS	Bureau of Labor Statistics
BMI	body mass index
BSE	bovine spongiform encephalopathy
CAFO	concentrated animal feeding operation
CBO	Congressional Budget Office
CDC	Centers for Disease Control and Prevention
CNPP	Center for Nutrition Policy and Promotion
CPI	Consumer Price Index
CPS	Current Population Survey
CR4	four-firm concentration ratio
CRP	Conservation Reserve Program
CRS	Congressional Research Service
CSP	Conservation Stewardship Program
CSPI	Center for Science in the Public Interest
D	Democrat
DGAC	Dietary Guidelines Advisory Committee
DHHS	Department of Health and Human Services
DOJ	Department of Justice
DSHEA	Dietary Supplement Health and Education Act
EBT	electronic benefit transfer
EPA	Environmental Protection Agency
EQIP	Environmental Quality Incentives Program
ERS	Economic Research Service
EWG	Environmental Working Group
FAO	Food and Agriculture Organization
FCC	Federal Communications Commission
FDA	Food and Drug Administration
FNS	Food and Nutrition Service
FOIA	Freedom of Information Act
FRAC	Food Research and Action Center

FSA	Farm Service Agency
FSIS	Food Safety and Inspection Service
FSMA	Food Safety Modernization Act
FTC	Federal Trade Commission
FTE	full-time equivalent
GAO	Government Accountability Office
GATT	General Agreement on Tariffs and Trade
GCFI	gross cash farm income
GDP	gross domestic product
GE	genetically engineered
GIPSA	Grain Inspection, Packers and Stockyards Administration
GMA	Grocery Manufacturers Association
GMO	genetically modified organism
GRAS	Generally Recognized as Safe
HACCP	hazard analysis and critical control points
HFCS	high-fructose corn syrup
HFFI	Healthy Food Financing Initiative
HHI	Herfindahl-Hirschman Index
IOM	Institute of Medicine
IWG	Interagency Working Group
MPS	market price support
NAD	National Advertising Division
NAFTA	North American Free Trade Agreement
NLEA	Nutrition Labeling and Education Act
NRCS	Natural Resources Conservation Service
NSLP	National School Lunch Program
OECD	Organisation for Economic Co-operation and Development
OIG	Office of the Inspector General
PDP	Pesticide Data Program
PLC	Price Loss Coverage program
PSE	producer support estimate
R	Republican
RACC	reference amount customarily consumed
ROW	Rest of World
RTE	ready-to-eat
SBP	School Breakfast Program
SFA	School Food Authority
SNAP	Supplemental Nutrition Assistance Program
SNDA	School Nutrition Dietary Assessment
SPS	sanitary and phytosanitary
STEC	Shiga toxin-producing *Escherichia coli*
TEFAP	The Emergency Food Assistance Program
TFP	Thrifty Food Plan
TPP	Trans Pacific Partnership
UEP	United Egg Producers
USAID	U.S. Agency for International Development
USDA	U.S. Department of Agriculture
WIC	Special Supplemental Nutrition Program for Women, Infants and Children
WTO	World Trade Organization

Supplementary Material

Additional Resources are available on the Companion Website for this book at www.routledge.com/cw/wilde, and include the following. Further items may be added to the website from time to time.

- Supplemental **economics appendices** provide additional insight into supply and demand functions at the market level, the concept of elasticity, competitive markets for agricultural commodities, and the economics of consumer demand in response to a price change. These build upon and connect with the 14 **economics boxes** in the text itself on topics including the economics of price supports, deficiency payments, labor markets for farmworkers, fishery overharvesting, international trade in corn, trade barriers, market power for sellers, market power for buyers, time use, monopolistic competition, consumer choice, food safety technology, and the economics of a targeted food benefit. Taken together, these materials offer great opportunities for teachers and readers who seek to use food policy examples to motivate study of economics, but without breaking the flow of the main narrative for other readers.
- Supplemental **program summary tables** provide additional quantitative and historical information about government programs that are important in U.S. food policy, including Price Loss Coverage (PLC), the Environmental Quality Incentives Program (EQIP), the Conservation Stewardship Program (CSP), The Emergency Food Assistance Program (TEFAP), the School Breakfast Program (SBP), and the Child and Adult Care Food Program (CACFP).
- **Problem sets** for each chapter provide questions and answer keys for deeper study of U.S. food policy. These may be used as examples or templates for instructors developing questions on all aspects of the course.
- **Activities and role-playing exercises** offer opportunities for lively class-room discussions. For example, in a power mapping exercise called "Who's the Boss?", students score the political power of leading industry and non-governmental advocacy constituencies in U.S. food policy, providing evidence and arguments for their assigned scores. Later, in two activities titled "Let's Make a Deal" these scores are used as voting weights in a role-playing coalition-building exercise.
- **Online links** connect with sources of information, news, and public discussion.

1 Making Food Policy in the United States

1.1 Introduction

This book offers an introduction to food policy in the United States. **Food policy** encompasses laws, regulations, decisions and actions by governments and other institutions that influence food production, distribution and consumption. While food policy is defined broadly, a **food program** is a more specific institution that provides or distributes food.

Food policy is intertwined with many of the fundamental economic and social decisions of the day. Will traditional farming in the United States disappear as an economically viable way of life? Can U.S. agriculture contribute to nourishing a growing world population without destroying the environment? What are the causes of low wages for farmworkers? Does globalization help or harm U.S. farmers and food consumers? How can the safety of food be protected without imposing unnecessarily burdensome rules and regulations? What can be done about the epidemic of obesity and chronic disease? How can school lunches be improved? Why do some families go hungry in such a rich country?

U.S. food policy is an important topic for readers in the United States and also in other countries. The United States is the world's largest exporter for some crops and a leading importer for others. The U.S. government position carries considerable weight in multinational policy decisions about globalization and international trade. Consumers around the world aspire to emulate some aspects of U.S. consumer culture, even as doubts arise about the nutritional merit and environmental sustainability of U.S. food consumption patterns. Some environmental constraints on U.S. agricultural production are local, but others are global. In these respects, the implications of U.S. food policy extend beyond national borders.

This book focuses on national-level food policy in the United States, but there are similarities with policy-making at other levels of government and in other institutions. **Federalism** refers to the division of authority between the national government and state and local governments. Policy innovations may be first attempted at the state and local level and later adopted at the federal level.

U.S. food policy is absorbing in part because it is dysfunctional. Just as other areas of politics in the United States suffer from partisanship and deep regional and cultural divisions, food policy can become mired down in bitter struggles across stagnant political lines in the sand. On topics ranging from genetically modified organisms (GMOs) to advertising that targets children, it can seem as if no policy actors have either changed their mind or persuaded an opponent in the past generation.

Faced with such challenges, it may be worthwhile to climb down from the ramparts and devote some time to reflection and study. To some extent, this book is a descendant of hefty agricultural policy textbooks such as traditionally were used in departments of agricultural economics in U.S. land-grant universities, but there are important differences. This book tackles both **normative questions** (about how decisions should be made) and **positive questions** (about how decisions actually are made) in U.S. food policy. Throughout the book, real-world policy struggles provide the contemporary hook to motivate the reader's attention to the more specialized details of economic principles, policy analysis, institutional structures and data sources. The study of these more academic topics may pay off even for readers whose primary interest is the policy arena. The hope for this book is that these principles and data sources hold some promise for knocking loose the logjam in policy-making.

Current data sources are particularly influential. Many of this book's tables and figures provide notes showing how to acquire and interpret the most recent data. In reading tables and figures, do not envision the author standing at a lectern, making an authoritative presentation of static numbers. Instead, envision the author and the reader sitting shoulder to shoulder at a computer screen, following the hyperlinks, poring over the most recently released data and discussing their interpretation.

The book takes a public interest perspective on food and agricultural policy. It assumes that the reader cares about the economic interests of farmers, and also about hired laborers, the environment, food safety, nutrition, consumer welfare and the poor. To introduce several themes and institutions that cut across the subsequent chapters in complex ways, this first chapter:

- connects the public policy perspective of this book to the social ecological framework used in nutrition and public health research (Section 1.2);
- provides an overview of key industries in the food marketing chain (Section 1.3);
- explores the role of both markets and governments in achieving economic and social objectives (Section 1.4);
- studies how interest groups and advocacy coalitions compete to influence food policy (Section 1.5);
- describes the policy-making process, with a focus on the legislative branch of the federal government (Section 1.6);
- describes the policy implementation process, with a focus on the executive branch of the federal government (Section 1.7); and
- describes the use of law in U.S. food policy, with a focus on the judicial branch of the federal government (Section 1.8).

1.2 An Interdisciplinary Approach

Economic and political science perspectives on the food system are especially useful for students of nutrition and public health. The advisory committee for the *2015–2020 Dietary Guidelines for Americans*, which is the federal government's most authoritative official statement on nutrition and health issues (discussed at length in Chapter 8), draws on a social and ecological framework for understanding food consumption and physical activity decisions (Figure 1.1). Similar models are found in many other high-profile nutrition policy documents (Institute of Medicine, 2012). To analyze major nutrition-related health outcomes, this framework goes far beyond immediate causes such

**Diet and Physical Activity, Health Promotion and Disease Prevention
at Individual and Population Levels across the Lifespan**

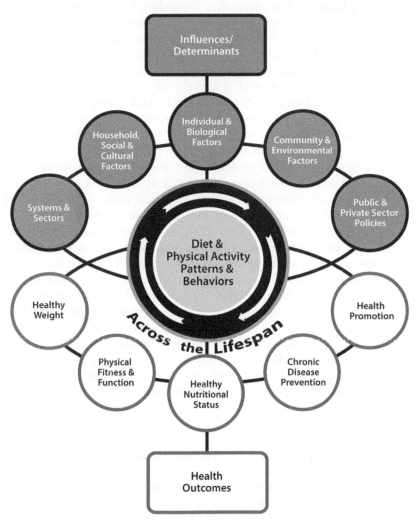

Figure 1.1 The Dietary Guidelines Advisory Committee's framework for understanding nutrition and physical activity in their social/ecological context

Source: Dietary Guidelines Advisory Committee (2015).

as food and beverage intake and physical activity. The framework calls attention to broader systems and sectors, including agriculture (Chapter 2), the food and beverage manufacturing industries (Chapter 5), the retailing and restaurant industries (Chapter 6), marketing and the media (Chapter 9) and socioeconomic factors (Chapter 10). Once nutrition and public health professionals begin to explore these more fundamental influences on food and beverage consumption, they find themselves engaged with the challenging topics in public and private-sector policies addressed in this book.

At first, this engagement can be unnerving. When interacting with patients, professionals in medical fields are rightly proud of their ability to diagnose problems and prescribe an appropriate remedy. It is tempting to adapt this medical patient approach to food policy applications. For example, if expanding food portion sizes contributes to rising rates of obesity, it is tempting to say government agencies should prescribe smaller portion sizes. If nutrient-dense foods cost too much, it is tempting to say government agencies should prescribe a price ceiling for fruits and vegetables. It is disappointing if policy-makers reject such proposals as politically infeasible. It is downright frustrating if policy-makers say with a straight face that a well-intentioned nutrition policy prescription is unwise. Yet, except in special settings such as school meal programs, determining portion sizes may be a decision that people do not want to delegate to their government. A price ceiling for fruits and vegetables may have unintended consequences, such as reducing the incentives to grow fruits and vegetables.

The upper orbits of the social ecological framework bring nutrition policy into contact with many other societal objectives, such as a thriving economy, a healthy environment, poverty alleviation and effective political governance. Powerful policy actors in these outer layers do not—and sometimes should not—behave as if food consumption and physical activity stood alone as the sun at the center of the social ecological solar system. Governments balance food and nutrition concerns against other considerations, just as individuals and families do. As we explore more deeply the normative question of what food policies best serve the public good, it will appear necessary to discern which decisions should be delegated to governments and which decisions should be made by individuals interacting in economic markets. And, as we explore more deeply the positive question of what policies can win political support, it will appear necessary to anticipate how a variety of producer and consumer interests will respond to such proposals. These interdisciplinary explorations are more difficult than simply prescribing the right policy medicine, but ultimately they offer both sharper policy insight and greater potential for political success.

1.3 The Food Marketing Chain

U.S. consumers spent approximately $1.3 trillion on food in 2014 (USDA Economic Research Service, 2017). Food spending has fallen over time as a fraction of all consumer spending, from 17 percent of personal disposable income in 1960 to only 9.7 percent of personal disposable income in 2014. The composition of food spending also has changed. As the U.S. standard of living increased, more women entered the labor force and time became more valuable during the second half of the twentieth century. A larger fraction of food spending went toward food away from home (for example, from restaurants and other food services), and a smaller fraction went toward food at home (from grocery stores). Even for at-home food, the process of industrialization has altered food consumption patterns and transformed the industries that provide Americans with food.

The **food marketing chain** is the linked sequence of industries that are responsible for food production and distribution (Figure 1.2). The Economic Research Service of the U.S. Department of Agriculture (USDA) illustrates the relative economic contributions of food industry groups using the widely recognized food marketing dollar (Figure 1.3). The food marketing dollar emphasizes that food production is about much more than just agriculture. Of each dollar of consumer food spending, only 8.6¢ is

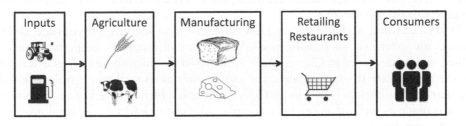

Figure 1.2 The food marketing chain

2015 Food dollar: Industry Group (nominal)

Figure 1.3 The USDA Economic Research Service food marketing dollar, 2015

Data note: USDA's Economic Research Service provides several variations on the food marketing dollar data series, providing breakdowns by industry group and factors of production, and explaining trends over time (www.ers.usda.gov/data-products/food-dollar-series.aspx).

Source: USDA Economic Research Service.

attributed to farm and agribusiness (Chapter 2), while 15.6¢ goes to food manufacturing and processing (Chapter 5), 12.7¢ goes to food retailing (Chapter 6) and 34.4¢ to restaurants and other food services (also Chapter 6).

1.4 Markets and Governments

In food policy, as in all policy-making, people acquire and use political power and influence for both principled and self-interested reasons. Some policy differences arise because people disagree about what should be done. Other differences arise because people seek to advance their own interests, regardless of what should be done. It would be naive to recognize only arguments about principle. It would be cynical to recognize only arguments about self-interest. Both motivations are important in U.S. food policy.

This section introduces a mainstream economic account of how policy decisions can be evaluated. This is the standard academic policy analysis perspective in the United States, but it is just one perspective. The reader certainly is not obliged to adopt this perspective, but to comprehend U.S. food policy, it is useful to become fluent with the language of this perspective.

In this account, a challenge for policy-makers is to identify appropriate circumstances for government action. In an idealized economic model of competitive markets, which will be discussed in Chapter 2, the prices and production quantities determined by the market are thought to serve the public interest as well as possible. Formally, the market equilibrium is said to be **Pareto optimal**, which means that each economic actor is made as well-off as can be accomplished without harming the economic interests of other actors.

Because competitive markets are thought to function this well on their own, this account advises governments to show some restraint. Government institutions should enact policies to remedy **market failures**, which are particular circumstances in which markets fail to serve the public interest. Note that markets need not collapse or cease to function; a market failure just means that markets fall short of their potential. The following examples commonly appear on lists of market failures:

- Insufficient **public goods**, which are goods that are nonexcludable (anybody can use them) and nonrivalrous (one person's use does not diminish another person's use). Traditional examples of public goods are roads and national defense. The economic account recognizes that governments must provide some public goods.
- **Externalities**, in which one actor affects the interest of another actor through some nonmarket mechanism. A positive externality is when one economic actor benefits others, such as when a farmer's use of land provides a beautiful landscape for others to enjoy. A negative externality is when one economic actor harms others, such as when water pollution from a factory causes illness for people who live downstream.
- **Imperfect information**, in which some economic actors lack the information they need to defend their own economic interests in the marketplace.
- Monopoly or oligopoly, in which a good's production is limited to one actor or a small number of actors, who thereby gain the power to choose noncompetitive prices and production quantities.

In addition to these archetypal market failures, governments also may act to remedy a different sort of problem:

- **inequality** or economic injustice or poverty.

Economic inequality is not classified as a market failure, but instead it reflects the severely limited meaning of Pareto optimality. Even if a well-functioning market achieves a Pareto optimal outcome, governments may decide to satisfy people's desire for fairness by redistributing some resources from the rich to the poor. In doing so, economists say, governments must weigh the value of income equality against the value of economic incentives for hard work.

This economic perspective is heard in policy arguments throughout this book. Externalities are important in discussing food production and the environment (Chapter 3). Monopoly and oligopoly arise in discussing the seed industry and food and beverage manufacturing (Chapter 5). Imperfect information is a central concept in food safety (Chapter 7), dietary guidance and health (Chapter 8) and food labeling and advertising policy (Chapter 9). Economic inequality and poverty are closely related to questions of labor conditions for farmworkers (Chapter 2), the food justice movement (Chapter 6) and hunger and food insecurity (Chapter 10).

In arguments about U.S. food policy, it is useful to notice whether participants adhere to variations on this economic perspective or whether instead they hold a different perspective altogether. Most participants in U.S. policy-making accept the mixed structure of the U.S. economy, which assigns important roles to governments and private-sector institutions. Under the big tent of this perspective, political liberals generally are quicker to perceive market failures and to call for government action, while political conservatives generally are more suspicious of government regulation and more reluctant to intervene in private-sector markets.

Moving outside this big tent, there are dissenters on both the right and the left. Some economic libertarians and some participants in the Tea Party movement call for more ambitious scaling back of the powers of the government, which is seen as fundamentally incapable and illegitimate. Some political progressives and some participants in the food justice and food sovereignty movements call for subjugating private-sector markets more firmly under the authority of the government. Among political philosophers, there are respectable alternatives to the standard economic perspective. For example, rather than thinking of people as individuals who interact mainly through markets, a long tradition in political philosophy describes people primarily as citizens joined by bonds of mutual obligation and collective interest into a political community or **polis** (Stone, 1997).

1.5 Interest Groups and Advocacy Coalitions

Food policies enacted by the government affect people's interests in different ways. Farm subsidy programs explicitly take money from taxpayers and give it to farmers (Chapter 2). Trade barriers implicitly take money from consumers and give it to producers (Chapter 4). Consumer interests and food company interests are at odds over many policies regarding food manufacturing (Chapter 5), food safety (Chapter 7) and dietary guidance and health (Chapter 8). Anti-hunger programs (Chapter 10) and nutrition assistance programs (Chapter 11) use taxpayer money to help meet the food and nutrition needs of children and the poor. Policy positions are strongly influenced by these interests. The saying is: "Where you stand depends on where you sit."

Some interests are easier to organize into political action than others (Olson, 1965; Stone, 1997). For example, farmers in the United States are greatly outnumbered by food consumers, so you might think that legislatures would be biased in favor of consumers. In the United States and other rich countries, the opposite is more generally true (Pasour and Rucker, 2005; Masters, 2011). Contributing to the political process is voluntary. Many farmers have their livelihood at stake when farm policies are discussed, whereas food is only about 10 percent of the typical consumer's household budget. Farmers in a particular agricultural industry frequently are concentrated in rural areas of the same region or a few regions, whereas consumers of each product live in cities, suburbs, towns and rural areas all over the country. Farmers are comparatively well informed about farm policy, and they are few enough in number that political organizers can keep in touch with them. Consumers are less informed about farm policy, they are internally divided by political differences, they are so numerous that organizing is difficult and, in many food policy debates, each consumer has less at stake in the outcome.

Many industry associations and public interest organizations seek to influence both Congress and the agencies of the executive branch in favor of particular policies. These organizations write position papers, hire lobbyists in Washington to visit with legislators and USDA officials, and make campaign donations. Some of these activities fall within the scope of open records laws, which require governments to share certain types of information about the policy process. For example, on the website for the Center for Responsive Politics (OpenSecrets.org), you can browse long tabulations of lobbying activities and campaign donations, categorized by legislator and election cycle. For particular committees, such as the House and Senate agriculture committees, the website makes it easy to identify donations from the most closely related industries. In 2010, the U.S. Supreme Court decided in *Citizens United v. Federal Election Commission* to limit the federal government's power to regulate presidential election advertising. At the same time, the decision upheld rules requiring advertising sponsors to disclose their identity.

Different organizations face different rules about lobbying and political activities. Most trade associations are allowed to hire lobbyists and make campaign donations. By contrast, nonprofit organizations may be incorporated under section 501(c)(3) of the Internal Revenue Code, which gives the organization a tax benefit and requires the organization to accept limits on lobbying and political activities. Sometimes, larger groups will divide their activities into separately incorporated organizations for tax purposes, with one arm doing the political work and a separate arm qualifying as a 501(c)(3) organization. For example, the American Farm Bureau Federation lobbies Congress on behalf of farmers, while the American Farm Bureau Foundation for Agriculture uses tax-deductible contributions for educational activities that seek to improve the public perception of farmers (Chapter 2). The Christian anti-hunger organization Bread for the World lobbies Congress, while the allied Bread for the World Institute uses tax-deductible donations for research and education on related themes (Chapter 10). Several of the biggest agricultural industries, including beef, pork and dairy, have both a trade association that may lobby and a semi-public check-off program that is prohibited from lobbying (Chapter 9).

Because there are so many interest groups, each with a particular agenda, no one interest group can successfully advance major legislation on its own. Instead, interest groups combine into **advocacy coalitions** for or against particular policies. In some nonagricultural areas of public policy, deeply felt social and political differences complicate advocacy coalition efforts, for example, pro-life versus pro-choice, gun control versus second amendment rights, gay rights versus the religious right. In other areas of public policy, where long-standing loyalties and identities are less relevant, interest groups have more freedom to sort themselves into different combinations for different policy issues.

Food and agricultural policy tends to fall into this second category, with interest groups freely working together on some causes but not others. Some exceptions are passionate divisions over the wisdom of local and organic agriculture (Chapter 3) and the safety of new food technologies (Chapter 7). There are also politically relevant cultural divisions between the agricultural heartland and more urban and coastal regions of the country. Generally, however, the interest groups with greatest influence over U.S. food and agricultural policy are led by thick-skinned political veterans who have witnessed a long history of incremental policy change, in which advocacy coalitions have been formed and re-formed with considerable flexibility.

1.6 The Legislative Branch

Introductory policy textbooks often present a **policy cycle,** a schematic model of the policy-making process (Howlett et al., 1995). Typical steps in the cycle include the following:

- **Agenda setting,** the process by which a select few policy issues are chosen from among the many possible issues one could consider.
- **Policy formulation,** the process of developing policy options.
- **Decision making,** choosing among the available options.
- **Policy implementation,** the more detailed process of carrying out policy decisions.
- **Policy evaluation** which completes a feedback loop, as each policy's successes and failures generate new issues of their own, which may influence the policy agenda anew.

As a literal chronology of events, this cycle rarely describes how actual policies are made, which is generally a more jumbled process. The policy cycle does provide a useful outline to several topics worth covering. For example, the policy formation step brings to mind the work of the legislative branch (discussed in this section), and the policy implementation step addresses the work of the executive branch (discussed in Section 1.7).

Here is a simplified account of the legislative process in the U.S. Congress. Although legislation may in fact follow a meandering path, it is useful to recognize the simple chords around which the more intricate improvisation takes place. A bill is proposed in one of the two chambers, the House of Representatives (with 435 voting members) or the Senate (with 100 voting members plus the vice president as a tie breaker). Tax legislation can only originate in the House of Representatives. After introduction, a bill is assigned to one or more committees for consideration. The committees may recommend the bill to the full chamber. Legislators in the full chamber may offer amendments. In the House of Representatives, a simple majority suffices to pass most bills. In the Senate, a three-fifths majority may be required in practice to shut off debate and pass important legislation. If a version of a bill passes both chambers, a conference committee with members from both chambers may be assigned to work out any differences. The conference committee's bill is returned to both chambers for a vote. If a bill passes both chambers, the president may either sign the bill to enact it into law, or the president may veto the bill. In the latter case, Congress may override a veto by passing legislation with a two-thirds majority in each chamber.

Much depends on the committees to which bills are assigned (Figure 1.4). In the U.S. Senate and House of Representatives, two important types of committees are (a) authorizing committees, including the **agriculture committees** in each house, and (b) **appropriations committees,** which decide annual funding levels. Within each appropriations committee, there is a subcommittee that specializes in agricultural and food policy.

The division of labor between authorizing and appropriations committees depends in part on the type of government program being discussed. For **mandatory programs** (about 80 percent of federal agricultural spending), an authorizing committee writes the rules under which the program will operate, and the federal government commits to providing whatever amount of funding is needed to meet that commitment. For

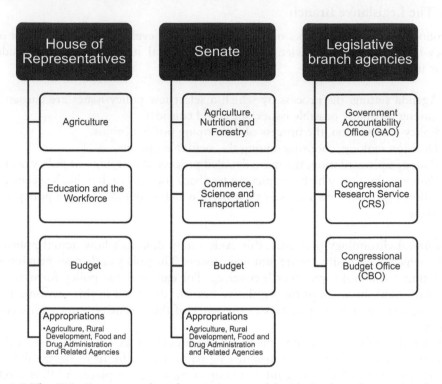

Figure 1.4 The U.S. Congress: selected committees and legislative branch agencies that are influential in U.S. food policy

example, deficiency payment farm subsidies (Chapter 2) and the Supplemental Nutrition Assistance Program (Chapter 10) are mandatory programs. For **discretionary programs** (about 20 percent of federal agricultural spending), the authorizing committee sets up a program that may be funded, but the appropriations committee has considerable leeway to choose the annual spending level. For example, several major agricultural conservation programs (Chapter 3) and the WIC program (Chapter 11) are discretionary programs. In general, agriculture committees have greater authority over funding decisions for mandatory programs, while appropriations committees have greater authority over funding decisions for discretionary programs.

This committee structure increases the influence over agricultural policy of citizens from more agricultural states. This pattern is seen in both houses but simplest to explain for the Senate agriculture committee, formally called the Committee on Agriculture, Nutrition and Forestry. Consider the example of Iowa's representation on this committee. Although it is unusual to have two senators from the same state on the same committee, from the 108th Congress (beginning in 2003) to the 113th Congress (beginning in 2013), the same two senators from Iowa served on the agriculture committee (Senators Charles Grassley and Tom Harkin). When Senator Harkin was replaced by Jodi Ernst (R-IA), she, too, was assigned to this committee, so the double representation continued in the 114th Congress (beginning in 2015) and 115th Congress (beginning in 2017). In 2016, Iowa had 1.0 percent of the U.S. population, but

Table 1.1 Authorizing legislation: spending projections in the 2014 Farm Bill for 10 fiscal years, FY2014–FY2023

Farm Bill title	10-year spending estimate ($ billions)			
	Baseline (if 2008 Farm Bill were continued)	CBO score (change to baseline)	Projected outlays	Chapters in this book
Nutrition (Title IV)	764	−8.0	756	10 and 11
Crop insurance (Title XI)	84	+6	90	2
Conservation (Title II)	62	−4	58	3
Commodities (Title I)	59	−14	44	2
All other titles	4	+4	8	
Total	973	−17	956	

Data note: CRS offers lucid explanations of federal legislative and budget issues. CRS reports are intended for congressional staffs, not for the general public, but many relevant reports are available from the National Agricultural Law Center (www.nationalaglawcenter.org/crs). The detailed content and history of federal bills and laws are available from Thomas (thomas.loc.gov), a service of the Library of Congress. Congressional Budget Office scores offer less explanation than CRS provides, but they are available immediately on the CBO website (www.cbo.gov/cost-estimates).

Source: Adapted from Chite (2016), Congressional Research Service (CRS).

the state receives 8.3 percent of federal farm subsidies, the second highest of any state. Overall, the 21 senators who served on the committee represented states with 32 percent of the U.S. population while receiving 52 percent of federal farm subsidies. Thus, as one would expect, farm-state senators have the greatest influence over agricultural policy. In making policy, agriculture committee members consider national objectives, the particular interests of their own state and local constituents, and the interests of political allies, such as other legislators and outside individuals and companies who provide political support.

A wide variety of legislation addresses food and agricultural policy. A leading example in this book is the **Farm Bill** (Table 1.1), although other examples encountered later in the book include legislation regarding health care, food safety and child nutrition programs. The Farm Bill authorizes agricultural programs (Chapter 2), conservation programs (Chapter 3), anti-hunger programs (Chapter 10) and many other relevant programs. Congress passes a Farm Bill approximately every five or six years. Food and agricultural policy is exceedingly complex, but legislators and other policy actors make the task manageable by thinking incrementally. Each revision of the Farm Bill may establish new programs, end old programs and modify continuing programs.

For the 2014 Farm Bill (formally, the Agricultural Act of 2014), Table 1.1 illustrates how legislators on the agriculture committees can use this incremental approach to weigh the advantages and budgetary costs of changes from one Farm Bill to the next. The **baseline** is an estimate of future costs over 10 years if existing policies were continued essentially unchanged. To reduce the risk of political manipulation, this baseline estimate comes from the Congressional Budget Office (CBO), a nonpartisan agency within the legislative branch (see Figure 1.4). After legislators draft a new Farm Bill, the CBO provides a **score**, which is an estimate of how much the legislation's costs over 10 years will differ from the baseline. For example, the 2014 Farm Bill had a total spending reduction of approximately $17 billion over 10 years. The Farm Bill achieved

Table 1.2 Appropriations: agriculture and related agencies in a single fiscal year, FY2017

Title in appropriations bill	1-year budget authority ($ billions)			
	Fiscal year 2016	Change	Fiscal year 2017	Chapters in this book
Food/nutrition programs	109.8	−1.7	108.1	10 and 11
Mandatory	103.0	−1.7	101.2	
Discretionary	6.8	+0.0	6.9	
Agricultural programs	23.1	+15.3	38.4	2
Mandatory	16.0	+15.2	31.3	
Discretionary	7.0	+0.1	7.1	
Conservation programs	0.9	+0.2	1.0	3
Foreign assistance	1.9	+0.0	1.9	4
Food and drug (FDA)	2.7	+0.0	2.8	7
Other	2.1	−1.0	1.1	
Total	140.5	+12.9	153.4	
Mandatory	119.0	+13.5	132.5	
Discretionary	21.5	−0.6	20.9	

Data note: Each year, the president releases a budget proposal for the entire federal government (www.whitehouse.gov/omb/budget), and USDA releases a departmental budget (www.usda.gov/budget). Congressional appropriations bills are available from Thomas (thomas.loc.gov).

Source: Adapted from Monke (2017), Congressional Research Service.

this target by cutting anti-hunger and nutrition assistance programs by $8 billion, conservation programs by $4 billion and commodity subsidies on net by $14 billion, offsetting some of the savings by increasing crop insurance spending by an estimated $6 billion over 10 years. The rightmost column of Table 1.1 provides a roadmap to the connections between this high-profile authorizing legislation and food policy topics covered throughout this book.

After agricultural and food programs are authorized, Congress must still make spending decisions each year. As noted earlier, appropriations committees must largely accept as given the forecast spending level for mandatory programs, but they have greater say over discretionary program spending. As with authorizing legislation, to keep the task manageable, legislators and other policy actors frequently think incrementally in terms of changes from the previous year. Table 1.2 shows fiscal year 2017 spending levels and the changes from the previous year. The appropriations bill anticipated mandatory program spending increases of $13.5 billion in fiscal year 2017. More directly, the appropriations bill proposed to reduce discretionary program spending by $0.6 billion, reflecting the tight budgetary climate. Again, the rightmost column of Table 1.2 provides a guide to the connections between this appropriations legislation and topics covered in later chapters.

1.7 The Executive Branch

The executive branch includes all the departments and agencies of the federal government that answer to the authority of the president. Counting both military and civilian agencies, the executive branch employs more than 4 million people. USDA is the department with greatest responsibility for agricultural and food programs, although later chapters of this book also will discuss other departments and independent agencies, including for example the Department of Health and Human Services (DHHS), the Environmental Protection Agency (EPA) and the Federal Trade Commission (FTC) (Figure 1.5).

The Secretary of Agriculture and the Secretary of Health and Human Services are members of the president's cabinet, and the administrator of the EPA also has cabinet rank. A departmental secretary and three or four tiers of the most important executives are **political appointees,** who usually are replaced when a new president is elected. In USDA, the political appointees include a deputy secretary, who reports directly to the secretary, and seven undersecretaries, who each oversee between one and five agencies

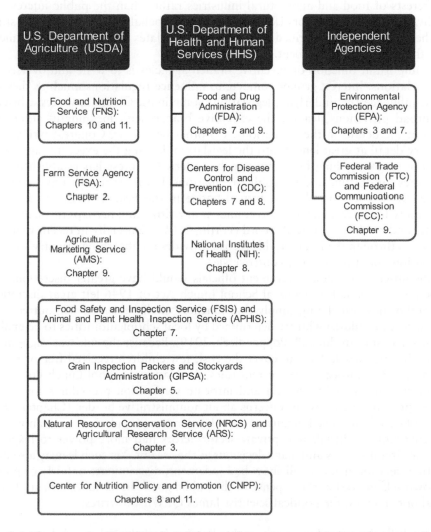

Figure 1.5 The executive branch: selected federal departments and independent agencies that are influential in U.S. food policy

in related areas of work. One undersecretary is responsible for farm subsidy programs (Chapter 2), one is responsible for the conservation and environmental programs (Chapter 3) and a third is responsible for the nutrition programs (Chapter 11). After the political appointees, most of USDA's remaining 106,000 employees are **civil service** employees who provide continuity from one administration to the next. There are rules designed to protect civil service employees from some kinds of political influence and to limit their political activities in some respects.

USDA agencies generally maintain collegial relationships with the food and agricultural industries. Senior USDA officials commonly rotate between government and industry positions at different times in their careers. When a writer questions the impartiality of USDA policy decisions, these career paths are described as a **revolving door** and the department is described as a **captured agency**, meaning that it reflects the interests of food and agricultural industries rather than the public interest more broadly. When a writer favors USDA's advocacy on behalf of agricultural constituencies, the department is described by a moniker that dates back to its establishment in 1862, the "People's Department."

One important function of executive branch agencies is to write and oversee rules and regulations. Interest groups compete to influence regulations much as they compete to influence the underlying legislation. Sometimes, Congress writes a brief law with broad provisions, leaving the executive branch with meaningful authority to work out the details in the regulations. On other occasions, Congress writes all the necessary detail at great length into the legislation, leaving the executive agency little flexibility to do anything but carry out the orders. Congress has established formal procedures for drafting and publishing regulations. For most regulations, due process requires the agency to publish a formal notice in the *Federal Register*, provide an opportunity for interested parties to comment in writing and perhaps through a public hearing, and publish an official record (Fortin, 2009). Especially in recent years, with easy access through the Internet, this record provides an absorbing primary source for information about food policy controversies.

In the absence of rules, government officials would have greater discretion, which can be good or bad. The National School Lunch Act of 1946 left great discretion to local authorities, stipulating simply that lunches "shall be served without cost or at reduced cost to children who are determined by local school authorities to be unable to pay the full cost of the lunch" (Poppendieck, 2010). Because the rule was vague and the local authorities would have to cover the cost, few children received free or reduced-price meals. By contrast, under current rules, the National School Lunch Program has detailed income eligibility criteria and intricate verification procedures for free and reduced-price lunches, raising concerns about administrative burden (Chapter 11).

In the face of excessive bureaucracy and burdensome regulation, one can wish that both government officials and private-sector actors had more power to respond to changing circumstances and make decisions as they see fit. Yet such leeway also carries risks that decision makers will show bad judgment, discriminate unfairly or promote their own self-interest at the expense of the public good. In his landmark study of the federal bureaucracy, the political scientist James Q. Wilson writes:

> The difficulty of striking a reasonable balance between rules and discretion is an age-old problem for which there is no "objective" solution any more than there is

to the tension between other competing human values such as freedom and order, love and discipline or change and stability. At best we can sensitize ourselves to the gains and losses associated with governance by rule rather than by discretion.
(Wilson, 1989)

In U.S. food policy, the tension between rules and discretion arises in arguments about permanent crop insurance programs versus ad hoc disaster relief, food safety rules versus private-sector liability, mandatory versus voluntary food labeling and narrow versus broad income targeting for nutrition assistance programs.

1.8 Food Law in U.S. Food Policy

Through one path or another, many disputes in U.S. food policy end up in court. In deciding cases, U.S. courts draw on two sources of authority: (a) laws passed by governments in conformance with the U.S. Constitution and (b) accumulated precedents in the common law tradition.

The U.S. Constitution provides the architecture for the stage on which U.S. food policy is performed. The Constitution established the three branches of the federal government—legislative, executive and judicial—and set the boundaries for the respective powers of the federal government and state governments (Pomeranz, 2016). All federal laws and regulations must conform to the Constitution. The Constitution gives the federal government the power to regulate interstate commerce and to tax and spend money, an essential task for all of the federal government programs discussed in this book. The Constitution also describes the procedures through which it could be amended and changed over time. As part of the political compromise that led to ratification of the Constitution in the 1780s, the new U.S. government ratified the first 10 amendments as a Bill of Rights, limiting the powers of the federal government. Two of these amendments arise in U.S. food policy litigation: (1) the First Amendment, protecting freedom of speech, is relevant for legal arguments about dietary guidance (Chapter 8) and food labeling and advertising (Chapter 9); and (2) the Tenth Amendment, assigning all powers to the states that were not given to the federal government, is relevant to arguments over the division of responsibility for food safety oversight (Chapter 7) and many other areas.

The legislative branch of the federal government includes courts in 94 federal judicial districts spread across the U.S. states and territories. Cases may be appealed to 12 circuit courts: 11 courts that are each responsible for one region of the country plus a federal circuit court, based in Washington, DC, which is responsible for appeals related to several federal government functions. Finally, cases may be appealed from the circuit courts to the U.S. Supreme Court, which has the final say in matters of U.S. law. Supreme Court decisions sometimes are key turning points in U.S. food policy.

1.9 Conclusion

Some readers may simply want to understand U.S. food policy better. Others may look for information that can be used in a business or government career related to food and agriculture. Still others may seek to improve the way the food system works. All these motivations are welcome here.

It is interesting to follow food policy debates at the national level, in part because these debates will affect the future of U.S. agriculture, the environment, food safety, public health, nutrition and household food security. But another part of the fun and challenge is to watch and learn how these debates are fought under the spotlight of national politics, the better to participate actively in whatever venue one can.

To participate in food policy-making, readers can think strategically about the settings in which their own additional effort can offer the most benefit. Much of the public attention on food policy is concentrated on a few high-profile controversies. Even if one does find something new to say on the broad wisdom of GMOs, the environmental merit of local food, the implications of globalization or the need for federal spending to address hunger and poverty, many listeners may have already made up their minds. In January 2012, while issuing new nutrition rules for child nutrition programs, USDA reported that it received more than 133,000 public comments (Chapter 11). It is hard to believe that one more comment would have carried much weight. It is good citizenship to participate in the debates of the day by writing and placing telephone calls to congressional offices and sending comments in response to *Federal Register* notices, but there are also other ways of making a difference.

By focusing on narrower topics, selected regions of the country and smaller institutions, readers can make a more immediate contribution on less crowded ground. Readers with a particular business or government career interest likely already have chosen—or have been channeled into—an emphasis on particular industries or topics within the broad coverage of this book. In a similar fashion, specialization may be useful for readers who are university students or who are motivated primarily by a sense of public interest purpose. In contrast with the thousands of public comments on a federal school meals policy, many local school districts around the country make important decisions about child nutrition programs with insufficient public input.

If you are studying or working in the fields of nutrition, public health, planning or government, you can speak up in the deliberations of your respective professional associations. If you are a dietitian, or studying to be one, the Academy of Nutrition and Dietetics (formerly the American Dietetics Association) has energetic internal debates on many nutrition policy issues. If you are a veterinarian, or studying to be one, the American Veterinary Medical Association must decide where it stands on important questions such as the role of antibiotics in meat production. If you are active in the organic or sustainable agriculture or animal welfare movements, you can be a voice for sound policy within the Organic Consumers Association or the Sustainable Agriculture Coalition or the Humane Society of the United States; and so forth for dozens of professional and advocacy organizations with influence over U.S. food policy. Likewise, if you are pursuing a career within the agricultural and food industries, you can take an interest in the role that your employer and your industry associations play in the larger food policy arena.

Whether in government or business or the nonprofit advocacy sector, you may face difficult choices in balancing your own career interests and alliances with your informed perception of the public good, but that is to be expected. A theme of this book is that all of U.S. food policy-making takes place in this manner, subject to the push and pull of competing private interests and public objectives. The resulting policies are sometimes wise and sometimes foolish, but the process of making them always is fascinating to watch and worthwhile to understand.

Summary List of Key Terms (identified in bold in the text)

- advocacy coalitions
- agenda setting
- agriculture committees
- appropriations committees
- baseline
- captured agency
- civil service
- decision making
- discretionary programs
- externalities
- Farm Bill
- federalism
- food marketing chain
- food policy
- food program
- imperfect information
- inequality
- mandatory programs
- market failures
- normative questions
- Pareto optimal
- policy cycle
- policy evaluation
- policy formulation
- policy implementation
- polis
- political appointees
- positive questions
- public goods
- revolving door
- score

2 Agriculture

2.1 Introduction

U.S. agricultural policy affects many important outcomes of the food system, including the well-being of farmers and farmworkers, environmental quality, the price of food in supermarkets and restaurants, and the nutritional quality of American diets. Yet this topic is widely misunderstood, in part because farm subsidy programs are complex and more heterogeneous than most people realize. The objective of this chapter is to make agricultural policy more comprehensible to outsiders, especially readers whose curiosity about the farm sector originates from public interest goals.

This chapter:

- offers a tour of the U.S. farm sector, emphasizing distinctions across five agricultural industries (Section 2.2);
- summarizes government interventions in the agricultural economy, unknotting the tangle of farm programs (Section 2.3);
- describes economic conditions for farm operators and hired farmworkers (Section 2.4); and
- introduces the advocacy coalitions that influence farm policy (Section 2.5).

2.2 Overview of the Farm Sector

Agricultural economists have developed many ways to categorize farms. Three important ways are reviewed in this section: by geography, by farm type and by commodity specialization.

Geographical differences provide insight into U.S. farm policy. Farm production patterns straddle state boundaries in complex ways, so USDA statistics divide the country into nine **farm resource regions**, based on climate and production patterns. Figure 2.1 shows the percentage of **net cash farm income** that comes from these farm resource regions. Net cash farm income equals **gross cash farm income** (from sales and from government programs, for example) minus the cost of purchased inputs (such as fertilizer, equipment, rent and wages paid, for example). The Heartland, including Iowa, Illinois, Indiana and Missouri, is the most productive region in terms of farm income and perhaps the most influential in agricultural policy. The Fruitful Rim, including California and Florida, is almost equal in terms of net cash farm income, but not as influential in agricultural policy.

In each region, farms also differ by farm type. USDA's broad **farm typology**, whose wording has been carefully negotiated and tweaked through years of political

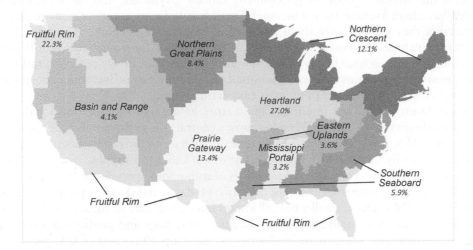

Figure 2.1 Percentage of U.S. net cash farm income from nine USDA farm resource regions, 2017

Data note: USDA's Economic Research Service provides annual farm income and wealth estimates and forecasts, including government program payments, by region and commodity (www.ers.usda.gov/data-products/farm-income-and-wealth-statistics/).

Map source: Park et al. (2010); data source: USDA ERS farm income and wealth estimates.

Table 2.1 U.S. farms, by type, 2015

USDA farm type		Annual gross cash farm income (GCFI)	% of all farms	% of gross cash farm income
Family farms				
Small	Retirement	< $350,000	17	2
	Off-farm occupation	< $350,000	42	5
	Farm occupation			
	Low sales	< $150,000	25	5
	Moderate sales	$150,000–$350,000	5	8
Midsize		$350,000–$1,000,000	6	22
Large		$1,000,000–$5,000,000	3	28
Very large		≥ $5,000,000	0.3	20
Nonfamily "corporate" farms		any sales level	1.3	10
All farms			100	100

Note: Aggregate U.S. number of farms (2.06 million), gross cash farm income ($342 billion).

Data note: Periodic updates are available from the farm economy page of USDA's Economic Research Service (www.ers.usda.gov/topics/farm-economy.aspx). Custom tailored reports on farm types may be generated online from USDA's Agricultural Resource Management Survey (ARMS) Farm Business Income Statement (www.ers.usda.gov/data-products).

Source: Hoppe and MacDonald (2016); data source: Agricultural Resource Management Survey (ARMS).

argument, suffices for the purpose of this chapter (Table 2.1). Large and very large family farms, with annual gross cash farm income greater than $1 million, are few in number, but they provided almost half of agricultural production as measured by gross cash farm income in 2015. As Section 2.4 will explain, these very large farms receive the largest fraction of government subsidy payments, and the farm house-holds have high average annual incomes. Small family farms are more numerous, but altogether they provide only about a fifth of gross cash farm income. The small family farms include residential and retirement farms whose operators rely on off-farm income, limited-resource farms whose operators are comparatively poor and full-time farm businesses that just happen to be small. Nonfamily farms, including "corporate farms," contribute just a tenth of gross cash farm income.

Small family farms are important innovators in organic farming and local food systems (discussed in Chapter 3) and occupy a central role in farm policy debates. Yet students of U.S. food policy should also seek to understand the economics of large and very large family farms, which provide most of the U.S. food supply.

This section focuses on five broad categories of commodity specialization: (1) grain and oilseeds; (2) fruits, vegetables and nuts, (3) cattle, (4) dairy, and (5) hogs, poultry and eggs (Figure 2.2). Other crops, smaller but still important, include cotton, tobacco and peanuts. We often think of the animal industries—cattle, dairy, hogs and poultry—as dominating U.S. agriculture. These animal industries do make up 39 percent of U.S. gross cash farm income. However, crop production deserves much of the credit for animal industry output, in the sense that grain and oilseed crops provide much of the feed consumed by all those cows, pigs and chickens. The animal industries therefore generate a somewhat smaller share of net cash farm income (after input costs are subtracted) and a still smaller share when industries are ranked by **value added** (a measure of the economic contribution more strictly within a particular industry, formally defined as the value of sales minus purchased inputs). In terms of both gross and net cash farm income for farm operators, the largest U.S. agricultural industries are grains and oilseeds, followed by high-value crops such as fruits, vegetables and nuts (Figure 2.2).

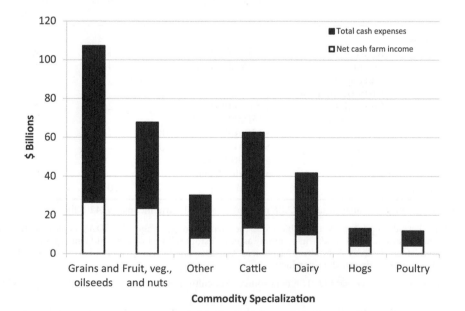

Figure 2.2 U.S. gross cash farm income and its components, by commodity specialization, 2015

Note: Gross cash farm income equals net cash farm income plus total cash expenses.

Data note: See the data note to Figure 2.1.

2.2.1 *Grain and Oilseeds*

Grain and oilseeds are the souped-up engine of the American agricultural economy and the original source of most of our food energy. The crop with the greatest total value is field corn, which is used mainly for animal feed, biofuels (ethanol), corn sweeteners and manufactured food (see Chapter 3 for a breakdown of the uses of U.S. corn). The next biggest crop is soybeans, used for animal feed, vegetable oil and manufactured food. Corn can also be consumed as fresh sweet corn (a distinct variety with higher sugar content), and soybeans are used as tofu and edamame, but these direct corn and soybean food uses are a tiny share of all grain and oilseeds produced. Of grains that are used directly for foods other than vegetable oil, wheat has the greatest total value in the United States, and rice is a distant second.

For corn and soybeans, the heaviest production region is in the Heartland. For wheat, which tolerates a drier climate, the regions of highest production are the Northern Great Plains and the Prairie Gateway. Heavily irrigated rice is grown around the Mississippi Portal region and in California. Climate and soils are the most important determinants of what crops are grown in what regions. Farm policy and market conditions are significant secondary factors. When you consider the possible impact of policy reforms or changes in market prices, do not imagine that most corn farmers will consider growing wheat, or vice versa. Instead, imagine that the geographical frontier between "corn country" and "wheat country" will shift eastwards or westwards over time as farmers at the margin respond to the incentives they face.

Large family farms are particularly prominent in grain and oilseeds. Farms with annual gross cash farm income of at least $350,000 provide three-quarters of all gross cash farm income in this industry. These farms are modern, high-technology ventures, very different from the quaint pastoral image of a bygone era. Compared to other agricultural industries, grain and oilseed farms make more intensive use of fertilizer and energy inputs. Grain and oilseed farms may supplement the labor of family members with hired workers, but typically not very many hired workers compared to similarly sized farms in other agricultural industries. Capital equipment, such as big tractors and harvesters, has replaced much labor in grain and oilseed farming, so each person working on these farms is highly productive.

A novice mistake in farm policy debates is to confuse large and very large family farms with nonfamily or "corporate" farms, which are responsible for less than 5 percent of gross cash farm income in grain and soybeans. The large and very large family farms, in USDA's typology, are sometimes incorporated, but ownership and management are retained by members of a family. The operational scale, technology and business strategies may be nearly unrecognizable to the grandparents of the family, but the large U.S. grain and oilseed farms remain, in an economically and politically relevant sense, family farms.

The grain and oilseed industry receives the lion's share of U.S. farm subsidies, as the next section will explain. Except for the distortions caused by these subsidies, grain and oilseed markets are globalized and highly competitive (see Chapter 4). The United States is a large net exporter of grain and oilseeds. Without these international markets, U.S. grain prices would be lower, and the industry would be less prosperous.

2.2.2 *Fruits, Vegetables and Nuts*

Fruit and vegetable farms occupied less than 2 percent of U.S. farmland in the 2012 Census of Agriculture, but their harvest is exceptionally valuable. Annual sales per acre for these high-value crops are about five times as high as sales per acre in grain and oilseed farming (one U.S. acre equals approximately 0.4 hectares). The fruit and vegetable industry provided a fifth of the 2015 gross cash farm income in U.S. agriculture (Figure 2.2).

Leading fruit and nut crops are grapes, oranges, apples, almonds and strawberries, and leading vegetables are potatoes, lettuce and tomatoes. Most of the fruit and vegetable industry is located in the Fruitful Rim, although Idaho is the leading potato state. The industry has deep internal divisions across products and regions, which make it difficult to exercise national political influence in the manner of other agricultural industries.

Despite years of endorsement in the *Dietary Guidelines for Americans* and other high-profile sources of nutrition guidance, the per capita fruit and vegetable supply has not been increasing (Krebs-Smith, Reedy and Bosire, 2010). In 2004, the annual per capita quantity of fruits and vegetables in the U.S. food supply, from production and net imports, adjusted for an estimate of loss and waste, was 703 pounds (fresh weight equivalent); a decade later, in 2014, it was only 645 pounds (Menus of Change, 2017).

Corporate farms play a bigger role in fruits and vegetables than in other agricultural industries, but large and very large family farms still are the farm structure with the greatest total sales. In contrast with grain and oilseed farming, hired laborers do most of the field work in the fruit and vegetable industry (see Section 2.5). Most hired farmworkers are immigrants, with the greatest number from Mexico and Central America (see Chapter 4).

The fruit and vegetable industry receives almost no traditional agricultural subsidies. The principal government interventions are in the form of subsidized inputs (such as water, discussed in Chapter 3) and marketing orders that regulate product characteristics and, to some extent, production volumes. International markets provide both export revenue and import competition. Production and international trade are both highly seasonal, as the world's major fruit and vegetable growing regions supply products to other parts of the world during the importing countries' off season.

2.2.3 Cattle

The beef cattle industry provides America with one of its most enduring iconic characters, the cowboy, and also with 19 percent of production as measured by gross cash farm income (Figure 2.2). The leading regions are the Prairie Gateway, the Northern Great Plains and the Heartland, but cattle production is widely dispersed throughout the country, increasing the industry's political importance.

The industry has two main parts: the farms or ranches where cows are born and the feedlots where they are fattened up for slaughter. Cattle farming or ranching uses an immense land area, about two-fifths of all U.S. agricultural land, including much dry land in the West on which crops are not economically feasible. Even when the acreage is large, the economic scale may be either large or small. Small farms, by USDA's definition, provide more than one-third of the gross cash farm income in cattle production, a higher fraction than in most agricultural industries. Most cattle farms and ranches breed cows and raise calves for sale to cattle feedlots.

The feedlots are economically bigger operations but are packed into a much smaller land area, less than 2 percent of U.S. agricultural land. Most feedlot production comes from operations classified by USDA as large and very large family farms and from nonfamily or "corporate" feedlots. Cows have been described as machines for converting grass into food that humans can eat, but in feedlots, most of the feed actually comes from the grain and oilseed industry. The major land use implication of feedlots is the cropland used for growing the animal feed inputs rather than the land for the feedlot operations themselves.

The cattle industry receives few direct subsidies and a modest amount of government protection against imports. Cattle markets are not as competitive as grain and oilseed or fruit and vegetable markets. The meatpacking industry (described in Chapter 5) is controlled by four large firms. Economists believe this high degree of concentration is sufficient to suppress the prices earned by cattle producers.

2.2.4 Dairy

The traditional dairy region is the Northern Crescent, including Wisconsin, Minnesota and New York, but much of the growth in recent decades has been in California, which is now the nation's biggest dairy state. As with cattle feedlots, the industry's main occupation is to convert animal feed into food products, including milk, cheese, butter, ice cream and yogurt. Dairy farms provide about 12 percent of U.S. aggregate gross cash farm income (Figure 2.2).

Like the grain and oilseed industry, the dairy industry is increasingly led by large and very large family farms. As the next section will explain, dairy producers are sometimes subsidized, but a more important government intervention is trade barriers that keep prices high and protect the domestic industry from imports (see Chapter 4). Dairy markets are particularly complex because regional marketing orders and farmer-owned cooperatives play a more central role in dairy than in other agricultural industries. In some ways, the cooperatives are like farm organizations that assist dairy farmers in marketing their product to the next stage of the supply chain. In other ways, the cooperatives are like manufacturing companies, for which the farmers' product is merely an input. The market share of the largest cooperatives has increased in recent decades.

2.2.5 Hogs, Poultry and Eggs

The industries in these animal production categories share some similar characteristics. They each have experienced dramatic changes in technology, geography, farm structure and environmental concerns in the past two decades. Together, these industries provide about 7 percent of U.S. gross cash farm income from the perspective of farm operators (Figure 2.2).

Traditionally, hog and poultry production was a side operation on crop farms, especially in the Heartland. Although the Heartland retains a leading role in the industry, hog production also boomed in North Carolina in the 1990s and in Western states more recently (Key and McBride, 2007). The hog, poultry and egg industries have experienced rapidly increasing market control by large corporations further up the food chain, even as large and very large family farms remain the most important type for the farm operations themselves.

Vertical integration is nonmarket coordination between different marketing levels (such as growers and food manufacturers), using contracts or ownership structures.

For example, in the hog and poultry industries, multiyear production contracts allow large branded food manufacturers, such as Tyson, Smithfield and Perdue, to influence prices and production decisions for growers. These contracts will be discussed further in the chapter on food manufacturing (Chapter 5). Critics say these contracts give the manufacturers undue control over farm production decisions and prices. Supporters give the contracts credit for facilitating production efficiencies, allowing the food manufacturers to produce at lower cost and pass along some of the savings to consumers. In either case, this vertical integration means that these agricultural markets operate very differently from the textbook model of a competitive market.

2.2.6 Interactions among Agricultural Industries

In one respect, the various agricultural industries are each other's competitors, eager to enhance their relative share of the consumer's food budget. In another respect, the industries are allies, working together to support policies and innovations that promote food demand or save input costs. In a third respect, these industries are buyers and sellers on opposite sides of the same business transactions, as one industry's harvest becomes another industry's input.

If a promotional campaign convinces consumers that daily slabs of beef are an essential source of protein, the change in animal feed demand also generates a bonanza for grain farmers. However, if Congress passes new ethanol incentives, which raise the demand for corn, the grain farmers will be delighted, but the animal feed industry will pass the higher corn price on to the beef industry, which will voice its alarm back to Congress. Hence, industries may be allies on the first issue and opponents on the second issue. The most important lesson of this section is that the agricultural industries are economically, geographically and structurally diverse and far from united in political purpose.

2.3 Agricultural Programs

The complex system of government interventions in agricultural markets may seem bewildering, but we should have some sympathy for its creators. Nobody ever sat down at a conference table, laid out a plan for the current system of farm subsidies and pronounced it good. Since the 1930s, programs have been added piece by piece, year by year. Repeatedly, modifications were designed to solve some problem with the existing policies, while they introduced new problems of their own (Glauber and Effland, 2016; Glauber, Sumner and Wilde, 2017).

No system of programs could simultaneously appeal to all stakeholders—farmers, consumers, nutritionists, environmentalists and taxpayer advocates, for example. Trying to satisfy them all, a policy-maker might feel like a laboratory mouse in a cruel maze that lacks an exit. This section provides a map to the twisted path policy-makers have followed. Then, the next section shows real data on subsidy amounts over the years. Throughout, this chapter emphasizes that farm policies are not homogeneous but have diverse effects on prices, production and consumption. The key to understanding the politics of farm subsidies is to identify whom a policy helps, whom it hurts and how it influences the quantities produced and consumed (Table 2.2).

Table 2.2 Seven broad categories of farm policy interventions

Category	What the government does	Effect on . . .		
		Farmers	Buyers	Quantity
1 Price supports	Buys commodity at the support price	Higher price	Higher price	More
2 Supply control	Limits how much is grown or imported	Higher price	Higher price	Less
3 Deficiency payments	Pays farmers the difference between a target price and the market price, on current production	Higher farm price	Lower market price	More
4 Direct payments	Pays farmers steadily, based on historical production	Higher income	—	—
5 Countercyclical payments	Pays farmers the difference between a target price and the market price, on historical production	Higher income	—	—
6 Insurance	Pays farmers if production suffers a loss	Higher income	—	—
7 Demand expansion	Promotes sales or develops new uses	Higher price	Higher price	More

2.3.1 Policy 1: Price Supports

A **price support** is a government policy that maintains a price higher than the market price. With price supports (unlike the deficiency payments discussed in Section 2.3.3), both buyers and producers face the new higher price. The goal is to help farmers, even at the expense of consumers or taxpayers.

Price supports played a major role in U.S. farm policy from the 1930s through the 1970s, especially for the grain and dairy industries. Because fresh milk is perishable, dairy price supports usually involve acquiring and storing butter and cheese. Since the 1970s, the importance of price supports in grains has been eclipsed by deficiency payments and direct payments, discussed later. Price supports still influence dairy markets in some years.

A price support must include some enforcement mechanism that prevents a return to the equilibrium price. Without an enforcement mechanism, the government's intended price is mere wishful thinking. One enforcement mechanism is a **purchase and removal** policy, in which the government offers to purchase whatever quantity farmers want to sell at a specified support price. When equilibrium prices are higher than this support price, no farmers will sell to the government, because the competitive market is more lucrative. However, when equilibrium prices are lower than the support price, some farmers will accept the government's offer. Because the government purchases reduce the volume that remains on the market, the market price rises until it reaches the support price. The government buys only some of the commodity, but it raises the price received by all farmers and paid by all consumers (see Box 2.1).

Box 2.1   The Economics of Price Supports for Corn

This box considers a hypothetical example of a price support for corn (maize). In this example, policy-makers have decided the market price of $1.75 per bushel is too low, so they have established a higher support price of $1.95 per bushel.

For background on the supply and demand tools used here, see three online appendices: "The economics of demand and supply at the market level" (Appendix S2.1; see the online Companion Website); "Elasticity" (Appendix S2.2); and "A Competitive Market for an Agricultural Commodity" (Appendix S2.3). International trade, which is ignored in this example, will be addressed in Chapter 4.

The upward-sloping **supply function** in Figure 2.3 describes how the quantity provided by U.S. corn producers (on the horizontal axis) would respond to different prices (on the vertical axis). The downward-sloping **demand function** describes how the quantity purchased by consumers would respond to different prices.

At the competitive market equilibrium price of $1.75 per bushel, producers would offer 15 billion bushels for sale. Consumers would want to purchase this same amount, so the market equilibrium is stable. Suppose the government declared an official price of $1.95 per bushel, which is higher than the market equilibrium. U.S. producers would freely supply 15.6 billion bushels of corn for the year, while consumers would freely buy only 14.4 billion bushels. There would be a surplus of 1.2 billion bushels. Some type of enforcement mechanism will be required, or else producers will begin to offer discounts rather than suffer from holding unsold stocks of corn, and the market price will soon return to the equilibrium price of $1.75 per bushel.

One enforcement mechanism is a purchase and removal policy. Suppose the government offered to purchase and store any quantity of corn at the support price of $1.95 per bushel. Because farmers now have the backup option of selling to the government, they will only sell corn to consumers at a price of $1.95 per bushel or more. At a support price of $1.95, consumers will purchase 14.4 billion bushels. The government will purchase the surplus amount of 1.2 billion bushels, at a total program cost of $2.3 billion for the year.

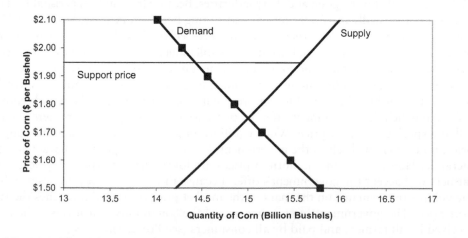

Figure 2.3 The U.S. corn market, with a support price of $1.95 per bushel (hypothetical)

A variation on the purchase and removal program is a **nonrecourse loan**. The government offers farmers a loan at a specified loan rate, similar to a support price. When farmers sell their crop, they may choose either to repay the loan or forfeit their harvest to the government as full payment for the loan. If the equilibrium price is greater than the loan rate, the farmers prefer to sell their crop on the market and repay the loan in cash. If the equilibrium price is less than the loan rate, some farmers choose to forfeit the crop to the government. In the end, a nonrecourse loan provides a different financial vehicle for achieving the same objective that a purchase and removal policy achieves.

With purchase and removal programs and nonrecourse loans, a serious challenge is figuring out what the government should do with the commodities it acquires. The government may not sell the commodity on the domestic market the same year, because such sales would push the market price back down, undermining the effect of the price support. The government may store the commodity for resale in a later year when equilibrium prices have risen above the support price, but the storage may be expensive, especially if the support price has been set too high and the equilibrium price fails to reach this height for many years. The government may give the commodity away in international food aid programs (see Chapter 4) or dispose of the commodity through food assistance programs, such as the National School Lunch Program (see Chapter 11). Each of these disposal options is controversial. In the meanwhile, immense piles of stored commodities make a great visual image for critical media coverage of the subsidy programs.

An unintended consequence of price supports is to stimulate production quantities greater than the equilibrium quantity, which raises concern about environmental impacts and trade consequences (see Chapters 3 and 4). Matters become even worse if price supports are maintained in the long run. Supply is more responsive to changes in price in the long run than in the short run. Thus, in the long run, a price support can generate significant overproduction.

Another unintended consequence of price supports is to increase rents on agricultural land. Many farmers rent the farmland they use. Even when farmers are landowners, economists think of their agricultural income as being partly a rent for the use of their own land. A limiting factor on how much rent landlords can charge is the profitability of the farm operation. If a price support program makes farm operations more profitable, landlords may charge higher rent, sucking up economic support that was intended for the farmers.

The advantage of price supports is that they place a floor under the market price, seeking to protect farmers from economic hardship in the years when farmers need help most. However, price support programs are expensive to taxpayers, they raise the price of food for consumers, they require the government to store commodities, they encourage overproduction and their benefits are absorbed in part by landlords instead of the intended beneficiaries.

2.3.2 Policy 2: Supply Controls

A **supply control** is a government policy to reduce the quantity planted or sold. All else being equal, the reduction in supply raises the price above equilibrium levels. Like the price support program, the goal is to help farmers, not consumers. Unlike price support programs, supply controls avoid encouraging overproduction.

As with price supports, there must be some enforcement mechanism. In one approach, each farmer in an industry could be given a **production quota** stating his or her share of the industry's national production quantity, as determined by the government. Such quotas were used for major grain crops in the United States from the 1930s to the 1970s. For some smaller farm industries, such as tobacco and peanuts, quotas lasted until more recently. Production quotas were difficult to enforce, there was no easy way to assign each farmer's quota fairly and production was intensified on the acres that remained in production. Moreover, it was politically unpopular to shackle the productive power of American farmers. Similarly, in the 1980s, the federal government sought to control dairy supplies through a "whole herd" buyout, paying farmers to cease production for a specified time period. This policy's effectiveness was undermined as farmers who remained in the industry increased milk output per cow.

For several major U.S. agricultural industries, which no longer have production quotas, federal conservation programs function as a lighter form of supply control. Such programs date back to the 1930s and remain important today. For example, the Conservation Reserve Program (CRP) compensates farmers who volunteer to take some land out of production (see Chapter 3). These programs are not linked to a particular price that the government seeks to achieve, but their price-enhancing effects are an essential element of their political support. For commodities that the United States imports, another option for controlling supply is restrictions on international agricultural trade (see Chapter 4).

2.3.3 Policy 3: Deficiency Payments

With a **deficiency payment**, the government offers to pay producers for the difference between a **target price** and the price to the buyer (typically a manufacturing company that uses crops as an input). In years when the equilibrium price is higher than the target price, no payment is made. Whereas a price support requires buyers to pay the same support price that farmers receive, a deficiency payment allows buyers to pay a lower price.

Producers use the target price as the basis for decisions about how much to grow. What matters to producers is the total revenue earned per bushel, regardless of how that revenue is divided between consumer sales and government payments. Thus, deficiency payments encourage overproduction just as price supports do. While the producers' target price is chosen by the government, the buyers' price is still determined by market forces. The increased production quantity stimulated by the government policy is dumped on the consumer market, suppressing the buyer price below equilibrium levels. Because the government must pay the farmers the difference between the target price and this artificially suppressed buyer price, deficiency payment programs can turn out more expensive than policy-makers anticipated in advance (see Box 2.2).

As with price supports, a government loan may be used as the financial vehicle for implementing the deficiency payment program. USDA offers farmers a **marketing assistance loan**, with a loan rate specified in dollars per bushel of crop harvested. If the equilibrium price is above the loan rate, the farmer simply repays the loan and there is no subsidy that year. If the equilibrium price is below the loan rate, USDA allows the farmer to repay the loan at a rate equal to the price farmers can earn on the market. Alternatively, even without taking out a loan, the farmer may request a **loan deficiency payment** equal to the difference between the loan rate and the market price, in which case the government writes a check directly to the farmer.

Box 2.2 The Economics of Deficiency Payments for Corn

With a deficiency payment, the government offers to pay producers for the difference between the target price and the consumer price. The deficiency payment only takes place when the equilibrium price is lower than the target price.

To continue the corn example from Box 2.1, suppose the government establishes a deficiency payment program with a target price of $1.95 per bushel (Figure 2.4). As before, producers will grow 15.6 billion bushels of corn. A buyer price of $1.56 clears the market of 15.6 billion bushels of corn (in Figure 2.4, see the horizontal line labeled "buyer price"). This price is stable, because there is neither a surplus nor a shortage of corn on the market. The government makes a deficiency payment of $0.39 per bushel, which is the difference between the target price of $1.95 per bushel and the consumer price of $1.56 per bushel. The government's deficiency payments on the 15.6 billion bushels total $6.1 billion for the year.

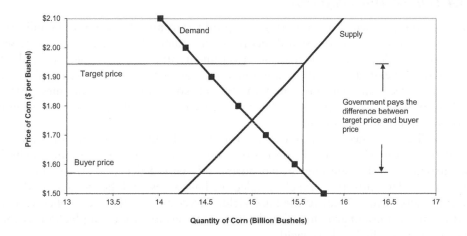

Figure 2.4 The U.S. corn market, with a deficiency payment target of $1.95 per bushel (hypothetical)

Does this high cost to the taxpayer seem surprising? Based on the free-market equilibrium of $1.75 per bushel for 15 billion bushels, one might have hoped for a deficiency payment of $0.20 per bushel, leading to program costs of only $3 billion for the year. Unfortunately, the higher figure of $6.1 billion is correct in this example. Do not forget that the deficiency payment scheme encourages a production quantity that exceeds the equilibrium quantity and hence a buyer price that falls below the equilibrium price. As a consequence, the deficiency payment program's budgetary cost may be high.

To avoid confusion, notice that the nonrecourse loan program described earlier under price supports (Section 2.3.1) raises the buyer price to the support price level, while the marketing assistance loan and the loan deficiency payments discussed here lower the buyer price. For USDA programs that have the word "loan" in the title, one must read carefully to understand the economic impact.

Deficiency payments remain on the books as one of several major forms of farm subsidies, especially for the grain and oilseeds industry. They provide billions of dollars of support in years when equilibrium prices are low, while their cost drops to almost nothing in years when equilibrium prices happen to be high (as in the recent years 2008 to 2013). A deficiency payment program has the same principal advantage as a price support, raising the farmer's effective price per bushel. The payments can complicate trade relations, impose large costs on taxpayers and promote overproduction, especially if the program is maintained with a target price higher than the equilibrium price in the long run. Like a price support, some of the benefits go to landlords instead of farmers. Unlike a price support, a deficiency payment lowers the buyer price and increases the quantity of sales, a pattern that benefits manufacturing companies' and consumers' economic interests while raising nutritional concerns about the impact of farm programs on overconsumption and obesity.

2.3.4 Policy 4: Direct Payments

To avoid the problems of promoting overproduction and distorting the equilibrium price, the government may use a **direct payment**, much like a welfare or social security check. With direct payments, the government support is designed to be **decoupled**, which means the payment amount does not depend on the farmers' current production decisions. Although the term "direct payments" was sometimes formerly applied to deficiency payments by check directly to farmers, the term is now generally restricted to decoupled subsidies.

Until direct payments were terminated as part of the 2014 Farm Bill, they were based on a farmer's historical production during several recent years, not including the current year. The amount grown during this period depends on the amount of farmland under cultivation, which is called the **base acres**, and the average production level per acre, which is called the **base yield**. Direct payments were applied to just a portion of the amount grown during the historical period—for example, 85 percent of base acres multiplied by base yield.

There are some reasons to be skeptical that direct payment programs are truly and completely decoupled. First, recognizing that the current year may someday become the historical reference period for a future direct payments program, farmers may engage in strategic behavior by maintaining a high production level in the current year. Second, the government sometimes establishes **planting limitations**, which restrict the ability of subsidy recipients to move into other crops (Balagtas et al., 2013). In particular, there are limitations designed to discourage grain and oilseed farmers from switching into fruit and vegetable production, even though greater fruit and vegetable production would be desirable from a nutrition perspective.

The original intention of direct payments was to replace market-distorting deficiency payments, although this transition was only partly accomplished, so the major grain and oilseed industries enjoyed a combination of several subsidy programs. The principal advantage of direct payments was that they helped farm incomes every year, which was an especially attractive policy outcome in years when prices were low. Direct payments sought to avoid promoting overproduction, so they were preferred by environmentalists and by trading partners overseas. Although the direct payments were expensive to taxpayers, they were predictable from year to year, which made budget planning easier. On the other hand, direct payments were politically unpopular with the nonfarming public in years when prices were high and farmers already were prospering. Direct payments were ended in the 2014 Farm Bill.

2.3.5 Policy 5: Countercyclical Payments

To avoid the problem of paying expensive direct subsidies in high-price years, the government in 2002 added a new type of subsidy called **countercyclical payments**. Like direct payments, countercyclical payments are designed to be decoupled, in the sense that the payments are based on historical production quantities and do not depend on production decisions in the current year. Yet, like deficiency payments, countercyclical payments are made only in years when the market price is comparatively low. Moreover, the countercyclical payments are typically supplemental for crops that also have programs of direct payments and deficiency payments.

The **Price Loss Coverage (PLC)** program, one of several new programs introduced in the 2014 Farm Bill, is a form of countercyclical program (see online supplemental Table S2.1). Comparatively few farms used this program after the 2014 Farm Bill, because eligible farmers were required to make a one-time selection of either the PLC or the more popular Agricultural Risk Coverage program discussed in Section 2.3.6. However, participation and payouts under the PLC could increase under the next Farm Bill if commodity prices are expected to be comparatively low, because the PLC offers comparatively generous protection against low prices (Schnitkey and Zulauf, 2016) (Chapter 12 discusses USDA forecasts for future commodity prices).

2.3.6 Policy 6: Crop Insurance

A leading motivation for farm subsidy programs is to protect farmers from economic risks. The classic irony, which has made a pessimist of many a farmer, is that farm income may suffer when weather is bad and harvests are poor, but farm income also may suffer when weather is good and abundant harvests lead to low prices.

Even in the absence of government programs, private companies could provide insurance policies that allow people to reduce their exposure to economic risks. For example, just as with automobile or medical insurance, a farmer could pay an annual premium for a crop insurance policy that guarantees a payment in the event of a crop loss due to weather, plant disease or insect infestation.

The presumption of federal crop insurance programs is that these private-sector insurance markets are inadequate, and farmers cannot afford to pay market-rate premiums. In federal crop insurance programs, private insurance companies continue to provide the insurance policies, but the federal government subsidizes the premiums and also covers some of the insurance programs' administrative costs. In principle, subsidized crop insurance is the category of farm subsidy program that is most open to a wide range of crops, even fruits and vegetables. In practice, most of the crop insurance subsidies still go to the traditional grain and oilseed crops. In addition to the permanent crop insurance programs, in many past years Congress provided disaster payments to compensate farmers who suffered in particular events, such as droughts or floods. The disaster programs required no premium from the farmer.

Some government-subsidized insurance programs pay out based on shortfalls in crop yields, while others pay out based on shortfalls in expected revenue (based on both yields and prices). An important program design question is whether payments are based on state-level conditions, county-level conditions or conditions on the specific farm that holds the policy. A policy that pays out based on state-level conditions has the advantage of simplicity, but it may fail to help a farmer suffering from a localized shortfall. By contrast, a policy that pays out based on each farm's own circumstances offers more precise protection, but it may be more expensive for the government.

The largest of the new farm subsidy programs in the 2014 Farm Bill, the **Agricultural Risk Coverage (ARC)** program, pays farmers when estimated revenue falls below a guarantee level (O'Donoghue et al., 2016; Schnitkey and Zulauf, 2016) (see Table 2.3). In the most common program option, the estimated revenue is computed each year from a county-level average rather than the individual farm's experience. The guarantee level is based on a moving average over several recent years, so this program is comparatively generous during a short-term drop in prices, but it would be less generous in a long-term low-price environment. After the 2014 Farm Bill, farmers had to make a one-time choice between the ARC and the PLC (discussed in Section 2.3.5). Hence, many farms were locked into the ARC (Table 2.3).

Because insurers and government agencies cannot easily monitor every farm, crop insurance programs and disaster programs that pay out based on farm-level conditions face considerable problems of fraud. Even in the absence of outright fraud, government and private-sector insurance programs may suffer from **moral hazard**, which occurs when the availability of insurance reduces the farmer's incentive to avoid potential shortfalls, leading to riskier farming practices or increased production in

Table 2.3 Program summary: Agricultural Risk Coverage (ARC)

Overview: A "shallow loss" program that protects farmers against revenue losses, ARC is the most widely used of the new farm subsidy programs established in the 2014 Farm Bill.	
Year begun	*2014*
Scale of operation	
Corn, farms electing, ARC—County Option, 2014 Farm Bill (million)	1.2
Corn, base acres, ARC—County Option, 2014 Farm Bill (million)	90.1
Soybeans, farms electing, ARC—County Option, 2014 Farm Bill (million)	1.0
Soybeans, base acres, ARC—County Option, 2014 Farm Bill (million)	52.6
Budget	
ARC payments, 2015 ($ billion)	7.8
Eligibility: Crop producers make a one-time selection of either ARC or the Price Loss Coverage (PLC) Program. Payments from ARC begin if estimated farm revenues fall below a historical benchmark for the county.	
Benefits: Provides farmers with payments, for 85% of base acres, equal to the difference between estimated farm revenue and the benchmark, up to a maximum.	
Maximum payment (as % of benchmark)	10

Note: See also Price Loss Coverage (PLC) Program (online supplemental Table S2.1).

Data note: OECD's PSE (www.oecd.org/agriculture/pse) provides country-level farm subsidy data. ARC/PLC election data are available from USDA's Farm Service Agency (www.fsa.usda.gov/programs-and-services/).

Source: USDA Farm Service Agency (FSA); O'Donoghue et al. (2016); OECD (2016).

environmentally stressed regions. Environmental organizations have noted that the 2014 Farm Bill excludes certain low-yield years when historical average yields are computed, which could insulate farmers from environmental signals that land may be unsuitable for producing a particular crop sustainably (Schechinger and Cox, 2017).

To summarize, crop insurance programs have their origins in the reasonable goal of protecting farmers from the production hazards and economic fluctuations of agriculture. Yet over the years, federal crop insurance programs have morphed into the leading mechanism for farm subsidies more broadly. These programs require farmers to compute their likely payouts under complex guesses about future prices and yields, and there is some evidence that farmers do not make these choices optimally (Du, Feng, and Hennessy, 2016). Although crop insurance programs are intended to be less distortionary than the price supports and deficiency payments discussed earlier, they do encourage farmers to increase production to some extent (Glauber and Effland, 2016).

2.3.7 Policy 7: Demand Expansion

The shortcomings of the preceding agricultural subsidies could be avoided if only the equilibrium price itself were higher. In principle, this outcome could be achieved through a policy of demand expansion. Recall that demand describes the quantity that consumers would buy at each possible price. With demand expansion, consumers are willing to buy a larger quantity at each possible price. The increased demand bids up the equilibrium market price.

For example, a large majority of U.S. corn production is used as inputs for other goods, such as ethanol and animal feed for beef, pork, dairy, poultry and egg production. Federal programs promote increased use of these end products, which could expand demand and raise the market price for corn. An example of demand expansion through the corn-based ethanol market is the federal Renewable Fuels Standard, which requires that an increasing quantity of renewable fuels is blended into gasoline for automobiles and other vehicles (see Chapter 3). An example of demand expansion through the animal feed market is the federal commodity checkoff programs, which support research efforts and advertising campaigns to promote beef, pork and dairy consumption, funded by a mandatory assessment collected from farmers (see Chapter 9). Another important type of demand expansion is export promotion programs for corn and food products created from corn (see Chapter 4).

Demand expansion programs are popular with agricultural constituencies because they simultaneously raise the market price and the quantity consumed, a feat accomplished by none of the other policies on our list. The opponents of demand expansion programs vary with the design of the program. For example, checkoff programs for beef, cheese, pork and eggs may appear in tension with the federal government's public health message in the *Dietary Guidelines for Americans* (see Chapter 8). The Renewable Fuels Standard is opposed by many environmentalists. Because corn-based ethanol is a nonfood use of a traditional food crop, international food aid charities are concerned about the impact of ethanol promotion on the price of food for the poor and hungry around the world.

2.3.8 Data on U.S. Farm Subsidies

Because the several types of farm policy reviewed in this section are so varied, one must look at real-world data in order to understand them collectively. Figure 2.5

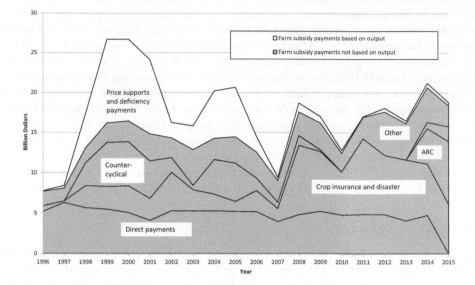

Figure 2.5 Government payments from U.S. farm programs, 1996–2015

Note: Payments based on output have greater implications for overproduction and for trade policy (see Chapter 4).

Data note: OECD's PSE (www.oecd.org/agriculture/pse) provides country-level data in a consistent format for international comparisons. Also, data on government payments are available from the ERS Farm and Commodity Policy page (www.ers.usda.gov/topics/farm-economy). Custom tailored reports may be generated online using ARMS (www.ers.usda.gov/data-products/). Data on payments to individual farmers are available from the Environmental Working Group (farm.ewg.org).

Source: Organisation for Economic Co-operation and Development (OECD), Producer Support Estimates (PSE) (2017).

illustrates government subsidy payments from 1996 to 2015, using producer support estimates (PSE) data from the Organisation for Economic Co-operation and Development (OECD).

Working upwards from the bottom of the figure, direct payments were comparatively stable over time, because they did not respond much to price fluctuations or weather, until they were ended by policy changes in 2014 (see Section 2.3.4). Crop insurance and disaster payments, which fluctuate due to weather and also political circumstances, were particularly high in 2008 (see Section 2.3.5). The ARC, a new program in 2014, quickly came to account for a significant part of federal farm subsidy payments (also in Section 2.3.5). Countercyclical payments cost billions of dollars in comparatively low-price years such as 1999 and 2005, while they cost nearly nothing in high-price years such as 2007 to 2010 (see Section 2.3.4). Price supports and deficiency payments (a category that has been dominated by deficiency payments in recent years) were high in the same low-price years that countercyclical payments were high. The PSE classifies these payments in a special category (identified by shading in Figure 2.5) because they are based on the farmer's current-year output. Such payments raise concern about encouraging overproduction, with potential consequences for the environment (see Chapter 3) and for international trade (see Chapter 4).

The Environmental Working Group (EWG), an environmental advocacy organization, each year requests from USDA a database of government payments. The Freedom of Information Act (FOIA) requires federal agencies to make such information available in many circumstances (there are exceptions for national security, for protecting individual privacy and for documents related to the internal decision-making process within agencies). With the EWG's online database, one can list the nation's top subsidy programs, individual recipients or Congressional districts. For example, the district of Rep. Mike Conaway (R-TX), chairman of the House Agriculture Committee in the 115th Congress, received $2.2 billion in 1995–2014, ranking 27th in the nation. The district of Rep. Collin Peterson (D-MN), ranking minority member of the committee, received $7.3 billion in 1995–2014, ranking eighth out of the nation's 435 congressional districts. For the legislators with greatest influence over U.S. agricultural policy, in either political party, farm subsidies are an intensely important local issue.

Real-world data on farm subsidy payments carry several important lessons. First, total government payments fluctuate greatly from year to year, because of variation in crop insurance programs and in payments that are a function of crop prices. Second, the relative shares for different programs also change from year to year. Third, the payments vary greatly across regions of the United States, based on agricultural production patterns. Instead of generalizing, it is essential to think quantitatively about the impact of farm subsidy programs in particular years and places. There is no other way to judge the many conflicting claims we hear in policy debates about whether farm subsidies serve the public well or badly.

2.4 Economic Conditions for Farm Operators and Farmworkers

To understand agricultural policy, we must contemplate important questions of economic justice and injustice for farm operators and hired farmworkers. From the rhetoric of farm policy debates, one would think that reducing poverty for farmers is a key objective of U.S. farm programs. Yet U.S. farm programs concentrate on providing economic security for farm owners and operators, who are today—with the important exception of small farms other than residence and retirement farms—a comparatively privileged population (Glauber, Sumner and Wilde, 2017). Meanwhile, farmworkers, who actually experience poverty in large numbers, are given little political weight in the design of U.S. agricultural policy.

2.4.1 Farm Operators and Their Households

Most farm subsidies go to large and prosperous family farms, because these farms are responsible for most agricultural production. Table 2.4 shows average annual income and percentage of government payments for the same farm types described earlier in Table 2.1. The operators of midsize, large and very large family farms had mean household income much above the U.S. average income, and together they received 55 percent of government payments in 2015. For example, large family farms (with gross cash farm income between $1 million and $5 million) earned several times the average income for all U.S. households in 2015, and yet they received 26 percent of all government payments (Table 2.4).

Table 2.4 U.S. government program payments and mean annual income for farm operators' households, by type, 2015

USDA *farm type*		*Farm household's mean annual . . .*			*% of government payments*[c]
		Total income	*Farm income*	*Total income as % of U.S. mean*	
Family farms					
Small	Retirement	$85k	$4k	107%	9
	Off-farm occupation	$127k	–$2k[a]	160%	12
	Farm occupation Low sales	$65k	–$2k[a]	82%	9
	Moderate sales	$96k	$42k	121%	11
Midsize		$192k	$123k	242%	27
Large		$430k	$368k	543%	26
Very large		$2,208k	$2,077k	2,785%	2
Nonfamily "corporate" farms		NA[b]	NA	NA	5
All farms					100

[a] 2013 data (not available from USDA for 2015). [b] Owned by a corporation, not a household. [c] Aggregate 2014 government payments in ARMS: $8.6 billion.
Data note: Custom tailored reports about farm household finances may be generated online from ARMS Farm Household Income and Characteristics (www.ers.usda.gov/data-products).

Even within the several categories of small farms, government payments are not targeted toward low-income farmers. For two types of small family farms (retirement and off-farm occupation farms), mean farm income was small or even negative, and yet their household income was higher than the U.S. average for all households because of their nonfarm income. For a third type of small family farm (farm occupation moderate sales farms, with annual gross cash farm income $150k to $350k), the operator had annual household income of $96k in 2015, somewhat higher than the U.S. average for all households. The only category of small family farm with below-average household income was farm occupation low sales farms (with annual cross cash farm income less than $150k). These farm households face considerable economic hardship, but they were responsible for a small fraction of U.S. farm output, so they received only 9 percent of government payments in 2015.

At one time in U.S. history, many more farm operators were poor. For example, the Great Depression and the Dust Bowl of the 1930s caused forced migration for more than 2 million rural Americans. In subsequent decades, through consolidation, the number of farms fell and average farm size grew. Through the long post-Civil War history of Reconstruction and Jim Crow, African American farmers in particular faced severe economic conditions and racial discrimination. From the 1930s to the 1990s, the number of black-owned farms declined at faster rates even than the steep declines for all farms (Gilbert, Sharp and Felin, 2002). In the 2012 Census of Agriculture, 95.4 percent of farm operators were white and 1.6 percent were black or African American.

The federal government has made some effort to address concerns of low-income farmers. A small program called "Section 2501" spends about $20 million annually for outreach and support to help limited-resource farmers apply for program benefits. However, in 2015, USDA's Office of Inspector General (OIG) criticized the Section 2501 program for "a pattern of broad and pervasive mismanagement." OIG said grant approval processes were "informal and undocumented" and "regulatory processes were disregarded." The federal government also in 1999 and 2010 reached landmark settlements (known as the Pigford cases) with African American farmers who faced discrimination in USDA programs just from 1981 to 1996, providing approximately $2.3 billion in compensation to these farmers (Cowan and Feder, 2008). Beyond the Section 2501 program and the Pigford settlements, the main U.S. farm subsidy programs have little beneficial impact for poverty reduction (Glauber, Sumner and Wilde, 2017).

2.4.2 Hired Farmworkers

Many people come to the United States from around the world to find employment as farmworkers. In the United States, only 29 percent of hired crop farmworkers are born in the United States (including Puerto Rico), and 68 percent are from Mexico. USDA estimates that approximately half lack legal authorization. Mean hourly wages in 2011 were low: $8.99 for crop farmworkers and $9.17 for agricultural graders and sorters, comparable to $9.32 for maids and housekeepers and $14.30 for construction workers, for example (Glauber, Sumner and Wilde, 2017). And farm work requires physical labor that cannot easily be sustained; hired farmworkers are much younger on average than farm operators.

An important question is what policy initiatives or economic changes could improve working conditions and wages? Because farming industries such as fruit and vegetable growing are highly competitive, firms that consider paying higher than average wages may find that they would be undercut by their more ruthless rivals. In response, some labor organizers in recent years have bypassed the growers and focused on downstream brand-name supermarkets and restaurant companies (see Chapter 6). Through high-profile campaigns that generated national attention, the Florida-based Coalition of Immokalee Workers has reached agreements with several leading companies to pay a bonus of more than a penny for each pound of tomatoes harvested. Such a bonus generates only a tiny increase in the eventual consumer price, but it can represent a substantial increase in wages for tomato harvest workers, who are paid on a piece-rate (per bucket) basis.

In addition to these direct initiatives, it is useful to consider the fundamental economics of wage determination for farmworkers (Box 2.3). In the long run, higher wages may originate from economic trends that make farm labor more scarce (such as improved opportunities in nonfarm sectors) or more productive (increasing the economic value to employers).

There is a lively debate about proposals to improve conditions for farmworkers directly. For example, federal labor standards do not require employers to pay overtime for agricultural work, and states have varying policies for covering farmworkers under minimum wage laws (minimum wages are discussed further in Chapter 6). Farm labor organizations raise public awareness about working conditions and advocate for higher wages (and higher piece rates, such as the payment per bucket for tomato harvest workers). The message of Box 2.3 is that, in addition to these direct proposals, it also is valuable to consider fundamental economic changes that affect farmworker wages and working conditions by influencing labor supply and labor demand.

Box 2.3   The Economics of Labor Markets for Farmworkers

In labor economics, a wage is the price of an hour of work. As with other markets, the labor market can be studied using supply and demand analysis. Figure 2.6 shows a simple model of the labor supply and labor demand for farmworkers in the United States, with a hypothetical equilibrium wage of $9 per hour. Counting a part-time job as just a fraction of a full-time job, there would be 1.2 million full-time equivalent (FTE) farmworker jobs in the United States (Martin, 2013). For higher wages, consider economic changes that shift the labor supply function leftward or shift the labor demand function rightward.

The **labor supply** function is upward sloping, because a higher wage attracts more workers. Labor supply could shift leftward for several reasons: immigration restrictions (see Chapter 4); better wages in other local industries, such as construction or services; and deteriorating local schools or higher local housing costs in farming regions. Any of these changes could require farmers to pay higher wages to attract workers, but only some of them are good for farmworkers.

Labor demand by farm operators is downward sloping, because lower wages lead farmers to hire more workers. In the traditional analysis, labor demand depends on the **value of the marginal product** of labor (a concept also discussed in Box 5.2). This value equals the marginal product of labor (how much farm output the employer can produce using an additional hour of a laborer's work) times the price of the agricultural product. The labor demand function will shift rightward when the price of a farm commodity rises. A complex and important question is what happens to labor demand with mechanization and new technology adoption (Huffman, 2014). These changes may in part displace workers (shifting labor demand leftward and lowering wages) and in part make workers more productive (shifting labor demand rightward and raising wages). Thus, mechanization and new technology sometimes help and sometimes harm farmworkers (Schmitz and Moss, 2016). Chapter 10 has more on how productivity improvement contributes to poverty reduction.

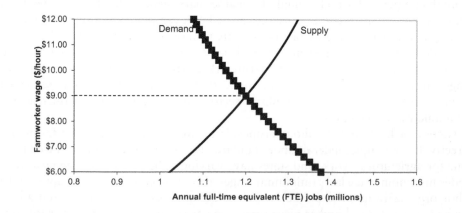

Figure 2.6 The supply and demand for farmworker labor (hypothetical)

2.5 Interest Groups in U.S. Farm Policy

Some farm lobby organizations address the agriculture sector as a whole. Among these, the American Farm Bureau Federation has a politically conservative reputation. The National Farmers Union and the National Family Farm Coalition have more liberal reputations. Many other farm lobby groups are connected to particular agricultural industries. The organization name typically identifies the industry, as in the National Corn Growers Association, the American Soybean Association, the National Association of Wheat Growers, the American Peanut Council and the Almond Board of California.

Consumer organizations take great interest in many aspects of U.S. food policy, such as food safety, but few devote much effort to farm policy specifically. Conservative think tanks, such as the American Enterprise Institute, sometimes oppose farm subsidies on grounds that they waste taxpayer money. Anti-hunger groups, such as Oxfam America and Bread for the World, encourage U.S. farm policy reforms that would help the interest of poor farmers overseas. Environmental groups take particular interest in the environmental impacts of farming and in farm conservation programs, both discussed in Chapter 3. Some sustainable agriculture organizations are critical of farm subsidy programs, while others endorse Farm Bills that provide subsidies to large-scale producers if they also provide support for conservation programs and small sustainable agriculture programs.

For several decades, Farm Bills have been supported by a coalition of rural interests focused on farm programs and urban legislators who care principally about the larger nutrition title. Because the food assistance programs are assigned to the same federal department and the same legislative committees who are responsible for farm policy, this coalition has been politically powerful and stable over time. This coalition is central to the politics of both agriculture programs and nutrition assistance programs.

2.6 Conclusion

This chapter has reviewed how the U.S. agricultural sector is organized, summarized seven types of government policies to influence agricultural markets, introduced leading data sources about government subsidies and farm incomes and described the advocacy organizations that influence agricultural policy.

One conclusion is that U.S. agriculture is not monolithic. Public health and nutrition advocates sometimes describe an agricultural establishment so united in purpose that it can dictate whatever policy it wishes. By contrast, this chapter emphasizes distinctions across regions, across industries and across different types of farm programs. In contemplating future improvements in U.S. agricultural policy, a fruitful question is to identify what new advocacy coalitions would support what particular policy proposals.

A second conclusion is that different farm policies have widely varying consequences for agricultural prices and quantities. Despite the price-suppressing effects of some farm programs, such as deficiency payments, U.S. farm interests do not more generally promote a "cheap food policy" (Miller and Coble, 2007; Glauber and Effland, 2016). The most important reasons for comparatively inexpensive food in recent U.S. history are not farm programs but abundant land and changes in agricultural technology (Chapter 3). A reliable principle of U.S. farm policy is that farmers favor an array of policies that raise agricultural prices. This principle may conflict with the objectives of food manufacturers, retailers, restaurants, consumers and food assistance programs, with consequences that are explored throughout this book.

Summary List of Key Terms (identified in bold in the text)

- Agricultural Risk Coverage program
- base acres
- base yield
- countercyclical payments
- decoupled
- deficiency payment
- demand function
- direct payment
- farm resource regions
- farm typology
- gross cash farm income
- labor demand
- loan deficiency payment
- marketing assistance loan

- moral hazard
- net cash farm income
- nonrecourse loan
- planting limitations
- Price Loss Coverage program
- price support
- production quota
- purchase and removal
- supply control
- supply function
- target price
- value added
- value of the marginal product
- vertical integration

3 Food Production and the Environment

3.1 Introduction

Food production connects us to each other and to the natural environment. In the 2006 bestseller *The Omnivore's Dilemma*, Michael Pollan writes, "Though much has been done to obscure this simple fact, how and what we eat determines to a great extent the use we make of the world—and what is to become of it" (Pollan, 2006).

In discussions of agriculture and the environment, a commonly stated goal is **agricultural sustainability**. In its original literal meaning, sustainability requires maintaining the resource base on which agriculture depends. More broadly, agricultural sustainability has become a shorthand term for a bundle of environmental, economic and social objectives (National Research Council, 2010; FAO, 2014): satisfying human food, feed and fiber needs and contributing to biofuel needs; enhancing environmental quality and the resource base; sustaining the economic viability of agriculture; and improving the quality of life for farmers, farmworkers and society as a whole. In this broader sense, agricultural sustainability involves environmental objectives addressed in this chapter and also other public interest objectives throughout this book.

This chapter:

- introduces economic principles for thinking about environmental externalities (Section 3.2);
- summarizes five environmental dilemmas in U.S. food production (Section 3.3);
- gives an overview of the global food situation, including trends in food needs and environmental constraints on global food production (Section 3.4);
- reviews current policies to address environmental challenges in the U.S. food system (Section 3.5); and
- discusses the contemporary explosion of interest in organic and locally grown food (Section 3.6).

3.2 The Economics of Environmental Externalities

At their best, markets create a strong incentive for environmentally sound decisions about resource use and the environment. At their worst, private-sector market incentives can generate environmental problems, such as pollution and over-use of valuable resources. This section explores the potential successes and failures of market incentives using a series of examples. In each example, food producers face a difficult decision about how much to produce, with potential environmental consequences.

3.2.1 Production Decisions Without and With Externalities

As the first example, consider a very large rancher's decision about how many cattle should graze on his or her 100,000-acre plot of grassland in Texas. If the rancher overgrazes the land, the grass will recover more slowly. If the rancher allocates too few cattle, valuable land resources will be underused. Finding the correct balance requires expertise about cattle, growth patterns for grass and the land. In the absence of externalities, market signals give the rancher a strong incentive to correctly discern the most environmentally sound number of cattle to graze, because this number also maximizes the rancher's long-term profits. In this first example, market incentives serve the environment well.

Second, consider the contrasting case of the Alaska salmon fishery. Like the rancher, the salmon fishing boats can misuse a valuable environmental resource either by overharvesting or underharvesting. With overharvesting, depleted salmon stocks will be slower to reproduce, causing a decline in future harvest potential. In this example, there is an obvious externality. Unlike the rancher, whose grazing decisions affected only his or her own future production, each salmon fishing boat's harvest decision affects the stock of fish available for future harvest by all boats in the fishery. Because of this externality, market signals give each boat's manager a strong incentive to overharvest (see Box 3.1). Unregulated markets would be an environmental disaster, so important decisions must be made collectively. In this example, the Alaska Board of Fisheries develops management plans, based on input from technical experts and policy meetings with affected parties, including the salmon fishers. When this important governmental function has failed elsewhere, such as Atlantic cod fishing in New England and Canada, fish populations have collapsed, leading to the destruction of businesses and coastal communities that had thrived on fishing for many generations.

These two examples show that understanding property rights is central to understanding environmental economics. In the rancher example, the environmental consequences of cattle-grazing decisions are said to be internalized, because the rancher owns the whole property. In the fishery example, there is an environmental externality, because no one fishing boat has a property right to the whole fishery.

3.2.2 Property Rights

The economist Ronald Coase suggested that, if property rights are clearly assigned, private-sector markets might provide an incentive for economic actors to negotiate their own solutions to environmental externality problems, making government intervention less necessary (Coase, 1960). For example, suppose a farmer in Massachusetts has an opportunity to build a new large-scale hog feeding facility. If the farmer builds the facility, neighbors will experience odors. A community meeting to discuss the matter may be loud and angry, because the farmer and the neighbors disagree on two key points.

- First, they disagree about whether the farmer has a right to build the facility. The neighbors say they have a right to clean air, so the farmer is not allowed to generate a harmful externality. The farmer says there is a long-recognized right to farm in Massachusetts, and neighbors in farm communities have always had to adapt to a certain amount of smell.

Box 3.1 An Economic Model of a Fishery

We can use an economic model to illustrate the potential for overharvesting when a fishery is shared as a common resource. Suppose fishing boat operators must decide their annual "effort" in terms of months of fishing activity. For example, if the legal fishing season is two months long each year, five fishing boats operating for two months per year would generate 10 months of effort (see Figure 3.1).

For simplicity, we consider a steady-state model to contemplate the consequences of maintaining a fixed annual effort year after year. As the annual effort increases from zero to 14 months, the annual harvest increases, but at a diminishing rate (because harvesting more fish leaves fewer behind to reproduce). Hence, as effort increases, total annual revenue also rises at a diminishing rate. With more than 15 months of effort, the overharvesting is so severe that total aggregate revenue actually declines with each additional month of fishing boat effort. If a single company controlled all the fishing boats, and had costs of $100,000 for each month of fishing boat effort, the company would maximize profits by choosing 10 months of effort. Notice that total revenue exceeds total cost by the largest amount when effort = 10.

By contrast, in a competitive market, it is rational to fish if profits are expected to be positive, meaning that the expected revenue exceeds the expected costs (see Appendix S2.3; see the online Companion Website). For example, if other boats already are working 18 months in a particular year, the operator of an additional boat might nonetheless put in a 19th month of effort, because profits are small but still positive. In this competitive market, with 19 months of effort, the fishing boats put in so much hard work that their overharvesting reduces total profits to nearly nothing.

In many settings, economists favor fully competitive markets Yet, the narrative point of this box is that unbridled competition is not optimal when there are environmental externalities or common resources, as in fisheries. Having some type of coordination mechanism to limit fishing to 10 months of effort would be better for total operator profits and for the local ecology.

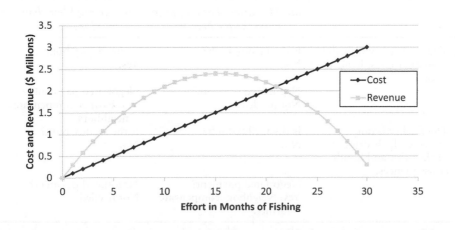

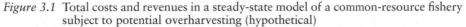

Figure 3.1 Total costs and revenues in a steady-state model of a common-resource fishery subject to potential overharvesting (hypothetical)

- Second, they disagree about whether the hog facility is a worthwhile endeavor. The farmer thinks of large-scale food production as a valuable activity and describes the smell as a minor nuisance. The neighbors have an unfavorable view of industrial food production methods, and they raise concerns about respiratory health consequences.

Let us consider whether the farmer and the neighbors can negotiate a sensible bargain. In Table 3.1, the columns show two possible property rights assignments: (a) the right to farm gives the farmer the power to build the facility, or (b) the right to clean air gives the neighbors the power to veto the construction of the facility. The rows show two possible assumptions about the value of the facility: (1) the facility is worthwhile on net, because the food production is valuable and the odor is a minor issue, or (2) the facility is not worthwhile on net, because it causes major respiratory health consequences for neighbors. In the cells of the table, the text in bold describes a sensible negotiated outcome. For example, even if the neighbors have a right to clean air, the farmer might negotiate a cash payment to convince the neighbors to tolerate a minor odor problem (see top right cell). Conversely, even if the farmer has a right to build the facility, neighbors who face health consequences might negotiate a cash payment to convince the farmer not to build (see bottom left cell).

Such negotiations may generate environmentally wise solutions, regardless of the property rights assignment. Supposing the new facility really is worthwhile, even after considering a minor odor problem, notice that both negotiated outcomes in the top row lead to the facility being built. On the other hand, supposing the new facility is not worthwhile, because of the health consequences of air pollution, notice that both negotiated outcomes in the bottom row lead to the facility not being built. Although farmers would rather have a right to farm and neighbors would rather have a right to

Table 3.1 The negotiated solution to a hypothetical argument between a hog farmer and neighbors depends on property rights and assumptions about the value of a facility

Assumption about value	*Property rights assignment*	
	(a) The farmer has a right to build the facility	*(b) The neighbors have a right to odor-free air*
(1) The facility is worthwhile, even after considering the odor.	Is the facility built? **Yes.**	Is the facility built? **Yes.**
	Negotiated payment? **Not needed.**	Negotiated payment? **Yes. Farmer compensates neighbors.**
(2) The facility is not worthwhile, because of the odor and health consequences.	Is the facility built? **No.**	Is the facility built? **No.**
	Negotiated payment? **Yes. Neighbors compensate farmer.**	Negotiated payment? **Not needed.**

clean air, any clear assignment of property rights would suffice to generate the correct decision about the actual construction of the facility.

In practice, there are many reasons such negotiations may not work as well as one might hope. For example:

- There are **transaction costs** and difficulties in reaching a negotiated agreement. A privately negotiated solution that may work with a small group of neighbors may not be achievable for larger-scale environmental externalities that affect thousands of people or whole ecosystems.
- People's moral sense of right and wrong may override their interest in reaching a negotiated solution. Even if property rights are clearly assigned, the farmer or the neighbors might be unwilling to make a compensatory payment that feels like a type of extortion.
- Property rights may not be assigned clearly. The farmer may believe in a right to farm, the neighbors may believe in a right to clean air, and both parties may be willing to take their chances that courts will decide in their favor.

Economists and political scientists have a well-developed body of thought about how such problems may be overcome. At the local level, informal traditions and formal management institutions can sometimes manage solutions to environmental externalities (Ostrom, 1990; Hanak et al., 2017). When negotiation is impossible, the initial assignment of property rights may determine the outcome. In Table 3.1, if negotiated payments cannot be agreed, then confirming a right to farm will lead to the construction of the hog facility, while confirming a right to clean air will lead to no construction, regardless of the severity of the pollution problem and the environmental worthiness of the facility.

3.3 Environmental Challenges in U.S. Food Production

U.S. agriculture faces many environmental challenges, including concerns about resource scarcity and environmental degradation. Of the many issues that one could consider, this section reviews just five leading challenges: water scarcity, water quality, soil quality, genetic diversity and climate change.

3.3.1 *Water Scarcity*

While water supplies are abundant in many regions of the United States, supplies are scarce in key production regions. USDA estimates that only 16 percent of U.S. cropland is irrigated, but this irrigated land is exceptionally important, producing more than 50 percent of the total value of U.S. crops. In some parts of the West, tensions over water supplies have generated a fierce standoff.

The Ogallala aquifer is a natural underground water reservoir that encompasses sections of eight states, including Nebraska, Kansas, Oklahoma and Texas. Irrigated corn, soybeans and alfalfa grown in this region are important inputs to feedlot beef production. Water withdrawals for irrigation exceed new water supplies from rainfall, leading to substantial declines in the water table, especially in the southern regions of

Box 3.2   Biotechnology

The most bitter controversy in agricultural technology surrounds genetically engineered (GE) or genetically modified organisms (GMOs), whose traits have been altered through direct changes to a plant's or animal's genes. Opponents fear that these technologies will endanger food safety, reduce biodiversity, cause environmental damage and increase corporate control over the food system. Proponents hope that they will improve agricultural productivity, facilitate environmentally sound tillage methods, protect against drought and enhance nutrition characteristics.

Adoption of GMO technology for agriculture is more widespread in the United States than in any other country. The dominant U.S. GMO food crops are corn and soybeans, and the leading GMO traits are (a) resistance to a broad-spectrum pesticide (glyphosate) and (b) protection from certain insects. The most hoped-for GMO innovations, such as drought-resistant corn for Sub-Saharan Africa or extra micronutrients for rice in South Asia, are not yet commercially important.

The three federal agencies with oversight responsibilities for GMOs largely make do with authority under laws that predated the new technologies. First, the Food and Drug Administration (FDA) is responsible for food safety issues. Companies that seek to commercialize a new GE food must notify FDA, which can issue guidance that is treated as regulatory approval or disapproval. FDA also may issue guidance about labeling for GMO foods. Second, USDA is responsible for GMO crops in the field and in practice can give or deny permission for commercial cultivation. Third, the Environmental Protection Agency (EPA) is responsible for GMO varieties that have pesticidal properties.

It is useful to consider GE or GMO foods within a broader spectrum of social decisions about food technologies (Tester and Langridge, 2010). The non-GMO and GMO categories each include diverse technologies:

• Non-GMO crop varieties range from traditional low-productivity varieties to higher-productivity varieties developed through generations of on-farm selection to modern scientifically developed breeds and hybrids. Even without manipulating genes, scientists have learned to scrutinize a plant's DNA to help select and breed promising varieties more efficiently, which saves the time-consuming step of actually growing out the selected plants.

• GMO technologies may be distinguished by whether they are controlled by a single corporation or are available for all to use, whether they have a low or high risk of spreading in the environment, whether they use genes from a related organism or an unrelated organism and whether they provide traits of value to farmers, consumers or the environment.

Non-GMO and GMO technologies both offer opportunities and risks. The strict line between non-GMO and GMO technology—the focus of so much argument—may be a distraction that prevents a more constructive discussion of these opportunities and risks.

the aquifer. As the National Research Council explains, "In effect, the Ogallala aquifer is a nonrenewable resource, similar to a coal mine" (National Research Council, 2010).

Irrigation is a leading contributor to water use in the Central Valley of California, where just 1 percent of U.S. agricultural land generates 8 percent of the total value of U.S. agricultural production. Irrigation needs are colliding with the demands of California's fast-growing urban population. Simultaneously, reduced water flows through the valley's Sacramento and San Joaquin Rivers have damaged the habitat of native fish, bringing some species to the brink of extinction (Hanak et al., 2017). Climate change is expected to increase the probability of drought, such as the unprecedented drought of 2013–2015 in California (Diffenbaugh et al., 2015). In drought years, water authorities must cut irrigation deliveries to farmers with junior water rights, sometimes driving them out of business. California water politics are fractured by regional, economic and philosophical differences that frustrate efforts to address these problems.

3.3.2 Water Quality

Agriculture affects the quality of water supplies in multiple ways, including sediment runoff, pesticide contamination, salinity, pathogens and heavy metals such as mercury. Some of these issues affect the productivity of the land, some generate health concerns for human populations and some affect natural habitats and wildlife.

A leading concern is the effect of excess nutrients from agriculture. Nutrients can come from manure applications associated with animal production and from nitrogen and other fertilizer applications on crops. Only 30 to 50 percent of the nitrogen fertilizer applied to crops is used by the plants. Through soil erosion and leaching, unused nitrogen can make its way into surface- and groundwater resources, impairing water quality both nearby and far away. When they reach the ocean, excess nutrients cause algae to grow, preventing sunlight from penetrating the water and oxygen from dissolving in the water, leading to a loss of habitat for fish and underwater plants (Diaz and Rosenberg, 2008).

These water quality problems have been severe in several regions of the United States. Agricultural runoff from much of the American heartland flows through the Mississippi, Ohio and Missouri Rivers, eventually reaching the mouth of the Mississippi River in Louisiana, contributing to hypoxia or "dead zones" in the Gulf of Mexico. Phosphate runoff from nearby agricultural land has severely damaged the ecology of the Florida Everglades. Excess nutrients from agriculture in the Central Valley in California put stress on aquatic habitats in the delta at the junction of the San Joaquin and Sacramento Rivers. On the East Coast, water quality in the Chesapeake Bay suffers from agricultural, and to a lesser extent residential, runoff in a large watershed. The Environmental Protection Agency in 2010 reached a legal settlement with the Chesapeake Bay Foundation and environmental advocacy organizations to establish the nation's most ambitious system of monitoring and permits to regulate concentrated animal feeding operations and urban and suburban storm water.

In 2014, the Des Moines Water Works brought a lawsuit against three upstream counties for allowing excess agricultural nitrate pollution into the Raccoon River, raising treatment costs for making the water drinkable (Vos, 2017). The suit was eventually dismissed because certain types of agricultural pollution are exempted from the Clean Water Act (see Section 3.5), but the suit raised the profile of the runoff issue in rural agricultural communities. In 2017, the Pulitzer Prize for editorial writing was awarded to the *Storm Lake Times*, a tiny rural Iowa newspaper, in part for its dogged investigation of the agribusiness funding sources for the three counties' legal defense costs.

3.3.3 Soil Quality

The soil itself is an essential part of the natural endowment that supports agriculture. Soil erosion negatively affects carbon balance, with potential implications for the rate of climate change, and affects food security by reducing agricultural productivity (Amundson et al., 2015). The soil that remains behind can suffer quality deterioration through compaction and other types of physical and chemical degradation (Wiebe and Gollehon, 2006).

Protecting soil from erosion has been a major policy concern since the 1930s, when erosion contributed to the mix of environmental and economic disasters of the Dust Bowl. In the past, USDA's periodic National Resources Inventory (NRI) compared actual soil losses to established tolerances, although it was difficult to determine what amount of soil loss would be sustainable without damaging future productivity. The NRI estimated that erosion removed 1.7 billion tons of soil in 2007, which was an improvement over higher rates of loss in earlier years. The NRI has not subsequently been updated to provide more recent statistics. USDA research suggests that the NRI may underestimate the risk of major soil erosion during heavy rain events (Walthall et al., 2013), which may become more common as a consequence of climate change (see Section 3.3.5).

Many promising methods have been developed for protecting and improving soil quality, including crop rotation, cover crops, contour-farming and buffers against erosion. In the past 20 years, an important development has been the increased adoption of conservation tillage, where farmers leave the soil surface partly covered by plant residue to avoid water erosion. Conservation tillage is usually accompanied by increased use of chemical herbicides, so soil conservation methods may involve trade-offs with other environmental goals.

3.3.4 Reduced Genetic Diversity

To develop new varieties of food crops, which are capable of increasing yields and adapting to a changing climate, farmers and plant scientists require diverse genetic resources. For example, traditional plant breeders build improved varieties by combining traits from existing varieties, each of which has some strengths and weaknesses. Even modern scientists using new genetic technologies require a diverse selection of existing plants, animals and microbes that have desired traits. These existing genetic resources are the building blocks that are used in future agricultural improvements. When crops lack genetic diversity, they become vulnerable to catastrophic failures if new pests or diseases develop that can exploit genetic weaknesses (Rubenstein et al., 2005). Yet genetic diversity has declined in the United States in recent decades and is especially low in the Heartland region (Aguilar et al., 2015; Hijmans, Choe and Perlman, 2016);

There are three main problems. First, traditional landraces (varieties that are bred by different farmers in different places over many generations) are being replaced by modern, scientifically developed varieties. Second, farmers are planting fewer principal varieties, and even these varieties may be less diverse, having a smaller "genetic distance" between them. Third, wild relatives of major food crops are being lost to habitat destruction in regions of the world that are major centers of biological diversity. These wild relatives are needed as a source of traits that can be used in cross-breeding.

An *ex situ* approach to protecting genetic diversity is to invest in gene banks, which are institutions that preserve seed collections and occasionally grow out the plants to make sure they are still viable. An *in situ* approach requires preserving wild relatives in their natural environment and encouraging farmers to grow a wider variety of crops and raise a wider variety of farm animals. The United States has signed, but not yet ratified, an International Treaty on Plant Genetic Resources for Food and Agriculture, which would require conservation measures and promote the sharing of genetic material.

3.3.5 Climate Change

Climate change is the most serious environmental challenge for the U.S. food system. It imposes on the U.S. food system the twin burdens of adaptation and mitigation.

Adaptation refers to the ways food and agriculture can adjust to climate change. Climate scientists project some beneficial changes from increased carbon dioxide and longer growing seasons in northern U.S. states, but most projected consequences will be harmful, including coastal flooding, hurricanes, and variable weather patterns, drought and heat waves, especially in the Southeast and Southwest (Pew Center for Global Climate Change, 2011; Walthall et al., 2013). These climate changes will alter the geography of agricultural production and may slow the overall rate of productivity improvement in U.S. agriculture.

Mitigation refers to the ways the food system can reduce greenhouse gas emissions in order to slow climate change. Greenhouse gases, including carbon dioxide, methane and nitrous oxide, have different effects on climate change, so atmospheric quantities are expressed in carbon dioxide equivalents. The U.S. Environmental Protection Agency (EPA) estimates that agriculture directly contributes about 570 million metric tons (MMT) of carbon dioxide equivalent emissions, 8.7 percent of the total inventory of U.S. greenhouse gas emissions (U.S. Environmental Protection Agency, 2017). If one includes agriculture's share of electricity production, this percentage rises to 9.3 percent of the U.S. total. The largest direct agricultural contributors are nitrous oxide released from fertilizer applications to soils, methane gas emitted by cows and other animals, methane gas released by animal manure applications and, to a lesser extent, methane gas released by flooded rice production.

In addition to soils and livestock emissions, the food system uses fossil fuels in agricultural machinery, transportation, manufacturing, commercial facilities and residential energy. Sustainable food advocates suggest that society's response to climate change should include changes in how we eat (Pollan, 2006; Lappé, 2010). USDA economists have estimated that energy use in the U.S. food system accounts for

13.6 percent of total U.S. fossil fuel carbon dioxide equivalent emissions (Canning et al., 2017). Using a model showing how changes in food consumption would ripple backwards through the economy, these economists found that substantially changing U.S. diets, especially eating less meat, could reduce food system energy use by as much as 74 percent (Canning et al., 2017).

The first edition of this book said that scientists, economists and government officials from both major parties treat climate change as an urgent challenge. It quoted Robert Zoellick, who served the first President Bush as U.S. Trade Representative and was nominated by the second President Bush as president of the World Bank: "We must act now. . . . The innovative technologies and crop varieties that we pilot today can shape energy and food sources to meet the needs of 3 billion more people by 2050" (World Bank, 2009). In the mid-2010s, however, divisions over how to address climate change became more partisan, with the U.S. President Donald Trump and most Republicans in Congress expressing skepticism of key elements of the global scientific consensus on climate change. In 2017, President Trump announced the U.S. decision to withdraw from the Paris Agreement (part of the United Nations Framework Convention on Climate Change), which committed signatories to setting national goals for net reductions in greenhouse gas emissions. If sustained, the U.S. federal government's inaction on climate change would increase the importance of other initiatives by state governments, local governments and nongovernmental civil society institutions in the United States.

3.3.6 Environmental Interactions Across Industries

In the preceding chapter, the section on "interactions among agricultural industries" (Section 2.2.6) described how industries are entangled in a network of alliances and competitions, as one industry's output becomes another industry's input. A similar pattern arises with biophysical and environmental links across agricultural industries (FAO, 2014). For example, ocean fisheries and aquaculture (fish farming) compete for consumer markets and also affect each other physically, as fish harvested in oceans are used as feed for aquaculture, and pollution from aquaculture impairs ocean fishing environments. Crops and animal production compete for food consumption shares; simultaneously, crops produce animal feed for livestock, and livestock produce manure that can be either a pollutant or a fertilizer for crop agriculture, depending on the quantity (Figure 3.2).

3.4 The Global Food Situation

There are two reasons to consider the global food situation in a book whose primary interest is U.S. food policy. First, U.S. food and agricultural markets are highly integrated with the global economy, as Chapter 4 will discuss. Second, debates about a sustainable food system in the United States stem from differing perspectives about global environmental issues. In particular, anybody who favors the expansion of organic and local food production (see Section 3.6) must be braced for the following question from skeptics: "If we do *that*, then how will we feed the world?"

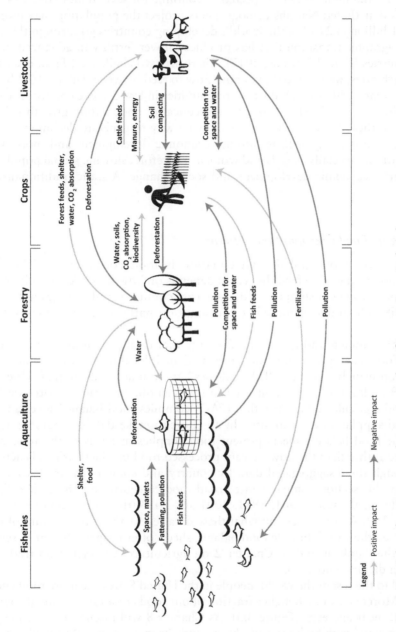

Figure 3.2 Selected environmental synergies and conflicts across agricultural sectors

Source: Food and Agriculture Organization, 2014; reproduced with permission.

3.4.1 Population Growth

The first part of the global food equation is population growth. The tough news about population is that the world already is a crowded place, with about 7.6 billion people as of mid-2017 and rapid growth expected to continue for several more decades. The good news is that United Nations demographers project the population may level off at around 11 billion in 2100 as the world's developing countries go through the same type of demographic transition that has produced lower fertility in advanced industrialized countries (United Nations, 2017). There are two challenges. First, even with slowed growth rates, we need to think about how to feed between 9.4 and 10.2 billion people in the year 2050. Second, if rural communities in low-income countries remain stuck with their current levels of poverty and education, population growth is likely to exceed even these forecasts. The most humane way to generate declining fertility and slowing population growth is through economic development and more widespread education, especially of girls and women. Therefore, slowing global population growth requires economic development and social change. A static traditionalism is not enough.

3.4.2 Changing Food Consumption Patterns

The second part of the global food equation is food consumption. The total amount of food required to feed the world depends on how much food each person needs. Yet, per capita consumption differs across countries and changes over time, making it difficult to determine what consumption pattern should be considered adequate.

Consider the amount and type of food energy that each person in the population consumes. Food energy is commonly measured in kilocalories (kcal) (which may somewhat confusingly just be called "calories" in common U.S. usage). One kcal equals 4,189 joules, the energy unit used in the scientific literature worldwide. The UN Food and Agriculture Organization (FAO) compiles **food balance sheets**, which describe food supplies in each country. In an effort to make data comparable across countries, the food balance sheets present food supplies in terms of the food commodities used rather than the downstream processed food products or meals actually eaten. Although the disaggregated data by country and commodity are fascinating, for simplicity this section compares just broad food categories for the United States and the world for the years 1961, 1981, 2001 and 2013 (the most recent year available) (Figure 3.3). We focus here on what these data reveal about the amount of food required to feed the world, but the food balance sheets offer insight relevant to several chapters of this book (including Chapter 2 on agriculture, Chapter 4 on trade and Chapter 8 on dietary guidance).

Compared to the rest of the world, people in the United States use more food energy per person. Moreover, a much higher fraction of our food comes from animal sources, such as milk, meat and eggs (Figure 3.3). As Chapter 8 will discuss, U.S. eating patterns are associated with high rates of obesity and chronic disease. Yet people around the world aspire to eat more like Americans do, having more food overall and consuming more meat and dairy.

Different food consumption patterns place different burdens on the environment, in terms of energy use, land use and greenhouse gas emissions (Canning et al., 2017). By

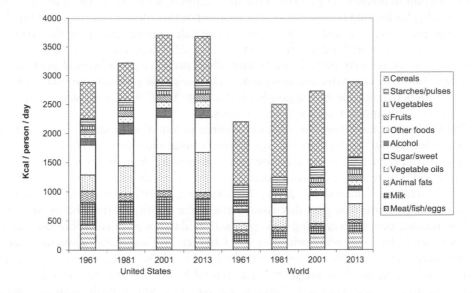

Figure 3.3 Food energy per person in the food supply of the United States and the world, 1961–2013

Data note: FAO's online statistics resource (FAOSTAT) provides a utility for generating customized food balance sheets for individual countries and groups of countries (faostat.fao.org). FAOSTAT also provides data for cross-national comparisons on many other issues related to agriculture, food prices and food security.

Source: UN Food and Agriculture Organization.

each measure, the environmental impact is lowest on average when we get our food energy from grains (such as rice and wheat) and starches and pulses (such as potatoes and beans). The impact is higher for food energy from eggs, poultry and dairy products, and highest of all for beef (Lusk and Norwood, 2009; Heller and Keoleian, 2015).

There are some partially offsetting nutritional and environmental advantages of animal food production. The environmental impact of both animal and plant food depends in part on the particular resources used in production. While red meat from typical U.S. production may be a comparatively damaging way to acquire food energy, grazing sheep and cattle is the most environmentally efficient use of some types of perennial grasslands. In rural areas of many low-income countries, animal production provides an important source of economic diversification and household savings, as families build up stocks during good-weather years and spend down the stocks in other years. In a more sustainable world food system, animal agriculture would still have an important role in food consumption, though surely smaller than its current role in U.S. food consumption patterns.

3.4.3 Food Loss and Waste

A third part of the global food equation is food waste. Much food is produced and never eaten. USDA economists estimate annual U.S. postharvest food losses at more than 130 billion pounds (31 percent of the food supply), with a retail value of $160 billion (Buzby, Wells and Hyman 2014). The amount of this food waste that could realistically be prevented or avoided is not known. The federal government for the first time in 2015 set a national food waste reduction goal: 50 percent by 2030. Some waste reduction measures may be technically infeasible (preserving nonbruised portions of damaged fruit), or expensive (hand separating below-grade products) or unacceptable to consumers (using stale baked goods), but a large fraction of food waste could be avoided through appropriate tools and policies.

The Environmental Protection Agency classifies potential approaches using a "food recovery hierarchy," with options ranging from source reduction and feeding hungry people (most preferred) to industrial uses and composting (less preferred) to landfill or incineration (last resort). For many potential approaches, there are complex tradeoffs (Neff, Kanter and Vandevijvere, 2015). For example, diverting food from landfills to food banks generates complex discussions about the quality of food being provided to low-income people. Preserving food past sell-by dates is promising, but only up to limits imposed by food safety priorities (see Chapter 7). Food waste reduction initiatives generate considerable enthusiasm at the local level. Schools, community organizations and emergency food programs such as food banks and food pantries have been involved, usually on a voluntary basis, but sometimes with a push from municipal government (Otten et al., 2016).

Another large fraction of U.S. food production is diverted into biofuels. Corn-based ethanol ballooned from 8 percent of corn use in 2000 to 38 percent of corn use in 2016. Animal feed was another 38 percent, and exports were 14 percent of corn use. All the remaining uses—including food and beverage manufacturing and seed—were only 11 percent of U.S. corn use in 2016. The largest of the food uses was high-fructose corn syrup.

U.S. ethanol production is only feasible because of large producer subsidies in the past and a current government mandate that specifies a fraction of gasoline must come from biofuels. Biofuels could be manufactured from plant material other than food crops, but in the United States these alternative fuel sources are not yet commercially viable on a large scale. Economists attribute rising global food prices in part to the use of food crops for biofuels, with price impact estimates ranging widely, from 15 percent (Chakravorty et al., 2017) to 70 percent (Rosegrant et al., 2008). Biofuel production from corn generates byproducts such as distillers grains, which can be used as animal feed, but these byproducts only partly reduce the large displacement of food uses for corn stocks. Without U.S. biofuels policy, it would be easier to produce enough food.

3.4.4 Increasing Food Production

The fourth part of the global food equation is increasing food production. Some of the most populous regions of the world, including South Asia and East Asia, have little unused land that can be brought into agricultural production. In other regions of the world, including South America and Sub-Saharan Africa, there are large tracts of forest and grassland that currently are not used for agricultural production. However, converting most of this land to agricultural use would have serious environmental consequences, including localized problems such as soil erosion and global problems such as raising the amount of atmospheric greenhouse gases, which contribute to climate change (World Bank, 2009). Moreover, while some new marginal land is brought into agricultural uses, other good farmland is converted to urban and industrial uses. Overall, the current amount of farmland is approximately all that will be available to feed a growing global population.

While land is limited, agricultural productivity per acre has grown rapidly in the past half-century. From 1961 to 2007, on average, global corn (maize) and wheat yields per acre increased 2.05 percent per year. This rapid improvement was enough to increase yields during this period by a factor of 2.6. Rice and soybean yields increased almost as quickly (Alston et al., 2009).

Unfortunately, that pace of yield growth will be difficult to maintain. The system of improving agricultural technology is showing signs of strain. Some new technologies require heavy water, energy and chemical inputs, which each raise their own environmental concerns. Resistance to chemical pesticides, exhaustion of water resources and global climate change may reverse some productivity gains. Some of the easiest technological advances may have already been discovered, and new advances may be more difficult. The field of biotechnology offers hope for some continued innovations, but these hopes should not be overstated, and the new genetically modified organisms (GMOs) face public resistance (Box 3.2). National governments and international organizations slowed the growth of their investments in agricultural technology and extension in recent years because the payoff to these investments appeared low when food seemed abundant and inexpensive. Globally, the rates of yield improvement quoted earlier have slowed in the most recent couple of decades. For example, from 1990 to 2007, the average annual rate of growth was only 1.8 percent for corn and 0.5 percent for wheat (Alston et al., 2009).

Agricultural productivity is important not just because it increases the total amount of food available globally but also because it improves economic conditions for the people with the greatest need for more food. Most of the world's poorest households are stuck in low-productivity agriculture and pastoralism (Bailey, 2011). For many, the tools required for higher productivity are adaptations of existing methods rather than new high-tech innovations. Agriculture-oriented rural economic development simultaneously addresses global food production needs and increases the spending power of the world's poorest households.

To avoid food crisis and famine, it seems likely that all elements of the global food equation discussed in this section will have to contribute a part: (a) population growth will slow as a result of economic development and expanded educational opportunity, (b) food and non-fuel demand growth will be moderate and will favor plant foods over meat, (c) food waste will be reduced and (d) agricultural productivity will increase through new technologies and through the spread of existing technologies to farmers who have been left behind so far.

3.5 Environmental Policies That Affect Agriculture

Policy-makers have a range of potential instruments for addressing environmental concerns, including direct regulation, conservation programs and changes to property rights assignments so that market incentives function better (Ribaudo et al., 2008). In different ways, contemporary U.S. environmental policy uses all of these instruments to address issues with agriculture and food production.

3.5.1 Regulation

Many environmental laws and regulations affect agriculture and food production. A distinctive feature of the regulatory approach is that compliance is mandatory. Three important examples are the Clean Water Act, the Federal Clean Air Act and the Endangered Species Act (National Research Council, 2010).

The Clean Water Act, which addresses water pollution, has diverse implications for U.S. manufacturing, municipal water utilities and land use. The law distinguishes between **point sources,** such as a drainage pipe that releases polluted water into a river, and **nonpoint sources,** such as cropland that might leach nitrogen from fertilizer. The Clean Water Act more strictly regulates point sources, while generally using more voluntary approaches for nonpoint sources. Most agricultural operations count as nonpoint sources, although large-scale confined animal feeding operations (CAFOs) may count as point sources and require a permit if they discharge water. Animal feeding operations may not require a permit if they keep all of their manure in lagoons and do not intend to discharge pollution into waterways. Environmentalists and farm interests disagree about what type of permit should be required if an animal feeding operation does not intend to discharge pollution but runs some risk of an accidental discharge. In addition to the Clean Water Act, some states have policies that address nonpoint sources in general, but they commonly provide an exception for farming (National Research Council, 2010).

The Federal Clean Air Act establishes air quality standards for many pollutants, such as carbon monoxide and particulate matter. It also puts limits on airborne hazardous chemicals. The law has sometimes led to restrictions on agricultural chemicals that could harm air quality, but in most cases it has not affected farms directly. Most farms do not emit sufficient quantities of pollutants to require a permit under the Clean Air Act (National Research Council, 2010). The major greenhouse gases that farms do emit, such as methane and nitrous oxide, are not currently classified by EPA as pollutants, although in principle EPA could classify them as pollutants in the future.

The Endangered Species Act seeks to conserve threatened plants and animals and to protect their habitats. There are rules against hunting or purposefully harming endangered species. A landowner who might accidentally harm an endangered species must get an "incidental take" permit to be assured of not violating the law (National Research Council, 2010). In California's Central Valley, court decisions have in some years used the Endangered Species Act to require greater water flows through the San Joaquin-Sacramento Delta to protect habitat for fish species such as the Delta smelt. These requirements reduce the amount of water available for irrigation.

3.5.2 Conservation Programs

A second major policy instrument is conservation programs, which offer producers a subsidy in return for voluntary action that helps meet environmental objectives (Figure 3.4). If the regulations discussed in Section 3.5.1 are the "stick," then these conservation programs are the "carrot." Conservation programs made up approximately 10 percent of the USDA budget in 2010. Two types of conservation programs are land

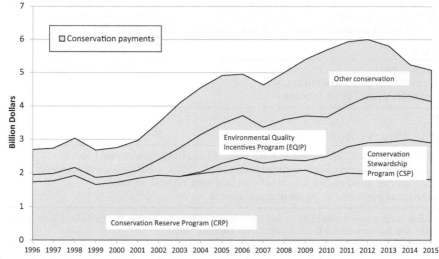

Figure 3.4 Government payments from U.S. agricultural conservation programs, 1996–2015

Note: Payments based on output are identified separately because of their implications for overproduction and for trade policy (see Chapter 4).

Data note: OECD's PSE (www.oecd.org/agriculture/pse) provides country-level data in a consistent format for international comparisons.

Source: Organisation for Economic Co-operation and Development (OECD), Producer Support Estimates (PSE).

retirement programs, which remove land from agricultural production, and working lands programs, which promote more sustainable practices on active farmland. Until the 2000s, land retirement programs were larger, but in recent years the working lands programs have grown, and the two strategies have become about equally important (Claassen et al., 2008; National Research Council, 2010).

Land retirement programs seek to address environmental goals, such as reducing soil erosion, preserving habitat and protecting water quality. The largest program is the Conservation Reserve Program (CRP) (see Table 3.2). In earlier years, the CRP paid a fixed price per acre, so farmers had an incentive to retire their least productive land. Since 1991, the CRP has used a bidding system, which allows payments to vary according to the economic sacrifice that farmers must make in retiring land. The new approach helps the government set appropriate payment levels based on information about market conditions. As noted in Chapter 2, land retirement programs also serve as a gentle form of supply control by reducing supply and encouraging a higher market price. Hence, land retirement policies are more popular with farmers and the taxpaying public during times of high production and low prices but less popular during times of food scarcity and high prices.

The leading working lands programs include the Environmental Quality Incentives Program (EQIP) (see Table S3.1 in the online companion website) and the Conservation Stewardship Program (CSP) (Table S3.2). EQIP provides technical and financial assistance to encourage producers to adopt sustainable practices. By design, a large part

Table 3.2 Program summary: Conservation Reserve Program (CRP)

Overview: Reduces erosion and environmental damage by paying farmers to replace crops on environmentally sensitive land with resource-preserving cover.	
Year begun	*1985*
Scale of operation	
Farms enrolled, April 2016 (thousand)	365
Acres enrolled, April 2016 (million)	23.9
Budget	
Funding, 2016 ($ billion)	1.9

Eligibility: For general participation, CRP solicits bids from farmers and scores them using an Environmental Benefits Index (EBI). Some CRP initiatives focus on issues of special concern, such as small isolated agricultural wetlands.
Benefits: Rental payments to participating farmers.

Note: Online supplemental materials provide corresponding tables for the Conservation Stewardship Program (CSP) and Environmental Quality Incentives Program (EQIP).

Data note: OECD's PSE (www.oecd.org/agriculture/pse) provides country-level farm subsidy data. Conservation program data are available from USDA's Natural Resources Conservation Service (NRCS) and Farm Service Agency (FSA) (www.fsa.usda.gov/programs-and-services/conservation-programs/).

Sources: Congressional Research Service (2016); OECD (2016).

of the support goes to animal producers. From 1996 until 2002, large-scale CAFOs were excluded, but this policy was changed in 2002, and these large-scale producers now receive much of the program's support. The purpose of this change was to influence the producers who actually have the largest impact on environmental quality, but a consequence is to subsidize producers who are substantial polluters. Using USDA administrative records on EQIP payments, Melissa Bailey estimated that the largest fraction of EQIP payments targeting improved water quality were to support improvements in waste storage, such as the manure lagoons used by large animal feeding operations (Bailey, 2010). Such subsidies only offer a net benefit if the environmental investments are "additional," meaning that they go beyond what producers would have made anyway as part of their business model or compliance with regulations.

3.5.3 Prices, Property Rights and Market Mechanisms

As discussed in Section 3.2, many environmental challenges in agriculture and the food system arise from externalities, public goods problems and incomplete or unclear property rights. Economic actors who would wisely manage their own resources may nevertheless make unwise decisions about resources that are shared. In response, governments may try to influence prices or assign property rights in such a way that private market incentives favor environmentally sound decisions.

For example, higher carbon prices could simultaneously address several environmental problems (Carbon Pricing Leadership Coalition, 2017). They would encourage consumers to reduce greenhouse gas emissions by conserving energy; promote conservation by food system intermediaries in the manufacturing, transportation and retail sectors; and motivate electric utilities to invest in renewable energy sources, which become economically competitive only when petroleum prices are high. Because energy inputs are the most expensive inputs in the production of nitrogen fertilizer, higher petroleum prices also would increase the comparative advantage of organic and low-input agriculture relative to conventional production.

Yet policies that would raise petroleum prices are profoundly unpopular. The most straightforward mechanism would be a higher petroleum tax, but in the United States, there is a well-developed political movement opposed to new taxes. Alternatively, under a **cap-and-trade** system for greenhouse gas emissions, producers that emit greenhouse gases would be assigned permits, which they could trade to the highest bidder. A farmer who was willing to cut his/her emissions by half could sell emissions rights to a power plant. The total amount of permits could be chosen to meet global emissions targets. From an economic perspective, such a system would have effects somewhat similar to that of a petroleum tax. In the United States, such systems are being developed only at the regional or state level so far. At the federal level, the House of Representatives in 2009 passed the American Clean Energy and Security Act, which contained a cap-and-trade proposal, but in 2010 the Senate let the proposal die. In 2015, the Obama administration developed a Clean Power Plan with some similarities to a cap-and-trade system, with state flexibility in choosing methods for meeting greenhouse gas targets; in 2017, however, the Trump administration paused this initiative and will review it skeptically.

For many issues related to food production and the environment, a key decision is how property rights should be assigned. For example, in California, water scarcity is related to problems with the assignment of property rights. Rights to water in rivers are comparatively well defined. Since 1914, these rights have been regulated through a system of permits, although a nagging exception is that owners of pre-1914 water rights require no permit even today. Rights to water in underground aquifers are even murkier. Market incentives lead farmers and residents in California to withdraw more water from underground aquifers than can be replenished. In 2014, California passed the Sustainable Groundwater Management Act (SGMA), which requires local water districts with severe depletion to develop environmentally sound plans by 2020 (or in some cases 2022) for managing groundwater resources (Hanak et al., 2017). It is not yet known how well these plans will work.

Likewise, continuing the fisheries example from Section 3.2.1, there is a lively ongoing debate over "catch shares," in which a total harvest target in each fishery is established and individuals are assigned tradable permits for their share of the total. To economists, such programs have great appeal, because they offer hope of meeting environmental objectives in the most efficient manner. Resource economist Chris Costello and colleagues argue that catch share programs are associated with a reduced risk of fishery collapse (Costello et al., 2008). Catch share programs are divisive among environmental advocates, with some in favor and some opposed.

3.5.4 Sustainable Dietary Guidelines

One of the mildest policy actions would be simply to advise the public on scientific evidence about environmental consequences of their food choices. A coordinated way to do so would be to cover sustainability issues as one part of the federal government's *Dietary Guidelines for Americans*, which are revised once every five years (see Chapter 8). This approach is opposed by animal production industries concerned about implications for consumer demand but supported by environmental and public health organizations (Merrigan et al., 2015).

The idea received a boost in late 2014 when the Dietary Guidelines Advisory Committee, an external committee that provides input on scientific matters for the guidelines, quietly noted evidence showing that health-promoting dietary patterns (including a healthier version of the typical American eating pattern, a Mediterranean eating pattern and a healthy vegetarian eating pattern) also had lower environmental impacts:

> All of these dietary patterns are aligned with lower environmental impacts and provide options that can be adopted by the U.S. population. Current evidence shows that the average U.S. diet has a larger environmental impact in terms of increased greenhouse gas emissions, land use, water use, and energy use, compared to the above dietary patterns. This is because the current U.S. population intake of animal-based foods is higher and plant-based foods are lower, than proposed in these three dietary patterns. Of note is that no food groups need to be eliminated completely to improve sustainability outcomes over the current status.
>
> (Dietary Guidelines Advisory Committee, 2015)

In the end, when the federal government released the most recent version of the *Dietary Guidelines* in January 2016, the official report omitted discussion of environmental sustainability. This policy decision means that the official federal government document cannot contribute a balanced summary of scientific evidence on sustainability issues as it does on nutrition issues. The decision will not stop consumers from contemplating and debating the environmental consequences of their food choices. Consumers just must turn to other sources for the information they seek.

3.6 Contemporary Food Movements

In addition to government policies, discussed in Section 3.5, farmers and consumers do voluntarily express concern about environmental issues, and this concern can affect their economic decisions. Consumers can vote with their fork to advance their interest in vegetarianism, animal welfare (see Chapter 9, Box 9.1) or community food security, for example. This section focuses on two such movements that have been influential in recent years: the organic and local food movements (see also Chapter 4 for discussion of the food sovereignty movement and Chapter 6 for discussion of the food justice movement). For the organic and local food movements, this section will discuss broad aspirations, narrower definitional details, prospects for growth and limitations to consider.

In some respects, these movements seek a radical departure from the conventional food system. Supporters frequently voice disenchantment with the modern food industry and suspicion of national-level policy-makers. At the same time, these movements are largely market oriented, driven by private-sector producer innovation and consumer passion. Major farm organizations have treated these alternative food movements as a dangerous threat that might overturn the more conventional food system. More realistically, for the foreseeable future, the potential expansion of organic and local food production will take place within a broader nonorganic and national food system.

3.6.1 Organic Food

The aspiration of organic agriculture is to use natural biological processes instead of synthetic chemical inputs to raise soil quality and control pests. Possible environmental benefits of organic production systems include reduced pesticide residues in water and food, reduced nutrient runoff, improved soil organic matter, lower energy use, carbon sequestration and enhanced biodiversity (Greene et al., 2009). The leading organic food sectors are fruits, vegetables and dairy.

In the United States, food labeled as organic must comply with the provisions of the 1990 Organic Foods Production Act and subsequent regulations that are administered by USDA's National Organic Program. The regulations are developed with input from a USDA-appointed National Organic Standards Board. The many provisions for crops include prohibitions against most synthetic pesticides, petroleum-based fertilizers, sewage sludge and genetically modified organisms. Organically produced animals must be given organic feed, and they may not be given antibiotics prophylactically as a growth promoter. They must have access to the outdoors, although some producers interpret this provision narrowly, providing only limited access. Individual farm practices are overseen by certifiers, who in turn must be approved by USDA or in some cases by a state agency. USDA provides support for research on organic agriculture and some modest cost-sharing for certification activities, but the costs of the certification system are mostly paid by the organic producers (Greene et al., 2009). The label "certified organic" has much tighter rules than other possible label claims, such as "natural," which influences the prices that consumers are willing to pay for organic food (McFadden and Huffman, 2017).

Organic food is more expensive to produce than conventional food. The price premium can range from 7 percent of the conventional price for lettuce to 82 percent for eggs (Carlson and Jaenicke, 2016). The organic movement has been transformed by its rapid growth, as large food manufacturers and retail chains have begun to sell organic food. Within the organic movement, there is a persistent tug-of-war between advocates for stricter rules, which distinguish organic production more sharply from conventional production, and advocates for less-burdensome rules, which reduce production costs and allow organic sales to expand more rapidly at the expense of conventional sales. Under current rules, organic food may be imported, transported long distances, harvested by low-wage laborers and produced by large corporations.

3.6.2 Local Food

The aspirations of the local food movement include reducing the food system's environmental footprint, reinvigorating rural economies, improving food quality and freshness and preserving the historical relationships between farmers and food consumers (Chase and Grubinger, 2014). Some "locavores" favor shorter supply chains to protect the environment and reduce resource use, while others simply want to make food production more visible and present to urban consumers. The poet and essayist Wendell Berry, an influential precursor to the local food journalists and activists of the 2000s, laments the sad fate of the industrial eater who "no longer knows or imagines the connections between eating and the land" (Berry, 1990).

The term "local" is used to describe a variety of direct marketing methods and geographical characteristics. The marketing approaches include farmers' markets, roadside stands, community-supported agriculture and farm-to-school programs. Among geographic characteristics, a popular benchmark is to define local food as food that comes from within a 100-mile radius. For some purposes, the federal government defines local food as food sold less than 400 miles from its origin or sold in the same state where it was produced. There are also more flexible definitions that take account of greater urbanization in some regions of the country (Martinez et al., 2010; Low et al., 2015).

Because local food has multiple definitions, there are multiple measures of its recent growth. USDA estimates that direct-to-consumer sales grew from $551 million in 1997 (0.3 percent of U.S. agricultural sales) to $1.2 billion in 2007 (0.4 percent of U.S. agricultural sales), leveling off to $1.3 billion (0.3 percent of U.S. agricultural sales) in 2012 (Low et al., 2015). Instead of direct-to-consumer sales, larger farms that sell locally are likely to market a greater share of their product through "intermediated" channels, such as through supermarkets, but these local food sales are difficult to measure.

In discussing the merits of the local food movement, one should not overstate the equivalence between local sourcing and low environmental impact. It is true that local sourcing can lower energy use in transportation, but a food product's environmental footprint depends on many factors in addition to transportation (Teisl, 2011). For example, energy use in agriculture, food manufacturing and food retailing exceeds energy use in food transportation (Canning et al., 2017). The environmental merit of consumer interest in local food stems from a wider variety of product qualities associated with local sourcing—such as production methods, seasonality, processing and packaging—in addition to transportation costs.

How much does local sourcing support local economies? Consider the impact of increased local sourcing from the perspective of a single agricultural county in the Heartland. In a scenario where one nearby city increases its local food purchasing, while the rest of the nation's consumption is unchanged, of course the increased local sourcing would benefit the local farmers in this agricultural county. By contrast, in a scenario where all U.S. consumers increased their local food purchasing and reduced their long-distance food sourcing, the agricultural county's farmers would suffer a loss of long-distance sales that could offset its increase in local sales. If all consumers increased their purchases of local food, some farmers would benefit and other farmers would lose.

Thinking about environmental and economic issues together, the case in favor of long-distance sourcing is strong for grain crops and oilseeds, which are more efficiently grown in some regions than others and which are comparatively inexpensive to transport. At its best, long-distance sourcing allows each region to focus on its comparative advantage (see Chapter 4), producing the products for which the local environment is most distinctively suitable. By contrast, the case in favor of local food sourcing is strongest when food products are expensive to transport (such as fruits and vegetables with a heavy water content) and when local food products provide the consumer with other valued qualities—such as freshness, taste and a sense of place—in addition to lower food miles per se.

3.7 Conclusion

This chapter reviews many ways in which decisions by food producers have consequences for other people and the natural environment. For example, the decisions that farmers make about chemical use affect their own health, air quality for nearby neighbors and also human populations and natural ecology throughout the farmer's watershed. Even if the world were a static and stable place, a textbook on U.S. food policy would require a chapter on food production and the environment, just to explain the various possible governmental and nongovernmental arrangements for coordinated decision making to address environmental externalities.

Agricultural sustainability requires both environmental awareness and a dogged pursuit of productivity. Internationally, the UN Food and Agriculture Organization uses the motto "Save and Grow" to describe the twin goals of environmental protection and pursuit of agricultural intensification. In the United States, discussion of environmental issues has become entangled with deeply felt political, regional and cultural divisions. Though some attempts are being made, it remains a daunting challenge to build an environmentally motivated food movement that resonates broadly with social conservatives, rural residents, commercial farmers and Heartland states.

Markets and government policy instruments each have strengths and weaknesses as tools for making important social decisions about food production and the environment. While it is true that environmental market failures are pervasive in the U.S. food system, this fact does not mean that government regulations always trump market approaches. In recent years, private-sector farm and food movements have far outpaced government initiatives as a source of innovation and inspiration for reconciling food production with the environment. The ultimate social goal is to harness and coordinate the efforts of millions of U.S. farms and food businesses, who must make food production decisions to meet the needs of millions of consumers, using environmentally sound choices of technology for each producer's and consumer's specific geographic and economic setting. To pursue this goal, governments have a variety of policy options for addressing environmental market failures while still seeking to assign to markets the tasks that markets do well.

Summary List of Key Terms (identified in bold in the text)

- adaptation
- agricultural sustainability
- cap-and-trade
- food balance sheets
- mitigation
- nonpoint sources
- point sources
- transaction costs

4 Food and Agricultural Trade

4.1 Introduction

U.S. food policy takes place in a global setting. American agricultural imports and exports affect food prices and market quantities around the world. Conversely, international trade and economic development in other countries influence food prices and consumption patterns in the United States.

Trade arguments do not always follow traditional partisan lines. Within U.S. agriculture, farmers themselves may be divided on trade policy. A wheat farmer who earns a living from exports to other countries may favor open trade, while a dairy farmer who competes with imports from other countries may disagree.

Similarly, within progressive food policy organizations and food movements, attitudes toward trade are mixed. According to the website for the nongovernmental organization Oxfam America, "Trade generates incredible wealth and connects people everywhere, yet millions of people in poor countries are not benefitting, and many are actually worse off, because trade rules are rigged against them" (Oxfam America, 2017). The loosely knit **food sovereignty** movement favors food self-sufficiency, denounces international trade regimes and demands power for countries and local communities to make their own decisions about food and agriculture. Yet, like Oxfam, the food sovereignty movement hedges its criticism of trade. In a much-cited definition, "food sovereignty does not negate trade, but rather, it promotes the formulation of trade policies and practices that serve the rights of peoples to safe, healthy and ecologically sustainable production" (Peoples' Food Sovereignty Network, 2002; cited in Patel, 2009).

This chapter explores how people in rich and poor countries alike can enjoy the potential advantages of international trade without falling victim to political powerlessness and a race to the bottom in a globalizing world. The chapter:

- summarizes the trade flows between the United States and other countries, noting that agriculture is a leading U.S. export industry (Section 4.2);
- introduces some economic principles of international trade, including gains from trade, government policies that promote or restrain trade and methods for measuring the impact of these government policies (Section 4.3);
- discusses international trade agreements that regulate the trade barriers that countries use (Section 4.4);

- describes U.S. food aid, including its intended benefits and unintended consequences (Section 4.5);
- considers farm labor and immigration, because international borders are permeable for people and not just for goods and services (Section 4.6); and
- reviews global food price trends (Section 4.7).

4.2 U.S. Food and Agricultural Trade Flows

The United States was a net exporter of agricultural products from 1980 to 2016, the most recent year available (Figure 4.1). In real inflation-adjusted terms (constant 2016 dollars), U.S. agricultural exports reached record levels in an environment of high world food prices from 2007–2014, before subsiding somewhat in 2015–2016.

People sometimes think of industrialization as a process that involves leaving agriculture behind, so the U.S. specialization in agricultural trade may seem surprising. The United States also is a major exporter of some comparatively high-technology industrial products, such as aircraft, and U.S. higher education and financial services draw customers from around the globe. Yet with a large endowment of land and efficient production practices, agriculture comprises a substantial part of modern U.S. international trade.

Most food around the world still is consumed in the same country where it is grown. For example, in the 2010/2011 crop year, global wheat exports were only 10.5 percent of global production, corn exports were 11.1 percent of global production and rice exports were 7.9 percent of global production. Some U.S. agricultural industries rely more heavily on trade as a major source of revenue for farmers. For example, in the same 2010/2011 crop year, wheat exports were 59.9 percent of U.S. wheat production.

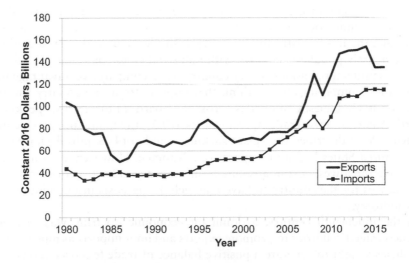

Figure 4.1 U.S. agricultural exports and imports, 1980–2016

Data note: The USDA data series on Foreign Agricultural Trade of the United States (FATUS) provides authoritative statistics on U.S. food and agricultural trade (www.ers.usda.gov/data-products).

USDA provides information about exports and imports through an ongoing data series called the Foreign Agricultural Trade of the United States (FATUS) (www.ers. usda.gov/data-products). U.S. agricultural export products in 2016 included soybeans ($22.9 billion), corn ($9.9 billion), wheat ($5.3 billion), beef and veal ($5.2 billion) and many other products from farms and food manufacturing industries. Leading import commodities, ranked by dollar value in 2016, included coffee, wine, cocoa, malt beverages, and beef and veal. The top destinations for U.S. agricultural exports in 2016 were China, Canada, Mexico, the European Union and Japan. Most of these same countries, with the exception of Japan, also are top sources of agricultural imports to the United States.

4.3 Principles of Trade Policy

4.3.1 Gains from Trade

Since ancient times, nations have reaped mutual economic benefits from trading with each other. With international trade, countries can specialize in the industries in which they are most capable. In this manner, groups of countries linked by trade networks can produce more goods and services with fewer resources than would otherwise be possible. The mutual advantages of this specialization are called **gains from trade** (Koo and Kennedy, 2005).

Under **autarky**, which is a situation without trade, each country would have to produce all of its own goods and services. A less industrialized country with plenty of arable land may be able to produce inexpensive food, but manufactured goods might be scarce and expensive. A densely populated country with industrial cities may produce inexpensive manufactured goods, but food might be scarce and expensive.

With trade, by contrast, each country can specialize in its **comparative advantage**, the industry or industries in which the domestic production costs are relatively low. For example, the less industrialized country with plenty of arable land could export food. The densely populated country with industrial cities could pay for this food by exporting manufactured goods. Every country has a comparative advantage in something. It is a common mistake to think that imports from one country can displace another country's domestic industries across the board. In the 1990s, speaking about the North American Free Trade Agreement (NAFTA), the billionaire presidential candidate Ross Perot described the "giant sucking sound" of U.S. jobs fleeing to Mexico, as if the United States had no comparative advantage. However, a country does not need to have the lowest cost in absolute terms in order to have a comparative advantage. It suffices for the country to have relatively lower costs in one industry than in another industry.

Until the nineteenth century, a dominant economic doctrine was **mercantilism**, which encouraged countries to promote exports and limit imports as much as possible. Such policies sought to generate a positive **balance of trade** (exports minus imports). This doctrine was thought to increase national wealth by inducing net inflows of gold from trading partners. We still commonly hear an echo of the spirit of mercantilism in modern trade policy arguments. The mercantilist thinks that the exporting nation always wins and the importing nation loses. Most contemporary economists believe instead that exporters and importers both benefit from trade.

Box 4.1   The Economics of International Trade in Corn

Figure 4.2 uses the same U.S. supply and demand functions that we began studying in Box 2.1. Under autarky, or the absence of trade, recall that the United States would have a competitive market equilibrium price of $1.75 per bushel. At this price, U.S. consumers would buy 15 billion bushels of corn from U.S. producers (left panel).

For simplicity, we treat the trading partner in this example as if it were a single country called "the rest of the world." Without trade, farmers in the Rest of World (ROW) would have to supply all the corn for consumers there. At a comparatively high market equilibrium price of $3.00 per bushel, foreign farmers would produce 20 billion bushels for use by foreign consumers (see the intersection of the supply and demand lines of the right-hand panel).

Suppose trade opens up. What new price would generate a global market equilibrium, where the new quantity supplied equals the quantity demanded? At a new world price of $2.20, the United States would want to export 2.5 billion bushels of corn, which is the horizontal difference between what U.S. farmers would supply (point B) and what U.S. consumers would demand (point A). At this same price, the rest of the world would want to import 2.5 billion bushels of corn, which is the difference between what foreign consumers would demand (point D) and what foreign farmers would supply (point C). This price is an equilibrium price, because the worldwide quantity supplied equals the quantity demanded at this price.

In this example, U.S. farmers profit from trade, because they get paid the world price, which is higher than the U.S. autarky price. Foreign consumers enjoy a lower foreign buying price than without trade. The losers from trade in this example are U.S. consumers and foreign farmers.

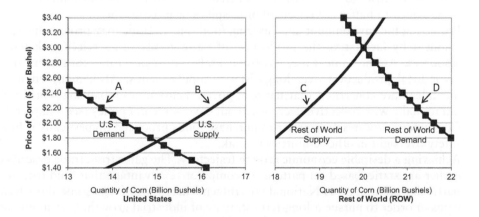

Figure 4.2 A model of trade in corn (maize) between the United States and the rest of the world (hypothetical)

Note: At the world price, the horizontal distance for U.S. exports (point B—point A) equals the horizontal distance for Rest of World imports (point D—point C).

International trade influences prices (Box 4.1 provides a numerical example). The magnitude of the price effect depends on the elasticities of supply and demand (Appendix S2.2; see the online Companion Website). The magnitude of the price effect also depends on whether a country is classified as small or large. A **small country** is one whose trade in a particular good, whether import or export, makes little difference for world prices. A **large country** can influence world prices. Classifying a country as small or large does not depend on population or land area. For example, a rice-exporting country of 70 million people in Southeast Asia may behave like a small country in global automobile trade and a large country in global rice trade. For brevity, this chapter focuses mostly on the large country case. Sometimes, several small countries can jointly be treated as equivalent to a large country, so the large country case has fairly wide application.

4.3.2 Motivations for Trade Policy

Economists frequently advocate comparatively **free trade,** with limited government intervention. Yet even mainstream economists also recognize several powerful reasons why governments restrict international trade.

- **Protecting certain economic sectors.** Trade generates domestic losers as well as winners (see Box 4.1). A manufacturing industry may suffer from increased competition, or consumers may suffer from elevated prices due to trade. For developing countries, free trade in agricultural products could provide new opportunities for farmers while raising food prices in rapidly growing cities. Even within the farm sector, trade may affect small farmers differently from large farmers. Economists believe that the gains for the winners exceed the hardship for the losers, so trade is a good deal in general. Nevertheless, the economic sectors that lose from trade may be sufficiently powerful to enact policies that limit trade.
- **Ensuring economic stability.** Because global prices fluctuate, international trade exposes countries to economic risks as well as benefits. Countries sometimes use trade policy to buffer the effects of price spikes or price crashes.
- **Protecting the environment and ensuring food safety.** Trade may protect the environment by facilitating the production of more goods and services with fewer resources. At the same time, environmentally conscious food consumers may favor local production over long-distance supply chains. Also, many environmentalists are concerned that national governments in a globalizing world will fail to make wise collective decisions about environmental policy (see Chapter 3). Consumer advocates may prefer to purchase foods produced domestically if food safety oversight in other countries is weak.
- **Achieving a desirable economic growth trajectory.** The gains from trade described earlier are static, based on patterns of comparative advantage that hold true at a particular point in time. National governments may try to forgo some short-term gains in order to pursue a long-term strategy of industrial growth. Continuing an example from Section 4.3.1, a rural agricultural nation may seek to promote industrialization by protecting new manufacturing industries from import competition.

It is difficult to distinguish well-motivated trade restrictions from unwise efforts to protect specific industries at the expense of other citizens. A country's trade restrictions

Box 4.2   The Economics of Trade Barriers in Corn

A tariff, or tax on imports, is an example of a trade barrier. Continuing the example from Box 4.1, farmers in the Rest of World (ROW) may seek a tariff on corn for protection against imports from the United States. Suppose ROW imposes an import tariff of $0.50 per bushel of corn, so that the foreign price would become $0.50 higher than the U.S. price (Figure 4.3).

What new price would generate a market equilibrium, where the new quantity supplied equals the quantity demanded? A U.S. price of $2.00 per bushel would generate export supply of just about 1.4 billion bushels in the United States, which is the difference between the amount supplied by U.S. farmers (point B) and the amount demanded by U.S. consumers (point A). A price of $2.50 per bushel in ROW, reflecting the $0.50 tariff, would generate import demand of the same quantity of 1.4 billion bushels, which is the difference between the amount demanded by foreign consumers (point D) and the amount supplied by foreign farmers (point C). So, in this new equilibrium, the tariff would suppress the U.S. price and elevate the price in the rest of the world, compared to the free-trade equilibrium. The tariff would limit trade and move the world partway back in the direction of autarky, where every country produces for itself.

Although the price gap in Figure 4.3 is labeled with the word "tariff," we can use the same illustration to explain other types of trade barriers. Instead of a tariff, suppose ROW imposed an import quota, or quantity limit, on imports from the United States. A quota of 1.4 billion bushels would have the same effect as the tariff, leading to the same $0.50 per bushel vertical gap between the U.S. price and the foreign price. Similarly, if the United States imposed an export tax of $0.50 or an export quantity limit of 1.4 billion bushels, the world trade situation would be the same as in Figure 4.3.

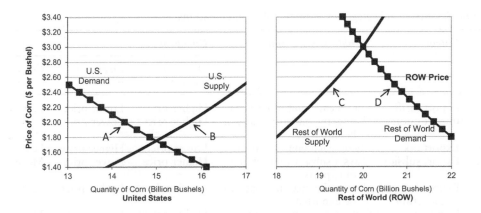

Figure 4.3 A model of trade in corn (maize) with a $0.50 tariff as a trade barrier (hypothetical)

Note: The horizontal distance (point B—point A) equals the horizontal distance (point D–point C).

for one commodity can affect the willingness of trading partners to permit trade in other commodities. Policy-makers must consider each proposed trade restriction in the context of a broader national decision about whether a country seeks to have a closed or open posture regarding international trade.

4.3.3 *Varieties of Trade Policies*

National governments employ a wide variety of trade policies. As Box 4.2 shows, trade barriers can elevate domestic prices for an import good. Similarly, trade barriers can lower domestic prices for an export good.

Six examples of trade policies illustrate the key concepts (Table 4.1):

1. An **import tariff** is a tax on goods entering a country. In developed countries, the main objective of a tariff usually is not to raise revenue but instead to influence prices and protect domestic industries.
2. An **import quota** is a restriction on the quantity that may be imported. Import quotas are an example of a **nontariff barrier.** Other nontariff barriers may include food labeling and food safety policies. A quota's effects are similar to those of a tariff. The quota limits the quantity available in the importing country, causing the price in the importing country to rise. Implementing a quota raises some of the same problems discussed in the context of production quotas in Chapter 2. The official document that entitles a particular firm to import the good becomes a valuable asset in its own right. Economists use the term **rents** to describe the surplus profits earned by quota-holders. Import quotas can encourage wasteful **rent-seeking behavior,** as firms expend resources trying to acquire these valuable quota rights (Box 4.3).
3. An **export tax** lowers the domestic price in the exporting country while raising the price paid by consumers overseas. The purpose is to protect domestic consumers or simply to raise government revenue.

Table 4.1 Six broad categories of trade policy interventions

	Category	What the government does	Effect on . . .		
			Domestic market	Overseas market[1]	Quantity traded
1.	Import tariff	Taxes each unit of imports	Higher price	Lower price	Less
2.	Import quota	Limits the quantity that can be imported	Higher price	Lower price	Less
3.	Export tax	Taxes each unit of exports	Lower price	Higher price	Less
4.	Export subsidy	Pays a subsidy on each unit of exports	Higher price	Lower price	More
5.	Export restriction	Limits the quantity that can be exported	Lower price	Higher price	Less
6.	Dumping	Sells a quantity overseas at less than the domestic price	Higher price	Lower price	More

1 Although trade policy always is capable of affecting the domestic market, it only affects the overseas market in the case of large countries.

Box 4.3 Sugar Politics

U.S. sugar production comes from sugar cane farms (in Florida, Louisiana, Texas and Hawaii) and sugar beet farms (principally in the Midwest and Great Plains). Sugar is just one part of a broader market for sweeteners, in which corn syrup is also a major player. The sugar cane production is concentrated in a few large corporations, while the sugar beet and corn production is distributed across many farms.

Trade barriers, production quotas and subsidy programs have kept U.S. sugar prices much higher than world prices for many years (USDA Economic Research Service, 2012b; McMinimy, 2016). Economic analysis published by the American Enterprise Institute estimated that U.S. sugar policy cost consumers $2.4 billion annually (in 2009 dollars), of which $1.4 billion was an economic gain for U.S. producers and $1 billion represented an outright loss to the economy (Wohlgenant, 2011). Using OECD's measurement approach, U.S. sugar production is more heavily supported in percentage terms than any other major crop (OECD, 2016).

U.S. sugar policies harm many sugar producers overseas by suppressing the world price while simultaneously enriching a small number of foreign producers who hold quota rights to import limited quantities without paying a punitive tariff. Even though the U.S. agreed in NAFTA to lower trade barriers over time, producers in Mexico have had to accept a series of temporary "suspension agreements" that limit Mexican sugar exports (McMinimy, 2016; Hendrix and Kotschwar, 2016). High U.S. domestic sugar prices led to new innovation and investment in sweetener technology, leading to the development and expansion of the high-fructose corn syrup (HFCS) industry. In Florida, especially, sugar production has generated environmental concerns, including phosphate runoff that damaged the Everglades ecology (see Chapter 3), requiring an expensive government buyout of sugar plantation holdings.

Yet the consumers and other constituencies who lose out from sugar policy are disorganized, widely dispersed and insufficiently motivated to get the policy changed. Even at the elevated price, sugar is not very expensive, so each consumer has only a little money at stake. Instead of consumers, the most powerful critic of sugar policy is the Sweetener Users Association, which represents manufacturers that buy sweeteners at elevated prices, but even this association does not usually prevail. There is little or no federal budget spending on the policies, because the main source of subsidy is an implicit tax on consumers in the form of higher prices, so taxpayer organizations also are only weakly motivated to oppose the policies. By contrast, the sugar cane industry is highly concentrated, giving a small number of wealthy producers a strong motivation to lobby for favorable policies (Carney, 2012).

4. An **export subsidy**, which pays exporters a certain amount per unit exported, raises the domestic price in the exporting country while lowering the price overseas. The purpose is to benefit domestic producers.

5. An **export restriction** is a limit on the quantity that can be exported. Sometimes, all exports are prohibited. For example, during the global food price spikes of the late 2000s, some countries restricted exports of key food staples (Section 4.7). Like an export tax, export restrictions lower the domestic price in the exporting country.

6. **Dumping** is when a product is sold overseas at below the production cost. In some cases, private companies use dumping as part of a strategy of price discrimination, charging a higher price domestically than they do overseas. In other cases, a government program may cover the loss. Dumping may arise as a consequence of a price support program in which the government buys up surplus product. When dumping is sponsored by governments, the purpose is to support prices and benefit producers in the exporting country. Dumping may suppress prices overseas.

Looking across countries, a consistent pattern is that low-income countries tend to adopt policies that tax agriculture and subsidize food consumption, while higher-income countries adopt policies that subsidize agriculture at the expense of food consumers and taxpayers (Masters, 2011). For example, export taxes are common in less-developed countries, while import tariffs and export subsidies are favored by the United States and European Union.

4.3.4 *Quantifying Policies That Influence Trade*

Faced with these multiple categories of trade policies, international organizations seek to measure their total impact. The Organisation for Economic Co-operation and Development (OECD), an international association of high-income countries, compiles data for multiple countries and presents them in a consistent format to show how all types of trade barriers transfer resources from consumers to producers. OECD's **market price support (MPS)** measure equals the price difference between domestic and world prices multiplied by the quantity produced. Under free trade, the domestic price would equal the world price (after accounting for transportation costs), so MPS would equal zero.

A quantitative example with real-world data illustrates in greater detail how OECD's MPS works in the presence of trade barriers:

- In 2005, the world price for milk was only $270 per ton, and trade barriers kept U.S. milk at a higher price of $334 per ton. Taking the price gap times the production quantity of 80 million tons, the MPS equaled about $5 billion.
- By 2010, the U.S. milk price was $359 per ton, almost exactly equal to the world price, which had risen to $357 per ton. Taking this small price gap times the 2010 production quantity of 87 million tons, the MPS equaled only $0.4 billion.

The most significant U.S. trade barriers block imports of milk, sugar and beef (OECD, 2016). The federal government intervenes in dairy markets through a complex set of price supports and marketing orders (see Chapter 2). As a side effect, these domestic dairy policies require the government to impose trade barriers. Otherwise, foreign producers would sell their product at the elevated U.S. price, causing the dairy program's budget costs to explode. For sugar, the MPS is smaller in aggregate, but this trade protection represents a large fraction of total earnings for sugar producers (Box 4.3).

Figure 4.4 shows OECD estimates of MPS in the United States from 1996 to 2015. OECD collects fairly detailed information about trade barriers for major commodities while making rough estimates about minor commodities. In the comparatively low-price years of the late 1990s and early 2000s, the milk and sugar MPS was greater than $12 billion, representing a large economic transfer to U.S. producers from U.S. consumers, who paid elevated prices. By contrast, in the comparatively high-price years of the late 2000s, the MPS for milk and sugar was less than $2 billion.

Total support for agricultural producers depends on the trade barriers discussed earlier and on other payments to producers, discussed in earlier chapters. International organizations use two leading approaches to measuring total support, with some similarities and differences.

- The OECD's **Producer Support Estimate** (PSE) is a research tool for measuring economic benefits to producers. As noted earlier, the market price support component (for assessing trade barriers) is based on the difference between the domestic price and the world price for leading agricultural products multiplied by the quantity produced. For the agricultural programs component, the PSE categorizes programs based on what the producers must do to gain the support. OECD's PSE is a good source for understanding the economic impact of farm programs and trade barriers.

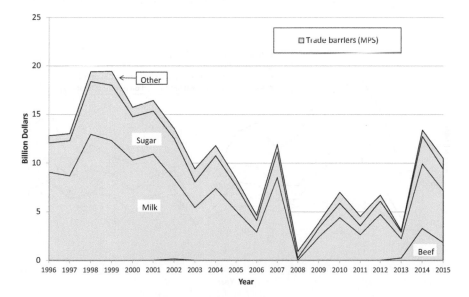

Figure 4.4 Market price support (MPS) shows the subsidy to U.S. producers generated by trade barriers, 1996–2015

Data note: OECD's PSE (www.oecd.org/agriculture/pse) provides country-level data in a consistent format for international comparisons.

- **World Trade Organization (WTO) notifications** measure support in particular categories that were the subject of trade agreements. The market price support component equals the gap between an administrative support price (which is a domestic price established by the government) and world prices multiplied by the quantity eligible for the administrative price. The WTO notifications include a wider range of agricultural programs, classified into color-coded categories or boxes. The **amber box** refers to trade-distorting policies, the **blue box** contains policies that are accompanied by quantity limits to temper their trade-distorting impact and the **green box** contains less trade-distorting policies. The green box includes most U.S. conservation programs (see Chapter 3), trade-neutral farm programs and nutrition assistance programs (see Chapter 10). WTO notifications are a good source for judging whether countries are complying with their obligations under international trade agreements.

Figure 4.5 shows trends in the PSE, combining information about policies that have been described throughout Chapters 2, 3 and 4. In 2000, the U.S. PSE was $52 billion, of which $27 billion was highly trade distorting. By 2010, the U.S. PSE was only $26 billion, of which less than $2 billion was highly trade distorting. Higher commodity prices in the late 2000s and early 2010s, rather than fundamental policy reform, were largely responsible for the fall in PSE. Subsequently, in the lower price environment of 2014 and 2015, the impact of trade barriers rebounded.

Some domestic programs that help farmers are not counted as part of either the OECD's PSE or the WTO notifications. For example, U.S. ethanol mandates influence food prices by increasing the scarcity of corn for food. Such policies favor the interests of the world's producers over the interests of the world's food consumers. However,

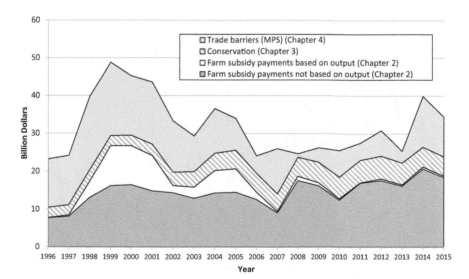

Figure 4.5 The producer support estimate (PSE) represents the total subsidy to U.S. producers generated by trade barriers and domestic programs, 1996–2015

Note: This exhibit combines information from Figure 2.5, Figure 3.4 and Figure 4.4.

Data note: OECD's PSE (www.oecd.org/agriculture/pse) provides country-level data in a consistent format for international comparisons.

unless these policies are accompanied by a trade barrier that favors some producers over others, they are not considered trade-distorting, because any global producer can take advantage of the higher prices they create. Although the OECD and WTO measures are useful for assessing policies that harm farmers overseas by suppressing world prices, new approaches may be needed to assess policies that harm the world's consumers by raising world prices.

4.4 Trade Agreements

4.4.1 Multilateral Agreements

Countries pursue **trade agreements** to coordinate reductions in the trade barriers they impose on each other. Typically, each country agrees to reduce its own trade barriers or trade-distorting domestic subsidy programs in return for a simultaneous commitment from trading partners to enact similar measures.

High-profile multilateral negotiations involve large numbers of countries at the same time. From the 1940s to the 1990s, several rounds of the General Agreement on Tariffs and Trade (GATT) established principles for all member countries (Koo and Kennedy, 2005). According to GATT principles, one country should treat another member country as well as it treats the **most favored nation**, a term that refers to whichever member nation enjoys the lowest import barriers. In practice, this standard rules out discrimination among member countries. An exception is that member countries may agree on special provisions for trade with low-income developing countries. GATT principles also say that nontariff barriers should be replaced by tariffs, which are more transparent and easier to measure.

Two multilateral agreements in the 1990s are most relevant for global trade in food and agricultural products.

- The Uruguay Round of GATT, completed in 1993, included limits on the most distorting trade barriers and subsidy policies for agricultural products and also introduced the colored box classification system for describing other domestic policies. It established the WTO as a more permanent forum for coordinating international trade policies.
- An accompanying sanitary and phytosanitary (SPS) agreement addressed national health and safety rules that could affect international trade.

The WTO coordinates trade relations among more than 140 member countries. Under WTO auspices, a new Doha Round of multilateral negotiations began in 2001. The Doha Round was supposed to improve oversight of trade agreements, continue to reduce trade barriers in agriculture, agree on trade-related aspects of intellectual property rights and further support the economic ambitions of less-developed countries. However, the negotiations foundered for many years, as rich countries demanded more unrestricted market access than poor countries were willing and able to offer.

4.4.2 Bilateral and Regional Agreements

In addition to multilateral negotiations through the WTO, countries may pursue bilateral agreements (with a single trading partner) or regional agreements (with a group of trading partners). Bilateral and regional trade agreements may increase global trade openness by reducing barriers among the member countries, but they also may decrease global trade openness by consolidating trading patterns into regional blocs.

The European Union has brought 28 member countries into an integrated regional market and a partial political union. The North American Free Trade Agreement reduced trade barriers between the United States, Mexico and Canada. For example, NAFTA led to increased U.S. corn exports to Mexico and increased Mexican produce exports to the United States. Several important regional agreements promote trade within groups of developing countries.

For U.S. food policy, the most important attempt at a new regional agreement in recent years was the Trans Pacific Partnership (TPP), signed by President Obama in 2015 but never ratified. The TPP reduced tariffs and nontariff barriers among 12 nations that border the Pacific Ocean—including the United States, Japan, Mexico, Canada, Australia and several smaller countries, but notably excluding China. The TPP was never really a "free trade" agreement but rather more modestly a "somewhat freer trade" agreement, because member countries agreed to let each other retain certain barriers. For example, Japan agreed to accept beef imports much more freely but made only partial concessions on rice, which is historically a sensitive issue in Japanese politics (Hendrix and Kotschwar, 2016). Economic assessments estimated moderately large positive economic impacts for member countries (Petri and Plummer, 2016), though such estimates always are disputed. Most U.S. farm organizations supported the agreement because of potential gains for U.S. agricultural exports, but others (including the National Farmers Union) opposed it out of concern for increased competition from agricultural imports for some products.

In the 2000s and early 2010s, bilateral and regional trade agreements had considerable momentum, especially by comparison to the subdued action on broader multilateral agreements during this period. From 2015 to 2017, even bilateral and regional agreements were in retreat. The European Union was shaken by the 2016 vote in the United Kingdom to exit the union, reflecting in part deeper public skepticism about trade and internationalism than had previously been recognized. The TPP became a major topic of debate in the 2016 U.S. presidential election, with vigorous and politically diverse opposition from Democratic primary candidate Sen. Bernie Sanders (Independent-VT) and Republican candidate Donald Trump, and eventually also some opposition from the Democratic nominee Hillary Clinton. The U.S. Senate delayed voting on ratification in 2016, and, in the first days of the new administration in 2017, President Trump withdrew U.S. support for the agreement, signaling the end of the decade's most notable trade initiative for the United States.

4.4.3 Safety and Labeling Provisions

The SPS agreement and similar SPS provisions in newer trade agreements provide rules for using nontariff trade barriers to protect humans, plants and animals while discouraging trade barriers that protect the economic interests of a domestic constituency at the expense of trading partners. In some cases, it is easy to distinguish policies that protect health from policies that unnecessarily inhibit trade. If a country forbids imported commodities that contain a certain pesticide residue, while allowing that same pesticide in domestic production, the policy clearly is a trade barrier posing as a food safety rule. The SPS agreement allows national policies that prohibit use of agricultural chemicals and food additives for which there is considerable scientific evidence of food safety risk, so long as these policies are applied equally to domestic producers and importers alike. However, major trade controversies have erupted when the scientific evidence is partial or incomplete (Sheldon, 2011; Hendrix and Kotschwar, 2016). In such cases, one party may see a food safety regulation as a legitimate precautionary measure, while another party may see it as an impermissible nontariff barrier.

For example, in the most significant trade dispute about the SPS agreement, the United States objected to the European Union's prohibition against livestock hormones that are commonly used in U.S. beef production. The scientific evidence of harm was inconclusive, but the European public was sufficiently worried for European regulators to ban the hormones. The WTO ruled that there was insufficient evidence of health risk and allowed the United States to impose trade penalties in response.

Similar issues arise when the United States refuses imports from a developing country based on production practices that authorities in the developing country considered adequately safe. Developing country authorities may at first bristle at having to meet U.S. safety standards. However, there may be offsetting advantages for developing countries that do take steps to develop export markets, as new production practices and safety oversight systems generate other benefits for the developing country's economy (Sheldon, 2011).

A particularly difficult challenge for the SPS agreement arises when an importing country imposes food label rules that apply equally to imported and domestic foods but which may lead consumers to favor the domestic product. For example, the United States in 2008 extended mandatory country of origin labeling (COOL) to a wider variety of food products, leading Mexico to file a complaint, which is not yet resolved (Johnecheck, 2010). The new rules identify Mexican products, such as tomatoes or beef, in the grocery store. Recall that the North American Free Trade Agreement struck a tough bargain, requiring Mexican farmers to compete with U.S. corn exporters. Even though better consumer information is always a desirable policy objective, one can see how Mexican farmers could object if U.S. labeling rules discouraged U.S. consumers from buying the tomatoes that Mexican farmers hoped to export in return (Johnecheck et al., 2011).

4.4.4 Dispute Resolution

The WTO has procedures for judging disputes about trade agreements. In such disputes, one country files a complaint saying that another country has failed to honor its trade commitments. If the dispute cannot be settled by negotiation, the WTO establishes a panel to make recommendations. If the panel upholds a country's complaint, the losing defendant country may decide to implement the panel's recommendations by changing its offending policy or by negotiating a compensating payment to offset the economic damage. Alternatively, if a losing defendant country refuses both options, the country with the complaint is allowed to impose an equivalent retaliatory trade barrier of its own.

The most famous example of such a dispute was a case brought by Brazil against U.S. subsidies and export credits for cotton (Sumner, 2011). U.S. cotton farmers enjoy large subsidies in part because of the regional politics of passing the Farm Bill, which requires support from legislators in the South, outside of the corn- and soybean-producing heartland. The United States functions as a large country on the global cotton market, which means that these subsidies can suppress prices paid to cotton farmers in Asia, Africa and South America. Brazil claimed, and the WTO confirmed, that the cotton subsidies and export credits violated U.S. commitments in the Uruguay Round of GATT. The WTO awarded Brazil the right to respond by imposing trade restrictions of its own, without having those restrictions count as a violation of GATT commitments. When the United States appealed, the WTO upheld its ruling in favor of Brazil. In the end, rather than change its own export credit policies, the United States agreed to make cash payments to Brazil. This outcome may provide some relief for Brazilian farmers, but it leaves poor farmers in yet smaller countries unsatisfied.

4.4.5 Ratifying Trade Agreements

International trade agreements raise concerns about the democratic process, both in international decision-making bodies and in domestic governments. Critics say the WTO threatens sovereignty by forbidding countries to implement their own trade and subsidy policies as they see fit. In this view, WTO dispute resolution panels are seen as international judges, capable of overturning democratically adopted safety and environmental laws.

Supporters of multilateral trade say instead that the agreements are voluntary, based on each country's appreciation of its gains from trade. The WTO is like a club, and adherence to the rules is a condition of membership. Other than allowing retaliation against countries that breach their commitments, the WTO panels have no policing authority over domestic laws and policies.

This milder view of trade agreements makes sense only if there really is a well-functioning democratic process for approving trade agreements in the first place. After treaties are negotiated by the executive branch (which answers to the president), they must be ratified by the legislative branch (Congress). In the United States, Congress may give the president **trade promotion authority**, which means that Congress promises to give the proposed agreement an up-or-down vote, without allowing amendments to selected sections. Without this procedure, each amendment by Congress could trigger renegotiation of the whole international treaty. Treaties require each participating country to make compromises, so trading partners might not agree to amendments that are adopted unilaterally by the U.S. Congress. Clearly, under the principles of democratic government, it is essential that Congress retain the power to approve and disapprove trade agreements. Yet the practice of giving trade agreements an up-or-down vote may be a necessary feature of international negotiations.

4.5 U.S. Food Aid

In the context of these policy decisions about trade policy, we can better understand **food aid**, a collection of government programs that provide agricultural products to other countries. In addition to being a vigorous participant in international agricultural trade, the United States is the world's largest provider of international food aid. While food aid flows are small by comparison to global agricultural trade, and tiny by comparison to global food production, food aid generates some notable dilemmas in U.S. food policy.

The World Bank estimates that perhaps 790 million people, 11 percent of the world's people, were undernourished in 2015 (World Bank, 2017). Contemplating the food needs of these undernourished people, one might entertain just shipping free food as a simple remedy. Yet food aid economics and politics turn out to be considerably more complex.

For several decades after World War II, U.S. food aid helped support friendly nations and simultaneously helped dispose of surplus commodity stocks. These stocks accumulated through the federal government's purchase of commodities that were in excess supply at the support price. As Chapter 2 explained, such stocks could not be sold on the U.S. domestic market because the sales would push commodity prices back down below the support level, so overseas disposal through food aid became an attractive option. This overseas commodity disposal could help needy consumers in recipient countries, but it also could harm the economic interests of farmers in the recipient countries if they faced increased competition from underpriced or free U.S. commodities.

After the 1970s, as the federal government began to hold smaller commodity stockpiles, the U.S. Congress appropriated money for direct purchases from U.S. farmers. In 2015, the total budget for U.S. food aid was only about $2.5 billion, a sum large enough to influence food security in a few low-income countries but too small to make a major difference in the global food situation. For comparison, as Chapter 10 will discuss, the budget for the Supplemental Nutrition Assistance Program (formerly known as food stamps) was almost 30 times as large, with $74 billion in outlays in 2015.

The terminology commonly used to describe the mechanisms of U.S. food aid can be confusing at first. U.S. food aid still is sometimes described by the public law number of the relevant 1954 legislation, P.L. 480, even though that legislation has been superseded. Programs are sometimes described by the title numbers of the 1954 legislation: Title I, which is no longer a large part of U.S. food aid, was direct aid to governments, while Title II encompassed most of the programs that remain in use today, administered either through governments or through nongovernmental organizations. In place of these terms, it is most helpful now to distinguish U.S. food aid programs according to the following categories:

- **Emergency food aid** (about 75 percent of Title II funding in recent years through 2014) provides short-term support to countries undergoing a crisis. It is the first part of the Food for Peace Program of the U.S. Agency for International Development (USAID). In recent years, projects have provided substantial emergency food to Sudan, Ethiopia, Kenya, Pakistan and Afghanistan (U.S. Agency for International Development, 2012).
- **Nonemergency food aid** (about 25 percent of Title II funding) provides development and related assistance through two mechanisms: (a) nonemergency Food for Peace aid is administered by USAID, and (b) nonemergency Food for Progress aid is administered by USDA. In recent years, recipient countries have included Ethiopia, Bangladesh, Haiti, Democratic Republic of the Congo and Guatemala.

A large fraction of the nonemergency food aid is **monetized**, which means that it is sold in recipient country markets to provide funding for development projects. It is highly inefficient to purchase U.S. food, ship it overseas and then sell the food again for money. It would be simpler just to provide the aid in the form of money, as the European Union now does. According to the Government Accountability Office (GAO), out of $722 million in nonemergency food aid through Food for Peace and Food for Progress in 2011, $219 million was lost to shipping and transactions costs, leaving only $503 million for development programs (U.S. Government Accountability Office, 2011b).

Although it is natural to think that free food would reduce poverty and hunger in recipient countries, one must consider people's livelihoods and earning capacity as well as food needs. In emergency situations, especially when local agriculture has failed during a famine or military crisis, additional food supplies clearly are beneficial. In nonemergency situations, U.S. food aid sometimes may risk suppressing local prices and harming people in farming and farm-related industries, who in many recipient countries comprise a large fraction of the people in poverty. GAO's 2011 report found that, in some cases, USAID and USDA monetized enough food aid to represent more than a quarter of a recipient country's total import volume. USAID and USDA conduct market assessments to develop limits on aid quantities in hopes of preventing displacement of commercial sales, but GAO found these limits sometimes are exceeded.

Despite these concerns, the current system is favored by some influential farm organizations, which seek to retain the requirements that food be purchased from U.S. sources. It also is favored by the U.S. maritime shipping industry, which seeks to retain a rule stipulating that at least 50 percent of U.S. food aid must be shipped in U.S. flag vessels. Some humanitarian assistance organizations endorse the current system out of concern that any changes would weaken the advocacy coalition that supports U.S. food aid. Many others, including scholars such as Chris Barrett and Daniel Maxwell (2005) and humanitarian assistance organizations such as Oxfam America, recommend that U.S. food aid be substantially reformed (Schnepf, 2016).

4.6 Immigration and Labor

Just as market incentives motivate international trade flows in goods and services, they also can motivate international flows in **factors of production**. The factors of production are the land, capital and labor that businesses employ to produce goods and services, such as food and agricultural products. Notably, land is immobile, so economic policy debates focus on international flows in the other two factors of production. International capital flows occur when U.S. companies build factories in other countries or when overseas investors buy U.S. financial assets. International labor flows occur when people from other countries move, generally from lower-income countries to higher-income countries, in search of better employment.

Immigration to the United States has grown in recent years. The number of U.S. immigrants doubled in two decades, from approximately 20 million people in 1990 to 43 million people in 2014 (Martin, 2013; Martin, 2017). Foreign-born persons represented 13 percent of the U.S. resident population in 2014, which is higher than in any decade since the 1920s.

Immigration policy has important effects on major food and agricultural industries, including meatpacking and farming. As meatpacking plants have increasingly located in rural areas of the United States, widespread employment of immigrant workers has transformed rural communities (Artz, 2012). In agriculture, approximately one-third of total U.S. farm labor is hired labor, and the proportion is much higher in selected industries such as fruits and vegetables (see Section 2.4.2). Immigrants make up about 70 percent of hired workers in agriculture (Martin, 2017). Many foreign-born farmworkers are in the United States legally, but unauthorized workers were 14 percent of hired farmworkers in 1989–1991, rising to 48 percent of hired farmworkers in 2007–2009.

One issue raised by these farm labor trends is whether immigration hurts the economic interests of U.S.-born workers by increasing the supply of labor and putting downward pressure on wages. Labor economists distinguish wage effects for different segments of the labor market, particularly less-educated and more-educated workers. To refute claims that immigrant farm laborers might displace native-born workers, the California-based United Farm Workers in 2010 developed a publicity campaign with the sarcastic slogan, "Take Our Jobs!" The UFW's point is that almost no native-born workers are willing to take nonsupervisory farm labor jobs, especially in the fruit and vegetable industries. This fact highlights the degree of segmentation between labor markets for immigrant and native-born workers. Immigrant workers in low-skill occupations may compete for jobs with each other and with some native-born workers in these same occupations, but they do not greatly affect the overall labor market for native-born workers (Card, 2009; National Academies, 2017).

A second issue raised by farm labor trends concerns justice for the immigrant workers themselves. On the one hand, the decision to immigrate often represents a worker's own judgment that economic opportunities are greater in the United States than in the home country. On the other hand, economic conditions for many foreign-born farmworkers in the United States are severe by U.S. community standards. Several factors make it difficult for immigrant farmworkers to advocate for improved wages and working conditions, as other groups of U.S. workers have done for many decades through private-sector initiatives, unionization and favorable government policies. Organizing efforts are complicated by frequent relocations, language barriers, physical intimidation and fear of deportation. Noncitizen workers cannot vote and hence cannot command much favorable attention from legislators. Even though farm labor is arduous and presents multiple workplace risks, from repetitive motion problems to chemical exposure, farmworkers in general and immigrant farmworkers in particular may have less adequate access to health care (Escalante and Luo, 2017).

Torn between farm operators' desire for inexpensive labor and the political liability of opening up legal immigration, the federal government has expanded a guest worker program known as H-2A. The program permits temporary immigration for farmworkers when agricultural employers cannot find nonimmigrant workers. Employers must keep records on wages and working conditions demonstrating that, in principle, the use of guest workers did not undercut and displace U.S. workers.

Congress has been sorely divided over immigration issues. Some proposals for policy reform take an enforcement-only approach, requiring increasing militarization of the U.S.–Mexico border and increased criminal enforcement against U.S. farmers who hire unauthorized workers. Alternative proposals combine heavy border enforcement with provisions that offer young and working immigrants without criminal records a path to permanent residence and citizenship. As with trade policy (see Section 4.4.2), immigration was a topic in the 2016 presidential election, with Republican nominee Donald Trump promising to build a wall on the U.S.–Mexico border and increase deportations. University of California economist Philip Martin argues that such policies "will be disruptive to U.S. agriculture" (Martin, 2017). One consequence of restricted immigration and higher labor costs could be increased labor-displacing technical changes, ranging widely from machines that assist with harvesting tree nuts to new varieties of fruits and vegetables that are easier to harvest. Martin writes, "It now seems that the period between 1980 and 2010 was one of abundance in Mexican farm labor, and that era is now largely over" (p. 4).

4.7 Global Trends in Agricultural Prices

From the 1980s through the first half of the 2000s, global agricultural commodity prices were generally quite low, which was bad news for farmers and good news for food consumers. Then global commodity prices spiked sharply upwards in 2007–2008 and 2010–2011, which was good news for farmers (and for the taxpayers who pay for subsidy programs whose costs were reduced) and bad news for food consumers. These food crises caused political unrest and even rioting around the world, and they generated new global concerns about food scarcity (Bourne, 2015).

Figure 4.6 illustrates a price index, a weighted average of individual commodity prices. This price index, from the UN Food and Agriculture Organization (FAO), is adjusted for inflation and scaled so that average prices in 2002–2004 are assigned a value of 100. Average prices in other years can be interpreted in comparison to this base period.

There were both long-term and short-term reasons for the two price spikes (Trostle et al., 2011; Baffes and Haniotis, 2016). The long-term reasons included the following:

- as discussed in Chapter 3, food demand has risen because the world population is growing and food consumption patterns are changing in ways that increase the per capita resource needs;

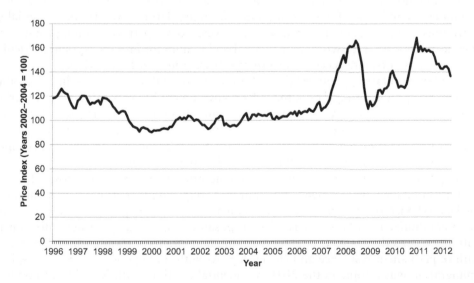

Figure 4.6 FAO real food price index (2002–2004 = 100), 1996–2017

Data note: The UN Food and Agriculture Organization (FAO) provides international data on agricultural commodity prices (www.fao.org/worldfoodsituation).

- food supplies are constrained by limited land and decelerating productivity growth; and
- biofuels, including corn-based ethanol, are competing with food supplies.

The short-term reasons included the following:

- bad weather in the mid-2000s led to temporary production shortfalls for several major crops;
- fluctuations in energy prices and international exchange rates; and
- once people began to perceive the crisis, national governments responded in ways that accelerated the price increases, as grain-producing countries restricted exports and food-importing countries bought contracts that locked in future purchases.

Ordinarily, governments and private firms hold substantial stocks of major food grains, which tends to stabilize prices. When supplies exceed demand, these stocks grow, tempering the potential price decline that otherwise might have occurred. When production falters, these stocks shrink, releasing supplies that temper the potential price increase. Unfortunately, if demand exceeds supplies for several years in a row, as in the mid-2000s, the stock quantities eventually reach a bottom below which they cannot be reduced further. Then the usual price-smoothing behavior ceases to function, leading to the very sharp price spikes that were observed in the late 2000s and early 2010s.

Although high food prices are sometimes seen as a problem in their own right, it may be best to focus on the underlying conditions of scarcity that generate high prices in the first place. For example, governments can end ethanol subsidies, fund research and extension to enhance agricultural yields, promote food consumption patterns that use fewer resources and provide nutrition assistance to the poor. To prevent sudden fluctuations in prices, governments can encourage the maintenance of adequate commodity stocks. Prices themselves are merely the messenger. If scarcity remains high, silencing this messenger may not solve the underlying economic conditions.

4.8 Conclusion

This chapter asks the reader to confront a question with both practical and moral implications. In your own conception of a fair and healthy food economy, what are the boundaries within which food and agricultural commerce should take place? Who is inside the border and who is outside?

Within the United States, trade goods and people flow freely between places as different as Boston, Massachusetts, and San Antonio, Texas, 2,000 miles apart. An international border lies between San Antonio and Monterrey, just 300 miles apart. Monterrey is a large city in northeastern Mexico with a comparatively high level of economic development. In each case, commerce between these places—and between the agricultural regions that surround them—is driven by the principles of specialization and gains from trade. From an economic perspective, the location of the border seems arbitrary, providing a shaky basis for using trade policies to address more fundamental social and environmental problems.

The challenge at the heart of this chapter is to move beyond "us" and "them" to discern the policy choices that best serve the long-term well-being of farmers and consumers in rich and poor places alike. For this purpose, this chapter has introduced tools and concepts for understanding trade flows, food prices, immigration and food aid. Because conditions vary from place to place and change from one year to the next, this chapter has highlighted regularly updated data sources for measuring trade flows, food prices and the impact of trade policies. These real-world data allow us to make key distinctions that would otherwise be lost among the passionate policy arguments for or against international trade and globalization.

Summary List of Key Terms (identified in bold in the text)

- amber box
- autarky
- balance of trade
- blue box
- comparative advantage
- dumping
- emergency food aid
- export restriction
- export subsidy
- export tax
- factors of production
- food aid
- food sovereignty
- free trade
- gains from trade
- green box
- import quota
- import tariff
- large country
- market price support
- mercantilism
- monetized
- most favored nation
- nonemergency food aid
- nontariff barrier
- producer support estimate
- rents
- rent-seeking behavior
- small country
- trade agreements
- trade promotion authority
- World Trade Organization notifications

---

5 Food Manufacturing

Parke Wilde and Daniel Hatfield

5.1 Introduction

Food in the United States comes not just from farms but also from factories. For example, grain elevators and mills convert corn into animal feed, flour, sweetener, vegetable oil and biofuels; crushing plants convert soybeans into animal feed and vegetable oil; and manufacturing plants convert flour, milk, meat, oils and sweeteners into many of the products we find at the grocery store.

While most of the food consumed in the United States is manufactured, this industry is not readily visible to the public. Even for highly processed foods and beverages, commercial marketing and advertising delicately avoid imagery of large-scale food manufacturing, processing or transportation. Instead, food companies recognize that consumers want to think of their food as coming directly from farmers.

The food and beverage manufacturing industry is important in the study of U.S. food policy for several reasons. As noted in Chapter 1, a small fraction of the consumer's food dollar goes to farmers, while a large fraction goes to food manufacturing and the other intermediate stages of the food marketing chain. Manufacturing is tied to several food policy concerns, including environmental impact (see Chapter 3) and nutritional quality (see Chapter 8). Furthermore, in some sectors of U.S. food manufacturing, a small number of firms have a large market share. Hence, although similar issues arise to some extent in other chapters, this chapter provides this book's principal discussion of less competitive forms of industrial organization. In sum, this chapter:

- provides an overview of the food and beverage manufacturing industry, emphasizing differences in value added and policy-relevant qualities across several sectors (Section 5.2);
- introduces the economics of imperfect competition, showing how food manufacturers may exercise market power over farmers, or buyers, or both (Section 5.3); and
- describes the legal tools for protecting **competitive markets**, using the history of meatpacking, contracting in pork and poultry, concentration in breakfast cereals and patented inputs such as seeds as examples (Section 5.4).

5.2 Overview of Food and Beverage Manufacturing

During the Industrial Revolution (1820–1870) and for several decades afterwards, many Americans moved to cities and took factory jobs that left less opportunity for home processing and preservation. The resulting consumer demand for preprocessed foods, combined with new industrial technologies, spawned some of the earliest manufacturing giants, including Borden (founded in 1857), H.J. Heinz (1869) and Campbell's (1869). Another wave of food manufacturing innovations occurred a century later, as a growing number of women entered the workforce in the 1940s and 1950s. Recognizing homemakers' desire for more "modern," convenient foods, manufacturers developed new product lines such as Betty Crocker's cake mixes and Swanson's TV dinners (Levenstein, 2003).

The industrialization of food manufacturing offers both advantages and disadvantages. For example:

- Packaging blocks harmful contamination and extends shelf life but also generates problems for environmentally sound resource use and waste disposal.
- Novel technologies, such as food irradiation and new chemical preservatives, can combat pathogens and preserve freshness, but they make many consumers uncomfortable.
- Packaged foods such as frozen entrees and ready-made cookies save consumers time and effort, but these products also displace culinary traditions.
- Processing can adapt foods' appearance, flavor, aroma and texture to a range of consumer preferences. However, these same processes may affect nutrition; minimally processed foods tend to retain nutritional qualities of their farm-level precursors, while highly processed foods tend to lose more of their nutritional value.

In 2012, the year of the most recent Economic Census at the time of this writing, U.S. food manufacturers generated over \$250 billion in value added, or about 13 percent of value added from all U.S. manufacturing sectors. Value added is a measure of the economic activity within an industry (Chapter 2). In manufacturing statistics, value added equals the shipment value, which is the aggregate amount that food manufacturers are paid for their product, minus the cost of purchased inputs used in production. For U.S. food manufacturing in 2012, this value added represents the sum of compensation to employees (40 percent), returns to the people who invested capital (47 percent) and net taxes after subtracting subsidies (13 percent) (Noonan, undated).

This section describes seven manufacturing sectors: (1) meat and poultry processing and slaughter; (2) milk and dairy processing; (3) grain and oilseed milling; (4) bakery; (5) fruits, vegetables and frozen foods processing; (6) soft drinks; and (7) sugar and sweets. Altogether, these sectors account for more than three-quarters of value added in U.S. food and beverage manufacturing. Manufacturers' value added varies by sector (Figure 5.1). For example, in the meat industry, the cost of inputs such as livestock is high, so manufacturers' value added is only about 26 percent of the shipment value. By contrast, in the bakery sector, the cost of inputs such as flour and oil is low, manufacturing transforms the product, and manufacturers spend heavily on branding and advertising, so manufacturers' value added reaches about 54 percent of the shipment value.

5.2.1 Meat

Meat manufacturers use animal inputs, including cattle, hogs and chickens, to make consumable goods such as steaks, bacon and chicken tenders. This sector generated about 19 percent of total value added from U.S. food manufacturing in 2012.

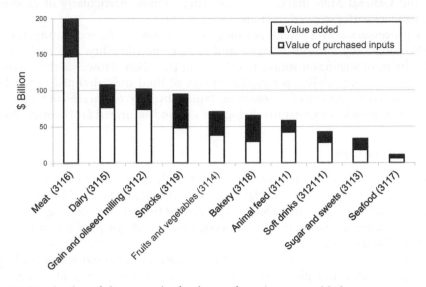

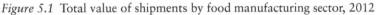

Figure 5.1 Total value of shipments by food manufacturing sector, 2012

Note: Industries are defined by North American Industry Classification System (NAICS) codes in parentheses.

Data note: Users can access Economic Census data through the online FactFinder tool (factfinder2. census.gov).

Source: U.S. Census Bureau, Economic Census, 2012.

Geographically, meat manufacturers are mostly concentrated in the Midwestern and Southeastern U.S., close to livestock production centers.

U.S. consumers tend to view meats as **commodities**, undifferentiated or interchangeable products that are sold without a strong brand identity. For example, many consumers will select whichever package of chicken breasts is priced lowest, paying little attention to whether the chicken breast was packaged by Perdue or by Tyson. As a result, meat processors invest relatively little in advertising and marketing. They operate on moderate **profit margins** (net income after subtracting costs, expressed as a percentage of total revenue). For example, the largest meat-processing company, Tyson, reported operating profit margins of 4 percent to 8 percent between 2014 and 2016.

In an effort to contain costs, meat processors may engage in practices that some consumers find undesirable. For example, industrial slaughtering processes raise concern about ethical treatment of animals (see Chapter 9, Box 9.1). Similarly, consumers may balk at the use of certain animal byproducts in processed meats. However, these practices also serve the economic interests of consumers, since much of the associated cost savings is passed on in the form of lower prices.

5.2.2 Dairy

Dairy manufacturers produce fluid milk, along with milk-based foods including cheese, butter, yogurt and ice cream. In total, dairy processors contributed about 11 percent of value added from U.S. food manufacturing in 2012. Because milk is heavy and perishable and therefore costly to transport, dairy processing tends to be more regionalized than other sectors. However, companies such as Dean Foods, Kraft

Heinz and General Mills market national dairy brands, particularly of cheeses and other products with extended shelf life.

Dairy processors deliver several advantages to consumers. Pasteurization, for example, kills potentially harmful bacteria and reduces perishability, and milk products provide the most significant source of calcium in U.S. diets. However, throughout the late 1900s and early 2000s, per capita intakes of fluid milk declined in the United States, while consumption of cheese rose, largely by way of cheese-containing items such as pizza, which is comparatively high in salt and saturated fat (Bentley, 2014).

5.2.3 Grains/Oilseeds

The grains and oilseeds manufacturing segment includes flour and rice milling firms; producers of plant-based starches, fats and oils; and breakfast cereal manufacturers. In 2012, the industry generated about 10 percent of food manufacturing value added, at facilities clustered mainly in the Midwest, near the major production regions for grain and oilseed crops.

Milling, refining and blending transform commodities into more user-ready products including flour and plant oils. These outputs, in turn, are sold to consumers and to other manufacturers as inputs for bakery items, snack foods and other goods. Because products such as refined grains and oils are fairly homogenous, the leading processors, Archer Daniels Midland, Cargill and Bunge, invest relatively little in consumer-focused marketing and advertising efforts. The cost-competitiveness of the industry also translates into narrow profit margins.

Processing grains and oilseeds into ingredients such as flour and vegetable oil tends to remove dietary fiber, vitamins and minerals while retaining food energy as carbohydrates and fat. Manufacturers may add nutrients back to foods, either in amounts equal to what was lost in processing (called **enrichment**) or in even higher amounts (called **fortification**). In the United States, FDA requires wheat flour to be enriched with iron and several B-vitamins and also fortified with folic acid. Still, enrichment does not fully restore all nutritional attributes of whole foods.

Breakfast cereal manufacturers also transform grain-based inputs, but they use a wider variety of processes—including puffing, flaking, shredding and extrusion—to produce diverse products that meet a range of consumer preferences. Although the nutritional quality of cereals varies, manufacturers recognize the consumer appeal of foods that promise a healthy start to the day. Manufacturers therefore often fortify ready-to-eat (RTE) cereals with nutrients and aggressively promote health messaging.

5.2.4 Bakery

Bakery manufacturers transform processed grains and other inputs into breads, pasta, cookies, crackers and tortillas. Firms in this segment generated about 13 percent of total U.S. food manufacturing value added in 2012. Market structures vary significantly among bakery sub-sectors. The bread and rolls industry, for example, includes numerous manufacturers, while the cookie and cracker industry is dominated by a few firms, such as Mondelez and Kellogg.

Bakery products offer consumers substantial convenience benefits. Opening a box of dried pasta or a sleeve of cookies, for example, requires far less time than making their equivalents from scratch. Companies seeking to attract health-focused consumers also may engineer products either to reduce nutrients perceived as undesirable or to increase nutrients perceived as health promoting. In any grocery store consumers can find low-fat or reduced-carbohydrate versions of traditional bakery goods. While these products may offer some advantages, public health experts worry that many merely replace one unhealthful component (such as solid fat) with another (such as sugar or salt). Even if the product offers no net nutritional benefit, consumers may perceive that they can consume the "improved" items with abandon.

5.2.5 Fruits, Vegetables and Frozen Foods

The fruits, vegetables, and frozen foods and juices sector produces a range of canned, frozen and dried items, from raisins and canned peas to frozen entrees and nondairy toppings. Altogether, this sector accounted for 12 percent of value added in U.S. food manufacturing in 2012.

Fruit and vegetable processing may increase U.S. consumers' access to these foods even when they are out of season. Because of their extended shelf life, such items can also be sold at a lower cost, and many manufacturing processes, such as freezing and canning, retain most of the nutritional value of fruits and vegetables. However, processing foods more intensively—as with TV dinners or french fries—can significantly compromise nutritional qualities.

5.2.6 Soft Drinks/Water

The soft drinks and water industry includes manufacturers of flavored nonalcoholic beverages (e.g., sodas, teas and sports drinks), bottled water and ice. In total, soft drinks generated about 5 percent of U.S. food manufacturing value added in 2012. Soft drink manufacturing, the largest subsector, typically begins with the production of concentrates (such as cola syrups), which may be sold directly to food service operations or delivered to beverage bottling facilities. Some major soft drink companies own bottling subsidiaries, while others partner with independently owned and operated bottlers. The leading U.S. soft drink companies, Coca-Cola and PepsiCo, maintain numerous brands that appeal to a range of consumer preferences. To motivate consumers to choose these brands, they invest heavily in marketing and advertising.

Costs for inputs used to make soft drink concentrates (mostly sugar and water) are typically very low. High-fructose corn syrup (HFCS), which is used widely by U.S. beverages manufacturers, has been a particular source of policy debate. Although some consumers worry about nutrition differences between HFCS and cane sugar, most nutrition scientists say that HFCS and cane sugar have similar health consequences. The more substantial policy questions have to do with the price of HFCS and the quantity used in the food supply. Some U.S. farm policies, such as deficiency payments, could in principle depress the price and increase the consumption of corn and corn syrup. However, as Chapter 2 explains, deficiency payments are just one of several major farm policies, and they had no influence on corn prices during high-price time periods such as most of the late 2000s and early 2010s. Moreover, HFCS is just one input into consumer products such as soda, so any price effects are further diluted (Beghin and Jensen, 2008). Hence, the problem of added sugars is not primarily attributable to deficiency payments or other farm policies, and yet it does generate broad and challenging nutrition policy concerns.

Soft drinks have drawn increasing attention as the prevalence of obesity has risen in the United States (Chapter 8). On average, sodas, energy drinks and sports drinks contribute over 100 kcal per day to U.S. diets, but they typically offer limited nutritional value and may also displace consumption of milk, a key source of dietary calcium. In recent decades, the beverage industry has responded to health-conscious consumers with innovations such as diet soda, sports drinks and vitamin-infused beverages. While marketing may endow such products with a health halo, they often contain high levels of sugar and offer few health benefits. The growth of the bottled-water segment offers a more healthful alternative but also generates environmental consequences from high levels of plastic use.

5.2.7 Sugar/Sweets

The sugar and confectionary industry includes both sugar processors and producers of chocolates, candies and other sweets. The sugar-manufacturing subsegment includes fewer than 100 facilities that process sugar cane and sugar beets into refined sugar. Confectionary companies transform inputs including sugar and cocoa into consumable items such as candy and chocolate bars. Altogether, sugar and confectionary companies generated about 6 percent of food manufacturing value added in 2012.

Because sugar is a relatively homogenous commodity, sugar processors spend little money on mass-market advertising. Confectionary companies, on the other hand, produce more unique items that are intensively advertised. Leading manufacturers market their products under multiple brands. Mars's product portfolio, for example, includes M&Ms, Milky Way, Snickers and Starburst, while Hershey owns brands such as Almond Joy, Reese's, Jolly Rancher and Twizzlers.

5.3 Market Structure in Food Manufacturing

The previous section shows that food manufacturing sectors have diverse economic characteristics and behaviors. Some sectors succeed better than others at meeting public interest objectives, such as producing safe and wholesome food at affordable prices. Economists describe relevant features of an industry's internal organization using the concept of **market structure**. Market structure encompasses three economic qualities of an industry or sector (Saitone and Sexton, 2012; Sheldon, 2017):

- the **degree of competition** among firms in the same industry or sector;
- **vertical coordination,** the extent to which firms in one industry (such as food manufacturing) control decisions in an upstream industry (such as farming) or a downstream industry (such as food retailing); and
- **product differentiation,** the degree to which the sector's products are distinct brands as opposed to commodities.

Figure 5.2 illustrates several key disputes about market structure in U.S. food policy as an overlay on the simple diagram of a food marketing chain that was introduced in Chapter 1. Later sections of this chapter will discuss several of these disputes as examples: (a) whether input suppliers, including biotech companies such as Monsanto, use patents to exercise monopoly power over farmers who buy seeds; (b) whether large food manufacturing companies can exercise market power over downstream buyers,

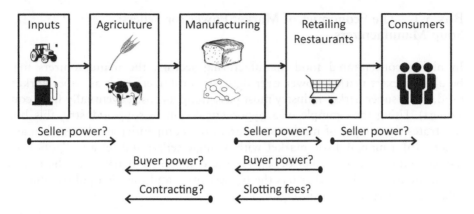

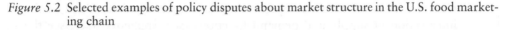

Figure 5.2 Selected examples of policy disputes about market structure in the U.S. food marketing chain

Note: For background see Section 1.3 on the food marketing chain.

including retailers and their consumers; (c) whether large retail companies can exercise market power over their vendors, including food manufacturers (for example
using slotting fees as a mechanism); and (d) whether meat and poultry manufacturers and processors take advantage of their growers (for example, using contracts as
a mechanism). Other disputes about the retail sector will be addressed in Chapter 6,
including whether retailers exert market power over customers or whether there is
anything wrong with the slotting fees they sometimes charge manufacturers as a condition for carrying certain food products.

A traditional organizing rubric for studying industrial organization is called the
structure-conduct-performance (SCP) framework. In this framework, market structure influences firms' conduct, and this conduct in turn influences how well the market
serves the economic interests of businesses and consumers. For example, a study using
the structure-conduct-performance approach may conclude that a highly concentrated
market structure with few firms leads to high prices for consumers. A newer body of
research, known as the new empirical industrial organization (NEIO), observes that
market concentration or vertical integration may offer other advantages that offset
harm to farmers and consumers (Saitone and Sexton, 2012; Sheldon, 2017). In the
following sections, we draw from both these traditions and contemplate the strengths
and weaknesses of alternative market structures.

5.3.1 Degree of Competition

A market's price and quantity depend on the degree of competition. Competition, in
turn, depends partly on the number of buyers and sellers. Assuming that there are
many buyers, three fundamental competitive structures are distinguished based on the
number of sellers (see Box 5.1 for a more detailed explanation, using the example of
a hypothetical soup manufacturing industry):

a. In **perfect competition**, there are many sellers. All else being equal, competitive
   markets are most efficient, generating the lowest consumer price and the highest

Box 5.1   The Economics of Market Power for Sellers: Soup Manufacturers

In highly concentrated food manufacturing sectors, the manufacturers may be able to exert market power over downstream buyers such as supermarkets (and, if the supermarket industry must pass along its costs, eventually food consumers). Using the example of a hypothetical canned soup industry, this box illustrates three types of market structure: (a) a competitive market with many sellers; (b) a monopolistic market with a single seller; and (c) an oligopolistic market with a small number of sellers. The competitive market has the lowest price, the monopoly market has the highest price and the oligopolistic market falls somewhere in between (Figure 5.3).

a.   *Competitive market.* In a competitive market, prices are determined by the intersection of supply and demand functions (see Appendix S2.1; see the online Companion Website). The supply function is based on the manufacturers' **marginal cost**, which is the cost to produce an additional unit. The demand function is based on the buyers' willingness to pay for an additional unit of soup. The competitive equilibrium price of $1.75 per can of soup motivates producers to supply precisely the 9 million cans demanded by consumers. At this price, competitive manufacturers earn no extra profits beyond what is required to cover their costs.

b.   *Monopoly.* In a monopoly, the single soup producer decides the price. For simplicity, we imagine that our monopolist happens to have the same marginal cost function as the multiple manufacturers did previously in section

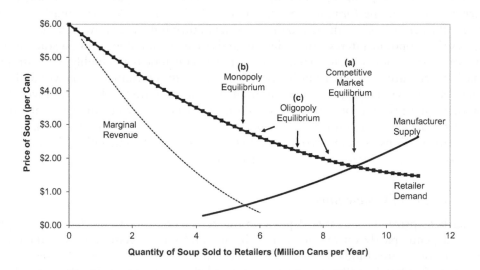

Figure 5.3 A model of food retailers selling soup under (a) competitive markets, (b) monopoly and (c) oligopoly

Note: A perfect competitor must accept the competitive equilibrium price, and a monopolist restrains the quantity supplied in order to be able to charge a higher price. Oligopoly is an in-between case.

(a). The monopolist chooses a quantity such that the **marginal revenue** from selling one more can intersects the supply function (reflecting the marginal cost). At the profit-maximizing price of $3.00 per can, buyers demand 5.6 million cans of soup, which is less than the competitive market quantity. The monopoly price far exceeds the marginal cost of $0.80 per can. In choosing a price, a monopolist must balance the advantages of a higher price (more revenue on every can sold) against the disadvantages of a higher price (fewer cans demanded by consumers). The monopoly equilibrium maximizes the monopolist's profits.

c. *Oligopoly.* In an oligopoly, the price and quantity fall somewhere on the demand curve in between the competitive equilibrium and the monopoly equilibrium. The exact price depends on particular circumstances, such as whether the soup producers are able to collude with each other by agreeing not to undercut each other's prices.

To summarize, when sellers have market power, they may increase their own profits by choosing to restrain the quantity they sell so that they can charge buyers a higher price.

quantity sold. In Chapter 2, corn farming was used as an example of a competitive industry. Perfect competitors generally have the lowest profits.

b. In a **monopoly**, there is a single seller. Monopoly generates the highest consumer price and the lowest quantity sold.

c. In an **oligopoly**, there are just a few sellers. If the sellers can behave strategically or cooperate, the oligopoly price and quantity will be more similar to those of a monopoly. If the sellers make independent decisions and cannot cooperate, the oligopoly price and quantity will be more similar to those of a competitive market.

We also can distinguish industries based on the number of buyers (see Box 5.2 for a continuation of the soup industry example):

d. Whereas in a monopoly there is just one seller, in a **monopsony** there is just one buyer. A monopsonist may be able to pay lower prices for inputs, reducing the well-being of input suppliers.

e. In an **oligopsony** there are just a small number of buyers. If the buyers cannot behave strategically, they must pay the full market price, but if they cooperate they can force a lower price much as a monopsonist does.

Competitive structure may be measured using **four-firm concentration ratios** (CR4), which show the market share for the top four firms as a percentage of all sales in the industry. Cheese manufacturing is an example of a relatively competitive industry: the top four cheese manufacturing firms account for about 30 percent of the cheese market. Breakfast cereal manufacturing is more concentrated: the top four breakfast cereal companies account for almost 80 percent of the breakfast cereal market (see Section 5.4).

Box 5.2   The Economics of Market Power for Buyers: Food Retailers

In contrast with Box 5.1, perhaps we should instead worry about the market power that major food retail chains can exert as buyers over their upstream vendors such as food manufacturers (and, if manufacturers pass along their revenues, eventually farmers). This box illustrates a competitive market and two more possible market structures: (d) a monopsonistic market with a single soup buyer; and (e) an oligopsonistic market with a small number of soup buyers. The competitive market with many buyers has the highest price, the monopsony market has the lowest price, and the oligopsonistic market falls somewhere in between (Figure 5.4).

(a) Competitive market. Just as in Box 5.1, the competitive equilibrium has a price of $1.75 per can of soup and a quantity of 9 million cans of soup. The retailer must pay the maximum price it can afford, while still just barely covering its costs.

(d) Monopsony. In a monopsony, the single retailer gets to decide the price. As a soup buyer, this retailer must consider how much soup it can then turn around and sell to its customers. Formally, for each additional marginal can of soup it buys, the retailer considers the additional revenue of selling an additional can (minus the retailer's operational costs for selling that can); this value is called the value of the marginal product (also discussed in Box 2.3). In our illustration, the monopsonist offers food manufacturers merely $0.75 per can. In choosing this price, a monopsonist balances the

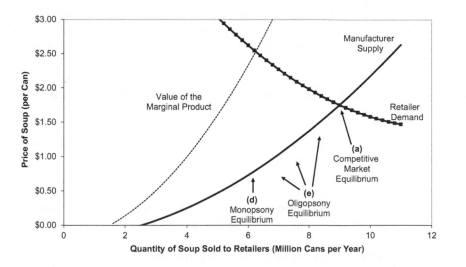

Figure 5.4 A model of food retailers buying soup under (a) competitive markets, (d) monopsony and (e) oligopsony

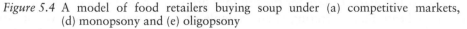

Note: A perfect competitor must accept the competitive equilibrium price, and a monopsonist restrains the quantity purchased in order to command a lower price. Oligopsony is an in-between case.

advantages of a lower price (lower cost for every can purchased) against the disadvantages of a lower price (fewer cans offered by manufacturers, which means fewer cans that the retailer may then sell to consumers). The monopsony equilibrium strikes this balance and maximizes the retailer's profits.

(e) ***Oligopsony.*** In an oligopsony, with just a few big retail chains as buyers, the price and quantity fall somewhere on manufacturers' supply curve in between the competitive equilibrium and the monopsony equilibrium. The exact price depends on particular circumstances, such as whether retail chains are able to collude with each other.

To summarize, when buyers have market power, they may increase their own profits by choosing to limit the quantity they buy, forcing sellers to accept a lower price. In terms of price paid to soup manufacturers, Box 5.2 is the exact opposite of Box 5.1. Yet, in terms of quantity, there is a similarity between market power for buyers and sellers. In both cases, exercising market power requires a powerful business to somehow restrain the quantity on the market. The important lesson: if there is no restraint on the quantity, then neither the seller nor the buyer is exercising market power. In U.S. food policy, there are many examples of market power and also many examples of fierce price competition with no significant market power.

An alternate measure of concentration, the **Herfindahl-Hirschman Index (HHI)**, is based on the market shares for more firms. It is calculated by taking the market share of each of the top 50 firms in an industry, squaring each value and summing those squared values. Like the four-firm concentration ratio, a higher HHI indicates a greater degree of concentration, but the HHI gives greater weight to firms with particularly large market share. In a convention used by the U.S. Department of Justice, few industries qualified as concentrated. An HHI less than 1,500 was said to indicate an unconcentrated market, an HHI of 1,500–2,500 indicated a moderately concentrated market and an HHI greater than 2,500 indicated a highly concentrated market. The HHI for cereal manufacturing is about 2,300, which is near the upper limit of moderately concentrated, according to the Department of Justice convention.

All such measures of concentration depend on how narrowly an industry is defined. For example, the degree of concentration appears much higher in the breakfast cereal industry than it is in the entire grain product manufacturing industry (Table 5.1). Concentration depends similarly on geographic boundaries. A particular regional market may be concentrated even if the national industry is fairly unconcentrated.

To assess the degree of competition in food manufacturing, a central question is how much **market power** firms have. Market power allows a food manufacturer to influence prices. As Box 5.1 illustrates for the example of a monopolist, we can recognize the presence of market power if the selling price exceeds the marginal cost (the cost to produce an additional unit). Likewise, a monopsonist demonstrates market power if it can suppress the price of purchased inputs below their competitive market price (see Box 5.2). When food manufacturers have market power, whether as sellers or as buyers, their profitability increases. Monopsonies in food manufacturing cause economic harm to input suppliers (such as farmers), while monopolies cause harm to output buyers (consumers).

Table 5.1 Four-firm concentration ratios (CR4) and Herfindahl-Hirschman Indices (HHI) for food manufacturing industries, 2012

Manufacturing Industry	CR4 % value added	HHI
Meat	43	580
Animal (except poultry) slaughter	61	1,085
Poultry	40	600
Dairy	22	263
Butter	75	2,245
Grains/oilseeds	51	839
Breakfast cereals	79	2,332
Fruits/vegetables and frozen foods	25	211
Frozen fruits/vegetables/juice	46	739
Sugar/sweets	32	370
Cane sugar refining	61	1,472
Bakery	24	227
Cookies/crackers	60	1,357

Note: Concentration ratios and HHIs differ substantially depending on how broadly or narrowly an industry is defined.

Data note: The U.S. Census Bureau's Economic Census once every five years gathers comprehensive economic data on the food industry and other sectors. Users can access data through the online FactFinder tool (factfinder2.census.gov).

Source: 2012 Economic Census.

The exercise of market power generally requires a **barrier to entry**, which prevents rival firms from entering a particular market. Possible barriers to entry include:

- Patents or other intellectual property rights. In U.S. food policy, patent rights are particularly important in the seed industry (Section 5.4.5).
- Specialized knowledge or other factors of production. Even without formal patent rights, existing firms may have specialized knowledge or equipment that potential rivals lack.
- Entry costs. If entering a manufacturing industry requires large investments in factories and technology, potential rivals may be reluctant to enter that industry and compete with existing firms. The rivals fear being unable to withdraw their investment if new competition eliminates the profitability that made the industry attractive in the first place.
- Limitations on market access. Even if no barrier prevents a potential rival firm from building a single factory, there may be barriers to marketing the food that the factory produces. For example, large multinational food manufacturers often maintain major investments in transportation and distribution. Food manufacturers build relationships with and negotiate payments to food retail chains to persuade the chains to carry particular brands. If large manufacturing firms can control distribution and retail access, smaller manufacturers may perceive barriers to entry.

Diagnosing possible barriers to entry is central to most policy arguments about market power. When there is no barrier to entry, economists are likely to disbelieve claims that a firm can really exercise market power, because it is implausible that potential competitors would overlook an opportunity to share in the profits enjoyed by the firms in the industry.

In other sectors of the economy, such as electricity production and distribution, one sometimes finds **natural monopolies,** where it is most efficient for production to be concentrated in a single firm. Natural monopoly may arise because of **economies of scale,** which are efficiency gains that come with larger operations. For example, if fixed costs of production, including equipment and facilities, are extremely high, it may be inefficient to duplicate those costs across many competing firms. Even in the absence of natural monopolies, large firms can gain competitive advantages through economies of scale by spreading fixed costs across a higher production volume.

Diversified firms may also experience **economies of scope,** which are efficiency gains associated with the production of two or more products. For example, before a corporate reorganization in 2012, the dozens of brands in Kraft Foods Inc. spanned categories including meat (e.g., Oscar Meyer), dairy (e.g., Philadelphia cream cheese), bakery (e.g., Oreo), beverages (e.g., Capri Sun) and confectionary (e.g., Cadbury). Such scope was thought to create efficiencies in activities such as sales and marketing. However, shareholders in fast-growing sectors such as snack foods may not want to share their investment with slower-moving food brands. In 2012, Kraft split into a food business now called Kraft Heinz and a snack food business called Mondelez, which kept brands such as Oreo and Cadbury.

5.3.2 *Vertical Coordination*

Vertical coordination encompasses various forms of organized exchange between different levels of the food marketing system. For food manufacturers, **upstream coordination** mainly describes connections with agricultural producers. **Downstream coordination** relates to connections with food wholesalers and food retailers. This section mainly deals with manufacturers' upstream relationships with agricultural suppliers, while Chapter 6 discusses vertical coordination between manufacturers and retailers.

The level of coordination between manufacturers and suppliers varies from almost no coordination in spot markets to high levels of control in vertical integration (MacDonald et al., 2004):

- In **spot markets,** buying and selling happens in open markets at a particular moment in time. The farmer maintains control over all farm assets and production decisions. The farmer (or another entity representing the farmer) brings the product to market and receives the market price plus or minus any adjustments based on product quality. Spot markets are the most traditional mode of exchange and remain important in many agricultural markets.
- In **contract exchange,** farmers and manufacturers negotiate prices and other terms before or during production. **Marketing contracts** may specify requirements for quantity, quality and timing of product delivery, but the farmer retains control over assets and production decisions. In **production contracts,** the manufacturer exerts some control over farm assets or production decisions and pays the farmer a fee for services provided. Contract exchange is becoming more common. Milk, chicken, hogs, sugar beets and tomatoes grown for processing now are exchanged mostly through contracts.

- In **vertical integration**, the manufacturer owns farm assets and controls production decisions. Today, other contractual arrangements are more common than outright vertical integration. Historical examples of integration include beef packers' owner interests in stockyards, railways and wholesale operations in the late nineteenth and early twentieth centuries (see Section 5.4.2).

Vertical coordination has some benefits. For example, coordination between manufacturers and suppliers may reduce transaction costs, including time and resources that would otherwise be required to negotiate spot-market sales. It also may reduce risk for both manufacturers and producers by guaranteeing, respectively, supplies and markets. On the other hand, vertical coordination raises concerns about market power just as horizontal coordination does. Manufacturers with vertical control may raise barriers to entry by new competitors. In addition, manufacturers' use of contracts, particularly production contracts, may compromise farmers' economic freedom. Because large farms tend to be best equipped to meet the terms of manufacturer contracts, contracting also raises concerns about the survival of smaller family farms and the well-being of rural communities (Sexton, 2013; Sheldon, 2017).

5.3.3 Product Differentiation

Competition also depends on the extent to which products are differentiated. As Section 5.2 describes, some food manufacturing industries offer highly differentiated products (such as branded breakfast cereals or candies), while others offer commodities (such as sugar, flour or vegetable oil). In commodity markets, consumers can readily switch between homogenous options. Price competition in undifferentiated products is fierce, leading manufacturers of such products to focus on finding production efficiencies in order to remain profitable.

By contrast, differentiated products may generate less competition and yield higher profit margins. Because these products do not have exact substitutes, consumers cannot switch to alternatives without sacrificing certain attributes. As a result, manufacturers can charge a higher price. For example, a consumer may be willing to pay a premium price for a particular brand of high-end ice cream rather than switching to a lower-cost brand.

Food manufacturers' motivation to create more profitable differentiated products is a key driver of innovation. Manufacturers spend millions of dollars on research and development and launch thousands of new products each year in an effort to command higher profits. However, differentiation is as much about consumer perceptions as about actual product attributes. In a 2007 USDA report, fewer than 10 percent of new products launched by food manufacturers were categorized as "innovative," with most instead being minor reconfigurations in packaging and branding (Martinez, 2007). Food manufacturers spend heavily to shape consumers' perceptions and, in turn, their willingness to pay premium prices. Chapter 6 will discuss in greater detail an economic model of monopolistic competition, in which product differentiation is the central feature.

5.4 Competition Policy

5.4.1 Legal Tools for Regulating Competition

Given the many potential shortcomings of imperfect competition, the U.S. government has long sought to use public policy to protect and enhance competition in food and agricultural markets. An early landmark in U.S. antitrust policy was the Sherman Act of 1890. The act prohibited anticompetitive collusion among firms selling similar products through interstate commerce, as well as anticompetitive behavior by individual monopoly firms. The Clayton Antitrust Act of 1914 built on the Sherman Act by stopping emergent anticompetitive actions, such as mergers and acquisitions that might impede competition. Today, the Federal Trade Commission (FTC) and the Antitrust Division of the Department of Justice (DOJ) share responsibility for enforcing these laws as they apply to food manufacturing and U.S. markets generally. The Packers and Stockyards Act of 1921 prohibited anticompetitive behavior specifically in meat, poultry and dairy industries and is administered by the Grain Inspection, Packers and Stockyards Administration (GIPSA) of the USDA.

These government agencies use multiple levers to maintain market competition. For example, they investigate anticompetitive behavior, such as price fixing or bid rigging, and take legal action against violating firms. In some cases, improper coordination between firms may be explicit, as when firms directly collude to fix prices. Coordination may also be tacit, as when competing firms follow a price leader to set inflated market prices. In addition to monitoring firms' current behaviors, regulators review proposed mergers and acquisitions between firms and, based on anticipated market effects, approve or reject them.

Regulating competition requires complex judgments. For example, to prosecute tacit collusion, regulators need to demonstrate anticompetitive action between firms that have not communicated directly. To evaluate mergers and acquisitions, they need to anticipate the likelihood of future anticompetitive behavior while balancing these considerations against potential efficiency gains from integration of firms.

As a starting place, regulators often look for signals of potential market power, such as elevated market concentration or high profit margins. However, these outcomes themselves are not unlawful. Judgments regarding whether anticompetitive behavior occurs are often made based on evaluation of harm to consumers. Adverse effects for sellers to concentrated firms (e.g., ranchers supplying livestock to meatpacking firms) may also be cause for government action, particularly when farmers' interests are threatened.

Enforcement of antitrust laws also depends in part on the posture of the government, including executive, legislative and judicial branches, at any given time. For example, members of Congress may insert competition-related language into the Farm Bill, and the president may choose to nominate Supreme Court justices, FTC committee members or USDA leaders who are more or less assertive on antitrust enforcement. As a result, the intensity of enforcement has ebbed and flowed over time. For example, a liberal Supreme Court helped to uphold antitrust regulation from the 1930s to the 1970s. During the subsequent decade, however, the Reagan administration loosened antitrust enforcement, leading to a rush of merger and acquisition activity during the 1980s. Partially in response to the declining influence of federal regulators, nonfederal enforcement mechanisms have emerged. In 1990, for example, the Supreme Court affirmed the rights of state attorneys general to prosecute corporations based on federal antitrust laws (*California v. American Stores*, 495 U.S. 271 (1990)). Private attorneys have also responded to food manufacturers' exertion of market power by bringing class-action lawsuits on behalf of injured parties.

5.4.2 The Beef-Packing Industry

The beef-packing industry played a central role in the development of early U.S. competition policy and continues to be a source of regulatory debate today. The rise of beef packing traces to the 1880s, when several new technologies, particularly in railway refrigeration, enabled the development of national firms that could slaughter and pack beef at a central location and ship it across the United States. The new national industry centered mainly in Chicago, the hub of the Eastern and Western railroads, which was quickly dominated by a small number of companies.

Large meatpacking firms capitalized on three main advantages over their smaller competitors (Aduddell and Cain, 1981). First, large beef-packing plants could use specialized labor, with workers completing focused tasks on animals moved by conveyer belt. Second, large firms had adequate scale to profitably use beef byproducts. And third, large companies had sufficient resources to integrate vertically, often by owning interests in stockyards, railways, cold storage facilities and local wholesalers. Such advantages fed rapid market consolidation, and by 1888 four firms handled 89 percent of beef slaughtered in Chicago and two-thirds of the dressed beef sold nationwide (Azzam and Anderson, 1996).

Initially, the large beef packers' efficiencies benefitted both consumers and ranchers: packers offered lower prices to customers, and as beef consumption rose farmers were able to command higher prices for cattle. By the late 1800s, however, large meatpacking companies were leveraging their market power to raise prices for beef consumers, even as they offered farmers lower prices for cattle. Speaking to Congress in 1890, Rep. Ezra Taylor complained that the major beef companies "fix arbitrarily the daily market price of cattle, from which there is no appeal, for there is no other market. . . . This monster robs the farmer on the one hand and the consumer on the other" (21 Cong. Rec. 4098 (1890) statement of Rep. Ezra B. Taylor).

Although the Sherman Act was passed in 1890, for nearly three decades the major beef packers evaded government attempts at curbing their market power. By 1916 the "Big Five" firms—Armour, Cudahy, Morris, Swift and Wilson—slaughtered 94 percent of cattle in the 12 cities that produced over 80 percent of U.S. beef (Horowitz, 2006). Finally in 1920, in response to consumer discontent over rising food prices, President Woodrow Wilson commissioned an FTC report to investigate the meatpacking industry. The report found strong evidence of anticompetitive behavior. The major packers, under threat of legal action, agreed to disband their vertical control by selling off all nonprocessing interests. Despite this victory, lingering concerns about the meatpacking industry led Congress to pass the Packers and Stockyards Act in 1921, which established a new USDA administration (today the Grain Inspection and Packers and Stockyards Administration, or GIPSA) to continue to monitor practices in the production of beef and other animal products.

Such regulatory developments alone were insufficient to dismantle the beef packers' power. In 1923, for example, the Big Five consolidated further after Armour acquired Morris, and in 1934 the new Big Four accounted for more than three-quarters of national meat sales. Ultimately, market developments played as important a role as regulation in reducing the firms' competitive advantages. For example, the development of the national highway system and lower-cost refrigerated trucks, as well as a new federal meat-grading program, lowered barriers to entry for new firms. The expansion of national grocery chains, which purchased meat directly from independent packers, further reduced the Big Four's market control. In 1971 the Chicago stockyards closed, and by 1977 the four-firm concentration ratio had fallen to under 30 percent.

The 1980s, however, saw a reemergence of large, powerful packing firms, fed by developments at both the market and policy levels. For example, U.S. consumers' declining intakes of red meat in the 1980s led to excess slaughtering capacity, making consolidation an attractive growth option relative to expansion. Also, new boxed-beef processes, which combined slaughtering, boning and breaking of meat into consumer-ready cuts, yielded new efficiencies through labor-specialization, mechanization and shipping, all of which favored larger firms. The Reagan administration's deregulatory position in the 1980s further facilitated consolidation. By 1990, the four-firm concentration ratio in beef packing had climbed to 81 percent.

Today, concentration in beef packing remains high, with four firms—Cargill, Tyson, JBS and National Beef—dominating the market. Like the Chicago packers a century before, these firms also gain efficiencies and market power through vertical integration, though today such integration is mainly achieved through contractual arrangements with farmers. The impact of these trends remains the subject of policy debate. A 2009 Government Accountability Office (GAO) report recognized the high level of market concentration in meatpacking but did not find that this concentration had an adverse effect on consumer food prices. GAO instead concluded that adverse impacts of market power generally were offset by efficiency advantages from vertical integration through contracting (U.S. Government Accountability Office, 2009). Some economists agreed with GAO's optimism that contracts offer production efficiencies for both growers and meatpackers, while still expressing serious concern that the contracting arrangements sometimes lack transparency (Saitone and Sexton, 2012). For example, if most cows are sold through contracts, there may not be enough of a spot market to provide growers with sound economic information about competitive prices for their products.

5.4.3 Overseeing Contracts in Pork and Poultry

As a large share of pork and especially poultry production has become vertically integrated through production contracts, there is an active debate about whether the upstream growers are treated fairly. For example, for broilers (chicken for meat), integrators (processors) provide inputs such as chicks and feed, give detailed instructions about equipment and methods and purchase the final product. Once growers begin working with a particular integrator and invest capital in buildings and equipment, they face economic pressure to continue to satisfy the integrator's requirements because it could be difficult or costly to switch to a competing integrator.

It is clear that consolidation in pork and poultry processing has dramatically transformed these industries, leaving just a few very large manufacturing companies in command of the market. There is some evidence that the upstream producers earn less as a consequence. For producers of broilers, for example, fees paid to the growers were estimated to be 8 percent lower in markets with just one integrator or processing company and 4 percent lower in markets with two or three integrators, compared to markets with four or more (MacDonald, 2016). On the other hand, working with an integrator may help a grower to control costs and, especially, to control risk from fluctuating prices for both inputs and outputs.

Based on concerns regarding market power and contracting terms, the 2008 Farm Bill instructed USDA to update the nearly century-old rules outlined in the Packers and Stockyards Act. Shortly thereafter, the appointment of new antitrust-focused leaders in DOJ and USDA, along with a series of government-hosted workshops on competition in meat and dairy industries, appeared to portend a shift toward tighter regulation. GIPSA proposed rules that would have restricted some contracting practices that farmers perceived as particularly abusive. One of the new provisions would have required manufacturers and meatpackers to collect and post sample contracts, bringing greater transparency and openness to the contracting arrangements. Another rule clarified that producers who claim to have been harmed by unfair contracts do not need to prove harm to competition in the entire industry (which is nearly impossible to prove); instead, they just need to show that they were unfairly harmed.

However, subsequently, Congress appeared to reconsider its support for stronger rules and took several steps to undermine the GIPSA proposal. In 2011, in its agricultural appropriations law for the next fiscal year, Congress instructed USDA not to issue regulations on several topics related to the GIPSA proposal, including the transparency provision. When USDA published a much milder rule in December 2011, omitting the most controversial policies, it explained in a press release that Congress' appropriations law "included language prohibiting the Department from moving forward on these important provisions." For the next few years, annual Congressional appropriations included a "GIPSA rider" that continued to restrain USDA from completing the process of issuing the new rules.

In 2014, the House of Representatives passed a version of the Farm Bill that would have fully quashed the USDA rule-making process, which previously had been merely stalled. The Senate was more supportive of the GIPSA rules, and the final bill produced by a House-Senate conference left the GIPSA rules alive, though still on pause. Then, for 2016, Congress did not pass a GIPSA rider, allowing the Obama administration in December, in its final two months, an opportunity to issue an "interim final rule" that could actually take effect even while the final rule was being prepared. However, in 2017, both Congress and the incoming Trump administration indicated that they are unlikely to support actually implementing these rules, on grounds that they reflect undue regulation of the free market for producers of beef, pork and poultry. As of 2017, there was little government support for strong measures to change contracting rules in ways that benefit growers, nor even for milder provisions that would merely increase transparency about contract terms to enhance competition in a market setting.

5.4.4 The Ready-to-Eat Cereal Industry

In 1995, then-House Rep. Chuck Schumer (D-NY) partnered with Rep. Sam Gejdenson (D-CT) to issue a widely publicized battle cry for regulation of the RTE breakfast cereal industry. "Why," Schumer asked, "should a box of cereal, made of cardboard and containing nothing more than grain, cost an arm and a leg?" (Gillespie, 1995). Cereal manufacturers' price-cost margins—that is, the ratio of retail prices to the cost of production—are among the highest in the food manufacturing industry, as are their levels of advertising spending and profit margins. These profits are mostly shared among a very small number of firms—particularly Kellogg, General Mills and Post—that have dominated the industry for nearly a century.

The lack of new firms entering the RTE cereals market—and, in turn, driving down prices—seems to point to impaired competition. However, most conventional barriers to entry seem not to apply to the industry:

- Intellectual property rights have a limited role among RTE cereal makers, which have rarely obtained patents since the 1950s. Branded cereals can be imitated by competitors with relative ease.
- While cereal production is somewhat complex, the level of specialized knowledge required is not sufficiently prohibitive to explain lack of entry.
- Cereal manufacturers have relatively little vertical control, and key inputs such as wheat and corn are readily sold to buyers willing to pay market prices.
- Up-front capital investments are a more sizeable barrier, given that an RTE cereal plant might cost about $300 million, according to one estimate (Nevo, 2001); however, given the size and profitability of the RTE cereals market, such sunk costs should not, on their own, prevent entry by new firms.

One alternative theory suggests that cereal manufacturers maintain barriers to entry by producing and aggressively advertising hundreds of different brands, which crowd the market and block new firms from entering. In 1972, FTC tried to use this premise as the centerpiece of a shared-monopoly case against top cereal manufacturers, contending that "practices of proliferating brands, differentiating similar products and promoting trademarks through intensive advertising result in high barriers to entry" (*F.T.C. v. Kellogg, et al.*, Docket No. 8883). In the end, though, after over 10 years of litigation, FTC was unable to make its case and dropped the suit.

In some respects, RTE cereal manufacturers do in fact face considerable competition. For example, lower-cost generic cereals are readily available in retail outlets but have failed to capture a substantial share of the cereal market. RTE cereals also may be viewed as a subsegment of a larger "breakfast foods" category, including competitive grocery items such as eggs or frozen waffles, as well as restaurant offerings such as fast-food breakfast sandwiches. While RTE cereal is one of the food manufacturing sectors with the most serious symptoms of industry concentration, the manufacturers' market power still is curtailed by significant competitive forces.

5.4.5 Patents and Market Power in the Seed Industry

U.S. antitrust policy usually treats competition as the ideal and monopoly as a problem. Yet intellectual property rights granted by the government can be an important source of monopoly power. For centuries, governments have assigned patent rights to motivate investments in new technologies. Patents allow an inventor (or a company that purchases rights from an inventor) to be the monopoly seller of a new product. It is a common mistake to think that a patent provides permission to make a product; instead, the purpose of a patent is to forbid rivals from making the product.

A leading example is patents in the modern seed industry. Patents over seeds are comparatively new. Improvements in agricultural technology are essential for achieving the food security of a growing world population (see Chapter 3). For most of human history, when new plant varieties were developed, farmers and seed manufacturers could adopt them freely. The 1980 U.S. Supreme Court decision *Diamond v. Chakrabarty* enabled inventors to exercise patent rights over new seeds. Such patent rights have become common for new genetically modified organism (GMO) traits and also for germplasm developed through more traditional plant breeding.

In the space of just 15 years, these patent rights allowed a single biotechnology firm, the Monsanto Company, to become the dominant U.S. seed producer for several crops. For example, seeds using Monsanto's traits were planted in 21.8 percent of U.S. corn acres in 2000 and 81.1 percent of U.S. corn acres in 2009 (Moschini, 2010; Carstensen, 2016). Similarly, Monsanto traits were planted in 94.5 percent of soybean acres in 2009. Although Monsanto and other biotechnology companies have explored a wide variety of promising traits, most of their business to date has come from just two new technologies: plants that contain protection against insects (the Bt toxin) and plants that are resistant to an herbicide (such as glyphosate, known by Monsanto's trade name Roundup).

The new seeds clearly are highly valued by farmers. Otherwise, farmers would not adopt them. The patent rights allow seed manufacturers to earn higher prices and licensing fees from farmers, capturing a large fraction of the economic benefit that farmers achieve by using the new varieties. To claim the profits that arise from patent rights, Monsanto has pursued a series of controversial lawsuits against farmers and smaller seed companies that were alleged to violate Monsanto patents or the terms of Monsanto licenses. For example, in 2013, the Supreme Court decided in *Bowman v. Monsanto* that Monsanto could prevent a farmer from planting soybean seeds that he had bought unlabeled from a grain elevator. This case was interesting, because the farmer had not signed any licensing agreement, as farmers must do when buying seed for planting directly from a Monsanto distributor. Hence, the farmer had not violated any agreement. Yet the court ruled that Monsanto's patent granted the ability to prevent farmers from planting even commodity soybeans that carried the patented trait (Carstensen, 2016).

As the agricultural economist Giancarlo Moschini explains, the new technologies provide great potential benefits, but "there remains an unresolved tension between the prescriptions of IPR [intellectual property rights] and antitrust laws" (Moschini, 2010). A World Bank report expressed concerns about having genetic technologies "largely controlled by a small group of multinational companies" (World Bank, 2007). Or, as antitrust law expert Peter Carstensen put it, "the market for commercial seeds remains . . . highly concentrated and encrusted with anticompetitive practices that both entrench the existing market leaders and exploit the buyers of their seeds" (Carstensen, 2016). Ironically, the very features that make monopoly unattractive to an antitrust regulator—restricted supply, higher prices for consumers and surplus profits for the producer—are central to the U.S. policy of using patent rights as the primary economic incentive for investments in biotechnology.

5.5 Conclusion

Food marketers and consumers alike sometimes appear to believe a fairytale account of the food system in which the factories and slaughterhouses of the food manufacturing industry have disappeared, as if removed by photo editing software. In the image left behind, food comes straight from farms. Yet the manufacturing industry plays a big role in creating most of the food and beverages that people consume in the United States.

This chapter provides tools for diagnosing what works well or poorly in U.S. food and beverage manufacturing. First, it emphasizes that manufacturing sectors vary widely in terms of production technology, nutritional impact, value added, competitive structure and market power. Second, it introduces economic and legal principles for analyzing the market structure and economic performance of industry sectors, using four industries as leading examples.

It is prudent for governments to monitor food manufacturing for signs of impaired competition. History tells us that market power among manufacturers can harm suppliers and consumers. In several industry sectors, high concentration indices appear to reflect market power. Especially in manufacturing sectors that use production contracts to control farm-level supplies, economists worry that there may not be enough transparency to ensure that markets function in a competitive manner.

Yet there is some contrary evidence as well. Firms in the food manufacturing industry have grown large in part because of genuine economies of scale in food manufacturing and economies of scope in food marketing and distribution. Manufacturers' food retailer customers (Chapter 6) are often large corporations with considerable bargaining power. The contracting arrangements between food manufacturers and their suppliers offer efficiencies in coordinating production decisions, assuring a buyer for growers and an input supply for food manufacturers. If food manufacturing firms were strongly monopsonistic or monopolistic, they would have to restrict the food quantity produced in order to be able to pay a lower price to farmers and charge a higher price to consumers. But that type of quantity restraint seems uncommon in the aggressively productive business of U.S. food and beverage manufacturing.

For farmers, some of the cruelest features of their economic circumstances may not originate from the monopoly or monopsony power of food manufacturers. Instead, they may originate from downward price pressure created by consumer demand in competitive markets. So long as consumers seek to choose less expensive foods over more expensive foods, intense pressure to squeeze out costs is passed backwards through the food marketing chain, affecting the fundamental character of the food manufacturing industry and eventually affecting the market for farm products. Consumer demand is a central topic in the next chapter.

Summary List of Key Terms (identified in bold in the text)

- barrier to entry
- commodities
- competitive market
- contract exchange
- degree of competition
- downstream coordination
- economies of scale
- economies of scope
- enrichment
- fortification
- four-firm concentration ratios
- Herfindahl-Hirschman Index
- marginal cost
- marginal revenue
- market power
- market structure
- marketing contracts
- monopoly
- monopsony
- natural monopoly
- oligopoly
- oligopsony
- perfect competition
- product differentiation
- production contracts
- profit margins
- spot markets
- structure-conduct-performance
- upstream coordination
- vertical coordination
- vertical integration

6 Food Retailing and Restaurants

Parke Wilde and Daniel Hatfield

6.1 Introduction

The *2015–2020 Dietary Guidelines for Americans*, published by the U.S. Department of Health and Human Services (DHHS) and USDA, emphasizes that our food behavior is influenced by the situation around us. "Having access to healthy, safe and affordable food choices is crucial for an individual to achieve a healthy eating pattern," the report explains (U.S. DHHS and USDA, 2015).

As the public face of the food marketing system, retailers and restaurants are central to policy debates about the food and beverage environment. Policy-makers may want to write zoning laws to attract supermarkets to low-income neighborhoods, limit the use of free toys to market restaurant meals to children or impose taxes on unhealthy food categories. To judge such proposals, we must understand: (a) how food retailers and restaurants make decisions related to the food environment and (b) how consumers respond to that environment when allocating time and money to food shopping and food preparation.

The two industries covered in this chapter are rapidly changing. Figure 6.1 shows that consumer spending on **food away from home** (from restaurants and other food service operations) recently surpassed spending on **food at home** (from supermarkets and other food retailers). These trends have important implications for food system outcomes. To help navigate the complex relationships among food retailers, restaurants and consumers, this chapter:

- provides a broad overview of the food retail industry (Section 6.2);
- discusses more specifically food retail access and the economics of store location decisions (Section 6.3);
- provides a broad overview of the restaurant industry and uses this industry as an example to introduce the economic concept of monopolistic competition (Section 6.4);
- summarizes recent labor policy debates in the food retail and restaurant industries (Section 6.5); and
- describes the economics of food price indices and inflation measurement, which shed light on the role of prices in nutritionally relevant food-spending decisions (Section 6.6).

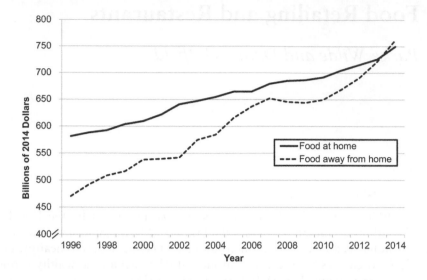

Figure 6.1 U.S. consumer food spending (in constant 2014 dollars), 1996–2014

Data note: USDA's Economic Research Service provides a wide variety of annually updated food expenditure data series, including this one (www.ers.usda.gov/data-products/food-expenditures).

Source: USDA Economic Research Service.

6.2 The Organization of the Food Retail Industry

Food retailers serve food manufacturers and consumers alike by reducing **transaction costs,** the time and expense that would be required for manufacturers and consumers to negotiate sales directly. In exchange for their services, retailers take a slice of the food dollar: the sector contributes about 13 cents of each dollar of value added in the U.S. food system. This section describes three categories of food retailers: (1) supermarkets, (2) supercenters and warehouse stores (together called big-box retailers) and (3) small outlets and other retailers.

6.2.1 Supermarkets

When the first U.S. supermarkets opened in the 1930s, they revolutionized the food retail sector. In traditional grocery stores, employees assisted customers with their selections; in supermarkets, customers moved products from shelves to shopping baskets themselves. This arrangement decreased supermarkets' staffing requirements, leading to lower store prices. Supermarkets were also larger than traditional markets, providing products ranging from fresh meat and produce to canned items and household goods. From the 1930s to the 1950s, automobile ownership spread to the middle class, allowing consumers to transport larger purchases. The combined appeal of low prices and one-stop shopping fed rapid growth of the supermarket format, which, by the 1950s, dominated food retail.

In the 1990s and 2000s, the supermarket segment faced new competition, particularly from supercenters, warehouse stores and the growing restaurant sector. The precise category definitions vary from source to source, but USDA economists estimate that the market share for supermarkets fell from 80 percent of food-at-home spending in 1999 to 62 percent in 2012 (Volpe, Kuhns and Jaenicke, 2017). To compete, leading companies such as Kroger, Albertson's, Supervalu and Ahold Delhaize have bought out many other chains. Such activity may go unnoticed by many consumers, however, since acquired stores often retain their regional brand names to avoid losing loyal customers.

Despite such cost-saving efforts, today the leading supermarket chains, such as Kroger, maintain profit margins of only about 1–2 percent. In an effort to boost margins, many chains have expanded their selection of prepared foods, which tend to be more profitable than other food items. Other supermarkets have added services—such as banking outlets, eateries or coffee shops—that help to draw customers into the store. Chains such as Whole Foods, Trader Joe's and Wegmans have differentiated from competitors with unique, high-quality foods and customer service, which enable them to command higher prices and profits.

6.2.2 Supercenters and Warehouse Stores

Supercenters and warehouse stores are types of **big-box outlets**, distinguished by their physically large spaces (often over 150,000 square feet), focus on competitive pricing and no-frills store formats. Big-box stores expanded rapidly in the 1990s and 2000s. Supercenters and mass merchandisers such as Walmart and Target generally sell food in addition to merchandise such as electronics, clothing and housewares. In some cases, supercenters' grocery offerings function as **loss leaders**, items sold at very low profit to increase traffic in other parts of the store. In comparison with supercenters, warehouse stores, including membership-based club chains such as Costco, generally sell fewer distinct products. Their products include high-end branded goods, often stacked unceremoniously on pallets on the store floor. Because warehouse stores typically sell food in bulk, prices per unit generally are lower than in other retail locations.

The price competitiveness of big-box stores is particularly pronounced for the largest chains. These firms leverage their size to negotiate discounts from suppliers and to capitalize on economies of scale in distribution. These cost savings, in turn, translate to lower prices for consumers. For example, one study found that food prices at Walmart Supercenters averaged 27 percent lower than at other stores and that entry of a Walmart Supercenter into a geographic market led to an average 4.8 percent reduction in prices at nearby supermarkets (Hausman and Leibtag, 2007).

Despite these advantages, the growth of big-box food retailers raises several concerns. Competition from highly efficient retailers such as Walmart may force smaller operations out of business. Labor organizations take issue with aggressive cost-containment strategies, which may translate into low wages, meager benefits or resistance to unionization.

6.2.3 Small Outlets and Other Retailers

About 20 percent of U.S. consumers' food-at-home spending is attributable to other, generally small outlets that cater to diverse consumer needs and preferences. Dollar stores, for example, have expanded food sales by targeting lower-income consumers with highly competitive prices. Convenience stores generally locate in high-traffic urban areas. Drug stores have also started to offer grocery products. Despite advantages in terms of cost and convenience, convenience stores and other small outlet stores raise concerns among health advocates, particularly since they tend to sell less of foods such as whole grains, lean proteins and fresh produce (Volpe, Kuhns and Jaenicke, 2017).

Local grocery stores and ethnic markets can play a particularly important role in providing food access for Americans who live far from supermarkets and also lack access to automobiles. Direct farm-to-consumer sales, mainly through roadside stands, farmers' markets and community-supported agriculture (CSA) programs, may also increase access to fresh local produce and other foods. The federal government has sought to support direct farm sales by making SNAP benefits redeemable at farmers' markets, and some municipal governments have developed dollar-for-dollar matching programs to augment SNAP purchases in farmers' markets. Overall, despite recent growth, direct sales continue to represent a relatively small proportion of the U.S. food retail market.

6.2.4 Market Power in U.S. Food Retailing

Despite rapidly increasing concentration, firms must aggressively contain costs to remain profitable. As in other segments of the food marketing system, many retailers have consolidated to capture economies of scale and scope. In 2009, for example, the top four firms captured 37 percent of U.S. retail food sales, more than double the 1996 figure of 17.5 percent. This trend reflects mergers among traditional food retailers and the growth of nontraditional giants, particularly Walmart. The four-firm concentration ratio is high enough to raise concerns about market power. In particular locations, retail concentration is much higher than these national statistics show (Sheldon, 2017). Because consumers shop locally rather than nationally for groceries, it may be local concentration that matters most.

Like manufacturers, some food retailers have captured savings by coordinating vertically. While wholesalers traditionally served as intermediaries between producers and retailers, large retail firms increasingly find it more efficient to negotiate contracts directly with food manufacturers and other suppliers. Wholesalers have become less powerful players in the marketing chain, and some have expanded into food retailing in order to remain profitable.

Most large food retailers also coordinate vertically by selling **private-label products**, store-brand lines that are typically priced lower than comparable national brands. Retailers often outsource production of private-label goods to manufacturing firms, sometimes the same companies that produce national brands. Such manufacturers capture a much smaller share of the consumer dollar on private-label items, so they carefully differentiate their own products from private labels through packaging and branding.

Some retailers charge manufacturers slotting fees or stocking fees, which are side-payments made in exchange for presenting the manufacturers' products on retail shelves, separate from the purchase price. Manufacturers may be willing to pay such fees in order to gain more consumer exposure through more shelf space in more retailers. It is not clear whether slotting fees serve as a vehicle for food retailers to exercise market power over manufacturers (Sheldon, 2017). Traditionally, some of the most competitive big-box retailers did not use slotting fees, preferring instead just to bargain hard for a low price on the goods they purchase from manufacturers. In this sense, oligopsony power seemed to be separate from the question of slotting fees.

However, in 2015, Walmart announced that it too would use such fees, which generated new concerns about the practice among suppliers (Layne, 2015).

A growth area for U.S. food retailing is online ordering. Long-time online sellers, such as Amazon, and long-time food retailers, such as Safeway and Walmart, have all been seeking to expand in this borderland between the two industries. In 2017, Amazon announced its intention to acquire Whole Foods, an upscale health-oriented food retailer. As of 2017, the full potential scale of online ordering and the implications for competitiveness are not yet known.

The economic tug of war between U.S. food manufacturers and food retailers involves two large industries whose members each want to exercise market power at the expense of the other, so the overall consequences for prices are unclear. First, because both manufacturers and retailers show considerable concentration, neither one is able to dictate prices to the other. Second, echoing an observation in Chapter 5 about concentrated food manufacturing industries, U.S. food retailers seldom behave like traditional monopolists or oligopolists, which must restrain the quantity sold in order to boost prices above competitive levels. Even when local concentration is high, food retailers usually behave as if they constantly fear the potential entry of new competitors, causing them to exhibit vigorous competitive energy and persistent downward price pressure.

6.3 Food Deserts and the Retail Environment

6.3.1 The Economics of Food Retail Location

National initiatives to improve the food environment have sought to address **food deserts**, which are neighborhoods or districts with inadequate access to healthy food retail options, especially for low-income residents. "In many communities across the country," former First Lady Michelle Obama said in a 2011 speech about food deserts, "there is no place to purchase any groceries, much less fresh fruits and vegetables" (Obama, 2011a).

In the economics of the food retail industry, geography matters for both demand and supply. On the demand side, consumers prefer to minimize time spent traveling to and from food outlets (Box 6.1). They also value product quality, variety and low prices. When choosing between two stores with the same characteristics, a consumer may reasonably prefer the one that is closer to home. Yet if a more distant store offers higher quality or lower prices, consumers with access to automobiles may prefer to drive to a store further away.

On the supply side, geography affects a retailer's costs and its competitive environment. Two types of costs are relevant. **Variable costs,** which increase in proportion to the quantity of food sold, include labor costs for checkout line clerks and the input costs of the food itself. **Fixed costs,** which occur once per store, include the cost of buildings and property. The fixed costs are comparatively low for a small corner store and quite high for a supermarket. Both types of costs vary from one potential location to another.

In the short run, a store must charge prices sufficiently high to cover variable costs. In the long run, to break even, a store must charge prices that are high enough to cover variable costs plus each customer's proportional share of the fixed costs. The ability to do so depends on the competitive environment in a particular location. A large retailer must spread the fixed costs over a sufficiently large customer base so that the fixed costs per customer are kept sufficiently low. To acquire this customer base, a supermarket chain's managers must consider the size, population density and purchasing power of the catchment area from which a store location could draw customers, along with the number and size of nearby competing stores.

If a supermarket in a small town is the only food retailer for many miles around, it can behave somewhat like a monopolist, raising prices above competitive levels. By contrast, if several supermarkets are located near each other in a city or suburban neighborhood, they are forced to behave like perfect competitors. There exists a full spectrum of in-between cases, where supermarkets compete to a certain degree with one another. The intensity of competition is proportional to the proximity of competing supermarkets.

Figure 6.2 illustrates key features of supermarket location decisions in a hypothetical community. The center of each circle represents a supermarket, and the circles represent neighborhoods lying less than 1 mile from a supermarket. Section 6.3.2 will provide a map of a real U.S. city. In the hypothetical community, assuming prices and quality are comparable, each resident (illustrated by a house icon) would want to shop at a food retailer located less than a mile away (at the center of the circle that contains the household). In a small community such as Our Town, a single supermarket may find a sufficiently large customer base (five residences). In a city such as Metropolis, two supermarkets may share an adequately large local customer base (at least five residences each). A rural location such as Quiet Hollow does not have enough residences to support a supermarket and could be considered a food desert. In this illustration, even with optimal food retailer location decisions, some residences have no supermarket nearby, some have one supermarket, and some have two supermarkets. Some customers can shop near home and others must drive longer distances.

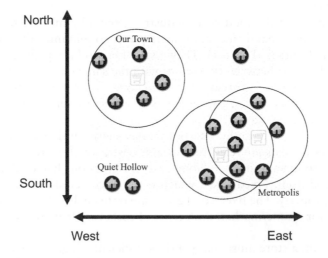

Figure 6.2 Map of a hypothetical community food retail environment

Note: The center of each circle represents a supermarket, and the circles represent neighborhoods lying less than 1 mile from a supermarket.

Box 6.1   Time Use

Food choices depend on how people allocate not just their limited money but also their scarce time. Dietary quality and obesity risk are connected to people's decisions about work and employment, grocery shopping, food preparation, eating and drinking, physical activity and television watching. For many Americans, time constraints bind more tightly than budget constraints do.

Food choices involve many tradeoffs between time and money. A wage is, in a fundamental economic sense, the price of an hour of time (Box 2.3). As wages for both men and women rose during the twentieth century, and as women moved into the labor force at higher rates, the value of time rose. People became more willing to pay extra for convenience food and restaurant food. The American Time Use Survey estimates time spent in many primary activities for people aged 15 and older in 2011 (Table 6.1) (Hamrick et al., 2011). The amount of time in food preparation and grocery shopping is lower for working women than for nonworking women, and time in these activities fell sharply for both groups of women from the 1960s to the 1990s. More severe time constraints are associated with higher fast-food restaurant spending, potentially leading to less healthy eating patterns (Hamrick and Okrent, 2014).

Economist Diego Rose points out that these trends have implications for estimating the cost of an adequate diet (Chapter 10). For households that do not have time to cook from scratch and for whom convenience and ready-to-eat foods are an essential part of an adequate food budget, current Supplemental Nutrition Assistance Program (SNAP) benefits might seem inadequate (Rose, 2007). It is difficult to set the SNAP benefit level in a way that is fair to households with different types of time constraints (Chapter 10).

Table 6.1 Mean time use in primary activities for U.S. persons (ages 15 and older), 2011

	Mean hours per day
Personal care activities	9.49
Sleeping	8.71
Eating and drinking	1.24
Household activities	1.77
Food preparation and cleanup	0.56
Purchasing goods and services	0.72
Grocery shopping	0.11
Caring for and helping household members and others	0.72
Working, work-related activities and education	4.04[a]
Leisure and sports	5.21
Watching TV	2.75
Other	0.81
Total time	24.00

[a] One might have expected the work hours to be longer, but this estimate is an average taken over both working and nonworking persons, on both weekdays and weekends.
Data note: The Bureau of Labor Statistics (BLS) tabulates primary activities from the American Time Use Survey (ATUS) for all U.S. adults and separately for working adults on a work day (www.bls.gov/tus).

Table 6.2 Program summary: Healthy Food Financing Initiative (HFFI)

Overview: A cross-departmental initiative with programs at the U.S. Department of Health and Human Services (DHHS), U.S. Department of Treasury, and USDA to improve food retail access in underserved areas.	
Year begun	2010
Scale of operation	
Number of DHHS Community Economic Development awards, fiscal year 2016	11
Number of DHHS Community Economic Development awards, fiscal year 2015	9
Number of Department of Treasury awards, fiscal year 2016	9
Number of Department of Treasury awards, fiscal year 2015	12
Budget	
DHHS Community Economic Development awards, 2011–2016 ($ million)	51.8
Department of Treasury awards, 2011–2016 ($ million)	113.3
Eligibility: Community Development Corporations (nonprofit organizations focused on community revitalization) with eligible community food projects (for DHHS awards) and Community Development Financial Institutions (private financial institutions that offer loans) with eligible food retail financing projects (for Department of Treasury awards).	
Benefits: Direct project funding (for DHHS awards) and food retail financing (for Department of Treasury awards).	

Source: U.S. Department of Health and Human Services, Office of Community Services (2016); Lang et al. (2013); Department of Treasury (unpublished).

In real-world policy debates about food deserts, a fundamental question is whether local food retail conditions arise from rational store location decisions such as those illustrated in Figure 6.2 or instead from poorly functioning markets. A poorly functioning market could arise if corporate managers underestimated local buying power, or were prejudiced against people of color or simply failed to notice opportunities in neighborhoods with which they were unfamiliar. Operating on the premise that current supermarket location decisions are mistaken in these ways, the federal government's Healthy Food Financing Initiative (HFFI) includes a collection of projects administered through multiple departments, all seeking to improve local food retail conditions (Table 6.2).

6.3.2 Identifying Food Deserts

To identify food deserts and estimate how many people have inadequate food retail access, researchers must first decide several technical questions:

- What type of retailer counts as providing adequate food access, in terms of price, variety and quality?
- What distance counts as being adequately close?
- What account should be taken of household income?
- What account should be taken of vehicle access or public transportation?

Numerous governmental and nongovernmental research efforts have taken different positions on these questions. The Retail Food Environment Index, developed by the California Center for Public Health Advocacy, is calculated by dividing the total number of fast-food outlets and convenience stores by the total number of supermarkets, produce stores and farmers' markets in an area (California Center for Public Health Advocacy, 2007). The Limited Supermarket Access score, developed by The Reinvestment Fund, uses a fairly complex method to compare access in lower-income block groups to a benchmark derived from comparable higher-income block groups (Reinvestment Fund, 2015). In some cases, the threshold distance from the nearest supermarket, which leads a neighborhood to be classified as having Limited Supermarket Access, may be smaller than a mile (Wilde, Llobrera and Ver Ploeg, 2014). The HFFI and USDA's online interactive Food Access Research Atlas have used an approach based on census tract characteristics, identifying census tracts that have high poverty rates and that have a substantial fraction of their populations living more than 1 mile from a supermarket (in urban areas) or 10 miles from a supermarket (in rural areas). Most of these approaches implicitly assume the critical issue is to locate the nearest supermarket within 1 mile or less from most low-income residents.

A new body of research provides more empirical information about how low-income food consumers actually make shopping decisions. In contrast to what one might expect from the earlier literature, it turns out that high-poverty census block groups are more likely than lower-poverty block groups to be close to the nearest supermarket (Wilde, Llobrera and Ver Ploeg, 2014; Ver Ploeg et al., 2015). The reason is that, notwithstanding the important issue of rural poverty, higher-poverty neighborhoods in the United States tend on average to have higher population density, and these higher-density neighborhoods in turn tend to have more supermarkets.

Moreover, most low-income households in the United States have access to an automobile. Among SNAP participant households, for example, 68 percent use their own vehicle for grocery shopping (compared to 95 percent in higher-income non-SNAP households), and another 19 percent of SNAP participant households use somebody else's vehicle for grocery shopping (for example, getting a lift, borrowing a car or taking a taxi) (Ver Ploeg et al., 2015). For households that are comparatively mobile, the distance to the nearest supermarket, which was the focus of so much attention in earlier research, may not even be the most salient feature of the local food retail environment. At all income levels, most shoppers bypass the nearest supermarket and conduct their primary shopping at a retailer farther from home. For example, for SNAP households, the mean distance to the nearest SNAP-authorized supermarket is just under 2 miles, but the mean distance to the primary store chosen for grocery shopping is about 3.4 miles (Ver Ploeg et al., 2015). Statistics are similar for higher-income households.

These insights may change how we perceive the geography of the local food retail environment. The map in Figure 6.3 illustrates supermarket access using real data for Houston, TX, following a map design developed in a USDA report to Congress (Ver Ploeg et al., 2009). As in Figure 6.2 earlier, the center of each circle represents a supermarket, and the circles represent neighborhoods lying less than 1 mile from a supermarket. In Figure 6.3, darker shading indicates greater population density. Three patterns stand out:

- Most densely populated neighborhoods, whether rich or poor, have fairly good access to supermarkets.
- Some outlying areas have poor access to supermarkets, but they are less densely populated (and most residents in these areas are likely to have access to a vehicle).
- The areas of greatest public policy concern may be the few high-density, high-poverty neighborhoods that lack a nearby supermarket.

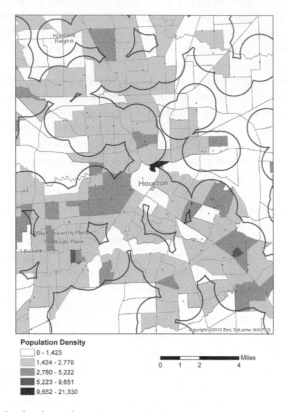

Population Density
- 0 - 1,423
- 1,424 - 2,779
- 2,780 - 5,222
- 5,223 - 9,651
- 9,652 - 21,330

Figure 6.3 Map of the food retail environment in Houston

Note: The center of each circle represents a supermarket.

Data note: The ERS Food Access Research Atlas provides a spatial view of census tracts with limited food retail access (www.ers.usda.gov/data-products/food-access-research-atlas/).

Source: Map by Joseph Llobrera and Parke Wilde, based on a design for a map of St. Louis in Ver Ploeg et al. (2009).

There are a couple lessons that arise from thinking empirically about local food retail access problems for low-income consumers in the United States. First, some low-income households really do have impaired food retail access. For example, the most serious access problems may arise for the comparatively small number of households that lack an automobile and live far from a supermarket. Second, a larger number of low-income households have access to a vehicle and use it to shop at stores of their own choosing, based on multiple store characteristics that may be important. For example, in addition to proximity from home, low-income consumers may care about a supermarket's low prices, good selection and respectful service.

6.3.3 Small Stores and Food Access

The federal government's food desert definitions focus mainly on access to supermarkets, but there also is considerable interest in other retail formats. These formats include smaller grocery stores with total annual sales less than $2 million, dollar stores and less-traditional formats ranging from warehouse club stores to fruit and vegetable stands on street corners. Formats other than supermarkets can be especially important for people without access to vehicles.

Various barriers can prevent some small stores from stocking healthful items, such as milk or produce. Small retailers may not have access to fresh-food suppliers, refrigeration equipment or marketing resources to publicize healthier options. Programs that provide grants, loans, marketing support or other assistance may improve availability of affordable, healthful foods in underserved communities. Some evidence suggests that such initiatives can improve healthy food offerings in small stores (Gittelsohn et al., 2012). Not every neighborhood can provide sufficient consumer demand to support a supermarket, so future improvements in low-income food environments are likely to depend on small stores as well as large stores.

6.3.4 *Food Deserts and Health Outcomes*

The earlier research literature on food deserts observed that households with greater access to supermarkets tend to have healthier diets and lower obesity rates than those with less access (Larson et al., 2009). Similarly, as Section 6.4.4 will discuss, households with less exposure to nearby fast-food restaurants tended to have better diets and lower obesity rates than households with more fast-food access (Larson et al., 2009; Giskes et al., 2011). These patterns suggested the potential importance of the local food retail environment, but there are plausible alternative explanations for these health and nutrition outcomes. Neighborhoods with more food stores may have other characteristics that improve diet-related health outcomes. When neighborhoods are selected for study based on having both poverty and lack of retail access, it is difficult to discern which factor is responsible for less favorable outcomes.

Some research has used strong designs to go beyond merely studying correlations between food retail conditions and health outcomes. One study compared the weight status of randomly assigned participants in Moving to Work, a U.S. Department of Housing and Urban Development (HUD) demonstration program, finding that women who had received low-poverty housing vouchers were less likely to be extremely obese, compared with women who had received no vouchers. This study provided experimental evidence that neighborhood location affects weight status. However, it is not possible to say if the food retail environment or some other characteristic of low-income neighborhoods was responsible for the observed results (Ludwig et al., 2011). In another study, researchers examined the outward expansion of Walmart Supercenters over many years from the company headquarters in Bentonville, AR, finding that each additional Walmart Supercenter per 100,000 residents (county-level) was associated with increased average body mass index (BMI) (Courtemanche and Carden, 2011). This apparent effect was strongest for women, low-income married individuals and those living in the least populated counties.

Studies in New York City (Elbel et a., 2015), Philadelphia (Cummins et al., 2014) and Pittsburgh (Dubowitz et al., 2015) compared changes in food-related outcomes for neighborhoods where a new supermarket was introduced to similar neighborhoods without a new supermarket. The effects on diet quality were small. Having a new supermarket made no difference in fruit and vegetable or whole grains consumption, for example (Cummins et al., 2014; Dubowitz et al., 2015). In Pittsburgh, the intervention community did have lower consumption of solid fats, alcohol and added sugars, but regular use of the new supermarket did not seem to be responsible for the improvement. In Pittsburgh and Philadelphia, the consumers had more favorable views of their neighborhood food environment after the new supermarket arrived.

A useful question is does the healthfulness of food choices depend mostly on the food retail environment or on idiosyncratic differences across households, even within the same retail environment? Several new studies have used data from ongoing "panels" of households that monitor their spending data over a longer period of time. Alcott, Diamond and Dube (2015) found that only a small percentage of the difference in the healthfulness of foods purchased can be explained by the census tract in which surveyed households live. Handbury et al. (2016) concluded that, of the differences in nutritional quality of purchases between low- and high-income households, about one-third can be explained by what county one lives in and another third can be explained by what census tract one lives in. Even when low- and high-income households shopped in the same store, the healthfulness of their food choices was different on average.

To summarize, although each of the available studies has limitations, social scientists are beginning to make progress in measuring the health consequences of the food retail environment. Food deserts are an important concern for some low-income consumers and not for others. It would be a mistake for policy-makers to assume that most low-income Americans do their grocery shopping on foot or that they usually shop within 1 mile from home. The diagnosis of food retail access problems requires highly localized empirical information about food retail locations and automobile access. Policy remedies to improve the food retail environment require careful attention to the hard economics of commercial food retail location decisions. When public policy initiatives attract new supermarkets to low-income neighborhoods, the new supermarkets must compete not just with local corner stores but also with existing supermarkets at greater distances from home that already have proven success in winning the business of low-income residents.

6.4 The Restaurant Industry

Today, Americans are eating out more than ever before. In 2014, just over half ($762 billion) of all U.S. food spending was for food away from home, compared with 43 percent in 1990 and 33.4 percent in 1970. Several demographic trends help explain increased spending at restaurants and other eateries (Stewart, 2011):

- Although wage growth in the United States has stagnated in recent years, mean incomes still have trended upward, providing increased discretionary income for luxuries such as dining out. As incomes rise, the value of saving time in food preparation and cleanup also increases (Box 6.1).
- Increased participation in the labor force improved economic resources for women and decreased time once allocated to at-home cooking.
- Decreases in the average number of people per household (2.6 in 2010, compared with 2.8 in 1980) translate to lower economies of scale to be gained in home preparation, making restaurant purchases relatively more desirable.

Box 6.2 The Economics of Monopolistic Competition

The chain restaurant industry offers an example of **monopolistic competition,** the final type of industrial organization discussed in this book (following earlier discussion of competition in Chapter 2 and monopoly and monopsony in Chapter 5).

In monopolistic competition, each firm is the monopoly producer of its own branded products, but it must compete to a certain extent with other firms that sell similar products. The competition is more intense for firms that are more similar.

Marketers think of brand identity as a position in a psychological space, defined by product qualities that are important to consumers. In Figure 6.4, restaurant brands are represented by positions based on how consumers might perceive the price (ranging from low to high on the vertical axis) and nutritional characteristics (ranging from more healthy to more indulgent on the horizontal axis). A brand manager's decision about a position in this psychological space is somewhat like a supermarket chain manager's decision about a location in physical space, discussed in Section 6.3. A brand that has a large region of this psychological space to itself may choose its own price much as a monopolist does. A brand that shares a particular position with multiple other brands must compete more intensely.

Monopolistic competition is like perfect competition in the sense that barriers to entry are absent. Competitive pressures force profit margins down to comparatively low levels. A monopolistic competitor differs from a perfect competitor by having a much greater incentive to advertise. In this form of industrial organization, advertising can help define a brand's psychological positioning. Effective advertising may benefit the company in part by stealing market share from competitors and in part by expanding overall consumer demand for a product category. Monopolistic competition offers an intuitive account of the go-go sell-more energy commonly observed in branded food marketing and advertising. In this economic model, the food may be healthy or unhealthy, but, at any given market price, the firms seek to sell more of it.

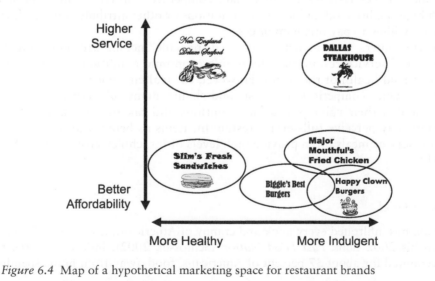

Figure 6.4 Map of a hypothetical marketing space for restaurant brands

Growing consumption of away-from-home foods in the United States has substantial implications for other players in the food marketing chain. Rising intakes of fast food, for example, may require some farm producers and manufacturers to shift their production patterns to meet increased demand for burgers, fries and pizza. Large restaurant chains, like large retailers, also may prefer to purchase homogenous inputs, favoring larger supplier organizations that can meet these requirements.

The chain restaurant industry provides a classic example of monopolistic competition, a type of industrial organization that is similar to monopoly in some respects (each firm is the sole producer of its own branded products) and yet highly competitive in other respects (it is easy for firms to enter the industry, driving down prices) (see Box 6.2). The following sections describe three categories of away-from-home food service providers: (1) full-service restaurants, (2) fast-food restaurants and (3) institutional food service and other outlets.

6.4.1 Full-Service Restaurants

Full-service restaurants include eateries ranging from greasy spoons to fine-dining establishments. Compared with other food-away-from-home operations, full-service restaurants typically provide customers with more diverse menus and amenities, including table service and nondisposable dinnerware. This business model demands specialized labor, such as chefs and servers. Higher-end restaurants tend to assume higher costs for skilled staff and quality supplies, which in turn translate to higher menu prices.

While the full-service restaurant industry includes many independent competitors, it has, like other segments of the food marketing system, grown more consolidated in recent years. National full-service restaurant chains have expanded, and in some cases multiple chains have consolidated under a common corporate umbrella. Darden Corporation, for example, operates several major chains, including Olive Garden and LongHorn Steakhouse. While such large operations do gain efficiencies through their large scale, smaller restaurants can remain competitive, differentiating themselves through high-quality food, unique ethnic traditions or other attributes for which consumers are willing to pay premium prices.

Since consumers with higher levels of disposable income are more likely to patronize full-service restaurants, favorable economic conditions are important to the financial health of the sector. However, to steal customers from low-price, high-convenience competitors like fast-food chains, many full-service restaurants have expanded their value-priced menu options and takeout operations. While consumers may perceive full-service restaurant items as being healthier than fast food, full-service meals often provide high levels of fat, cholesterol and salt (Stewart, 2011).

6.4.2 Fast Food

"Fast food has infiltrated every nook and cranny of American society," Eric Schlosser wrote in his 2002 book *Fast Food Nation* (Schlosser, 2002). Indeed, in 2014 fast food accounted for about 37 percent of Americans' food-away-from-home spending, compared with 10 percent in 1963. Such growth largely resulted from fast-food outlets' exceptional ability to meet consumers' demand for quick, inexpensive, convenient food. Unlike full-service operations, quick-service restaurants limit their menus to a small number of items and employ assembly-line-style operations that minimize requirements for skilled labor. Restaurants also employ more minimum wage earners than any other major industry sector.

Many quick-service restaurant brands operate as chains, which enables certain costs, such as marketing and advertising, to be spread across many outlets. Some chains, such as Burger King, are operated through a centralized corporate owner. Others, such as McDonald's and Subway, operate under a **franchise model**, where individual outlet owners (franchisees) pay the corporate entity (the franchisor) a fee for the right to use the company brand name, along with resources that enable the franchisee to replicate the franchisor's business model. Franchise contracts also typically require that franchisees adhere to standards to ensure consumers have a consistent brand experience at all outlets.

In recent years, fast-food chains have reported a relatively slow rate of new store openings, suggesting that consumer demand for fast food may be nearly saturated. However, fast-food chains have responded with innovations designed to prop up revenue and profits. Chains such as Starbucks and Panera Bread, for example, have grown mainly by catering to consumers seeking higher-end food, beverages and services. Other traditional fast-food chains have expanded their menus into higher-margin items, including salads and coffee drinks. At the same time, many major fast-food chains are also focusing on expansion in less saturated international markets as an engine of company growth.

6.4.3 Institutional Food Service and Other Outlets

A quarter of U.S. food-away-from-home spending is spread across a range of other types of outlets. For example, many hotels and recreational facilities sell prepared food as a secondary revenue source. The USDA Economic Research Service (ERS) also includes noncommercial food service operations, such as schools and nursing homes, in its figures on food away from home. Government-funded food service operations, particularly those that reach children, are a key target for many nutrition advocates. As discussed in Chapter 11, the National School Lunch Program (NSLP) reaches millions of American children each school day.

6.4.4 Restaurants and Health Outcomes

On average, meals away from home contain more calories, fewer fruits and whole grains and more solid fats and added sugars than do equivalent meals prepared at home (Todd et al., 2010; Lin and Guthrie, 2012; An, 2016). Improved public health may depend not just on increased access to more healthy food but also on decreased access to less healthy food. This view has generated growing attention to **food swamps**, neighborhoods where less healthy foods are more readily accessible than healthier options.

Former FDA commissioner David Kessler argues that restaurants engineer foods with high levels of fat, sugar and salt to give their products great appeal (Kessler, 2009).

Pricing strategies, such as bundling items together into discounted value meals, and aggressive advertising practices may also encourage overconsumption. McDonald's, for example, spent about $735 million on advertising in 2016. This raises particular concern when marketing is directed at children, who may not understand advertising's persuasive intent (see Chapter 9).

The restaurant industry has taken some self-regulatory measures to improve its impact on public health. Walt Disney and McDonald's, for example, changed default options in children's meals, replacing less-healthful items, such as soda and french fries, with nutritionally superior ones, such as milk and apples. Similarly, in 2011 the National Restaurant Association created the Kids LiveWell program, through which participating restaurants offer at least one children's meal that meets several nutrition requirements, including a ceiling of 600 calories.

Government may intervene in the restaurant market if industry self-regulation fails to meet important public health goals. State and municipal governments often have been the first to test regulatory options. In 2008, for example, when the Los Angeles City Council placed a two-year moratorium on new fast-food outlet openings in South L.A., a low-income area with a high prevalence of obesity, some observers asked why middle-income or high-income neighborhoods that also had many fast-food outlets were not included. Two years later, the city of San Francisco banned fast-food restaurants from providing free toys in children's meals with high levels of calories, fat and sugar. At roughly the same time, McDonald's faced a class-action lawsuit from the Center for Science in the Public Interest (CSPI), a nutrition-focused advocacy group, contending that Happy Meals unfairly used toys to lure children into their restaurants. Ultimately, the CSPI suit was dismissed in court, and McDonald's sidestepped the San Francisco toy ban by adding a 10¢ toy charge.

Mandatory calorie labeling policies for restaurant menus have captured national attention. Throughout the late 2000s, New York and several other U.S. cities issued regulations requiring calorie labeling on chain restaurant menus. The federal government adopted a similar law in 2010, mandating that restaurant chains with 20 or more outlets clearly disclose calorie information, but implementation was repeatedly delayed and the final regulations had not yet come into effect as of 2017. Research on the impact of menu labeling on consumption patterns has been mixed. One study found that mandatory menu labeling in New York City had no effect on the number of calories purchased in fast-food outlets (Elbel et al., 2009). Another study found that the same New York labeling policy led to a 6 percent decrease in calories purchased per transaction at Starbucks locations (Bollinger et al., 2010).

As discussed later in more detail (Chapter 9), policy-makers weigh the merits of labeling requirements against political disadvantages (including opposition from industry organizations) and substantive concerns about policy overreach (including the risk of intervening ineffectively or counterproductively in commercial business decisions). In addition to helping some consumers make more informed choices, labeling requirements may prompt restaurants to develop healthier options. More restaurant chains now offer healthy options, such as milk, in addition to sugar-sweetened beverages, and a fruit or vegetable in addition to french fries, but the practice of making the healthy choice the default choice has not yet been widely adopted (Mueller, 2017).

6.5 Labor Policy in the Restaurant Industry

Along with farmworkers (discussed in Chapter 2), the labor conditions for employees in the food retailing and restaurant industries raise some of the most pressing questions of fairness in all of U.S. food policy. These industries account for a large fraction of total employment in the food system, and workers have some of the lowest wages. While agricultural production has approximately 2.5 million workers and food manufacturing has 1.8 million, the food retail sector employs more workers, approximately 3.1 million. Employment in the restaurant industry is more than four times as large as in agricultural production, with 11 million workers (Food Chain Workers Alliance, 2016).

While the organic food and local food movements (discussed in Chapter 3) link farmers and food consumers, a broader **food justice** movement extends its boundaries to also include wages and working conditions for employees in sectors of the conventional food system that are responsible for a larger fraction of total employment. In a 2016 report, the Food Chain Workers Alliance criticized organic and local food activism that emphasizes "the role of small farmers and producers who are often white" if it ignores the struggles of food workers, "especially workers of color." Food justice and food sovereignty, by contrast, "seek to inject questions of equity into the wider movement" (Food Chain Workers Alliance, 2016).

As a consequence of its high employment and low mean wages, the restaurant sector has long been the most central industry in national debates about the minimum wage. The federal minimum wage of $7.25 has not been increased since 2009, and it includes an exception allowing a much lower hourly wage for workers who rely on tips, which especially applies to full-service restaurant workers (so long as tips plus the wage reach at least the federal minimum). Some states have higher minimum wages.

The likely impact of increasing the minimum wage is much disputed. A traditional labor economics model of wage determination suggests that a higher-than-equilibrium minimum wage could generate a labor surplus (labor quantity supplied that exceeds labor quantity demanded) at the target wage (see Box 2.3 for an illustration of the traditional model, applied to farmworkers). According to this theory, a modest minimum wage is relatively harmless, but a minimum wage that substantially exceeds the typical wage in the industry could generate increased unemployment.

In contrast with this theory, a large body of empirical research dating back to the early 1990s (Card and Krueger, 1994), using data from the restaurant industry, mostly showed only small impacts of minimum wages on unemployment. This research was heavily debated, and the key results could vary depending on the statistical methods used. Most economists were persuaded that the existing minimum wage had little harmful effect on unemployment in general. However, it was recognized that minimum wages could affect employment for particularly low-wage segments of the labor market, such as teenagers and other people without much employment history, and the effect of a hypothetical higher minimum wage was a contentious question. More recently, the city of Seattle implemented higher minimum wages, reaching $11/hour in 2015 and $13/hour in 2016. New research finds that this higher minimum wage had larger impacts on unemployment than had been found in earlier empirical research (Jardim et al., 2017).

Much as in our earlier discussion of farmworker wages, the lesson is that, in addition to thinking about statutory minimum wages, it is useful to consider the fundamentals of supply and demand that determine restaurant industry wages. Up to a point, minimum wages may serve as a useful floor to help just a small group of workers with the very lowest wages. At higher levels, evaluating proposed minimum wages requires carefully thinking through the potential employment consequences.

6.6 Food Prices and Inflation

Economists have a well-developed theory of how consumer spending responds to income and prices (Box 6.3). Spending typically falls when the price of the good rises, which is why demand functions are downward sloping. The effect of income may vary. For a **normal good**, spending rises when income rises. For an **inferior good**, spending falls when income rises.

As a natural outgrowth of this simple theory, one might hypothesize that the current epidemic of overweight and obesity stems from long-term technological changes that raised U.S. incomes, made food intake cheaper and made physical activity more expensive (Cawley and Datar, 2017; Lakdawalla et al., 2005). A variation on this theory focuses on relative food prices. Perhaps relative prices fell for comparatively less-healthful foods, such as baked goods or sugar-sweetened beverages, while prices increased for comparatively more healthful foods, such as fruits and vegetables and low-fat milk (Drewnowski, 2010; Monsivais et al., 2010).

To understand U.S. national price data, we need to discuss **price indices**, the tools economists use to summarize price changes for whole categories of goods. Table 6.3 uses a hypothetical example to illustrate how a price index for fruit can be created. Suppose apples cost $0.80 per pound in 1993 and $1.10 in 2010 (a 38 percent increase). Suppose prices for bananas rose somewhat faster (a 60 percent increase) and prices for strawberries rose faster still (a 200 percent increase). The simple mean price increase from 1993 to 2010 was about 99 percent for the three fruits. The problem with this simple mean is that U.S. consumers buy apples and bananas frequently and strawberries less frequently, but the simple mean price increase gives equal weight to all three fruits. A more sensible approach gives greater weight to the fruits with greater consumer expenditures. For example, if apples and bananas each represent 45 percent of fruit expenditures for fruit, while strawberries represent only 10 percent of consumer expenditures for fruit, then a weighted mean price change would be 64 percent for the three fruits combined. This expenditure-weighted mean price change is much lower than the simple mean reported earlier, because the most commonly consumed fruits in this hypothetical example have slower price increases.

The federal government's Bureau of Labor Statistics (BLS) uses a more elaborate version of this approach to estimate price indices for many categories of consumer goods, including foods and beverages. The Consumer Price Index (CPI) follows a numbering convention in which each category's price index is set to equal 100 in a base time period (currently 1982–1984). In subsequent years, the price index shows how prices

Table 6.3 A hypothetical example of a price index for three fruits and the actual Consumer Price Index (CPI) for fruits and vegetables, 1993–2010

Hypothetical example	Expenditure share, May 1993 (%)	Price in May 1993 ($/lb)	Price in May 2010 ($/lb)	Relative change 2010/1993
Apples	45	0.80	1.10	1.38
Bananas	45	0.50	0.80	1.60
Strawberries	10	1.00	3.00	3.00
Simple mean		0.77	1.63	1.99
Expenditure- weighted mean		0.69	1.16	1.64
Actual CPI for fruits and vegetables				
		CPI 1993	CPI 2010	Relative change 2010/1993
All fruits/vegetables		163.1	268.0	1.64

Note: A relative change of 1.38, for example, means that prices rose by 38 percent from 1993 to 2010. The CPI for each year is expressed relative to the base year (1982–1984 = 100).

have risen or fallen relative to the base year. For example, Table 6.3 shows that the actual official CPI for fruits and vegetables was 163.1 in May 1993 (a 63.1 percent increase since the base period of 1982–1984). From May 1993 to May 2010, this index increased another 64 percent.

Figure 6.5 illustrates relative price index trends from the early 1980s through 2016 for seven major food and beverage categories. Price increases were fastest for fruits and vegetables and slowest for nonalcoholic beverages (the category that includes sugar-sweetened beverages). Other food categories fell in between. These broad trends reinforce the concern that healthier food became relatively more expensive over these years.

In reaching this conclusion, there are some technical complications to consider. As Table 6.3 illustrated, price indices are based on weighted average price changes, where the weights depend on expenditure shares. Economists expect that expenditure shares will themselves be changing over time. Inflation estimates differ depending on the method used to update these expenditure shares. Some USDA economists suggest that the BLS fruit and vegetable price index could overstate food price inflation by failing to account fully for increased spending over time on innovative products, such as bagged spinach or miniature carrots (Kuchler and Stewart, 2008). Higher prices for such items reflect not only inflation but also real changes in consumer value. Then again, the BLS economists who create the official price indices do seek to measure changes for identical products from one period to the next as well as possible while trying to choose reasonable weights for categories that are undergoing rapid technological change and new product introductions. Although we take for granted the federal government's official estimates of price inflation, the actual methods used to generate them are still much debated (National Research Council, 2002).

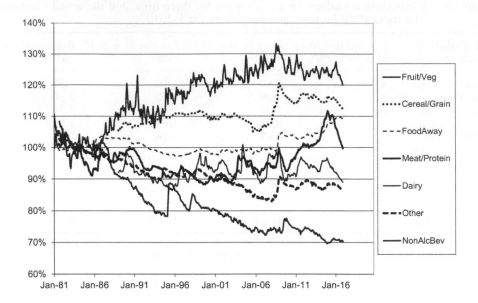

Figure 6.5 Changes in the official U.S. Consumer Price Index (CPI) for major food categories from the early 1980s through 2016

Data note: The U.S. Bureau of Labor Statistics (BLS) provides national price indices (www.bls.gov/cpi). A commonly used index for overall price inflation is the seasonally adjusted CPI for All Urban Consumers. BLS also provides indices for particular categories of goods, including foods and beverages.

Box 6.3   The Economics of Consumer Choice

Economists have a systematic theory connecting rational consumer choices to three factors: prices, income and preferences. The theory of consumer choice provides behavioral foundations for the idea that demand functions are downward sloping (see Chapters 2 and 5), and it offers insight into the role of food assistance benefits in household budgets (see Chapter 10).

Figure 6.6 illustrates a simplified version of this theory with just two goods. Any point in the figure depicts a combination of food (measured in grams per day on the horizontal axis) and other goods (measured in one-dollar units per day on the vertical axis). The consumer has an income of $12 per day, and the price of food is $2.40 per thousand grams of food. The **budget constraint** (the straight line) illustrates all the combinations that the consumer can just barely afford (for example 1,000 g of food plus $9.60 of other goods or 3,000 g of food plus $4.80 of other goods).

From among the affordable combinations on the budget constraint line, the consumer selects the one that is most preferred. For example, the consumer prefers point A to other combinations that offer less food and less other goods (down and to the left of A). Likewise, point A is inferior to other combinations that offer more food and more other goods (up and to the right of A).

The **indifference curve** (the curved line) illustrates all the combinations that the consumer likes exactly as well as point A. Point A is the optimal affordable combination when income is $12 per day and the price is $2.40 per thousand grams of food.

Naturally, the consumer would make different choices as prices and income change. For example, if the price of other goods were higher, and the price of food were lower, the consumer would shift some spending from other goods to food. Appendix S6.1 (see the online Companion Website) provides the details, showing how the changes in prices would affect the budget constraint. If the relative price of food falls, as happened in the United States over the course of the twentieth century, it makes sense that consumers would choose to purchase more food.

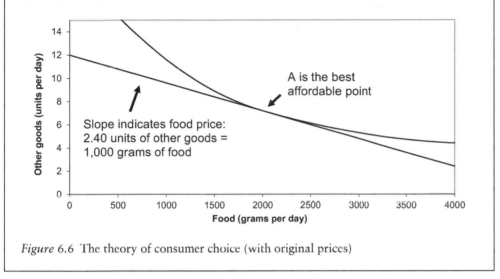

Figure 6.6 The theory of consumer choice (with original prices)

6.7 Conclusion

This chapter provides an overview of the food retail and restaurant industries, and it also offers this book's principal discussion of the economics of consumer choice. Consumer choices matter for some of the biggest nutrition policy challenges of modern times.

It is sometimes said that the consumer is sovereign in the American food system. If that is true, then retailers and restaurants are the courtiers who communicate the sovereign's commands to the rest of the realm. But not everybody sees the consumer as sovereign in the first place. In some accounts, consumers respond more like puppets to price signals, marketing messages and other features of the surrounding food environment. In this view, retailers and restaurants are the strings that move the puppets. In either perspective, the food retail and restaurant industries play a central role as the food sectors that have the most direct connections to consumer decisions and nutritional outcomes.

Summary List of Key Terms (identified in bold in the text)

- big-box outlets
- budget constraint
- fixed costs
- food at home
- food away from home
- food deserts
- food justice
- food swamps
- franchise model
- indifference curve
- inferior good
- loss leaders
- monopolistic competition
- normal good
- price indices
- private-label products
- transaction costs
- variable costs

7 Food Safety

7.1 Introduction

The Centers for Disease Control and Prevention (CDC) estimate that each year 48 million Americans get sick and 3,000 die from foodborne illnesses caused by microorganisms such as *Campylobacter*, *Salmonella*, norovirus and Shiga toxin-producing *Escherichia coli* (STEC) (Scallan et al., 2011; Johnson, 2016). Unknown numbers of people are harmed by toxic chemical additives and pesticide residues. New technologies, such as GMOs, and comparatively new hazards, such as mad cow disease (bovine spongiform encephalopathy, BSE), can stress regulatory systems that were designed with more traditional hazards in mind. In regulating food safety risks, policy-makers inevitably make vital decisions based on uncertain information.

In U.S. food safety policy, there is a philosophical divide between those who are principally concerned about foodborne illness and those who are principally concerned about toxic chemicals and new technologies. For example, the food safety discussion in the federal government's *Dietary Guidelines for Americans* gives primary attention to foodborne illness. Taking a different view, some environmental groups and sustainable agriculture advocates are most worried about chemical use and new technologies such as GMOs.

Many food safety problems stem from information failures. Hence, this chapter is related to subsequent chapters on dietary guidance (Chapter 8) and food labeling (Chapter 9), which also center on information issues. This chapter:

- presents economic principles for food safety (Section 7.2);
- introduces risk assessment methods for food safety (Section 7.3);
- summarizes policy issues related to foodborne illness (Section 7.4);
- describes the regulation of foods that are Generally Recognized as Safe (Section 7.5);
- summarizes policy issues related to pesticides and GMOs (Section 7.6); and
- explains the jurisdiction of federal agencies that oversee food safety in the United States (Section 7.7).

7.2 Economic Principles for Food Safety

One could think of food safety problems only as moral failures, attributable to greedy meatpackers or indifferent bureaucrats or unhygienic home cooks. Frequently, however, the most fruitful question is not who to blame but rather what policies best serve public interest objectives, given that producers rightly seek profits, government officials have limited options and consumers lack the information they need to protect their own interests. Section 7.2.1 explains that optimal food safety practices must balance food safety and other economic objectives in a setting where not all objectives can be achieved perfectly. Section 7.2.2 discusses several policy instruments that might compensate for information failures and bring private-sector market incentives more closely in line with public interest goals.

7.2.1 Optimal Food Safety Practices

Economic thought suggests two principles for choosing an optimal food safety technology from among the available options:

• The technology should be efficient. Of all the options for achieving a particular level of food safety, an efficient technology has the lowest cost. This principle is uncontroversial.
• The technology should achieve a level of food safety that strikes the right balance between costs and benefits of further improvements. Under this principle, society makes tradeoffs between food safety and other economic objectives. This principle is more controversial.

An example of how these two principles can be applied is provided in Box 7.1: the economics of choosing the right food safety technology in meat production.

There are at least two reasons to believe that some level of risk must be tolerated. First, any regulatory policy has both costs and benefits (Cash, 2011). Although some food safety improvements are easily affordable, others are expensive. One could disregard these costs as merely crass financial considerations. However, society can use economic resources in many ways to reduce the risk of death. Rather than pay a very high price to prevent every last death from foodborne illness, government might more efficiently use the same money to purchase an ambulance, or build a roadside guardrail, or make some other investment that would prevent even more deaths. This reasoning balances injury against injury and death against death, with no denomination in mere dollars.

Second, some policy dilemmas pit food safety goals against other public interest objectives, not only against economic considerations. For example: (a) production standards for spinach farmers must balance food safety with environmental and ecological goals (see Box 7.2); (b) dietary guidance about fruits and vegetables must balance nutritional advantages against safety risks from pesticides; and (c) FDA rules for very small producers and farmers' market vendors must balance consumer safety concerns against the goal of promoting local food systems.

Box 7.1   The Economics of Choosing the Right Food Safety Technology in Meat Production

There are many technologies that a pork-processing plant could use to improve food safety (Unnevehr and Jensen, 2005). For six options, Figure 7.1 shows the cost per carcass of pork and the percentage of pathogen contamination that is

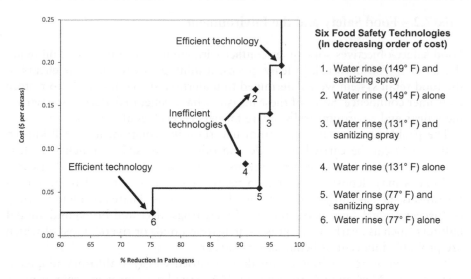

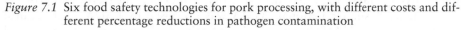

Figure 7.1 Six food safety technologies for pork processing, with different costs and different percentage reductions in pathogen contamination

Source: Image by the author, based on information in Unnevehr and Jensen (2005).

removed. For example, the most expensive technology is a water rinse at 149° F plus the sanitizing spray, for a total cost of $0.20 per carcass. The least expensive technology is just a water rinse at 77° F and no sanitizing spray, for a total cost of $0.03 per carcass. Which food safety technology is optimal?

To answer this question, the first issue is efficiency. The least-cost method for achieving a particular level of food safety is efficient. In Figure 7.1, there are some inefficient technologies. For example, it is a bad idea to choose a water rinse at 149°F alone (2), because another technology is simultaneously more effective and less costly (3). The technologies connected by the solid black line are efficient. For example, to achieve a pathogen reduction of at least 75 percent, an efficient method is just the water rinse at 77°F and no sanitizing spray (6).

The second issue is the best choice among efficient technologies. Given that consumers ultimately will bear the burden of any cost increase, how much money are consumers willing to pay for additional safety? To achieve a 75 percent reduction in pathogens, the cost is $0.03 per carcass. To achieve a 93 percent reduction, the cost is only $0.05 per carcass. But, to increase food safety even further and achieve a 97 percent reduction in pathogens, one must use a very hot water rinse (149° F) plus a sanitizing spray. The cost is $0.20 per carcass, about four times as high as the cost of achieving a 93 percent reduction.

In this particular example, many readers may decide that $0.20 per carcass is a reasonable cost for safety. In other settings, efforts to achieve yet higher levels of safety may be even more costly. Although it is discomforting to contemplate tolerating some nonzero amount of risk, the alternative of seeking perfect safety is unbearably expensive.

Box 7.2   Food Safety and the Environment

Food safety objectives sometimes conflict with environmental goals. Following the 2006 *E. coli* outbreak in leafy greens, leading growers and their clients in the food retail system were determined to undertake strong measures to restore consumer confidence. Some of these measures have generated alarm for environmentalists and environmentally aware farmers (Lowell et al., 2010).

The problem, as usual, stems from uncertain information. It is well known that *E. coli* can be carried by cattle and other animals. It is much less clear how contamination reaches leafy greens fields. Humans or animals that carry pathogens may deposit feces in crop fields, or water may travel from animal operations such as cattle feedlots to nearby crop farms. There are a wide variety of suspect animal sources (such as feral pigs, frogs, deer and birds) and animal habitats (such as nearby trees, grasses, irrigation ponds or rivers), most of which are probably innocent of being serious dangers.

The responses to the 2006 outbreak have varied widely. California adopted a Leafy Greens Marketing Agreement (LGMA), stipulating measures that growers should take. A similar national LGMA was proposed by USDA's Agricultural Marketing Service (AMS) but has not been finalized. The national LGMA would be overseen largely by industry representatives. It would be voluntary in principle, but in practice growers would be expected to participate if they intended to market their produce through major retail outlets. Leading corporate purchasers, such as retail and restaurant chains, may require their own additional checklists of food safety practices. Finally, following the 2011 Food Safety Modernization Act (FSMA) legislation, FDA is expected to propose new regulations for leafy greens.

To meet the various new standards, farmers report that they dug up windbreaks containing trees and bushes, filled in water sources, established bare ground buffers at the edges of fields and fenced off rivers to block wildlife access. Throughout the Central Coast of California, one can see from the roadside white T-shaped poison bait stations, made from PVC pipes, planted every couple dozen yards along the edges of fields. The bait stations contain a powerful rodenticide, which is expected to eliminate populations of small mammals and which may also affect birds of prey that feed on such mammals. According to a study by the Georgetown University Produce Safety Project and the Nature Conservancy:

> [G]rowers report yielding to tremendous pressure from auditors, inspectors and other food safety professionals to change on-farm management practices in ways that not only generate uncertain food safety benefits, but also create serious environmental consequences.
>
> (Lowell et al., 2010: 5)

Instead of focusing on foodborne illness to the exclusion of other objectives, the authors say a superior approach would be "co-management" for food safety and ecological health together. Co-management is quite different from the pre-cautionary principle. With the precautionary principle, food producers carry the full burden of proving that their food is safe. With co-management, the burden of proof is split: advocates for a food safety measure must show some evidence that the measure is effective and not too harmful to the environment.

Seeking to prevent every last food safety hazard may be a recipe for policy over-reach. Yet, as the next subsection will discuss, doing nothing and accepting all free-market outcomes also would be disastrous. The public policy challenge is to choose policies that are neither too lax nor too strict.

7.2.2 Food Safety Failures as a Problem of Information

Many food safety problems stem from information failures. Imagine if everybody had special sunglasses allowing us to see dangerous microbial contamination as hot pink coloration on any food product. Wearing these glasses, every consumer could pick through the meat case in the supermarket, choosing the cleanest and safest packages. Every supermarket chain's buying agent, in turn, could require safer food from man-ufacturers. With perfect information, consumers could defend their own economic interests in the marketplace, and federal safety rules for microbial contamination would be almost irrelevant.

In the real world, we have no such sunglasses. In the language of the economic perspective on public policy (Chapter 1), imperfect information is the market failure that justifies most government efforts to regulate food safety. A wise policy response to a food safety problem depends on correct diagnosis of the corresponding informa-tion failures. In particular, the recommended policy response differs based on whether imperfect information is symmetric or asymmetric.

- With **symmetric imperfect information**, the producer and consumer both lack important information about food safety qualities. For example, expensive research is required to determine the hazard from many pesticides. Even if both the producer and consumer know that a particular chemical was applied to a fruit crop, neither may be sure of the implications for food safety. Government invest-ment in improved information and better food safety technologies may be seen as a public good whose benefits accrue to many producers and consumers. With symmetric imperfect information, it is difficult for any stakeholder to know what food safety practices best serve the public interest.
- With **asymmetric imperfect information**, one party to a transaction has more information than another about the safety of a product. In practice, asymmetric information means that the producer knows more than the consumer does. For example, a farmer knows exactly what chemicals were applied to a crop, and a meatpacker knows whether procedures for safe plant operation were followed, but the consumer lacks this information. Comparatively unsafe foods are not suf-ficiently penalized in the marketplace because the consumer does not know which

producers are less safe. With asymmetric imperfect information, producers under-invest in protecting food safety.

Under both kinds of information failure, private-sector market incentives provide insufficient motivation to protect food safety. Because information failures are central to food safety problems, many food safety arguments revolve around who gets access to what information (Box 7.3).

Depending on the nature of the food safety problem, governments can choose from several policy instruments as potential remedies. They are listed here in order from most strict to most market oriented:

- **Process rules** describe exactly what practices and ingredients a farmer or manufacturer may use. For example, the government may stipulate procedures for cleaning equipment in a meatpacking plant.
- **Performance standards** describe how a food safety quality will be measured and what level of safety must be achieved. At the most basic level, federal government agencies have long been permitted to seize a food product or forbid its sale if it is **adulterated**, a legal term for food that contains harmful substances or is unsafe or deficient in particular ways. More recently, USDA's FSIS has begun to set tolerance standards for *Salmonella* in samples from chicken processors (see Box 7.3). Performance standards are less burdensome than process rules, because they allow the producer to make decisions about production practices and ingredients, so long as these decisions succeed in achieving the desired level of food safety.
- With liability enforcement, the court system can strengthen the incentive for producers to maintain a high standard of food safety. The government might not tell producers exactly what methods and ingredients to use, but the courts may help victims collect damages from producers in the event of a food safety failure that can be traced to its source. The application of liability enforcement may be arbitrary: some producers may get away with poor food safety practices, while others pay a very high financial penalty.
- Food labeling rules (discussed further in Chapter 9) encourage or require manufacturers to include certain information on food packages. Food labeling may repair a situation of asymmetric imperfect information by providing the consumer with information that ordinarily would be limited to the producer. Once the consumer is better informed, market incentives may encourage producers to offer a higher level of safety.
- Through food safety research, governments can supply a public good that private firms might not have sufficient incentive to provide. The government may support basic scientific research, such as studies of chemical toxicity. The government also may support more applied efforts, such as developing testing kits for microbial contamination and supporting the publication of **good agricultural practices** and **good manufacturing practices**, which include checklists of food safety best practices (see Box 7.2).
- Finally, consumer education provides consumers with information about the safety of different foods. Guidance from the EPA on sensible food practices notes that consumers may be exposed to pesticides in a variety of ways. It recommends

---

Box 7.3 Public Access to Information About Food Safety

Questions about information access frequently accompany policy debates about food safety. Some policies seek to make information more widely available, directly addressing the information failures that generated food safety problems. With better information, market incentives might suffice to protect consumers.

As a first example, food safety is affected by hygiene practices in restaurants. The consumer gets only partial information from observing cleanliness or from knowing the reputation of a restaurant chain. Local health inspectors have far more detailed observations of cleanliness, equipment, cooking practices, chilling temperatures and vermin in both public and nonpublic spaces of the restaurant. Traditionally, these inspections only come to public attention if problems are so severe that the restaurant must be temporarily closed. Beginning in 1998, a novel program in Los Angeles required restaurants to post grade cards from official inspections in the window by the entrance. An economic analysis found increased consumer awareness improved hygiene scores on inspection reports and reduced hospitalizations for foodborne illness (Jin and Leslie, 2005). Similarly, in 2010 New York City introduced a searchable web application that links information from inspection reports with maps and store-front images.

As another example, USDA's Food Safety and Inspection Service (FSIS) has long sampled poultry products for Salmonella contamination, but for many years information from these tests did not reach the public. Salmonella is not technically classified as an adulterant, and it occurs in much of the poultry that is sold in the United States, so FSIS officials do not request recalls based on tests alone, in the absence of an outbreak of illness. However, in 2008 FSIS did begin to share selected exceptionally poor test results on the public website for the Salmonella Verification Testing Program. USDA research suggests that the disclosures succeeded in motivating producers to reduce the extent of Salmonella contamination on their products (Ollinger et al., 2017).

In the preceding examples, government agencies acted to increase public access to information. Yet in other circumstances, government agencies may restrict access to information. After a cow in Washington state was identified with BSE in 2003, export markets for U.S. beef were closed. USDA instituted new animal feed rules and also began testing a larger sample of U.S. cattle. Food safety advocates and industry organizations argued over whether USDA's sample should be expanded even further. In this tense setting, Creekstone Farms, a specialty beef producer, sought to begin voluntary testing of all of its cattle, with an eye toward reassuring both domestic consumers and export markets about food safety. Other beef industry organizations worried that they would face pressure to institute similar testing. Arguing that the 100 percent testing approach was unscientific, USDA denied Creekstone access to the testing kits the company would need (Vina, 2006). Creekstone sued unsuccessfully, as courts ruled that USDA did indeed have authority to regulate the sale of the testing kits. In this case, federal policy-makers perceived an important public interest in preventing voluntary testing for an important food pathogen.

washing, peeling and trimming fruits and vegetables and eating a variety of foods to reduce the likelihood of exposure to a single pesticide. Meanwhile, the *Dietary Guidelines for Americans* (Chapter 9) suggest four safety practices for consumers to reduce the risk of foodborne illness: (1) clean hands, surfaces, vegetables and fruits; (2) separate raw, cooked and ready-to-eat foods; (3) cook foods to a safe temperature; and (4) chill perishable foods properly.

Each of these policy instruments has advantages and disadvantages in a particular application. It is possible to combine these policy instruments in multiple ways, assigning important roles to both government and industry actors (Garcia Martinez et al., 2007). The challenge for food safety policy-makers is to identify the best tool for each situation, so that economic actors have an incentive to choose production practices that are optimal from the perspective of society as a whole.

7.3 Risk Assessment Principles for Food Safety

Managing food safety risks requires high-quality scientific evidence. Traditionally, the scientific community has distinguished risk assessment from risk management:

- **risk assessment** is the scientific methodology for determining a population's level of risk from potential hazards;
- **risk management** is the process for deciding appropriate policy responses to hazards.

While risk management is recognized as a political process, risk assessment is supposed to be entirely free of political influence.

However, risk assessment and risk management have always been intertwined to some extent. Risk assessment is an applied mix of science and craft whose principal purpose is to inform risk management. Risk managers have long taken a keen interest in the detailed assumptions and methodologies used in risk assessments, recognizing their potential influence on policy outcomes. In a high-profile report, the National Academies acknowledged these interrelationships, saying that risk assessment should "be viewed as a method for evaluating the relative merits of various options for managing risk rather than as an end in itself" (National Research Council, 2009).

Risk assessment has four steps:

1. **Hazard identification** is the initial collection of information showing whether an agent is hazardous (an agent could be a chemical, production process or microbe).
2. **Hazard characterization** quantifies the relationship between an agent and the outcomes of concern.
3. **Exposure assessment** estimates how many people would be exposed to an agent, with or without regulatory controls.
4. **Risk characterization** describes the resulting extent of human health risk.

The overall level of risk depends on both toxicity (the harmful consequence to an exposed individual) and exposure (the number of individuals who could be affected):

risk = toxicity × exposure. Scientific risk assessment procedures have a long history of use in evaluating chemical hazards such as pesticides and food additives, and they have been applied more recently to the microbial hazards that cause foodborne illness (Buchanan and Suhre, 2005).

A complete risk assessment requires scientists to combine dozens of estimated quantitative factors that describe toxicity and exposure. Some quantitative factors are based on strong scientific evidence, while others require assumptions that cannot be confirmed. For example, in some cases scientists have direct evidence of toxicity in humans, while in others they must convert data on toxicity in laboratory animals into estimates for humans. In many fields of research, scientists faced with this type of uncertainty would simply acknowledge what they do not know. However, to be complete, a risk assessment requires some estimate for every quantitative factor. Hence, risk assessments necessarily make bold and unproven assumptions.

There is a lively debate about the quantitative factors used in risk assessment (National Research Council, 2009). As a purely scientific matter, one would want risk assessors to freely question all assumptions and adapt them as needed to the study of a particular hazard. For example, if an agent causes tumors in a certain percentage of rats, the scientists could develop new and innovative methods for estimating the corresponding risk of similar tumors in humans. However, to ensure transparency and consistency, risk assessors may be expected to use the same procedures and assumptions in each assessment. For example, given that an agent's consequences in mammals are systematically related to body weight, risk assessors may be expected to follow a stable and consistent procedure for extrapolating from rat tumor outcomes to generate estimates of likely tumor outcomes in humans. As a policy matter, major decisions and many millions of dollars may be at stake, so the "default" assumptions are the topic of heated scientific and legal arguments.

7.4 Foodborne Illness

This chapter's introduction cited CDC estimates that 48 million Americans get sick and 3,000 die each year from foodborne illness (Scallan et al., 2011), but there is some uncertainty about the precise number. For 31 leading pathogens, the CDC researchers used information from the federal government's food safety surveillance system, called FoodNet. In selected geographical locations, FoodNet collected data on all laboratory-confirmed cases of foodborne illness. For some illnesses, it was easy to tell which pathogen is responsible. For many other illnesses, it was not clear which pathogen to blame. To fill in the gaps, the CDC researchers estimated the number of serious cases of gastrointestinal illness and made educated guesses about the proportion that could be attributed to each of the potential foodborne pathogens.

To prioritize possible government responses to foodborne illness, policy-makers rely in part on these scientific estimates of foodborne illnesses, but they also respond to public concern over outbreaks that receive particular attention in the media. Food safety episodes in the 2000s and 2010s suggested diverse potential implications for public policy:

- A 2006 outbreak of *E. coli*, associated with spinach, led to at least 200 reported illnesses and three deaths. Foodborne contamination in fresh produce raises particular concerns, because consumers do not cook the product. The episode led to new food safety practices for farms that grow leafy greens (see Box 7.2).

- In 2007 and 2008, FSIS announced recalls of millions of pounds of beef from several companies, including the Kroger Co. and its supplier, Nebraska Beef. CDC reported 49 confirmed cases of *E. coli* and 27 hospitalizations. The outbreaks heightened attention to shortcomings in the procedures that private companies and FSIS employ to test for *E. coli* (Moss, 2009).

- A 2008 *Salmonella* Saintpaul outbreak caused an estimated 1,300 illnesses in 43 states and the District of Columbia. This outbreak prompted proposals to increase scrutiny of imported foods.

- A *Salmonella typhimurium* outbreak in 2008 and 2009, traced to peanut products, included more than 700 cases in 46 states and was blamed for nine deaths. FDA traced the outbreak to a manufacturer of peanut paste, the Peanut Corporation of America, which in turn sold its product to a large number of companies using many different brand names. FDA reported that the company had sold its products even after tests showed the presence of *Salmonella*. Faced with lawsuits, the company filed for bankruptcy in 2009. This outbreak showed the inadequacy of relying just on litigation through the courts.

- In July and August 2010, an FDA investigation of *Salmonella* outbreaks led to the identification of contamination at two large Iowa egg producers. The findings led to a voluntary recall of more than 300 million eggs that were sold at retail locations under more than a dozen different brand names. FDA suspected about 1,900 related illnesses. Later in 2010, Congress gave FDA the authority to require mandatory recalls in such outbreaks (see Section 7.8).

- A serious outbreak of *Salmonella* Poona in cucumbers caused 907 illnesses and six deaths in 2015 and 2016. FDA and CDC investigators focused on Baja California, Mexico, as a source of the cucumbers, but the source was never identified firmly, and the outbreak was over by March 2016. The event indicated some of the continued difficulties in ensuring safety for produce with international supply chains.

Commonly, policy-makers respond to public distress over particular outbreaks by prioritizing the hazards that have been in the news most recently.

To prioritize food safety policies more systematically, government researchers seek to quantify and rank foodborne illness hazards (Hoffmann, Maculloch, and Batz, 2015). Of the most harmful pathogens, each of which costs the United States at least 2 to 3 billion dollars annually, some occur frequently but have comparatively low death rates (Table 7.1). For example, there are approximately 5.5 million cases annually of norovirus (of which less than 1 percent lead to death) and about 3.7 million cases annually of *Salmonella* (of which about 4 percent lead to death). Other pathogens are more rare but cause serious illness and high risk of death. For example, there are only about 1,600 cases annually of *Listeria monocytogenes*, but about 16 percent of these cases lead to death. USDA researchers estimate annual costs of approximately $15.5 billion attributable to foodborne illnesses for which the pathogen can be identified.

A leading approach to managing foodborne illness risks is **hazard analysis and critical control points** (HACCP, pronounced "hassip"). HACCP "is designed to prevent the occurrence of problems by assuring that controls are applied at any point in a food production system where hazardous or critical situations could occur" (USDA Food Safety Inspection Service, 1999). For example, to control the risk of *Campylobacter*

Table 7.1 Annual cost and incidence for leading pathogens for foodborne illnesses whose cause is identified

15 Leading pathogens	Cost of illness ($ mil.)	Mean incidence	
		Cases	Deaths
Campylobacter	1,928.8	845,024	76
Clostridium perfringens	342.7	965,958	26
Cryptosporidium	51.8	57,616	4
Cyclospora cayetanensis	2.3	11,407	0
Listeria monocytogenes	2,834.4	1,591	255
Norovirus	2,255.8	5,461,731	149
Salmonella, all non-typhoidal	3,666.6	1,027,561	378
Shigella	138.0	131,254	10
STEC O157	271.4	63,153	20
STEC non-O157	27.4	112,752	0
Toxoplasmsa gondii	3,304.0	86,686	327
Vibrio vulnificus	319.9	96	36
Vibrio parahaemolyticus	40.7	34,664	4
Vibrio, other non-cholera	72.8	17,564	8
Yersinia enterocolitica	278.1	97,656	29
16 other identified pathogens	n/a	473,362	29
Total	15,534.6[a]	9,388,075	1,351

[a] Total $ for the 15 identified pathogens.

Source: Hoffmann, Maculloch, and Batz (2015).

and *Salmonella* in a large-scale manufacturing plant that slaughters and packages poultry, managers may analyze several hazards:

- when chicken are eviscerated, it is common for fecal matter from the gut to spread to the chicken meat;
- when the chicken is reprocessed into food products, contaminated meat may be mixed with uncontaminated meat;
- when the final product is chilled and stored, pathogens may reproduce and multiply.

For each identified hazard, a written HACCP plan must explain the critical points where the hazard may be controlled. To continue the example of a large-scale poultry plant:

- visual inspection may be used to identify fecal contamination from evisceration;
- an antimicrobial wash may be used to control pathogens during product manufacture;
- temperature maintenance within specified limits may control pathogen reproduction during storage.

In the United States, food manufacturing plants must have HACCP plans, but they have flexibility in tailoring the plans to their specific production process.

Many pathogens are known sources of foodborne illness, yet surprisingly, *E. coli* is the only pathogen that the federal government treats as an adulterant. In 1993, an outbreak of illness attributed to hamburgers from the Jack in the Box restaurant chain in Washington and nearby states sickened hundreds of people and led to four child deaths. In the resulting public policy response, the culpable strain of bacteria, known as *E. coli* O157:H7, was declared an adulterant, so food contaminated with it may not legally be sold. In 2011, six other strains of *E. coli* also were officially named as adulterants.

After the Jack in the Box case, the U.S. meat and poultry industries began testing for a variety of pathogens as part of the adoption of HACCP procedures in the 1990s. However, if these tests reveal the presence of pathogens other than *E. coli*, the food still may legally be sold to the public. Indeed, USDA lacks the legal authority to restrict such sales unless an actual outbreak of illness occurs. In 1999, after repeated tests showed excessive levels of *Salmonella* in ground beef sold for use in school lunch programs, USDA sought to halt the production line at the responsible meat plant. The plant's owner, Supreme Beef, successfully sued USDA. The case *Supreme Beef v. USDA* went to the U.S. Supreme Court, which concluded that *Salmonella* is commonly found in meat and is harmless if proper cooking and chilling procedures are used. Hence, although *Salmonella* is one of the most serious pathogens in terms of cost and incidence (Table 7.1), USDA is not allowed to regulate it as an adulterant. Instead, when pathogen tests show contamination, USDA works cooperatively with plant operators to improve hygiene and production methods.

7.5 Generally Recognized as Safe

All food, whether traditional or recently invented, is composed of chemicals. It would not be possible to test all of the chemicals that occur naturally in foods for safety. Instead, regulators classify many traditional food ingredients under the heading **Generally Recognized as Safe** (GRAS). The concept of GRAS was developed so that producers would not be forced to conduct unnecessary safety tests for many long-accepted food additives, such as vinegar, baking powder or black pepper.

Many food additives have GRAS status because they were already in use at the time of the 1958 amendments to the Food, Drug and Cosmetic Act, the principal law that governs FDA oversight activities. A food additive qualifies for GRAS status if it was in use already in 1958, there is a reasonable certainty of no harm, and experts generally accept the additive as safe based on publicly available evidence.

As scientific knowledge changes, an additive's GRAS status may be called into question. For example, a long-used GRAS flavoring agent called cinnamyl anthranilate was banned in 1985 because of evidence in mouse studies linking it to liver cancer. In many other cases, the food industry develops new variations on existing GRAS additives. FDA has a program for reviewing evidence voluntarily submitted by food companies, but the companies make their own determination that a use is GRAS. In theory, FDA does not certify the GRAS determinations, but in practice one can read between the lines to discern FDA's conclusions. If FDA issues a letter saying the agency has "no questions" about the additive's safety, it amounts to FDA approval. If FDA issues a letter saying that the manufacturer withdrew the notification, it provides a hint that the discussions with FDA were not going well.

FDA posts online a large database, called the GRAS Notice Inventory, with the company notifications and FDA response letters. Some of the notifications make claims for GRAS status that seem to stretch the original intent of the concept. For example, the chemical lysozyme is a component of human breastmilk, and breastmilk has been consumed since before the dawn of humankind and certainly since before 1958. Yet this long use did not ensure success for a 2006 GRAS notification for lysozyme produced from genetically modified rice as an ingredient for infant formula (number 191 in the FDA inventory). Likewise, caffeine has long been consumed in coffee and tea, but manufacturers were not successful in submitting a 2010 GRAS notification for new caffeinated alcoholic drinks (number 347 in the FDA inventory).

One GRAS additive that presents a particular quandary is table salt, sodium chloride. In the 1970s, the federal government asked a panel of scientists, called the Select Committee on GRAS Substances (SCOGS), to review new evidence on old additives. FDA posts the several hundred reviews online as the SCOGS Database. The Select Committee found that salt might be "deleterious to the public health." Based on this decision, the CSPI, a health policy advocacy organization, in 1978 petitioned FDA to agree that salt is not GRAS. FDA did not respond to the petition in the following three decades. A 2010 panel of the Institute of Medicine, which is affiliated with the National Academies of Science, recommended that FDA consider amending salt's continued GRAS status, allowing for certain additional labeling requirements or marketing restraints to be considered for products with excessive amounts of sodium (Institute of Medicine, 2010c).

GAO concluded in 2010 that FDA should strengthen its oversight of food ingredients with GRAS status (U.S. Government Accountability Office, 2010). GAO cited as examples salt, partially hydrogenated vegetable oils containing *trans* fats and food ingredients created using nanotechnology (products manufactured at a microscopic scale to have novel properties). All of these types of ingredients had GRAS status at the time. FDA ended GRAS status for *trans* fats in 2015, so they may no longer be used in foods after June 2018.

In the 2010 report, GAO recommended that companies be required at least to report their GRAS self-certifications. However, in fall 2016, FDA issued a final rule confirming that companies may self-certify ingredients as GRAS. Notification of FDA is voluntary, so the agency cannot know all of the products that have been certified. A group of consumer and environmental organizations, including CSPI and the Environmental Defense Fund, filed a lawsuit in May 2017, arguing that FDA's final rule was inconsistent with the food safety protections in the Federal Food, Drug and Cosmetic Act. The organizations noted that companies may use unpublished information to support their GRAS determinations, without letting the public review the information, so it is difficult to understand how such determinations could satisfy even the literal meaning of the words "generally recognized" as safe.

7.6 Pesticides and GMOs

For chemicals that are not GRAS, federal food safety agencies focus most of their regulatory attention on several categories that policy-makers have identified as particular concerns: (a) pesticides, (b) food and color additives, (c) environmental contaminants and (d) veterinary drugs. Also, food safety authorities must address concerns about new technologies such as GMOs.

Farmers and food manufacturers use pesticides to control weeds, prevent molds and fungi and protect against insects. The whole point of a pesticide is that it should be toxic to some plant, fungus or insect. It is not surprising, therefore, that many pesticides are toxic for humans also. Pesticides are a major safety concern for farm-workers (Das et al., 2001). In addition, possible food safety concerns include carcinogenicity (the ability to cause cancer), neurological consequences, reproductive problems for mothers and developmental problems for children. Federal law requires that all pesticides sold in the United States be registered with the EPA. Using the risk assessment procedures discussed in Section 7.3, EPA sets **tolerances** for the amount of residue that may be found on food. For some pesticides, there is no EPA tolerance, meaning that no residues are supposed to appear on food.

EPA uses data collected through USDA's Pesticide Data Program (PDP) to assess consumers' exposure to pesticides. A special focus is children's exposure to pesticides. This program collects about 12,000 samples each year for a variety of food commodities and drinking water. Data for selected fruits and vegetables are shown in Table 7.2. These residue detections have mixed implications for food safety risk:

- First, most fruits and vegetables had some pesticide residues. However, most of these detections were not violations (for example, small amounts on foods where the pesticide's use was permissible). Depending on the crop, the rate of samples with violations ranged from 0 percent (bananas) to 5.4 percent (green beans) (Table 7.2, column 4).
- Second, some samples had violations detected for pesticides with no tolerance, for which the use of that pesticide was not even permitted (Table 7.2, column 5). These violations were rare for most crops, but common for some crops (such

Table 7.2 Pesticide residue detections for selected fruits and vegetables sampled through USDA's Pesticide Data Program, 2008–2012

Commodity	Samples	Violations			
		Samples with 1 or more violations	Violation rate (percentage)	Violation type[a]	
				No tolerance (pesticide not allowed)	Detection exceeds tolerance
Apples	623	5	0.8%	6	2
Bananas	72	0	0.0%	0	0
Broccoli	308	4	1.3%	3	4
Cantaloupe	92	3	3.3%	4	2
Green beans	589	32	5.4%	59	1
Lettuce	289	3	1.0%	3	0
Peaches	222	10	4.5%	8	3
Pears	147	6	4.1%	8	0
Potatoes	480	10	2.1%	9	15
Sweet bell peppers	550	21	3.8%	38	3

[a] There may be more than 1 violation detected on a single food sample.

Data note: USDA's Pesticide Data Program publishes online annual reports summarizing pesticide residue detections from a national sample of selected agricultural products (www.ams.usda.gov/about-ams/programs-offices/science-technology-program). FDA's Total Diet Study, sometimes called the market basket study, offers an online database of pesticides and toxic chemicals found in foods (www.fda.gov/food/foodscienceresearch/totaldietstudy/). EPA's Pesticide Product Information System provides an online database about each registered pesticide (www.epa.gov/opp00001/PPISdata).

Source: U.S. Government Accountability Office (2014), using data from USDA Pesticide Data Program.

as green beans and sweet bell peppers). These pesticides with no tolerance level included some comparatively potent chemicals, but most of the detected residue amounts were very small.

• Third, other samples had violations detected for pesticides that exceeded a tolerance level (Table 7.2, column 6). For example, for potatoes, there were 15 such detections in 480 samples. These were more significant residue amounts, but they occurred in fewer than 1 percent of samples for most crops.

USDA's annual PDP report does not provide the information one really needs to assess the safety implications of the pesticide detections. For example, it offers no comment about which detections of pesticides with no tolerance represent the greatest danger. The accompanying narrative from USDA suggests minimal concern: "In most cases, these residues were detected at very low levels and some residues may have resulted from spray drift or crop rotations."

Environmental organizations and some cancer researchers are more concerned about these detections. The Environmental Working Group, a nongovernmental organization, uses the PDP data as one of several sources for its lists of the "dirty dozen" and "clean fifteen" fruits and vegetables. A 1998 report from the Organic Center, using the PDP data, noted fewer residue detections on domestic produce than on imported produce and fewer detections on organic produce than on conventionally grown produce. The 2008–2009 annual report from the President's Cancer Panel, issued by the federal government's National Cancer Institute (NCI), also used USDA's PDP data. It described a fairly high level of concern: "The entire U.S. population is exposed on a daily basis to numerous agricultural chemicals. Many of these chemicals are known or suspected of having either carcinogenic or endocrine-disrupting properties" (Reuben, 2010). The President's Cancer Panel identified several problems that hinder the U.S. government's regulation of environmental chemical contaminants, including undue industry influence and the overlapping responsibilities of agency authorities, discussed in the next section.

As with pesticides, there are heated public policy debates over how rigorously the safety of new GMOs should be assessed. In the European Union, genetically engineered products are regulated as "new foods," subject to substantial mandatory food safety testing in advance of approval (Davison, 2010). In the United States, by contrast, genetically engineered foods have traditionally been presumed to be as safe as the corresponding conventional foods, unless there is a particular reason to expect a difference (for example, if the genetically engineered food contains an allergen or a pesticide that is not present in the conventional food). In most cases, U.S. producers of a new GMO enter into a voluntary consultation with FDA, providing FDA with food safety data, after which FDA may publish a summary of the agency's evaluation of the evidence. A high-profile review by the National Academies "found no substantiated evidence that foods from [genetically engineered] GE crops were less safe than foods from non-GE crops" (National Academies, 2016). There is little reason to believe the U.S. approach to GMOs has caused any major food safety problems, but FDA's voluntary consultation process and the National Academies' report have not sufficed to alleviate public concerns (Box 7.4).

Given the current level of scientific uncertainty, differing policy perspectives on food safety hazards depend substantially on different attitudes toward risk. Under a precautionary approach, the government would more strictly regulate pesticides and other agents whose safety is unproven. By contrast, under an approach that accepts the risks from new technologies and takes market outcomes as the presumed optimum, current procedures for approving food chemicals and GMOs are too burdensome already.

7.7 Federal Food Safety Oversight in the United States

Food safety oversight in the United States is distributed across a large number of federal agencies and departments (see Table 7.3). The two most important food safety agencies are USDA's FSIS, which oversees most meat, poultry and processed eggs, and FDA, which oversees most other food products. Beyond the big two agencies, this chapter has already encountered some other federal agencies with secondary food safety responsibilities: CDC, which monitors the epidemiology of foodborne illness (see Section 7.4), and EPA, which sets tolerances for pesticides (see Section 7.6). Table 7.3 lists several more federal food safety agencies with narrower jurisdiction. Some food safety responsibilities are split between the federal government and state and local governments.

Table 7.3 Selected major U.S. food safety agencies

Agency	Major responsibilities and activities
Department of Health and Human Services (DHHS)	
Food and Drug Administration (FDA)	Primary agency responsible for the safety of most food products (except meat, poultry and processed eggs). Also oversees animal drugs and livestock feed.
Centers for Disease Control and Prevention (CDC)	Monitors and investigates foodborne diseases. Conducts epidemiological and scientific research.
Department of Agriculture (USDA)	
Food Safety Inspection Service (FSIS)	Primary agency responsible for the safety of most meat, poultry and processed eggs.
Animal and Plant Health Inspection Service (APHIS)	Oversees prevention of animal and plant diseases, including foreign diseases and pests.
Agricultural Marketing Service (AMS)	Establishes quality and marketing grades and standards for dairy products, fruits and vegetables, meat and other products. Quality and grading services may include food safety functions.
Environmental Protection Agency (EPA)	Regulates pesticide products. Sets maximum allowable tolerances for residue levels.
Department of Commerce	
National Oceanic and Atmospheric Administration	Oversees voluntary seafood safety and quality inspection services on a fee-for-service basis.
Department of Homeland Security	
U.S. Customs and Border Protection	Conducts border inspections and coordinates other activities to protect food from intentional harm, such as bioterrorism.

Source: Johnson (2016); U.S. Government Accountability Office (2017).

Box 7.4   FDA Safety Review of Genetically Engineered Salmon

Public interest groups have been particularly critical of the FDA summary of food safety evidence for the most controversial new proposed GMO food in recent years: a genetically engineered variety of Atlantic salmon, produced by a company called AquaBounty Technologies. The new AquAdvantage salmon contains genes from Chinook salmon and other fish species. These genes produce increased quantities of a hormone that accelerates growth. FDA granted approval in 2015.

FDA's review of the food safety evidence submitted by AquaBounty focused on whether elevated levels of growth hormone were found in the fish's flesh, because this hormone was by design the key intended difference between conventional salmon and the new fish (Food and Drug Administration, 2010). However, FDA's review showed that the relevant study submitted by AquaBounty did not detect any amount of the growth hormone, either in the genetically engineered fish or in conventional fish.

Nevertheless, from this evidence, FDA reported, "Food from AquAdvantage Salmon is the same as food from other Atlantic salmon. No biologically relevant differences were detected in the levels of the gene product (the Chinook salmon growth hormone)." It seems quite possible that the new salmon is safe for humans, but the evidence submitted by the petitioner did not support FDA's summary statement. The public interest group Consumers Union likened FDA's conclusion to "the police using a radar gun that cannot detect speeds below 120 mph and concluding that there is no 'relevant difference' in the speed of cars versus bicycles" (Hansen, 2010).

As of this writing, in 2017, small amounts of the GMO salmon have been sold in Canada, but not yet in the United States. FDA has not issued mandatory labeling rules for U.S. sale. Shortly after the FDA approval for the new technology, *Washington Post* columnist Tamar Haspel argued that the product was most likely safe, or at least safe enough to deserve approval, but she described the lack of a labeling rule as unfortunate: "One of the reasons GMOs became such a brouhaha is that consumers feel the technology was foisted, in secret, on an unsuspecting public" (Haspel, 2015).

GAO, a nonpartisan auditing and investigations agency that answers to the U.S. Congress, has found that "fragmentation in the nation's food safety system results in inconsistent oversight, ineffective coordination and inefficient use of resources" (Dyckman, 2004). A comparison of FSIS and FDA responsibilities indicates some of the coordination challenges (see Table 7.4). Regulators must define the exact line between a meat product (overseen by FSIS) and a nonmeat product (overseen by FDA). For example, the two agencies stipulate in writing exactly how many ounces of pepperoni qualifies a pizza as a meat product. The FSIS has a much higher funding level and a greater number of inspectors, because by law its inspectors must be on site at each slaughterhouse during operation. FDA, by contrast, has far fewer inspectors,

Table 7.4 Selected comparisons of USDA Food Safety Inspection Service (FSIS) and Food and Drug Administration (FDA) activities and responsibilities

Topics	Food Safety Inspection Service	Food and Drug Administration
Primary laws	Federal Meat Inspection Act, Poultry Products Inspection Act, Egg Products Inspection Act	Federal Food, Drug and Cosmetic Act; Public Health Service Act; Egg Products Inspection Act; Food Safety Modernization Act (FSMA)
Foods regulated	Meat, poultry, processed eggs and other foods	Most domestic and imported foods other than meat, poultry and processed eggs
Funding (fiscal year 2015)	Appropriated: $1,017 million for food safety (plus $190 million in other funding and fees)	Appropriated: $903 million for food safety (plus $312 million in other funding and fees)
Staff (fiscal year 2015)	8,900 federal full-time equivalents	3,700 federal full-time equivalents
Domestic facilities (fiscal year 2015)	6,390 slaughter and/or processing establishments	88,000 subject to inspection
Inspection approach	Traditionally, for slaughter, inspection of every animal and carcass before and after slaughter. Inspector is on site at all times of operation.	Facilities must register and follow rules. Inspection frequency may range from once each year (for 10 percent to 30 percent of facilities) to once every five or 10 years (for other facilities).

Source: Johnson (2016); U.S. Government Accountability Office (2017).

even though it oversees a larger portion of the food supply. As a consequence, FDA can inspect each food manufacturing plant in its jurisdiction only once each year for some plants and once every five or 10 years for many other plants.

GAO and many food safety advocates have long hoped for food safety oversight responsibility to be consolidated into a single agency, as several other countries have done. However, there are many bureaucratic and political hurdles to such consolidation in the United States. For example, hiring enough inspectors to monitor FDA-regulated manufacturing plants as intensively as FSIS-regulated manufacturing plants would require a large budget increase. If, instead, policy-makers aimed for cost neutrality by reducing the level of FSIS monitoring, the proposed consolidation would generate concern in light of recent food safety outbreaks in meat and poultry. Consolidation into a single agency also would be an immense administrative challenge. As a consequence, more attention in recent years has focused on policy reforms to modernize each agency separately, combined with efforts to integrate oversight across agencies through coordination procedures that fall short of a full merger.

An interagency Food Safety Working Group was formed in 2009, but GAO continues to recommend more vigorous coordination efforts to establish national food safety objectives and to quantitatively monitor progress toward those objectives. In a 2017 report on "fragmentation" in federal food safety oversight, GAO summarized three worrisome trends: food imports, which are particularly difficult to monitor, are increasing; consumption of raw fruits and vegetables, without cooking as a "kill step" to protect against pathogens, is rising; and a growing fraction of the population is older or more susceptible to foodborne illness. Without a more focused national strategy, food safety remains on the agency's list of "high-risk" government-wide challenges.

7.8 The FDA Food Safety Modernization Act

In late 2010, Congress passed the FDA Food Safety Modernization Act (FSMA), making some of the biggest changes to FDA's food safety authority in several decades. FDA has primary responsibility for safety of most food products other than meat, poultry and processed eggs. The new law:

- enhances FDA's authority to inspect food manufacturing facilities;
- gives FDA the power to order mandatory recalls of unsafe food;
- strengthens FDA oversight over imported food (see Chapter 4);
- requires a wider range of FDA-regulated food manufacturing facilities to have HACCP plans (see Section 7.4); and
- requires FDA to issue new regulations for safe production and harvesting of fruits and vegetables (see Box 7.2).

The 2010 passage of the FSMA illustrates the complexity of compiling an advocacy coalition that is sufficiently broad-based to win a majority of votes in Congress. Legislators are closely attuned to the U.S. public's concern about food safety, the public's suspicion of increased government regulations and the financial interests of food companies that may be political supporters.

It may be tempting to analyze policy debates as principally arising from divisions between political parties or divisions between industry organizations and public interest groups. However, food safety arguments, like many U.S. food policy arguments, are difficult to classify in this manner, because they cut across these political divisions in unusual ways. As initially proposed, the FSMA legislation was strongly supported by consumer groups and food safety advocates. In addition, many industry representatives recognized that the recent series of outbreaks and food safety failures (summarized in Section 7.4) had generated sufficient public pressure that some legislation was inevitable. Meanwhile, perhaps surprisingly, advocates for sustainable agriculture and small farms opposed the legislation. They were concerned that the law would increase regulation of small producers, forcing them to adopt HACCP plans and register with FDA in the same fashion as larger food manufacturers.

An amendment brokered by Sen. John Tester (D-MT) and Sen. Kay Hagan (D-NC) relaxed the law's requirements for small-scale businesses that have annual gross sales less than a half-million dollars and sell more than half of their products directly to consumers or local restaurants and retailers. This Tester-Hagan amendment was revised and renegotiated several times until its language sufficed to allow most consumer groups and sustainable agriculture groups to agree on their support. However, the amendment had by this time generated new opposition from larger producers, who were upset about facing burdensome rules that their smaller competitors did not face. Eventually, the bill's sponsors found compromise language for the small business exemptions that succeeded in winning majority support in Congress. President Barack Obama signed the FSMA on January 4, 2011.

7.9 Conclusion

Food safety problems stem from information failures that prey on the weaknesses of both markets and government actors. Because of imperfect information, market forces fail to serve the public interest in food safety as well as one might hope. At the same time, information problems hinder an effective regulatory alternative to market forces.

Much of the time, food producers exert more influence over food safety policy-makers than consumer groups do. During these ordinary noncrisis times, the food industries appear able to veto reasonable measures to strengthen food safety oversight. By contrast, during periodic food safety crises, consumer groups enjoy the full attention of policy-makers and the public. During these crisis times, however, it is difficult to enact measured policies that balance food safety objectives with competing objectives, such as protecting the environment, producing food efficiently and providing businesses with a stable and predictable regulatory regime.

Because of these multiple challenges, sound food safety policy requires using imperfect market incentives and imperfect governmental capabilities as well as possible. Progress in using market incentives happens when business innovators learn to convert the consumer's desire for safe food into a feasible business proposition. Progress in strengthening government capabilities happens when policy innovators learn to assemble new advocacy coalitions that overcome their internal divisions and translate the public's desire for safe food into sufficient political power to enact reforms.

Summary List of Key Terms (identified in bold in the text)

- adulterated
- asymmetric imperfect information
- dose–response assessment
- exposure assessment
- Generally Recognized as Safe
- good agricultural practices
- good manufacturing practices
- hazard analysis and critical control points
- hazard identification
- performance standards
- process rules
- risk assessment
- risk characterization
- risk management
- symmetric imperfect information
- tolerances

8 Dietary Guidance and Health

8.1 Introduction

It is sometimes said that there is no need for a government role in dietary guidance, because people know how to eat well and simply lack the willpower to do so. Is it true that people in the United States already know how to eat healthfully? While many nutrition and health experts say that something is wrong with U.S. eating patterns, they disagree about what is unhealthy.

Consider four perspectives that each have a large public following:

- A long tradition blames carbohydrates for weight problems and recommends a diet that may be high in meat and saturated fat. Examples include the Atkins diet and, more recently, most versions of "paleo" diets (Taubes, 2007; Taubes, 2011; Teicholz, 2015).
- A directly opposed tradition encourages a plant-based diet and blames meat consumption for health problems (Campbell and Campbell, 2007). In a 2016 position paper, the Academy of Nutrition and Dietetics (AND) called appropriately planned vegetarian diets "healthful" and "nutritionally adequate" (Melina, Craig, and Levin, 2016).
- Other leading researchers and nutrition organizations encourage the Mediterranean diet and similar diets that are comparatively low in meat and high in fruits and vegetables, but not necessarily low in fat, allowing plenty of vegetable oils (Willett et al., 2005). Dariush Mozaffarian, dean of the Friedman School of Nutrition Science and Policy at Tufts University, notes, "consistent and compelling evidence indicates that traditional Mediterranean-style diets produce substantial health benefits" (Trichopoulou et al., 2014).
- Still others, including former FDA Commissioner David Kessler and journalist Michael Moss, are most concerned about the highly palatable artificial creations of an industrial food system (Kessler, 2009; Moss, 2013).

These views about diet and health are partly overlapping and partly contradictory. Yet at least some scientific research in peer-reviewed journals can be found to support each one. To make sound judgments, a layperson needs a skeptical attitude towards dietary fads and a trustworthy summary of the balance of the scientific evidence.

One influential summary of the scientific evidence is the federal government's *Dietary Guidelines for Americans* (U.S. Department of Agriculture and U.S. Department of Health and Human Services, 2015). The federal government issued the first

Dietary Guidelines in 1980 and has revised the document every five years since then. Regardless of a reader's own views on diet and health, it is useful to understand the mainstream position of the *Dietary Guidelines* on controversial questions in nutrition science.

The *Dietary Guidelines for Americans* is used as a source of evidence for claims about diet and health on food labels (see Chapter 9). It provides key inputs for USDA's Thrifty Food Plan and other model diets for people at different income levels (see Chapter 10). It informs policies and regulations for nutrition assistance programs, including school lunch and school breakfast (see Chapter 11).

This chapter covers how the federal government develops and uses dietary guidance. The chapter:

- reviews historical trends in chronic disease and nutrition, so that we can pay the most attention to the most important health concerns (Section 8.2);
- considers several market failures that have been cited as motivation for a government role in dietary guidance (Section 8.3);
- explains the process of creating the *Dietary Guidelines for Americans* and related consumer-oriented graphics (Section 8.4);
- compares current U.S. consumption patterns to the *Dietary Guidelines* (Section 8.5); and
- explores several policy instruments that have been proposed to guide Americans toward healthier food choices (Section 8.6).

8.2 Trends in Health, Obesity and Food Choices

Major changes in food consumption, dietary quality and health from the 1970s to the 2010s provide the setting for contemporary debates about dietary guidance. During these decades, there were rapid advances in medical science and treatment, and rates of smoking decreased, but these advances were partly offset by unhealthy changes in eating patterns and increasing rates of overweight and obesity.

Diet is linked with four of the top 10 leading causes of death in the United States (National Center for Health Statistics, 2016):

1. heart disease (23.4 percent of deaths in 2015),
2. cancer (22.5 percent),
5. stroke (5.1 percent), and
7. diabetes (2.9 percent).

The rate of death from these diseases declined from 1970 to 2015 (Figure 8.1), but declining death rates do not imply that all is well.

Fist, the pace of improvement in mortality from diet-related disease has slowed in recent years. The prevalence of heart disease and cancer has remained high, and the prevalence of diabetes has increased from the 1990s to the 2010s (Figure 8.1). In addition to the effects of reduced smoking, the number of deaths fell because of earlier detection of disease and a variety of improved medical treatments. These treatments include better surgery to address heart disease, chemotherapy and radiation to address cancer and drugs to lower blood pressure and reduce the risk of stroke. Even when not fatal, these diseases cause hardship, pain and disability. The treatments themselves

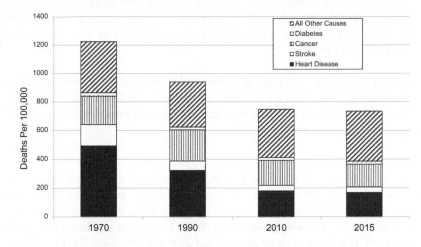

Figure 8.1 Annual deaths from leading causes, per 100,000 population, 1970–2015
Source: National Center for Health Statistics (2016).

Table 8.1 Age-adjusted death rates (per 100,000 population) for leading diet-related diseases in U.S. adults, by race and ethnicity status, 2015[a]

	Total	White	Black or African American	Native American	Asian	Hispanic[b]
			(deaths per 100,000 population)			
All causes	733	735	852	597	395	525
Heart disease	169	168	205	119	87	117
Cerebrovascular	38	36	51	25	30	32
Cancer	159	159	180	108	99	110
Diabetes	21	20	37	34	16	25
All other	346	352	379	311	163	241

[a] The age adjustment allows for meaningful comparison across population groups. [b] Hispanic persons may be any race.
Data note: The easiest source of data for U.S. health and mortality is the online spreadsheets that accompany the annual report series *Health, United States* from CDC (www.cdc.gov/nchs/hus.htm). For greater detail, CDC also offers an interactive utility called the "Wide-ranging Online Data for Epidemiologic Research" (CDC Wonder) (wonder.cdc.gov).

Source: National Center for Health Statistics (2016).

are expensive, contributing to rapid increases in medical costs (Finkelstein and Strombotne, 2010). Instead of just improving treatment enough to postpone death, it would be valuable to improve prevention through better nutrition so that Americans could live healthier lives in the first place.

Second, the improvements in mortality, such as they are, have not been enjoyed equally by all Americans. According to the National Center for Health Statistics, mortality rates for the leading causes of death were higher for black Americans than for white Americans (Table 8.1). For example, rates of death from diabetes were almost twice as high for black Americans as for white Americans. Such differences have multiple causes (Neff et al., 2009), including differences in food consumption patterns, retail environments and exposure to poverty and food insecurity. In light of such statistics, the U.S. *Healthy People 2020* objectives recognize a need for greater **health equity**. As explained by Shiriki Kumanyika, the president of the American Public Health Association in 2015,

> Health equity invokes human rights principles and creates a sense of commonality with a diverse human rights advocacy community. In this sense, health equity speaks to the process of creating opportunities for all population groups and each person to improve his or her health.
>
> (Kumanyika, 2016)

Overweight and obesity are linked with the leading diet-related causes of death: heart disease, some cancers, stroke and diabetes. Rates of overweight and obesity climbed to record levels from 1988 to 2014 (Figure 8.2). Weight status is most commonly measured using the **body mass index** (BMI) (weight in kg/the square of height in m). Among men, the prevalence of overweight and obesity (with BMI ≥ 25) rose from 61 percent in 1988–1994 to 73 percent in 2011–2014. Similarly, among women the prevalence of overweight and obesity (using the same cutpoint) rose from 51 percent in 1988–1994 to 66 percent in 2011–2014. Among children and youth, the prevalence of obesity increased proportionately even faster from 1988–1994 to 2003–2004, and then was more stable through 2011–2014 (National Center for Health Statistics, 2016). As with total deaths from chronic disease, there is considerable inequality across race and ethnic groups in rates of overweight and obesity (Table 8.2).

These trends have generated great interest in explanations for obesity, but not all explanations are equally relevant for the study of U.S. food policy. A proximal (near-at-hand) explanation is that obesity is caused by a food energy imbalance: too much food energy intake and not enough physical activity. One could say that obesity results from more eating occasions each day and increased portion sizes at each eating

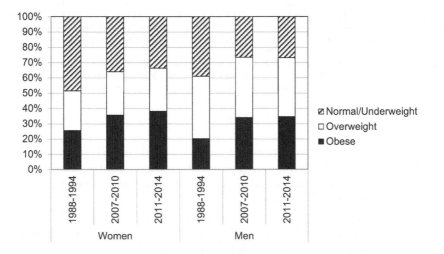

Figure 8.2 Age-adjusted prevalence of overweight and obesity for men and women, as a percentage of the adult population, 1988–2014

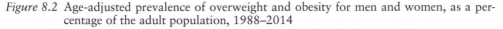

Source: National Center for Health Statistics (2016).

Table 8.2 Age-adjusted prevalence of overweight and obesity (as percentage of population) in U.S. adults, 1988–2014[a]

		Non-Hispanic White	Non-Hispanic Black	Hispanic
Men	1988–1994	61.6	57.8	68.9[b]
	2011–2014	73.7	69.6	79.6
Women	1988–1994	47.5	68.2	68.9[b]
	2011–2014	63.5	82.0	77.1

[a] Overweight and obesity is defined as having body mass index (BMI) ≥ 25.
[b] In 1988–1994, NCHS data reported just persons of Mexican origin, not all Hispanic persons.
Source: National Center for Health Statistics (2016).

occasion. However, this explanation leaves open questions about the more fundamental causes of increased eating occasions and portion sizes.

A distal (far-removed) explanation is that obesity is caused by innate human desires for highly palatable foods and beverages, whose energy can be stored in fat tissue for later use. These desires and storage mechanisms evolved in prehistoric times as an adaptive response to periodic food scarcity. However, this evolution took place over many thousands of years and cannot explain social changes from the 1970s to the 2000s.

Setting aside explanations that are too proximal and too distal to have much policy consequence, there still remains a long list of possible explanations for trends in overweight and obesity (Lakdawalla et al., 2005; Taubes, 2007). For example:

- welfare-improving technological change in the twentieth century made food cheaper on average while simultaneously making work less strenuous, and the resulting change in energy balance led to weight gain;
- social trends, including the movement of women into the labor force and increased television watching, reduced the time available for home cooking and increased consumer demand for convenience food and restaurant food;
- changes in food marketing and distribution have made desirable energy-dense food and sweetened beverages ubiquitous, available in every possible setting at every moment (Kessler, 2009).

8.3 Economic Motivations for Dietary Guidance

Private-sector markets have a remarkable capacity to produce a great diversity of foods, establish prices that reflect scarcity and provide consumers with food that satisfies their desires and perceived needs. Economists recognize that private-sector markets also have several shortcomings that are relevant for nutrition and dietary quality. The appropriate policy response to poor dietary quality and chronic disease depends in part on how one assesses these shortcomings.

1. Imperfect information. Market outcomes are optimal only if consumers have the information they need to make purchases that satisfy their preferences. Consumer preferences pertain to nutritional qualities (this chapter) and food safety (Chapter 7), which are difficult to observe directly in a retail environment. Private-sector markets may offer an insufficient incentive to supply accurate information about

nutrition qualities. Possible policy remedies include dietary guidance (Section 8.4) and rules to govern food labeling and advertising (Chapter 9).

2. Negative externalities. Market outcomes may be unsatisfactory if there are externalities, where one person's decisions affect other people's well-being through nonmarket mechanisms. Some economists argue that diet-related diseases impose negative externalities through the operation of insurance programs. For participants in the Medicaid or Medicare programs, the financial costs of illness are paid largely by taxpayers. Even for people who use private insurance, through their employer or by paying their own insurance premiums, financial costs of illness are shared with other people in the same insurance risk pool. If health insurance externalities are perceived as serious, governments may consider policies that are more assertive than mere guidance, such as a proposed system of taxes or subsidies (Section 8.6). However, the externalities from diet-related diseases are not as direct as those from communicable diseases. A person who makes poor decisions about risk factors for communicable diseases (such as not washing hands when ill or not getting vaccinated) directly endangers other people, while a person who makes poor nutritional choices suffers many of the consequences of diet-related disease himself or herself (Finkelstein and Strombotne, 2010; Bhattacharya and Bundorf, 2009).

3. Food choices of children. The traditional economic perspective assumes that consumers are rational adults who can make their own spending decisions. The justification for government efforts to promote nutrition is stronger for children than for adults. For example, policy-makers may be willing to consider restrictions on marketing unhealthful food to children (Chapter 9) even when similar advertising targeting adults would be permitted. Likewise, public schools are government institutions that are expected to educate children, not just provide children with goods and services, so schools may take stronger measures to promote good nutrition (see Chapter 11).

8.4 How Federal Dietary Guidance Is Created

Developing useful dietary guidance requires decision making under uncertainty. On many important nutrition issues, it is possible to distinguish sound from unsound judgments but not possible to know the certain truth.

This section describes five stages in developing federal dietary guidance:

1. Scientists conduct original research in multiple fields.
2. Scientists, the food industry and public interest organizations filter this research, seeking to discern broader implications for nutrition and health.
3. An external Dietary Guidelines Advisory Committee, commissioned by the federal government, critically reviews and summarizes the conflicting scientific evidence and distills it into a formal committee report.
4. Federal government agencies write the *Dietary Guidelines for Americans*.
5. These federal agencies prepare accompanying nutrition education materials, such as the MyPlate graphic.

Although this section focuses specifically on the example of the *Dietary Guidelines for Americans*, it offers lessons for many other applications in U.S. food policy where the process used to develop scientific evidence becomes an issue in policy debates over how that evidence should be used.

8.4.1 Scientific Research

The design of scientific research affects how the results are interpreted. Whenever nutrition science evidence is reported in the media or in policy documents, the following distinctions are critical:

- Subjects. Clinical studies of human subjects are more authoritative than laboratory studies of animals or chemical analysis of isolated cells.
- Research design. There are strengths and weaknesses to a wide variety of research designs, including these leading examples. **Experimental designs**, which randomly assign subjects to a treatment group and a control group, offer the greatest ability to discern cause and effect rather than just statistical associations. **Prospective cohort designs** (which follow a group of people over time) or **cross-sectional designs** (which compare different people at the same point in time) offer larger sample sizes and other advantages and hence remain an important part of the scientific literature. Larger sample sizes produce more precise statistical estimates, but these designs have weaker ability to determine cause and effect.
- **Representativeness.** The subjects of a study may or may not represent the general population. Some research outcomes, such as heart attacks, occur only rarely in healthy populations, so scientists commonly study special populations with elevated risk of disease, such as men who have previously experienced a heart attack. Also, if many participants withdraw from a study, perhaps because they get tired of the meddlesome questions or didn't like the food, the representativeness of the sample is weakened. To assess this problem, all studies should report their **response rate**, which is the percentage of sampled subjects whose data were actually used in analysis.
- Outcomes. Studies showing the risk of disease and death are more authoritative than studies showing an intermediate marker, such as elevated blood cholesterol. A well-designed study will specify the main outcomes in advance, because otherwise researchers may find spurious associations by testing a large number of outcomes in a scattershot manner.
- Bias due to sponsorship. Some research is supported by government agencies; other research is supported by the food, beverage and dietary supplement industries. Sources of financial support should be disclosed and potential conflicts of interest should be transparent (see Box 8.1). Because nutrition science research is expensive, there are more and better industry-funded studies on research topics that are easier to pursue and may lead to profitable food product innovations. For example, it may be easier to acquire industry funding for a study about the positive effect of calcium on bone health than about the negative effect of red meat on the risk of colon cancer.

Much of the evidence that popular writers cite in favor of diet and health beliefs fails to survive scientific scrutiny. Journalists cover recent scientific research without having time, space or motivation to explain the strengths and limitations of new studies. Most diet books include anecdotes about people revolutionizing their lives by adopting a new diet. These stories can be inspirational yet entirely misleading. They can be used to support every possible theory about nutrition and health.

8.4.2 *Filtering*

Filtering is the process of reading a large body of research and concisely summarizing its relevant points. Because the scientific literature is so heterogeneous, its policy impact depends heavily on how the research is filtered.

Filtering may be biased toward certain types of conclusions. Food industry organizations hire scientists and public relations specialists to spread the good word about favorable studies without mentioning unfavorable studies. The public relations specialists are evaluated according to their success in placing favorable stories in the mass media. Reporters do not purposely seek to serve as a vehicle for industry public relations, but they face intense pressure to generate buzz by reporting novel and surprising findings. Hence, even though the balance of evidence in the scientific literature changes only slowly, headlines each week tell the public that everything they previously believed about nutrition and health was a big fat lie.

To summarize a complex scientific literature with less bias, scientists prefer to rely on systematic evidence reviews. In a systematic evidence review, an interdisciplinary team establishes a protocol, a document that describes in advance the procedure for selecting relevant research studies, reducing the temptation to concentrate on studies that are favorable to the team's prior expectations. For each selected study, the team evaluates the strength of the evidence, again using criteria established in advance. Systematic evidence reviews do have some limitations. While they can avoid errors that stem from selective reading of just favorable parts of the scientific literature, systematic evidence reviews cannot fix misinterpretations that are widespread in the literature. Also, such reviews may not reflect recent improvements in scientific research. Still, because of their transparency and replicability, systematic reviews can clarify the state of the evidence on contentious scientific issues.

For U.S. dietary guidance policy, three influential collections of systematic evidence reviews are:

- The Nutrition Evidence Library from USDA's Center for Nutrition Policy and Promotion (CNPP). For most outcomes other than risk of cancer, the Dietary Guidelines Advisory Committee treats USDA's new evidence library as authoritative. This evidence library is available online at no cost (www.cnpp.usda.gov/nutritionevidencelibrary).
- Systematic evidence reviews regarding cancer risk from the World Cancer Research Fund and the American Institute of Cancer Research (2007). The Dietary Guidelines Advisory Committee has treated the WCRF/AICR evidence reviews as authoritative summaries for some issues related to nutrition and cancer. The Continuous Update Project (CUP) provides links to the most recent evidence reviews (www.wcrf.org/int/research-we-fund/continuous-update-project-cup).
- The Evidence Analysis Library from the Academy of Nutrition and Dietetics. This library represents the assessment of the dietetics profession in the United States (www.andeal.org).

Box 8.1   Conflicts of Interest in Nutrition Science and Dietetics

To be trusted, scientific research must be unbiased. Much of the research in nutrition science and dietetics is funded by the food and supplement industries. A vigorous argument has arisen over how the resulting conflicts of interest should be managed.

One mainstream view is that conflicts can be managed successfully if scientists disclose their sources of support and adhere to guidelines requiring them to maintain responsibility for research design decisions and to be objective (Rowe et al., 2009). Some researchers are outspokenly skeptical. David Ludwig and Marion Nestle argue, "The food industry, with its enormous financial resources, has an especially insidious influence on the conduct of research and development of public health policy" (Ludwig and Nestle, 2008). In this view, bias may creep into a research literature even if each scientist discloses his or her funding sources and seeks to adhere to a principle of objectivity. Financial sponsorship has recently become an interesting topic of research in its own right. Lesser et al. (2007) reviewed 206 studies of soft drinks, juice and milk, of which 111 disclosed financial sponsorship. Those studies with industry funding were significantly more likely to reach conclusions favorable to the industry.

In contrast with this concern about industry sponsorship, Cope and Allison (2010) warn of a "white hat" bias in favor of whatever opinion represents the conventional wisdom. They reviewed citations to two well-known studies, which found both statistically significant and insignificant results about the effectiveness of interventions to reduce consumption of sugar-sweetened beverages. Out of more than 200 citations to these two studies, the majority of citations only mentioned the results that confirmed the effectiveness of the beverage-reducing programs but did not mention the statistically insignificant results.

Many journals' disclosure requirements apply to all relevant financial interests, but in practice it is common only to disclose funding sources for the specific study being submitted. For example, Michael Zemel, whose research supports the hypothesis that high-calcium diets accelerate weight loss, has a patent on the use of high-calcium and high-dairy diets for weight-loss purposes. This hypothesis is not endorsed in the *Dietary Guidelines* (Dietary Guidelines Advisory Committee, 2015; U.S. Department of Agriculture and U.S. Department of Health and Human Services, 2015). Based on Zemel's patent, dairy industry organizations charge food manufacturers money for the right to use dairy weight-loss claims on food labels. In 2005, the editor for the *International Journal of Obesity* concluded (Atkinson, 2005) that Zemel's patent was a financial interest that should have been disclosed in connection with his article in that journal (Zemel et al., 2005). Zemel responded, "My patents and patent applications are well known and are a matter of public record, and no attempt has ever been made to obscure their presence or my interest in them." As it becomes more common for universities and their faculty to seek to profit from their scientific innovations, it will become more important for journals to ensure that all potential financial conflicts of interest are disclosed.

8.4.3 *The Dietary Guidelines Advisory Committee*

As was done for previous editions of the *Dietary Guidelines*, USDA and DHHS appointed an external Dietary Guidelines Advisory Committee (DGAC), composed of leading scientists, for the 2015 guidelines (Dietary Guidelines Advisory Committee, 2015). All of the scientists were respected researchers, and most members had received research funding from both industry and government sources. In contrast with previous editions, the USDA and DHHS did not share much information about potential conflicts of interest for members of the 2015 advisory committee (Teicholz, 2015).

The advisory committee and its subcommittees read and considered the systematic evidence reviews. The committee's report, released in 2015, reiterated time-honored themes from previous editions of the *Dietary Guidelines*, but it also included several distinctive new features (Dietary Guidelines Advisory Committee, 2015). For individuals and families, the committee recommended, "Seek to make gradual and sustainable changes in your dietary behaviors to achieve one of several sound healthy dietary pattern options (e.g. Healthy U.S.-style Pattern, the Healthy Mediterranean-style Pattern, or the Healthy Vegetarian Pattern)." For communities and populations, the committee made novel recommendations related to topics covered throughout this book. For example, the committee recommended making healthy lifestyles and prevention a national priority (Chapter 1), promoting environmentally sustainable diets (Chapter 3), establishing healthy food retail environments (Chapter 6), improving nutrition facts labels and front-of-package labels (Chapter 9) and more vigorously supporting dietary quality through federal nutrition assistance programs (Chapters 10 and 11).

8.4.4 *The Dietary Guidelines for Americans*

After the advisory committee completed its work, federal government officials from USDA and DHHS issued the actual *Dietary Guidelines for Americans, 2015–2020* (U.S. Department of Agriculture and U.S. Department of Health and Human Services, 2015). This two-stage process is designed to separate scientific and policy judgments. Because the document is an important input for federal policy, it would be difficult, and not necessarily even wise, to delegate the policy decisions entirely to research scientists without policy expertise or accountability to democratically elected authorities.

The process of developing the *Dietary Guidelines* explicitly welcomes public input. Several rounds of public comment were considered by the DGAC. After the publication of the external advisory committee's report, there was another round of formal comments. Not surprisingly, there are sharp differences between the comments from public interest organizations and the food and beverage industries. It is perhaps more surprising that the food industry was itself deeply divided on many recommendations (Box 8.2).

With each revision, the *Dietary Guidelines for Americans* is scrutinized for its economic and food policy implications. Each recommendation to increase or decrease consumption of a food or nutrient implies a suggested reallocation of resources in government food assistance programs and the food economy. Table 8.3 compares and contrasts selected conclusions from the 2015 advisory committee and the official guidelines, noting some implications that would be perceived by food industry and food policy audiences.

Nutrition experts have long observed that the guidelines trumpet easily recognized foods in "eat more" messages while using more technical terminology for nutrients and food components in "eat less" messages (Nestle, 2003). It is politically uncontroversial to recommend increased consumption of healthy foods or to encourage physical activity. It is politically more difficult to recommend less of nutrients (such as saturated fats) or ingredients (such as salt or added sugars), but the *Dietary Guidelines* nonetheless have fairly pointed recommendations on these topics. It is most difficult of all to make specific recommendations to reduce consumption of particular foods, because such recommendations generate vociferous opposition from producers. For example, the 2015 Dietary Guidelines Advisory Committee recommended that most Americans should reduce consumption of red meat and processed meat, but these recommendations were not included in the official guidelines (Table 8.3).

Table 8.3 Policy significance of selected recommendations in the Dietary Guidelines Advisory Committee (DGAC) report and *Dietary Guidelines for Americans, 2015–2020*

Advisory committee	Official guidelines report	Policy significance
Recommends a healthy dietary pattern, "including" consumption of vegetables, fruits, whole grains, seafood, nuts, legumes and low/nonfat dairy or dairy alternatives.	Agrees.	Producer groups are delighted with suggestions for increases. A strong guideline could mean increased demand for these foods.
Recommends "following" physical activity recommendations.	Agrees.	The food industry approves of promoting physical activity, which leads to higher food energy needs.
Recommends "reducing" added sugars.	Recommends "limit[ing] calories from" added sugars. The recommendation about added sugars (an ingredient) is accompanied by an illustration of a sugar-sweetened beverage (an actual food).	The guidelines were long criticized by some for being too strict on fats and too gentle on sugars, but recent editions have been fairly blunt on sugars. Following the guideline would mean reduced demand for sugar-sweetened beverages.
Recommends "reducing" sodium.	Agrees. The recommendation about sodium (in salt, an ingredient) is accompanied by an illustration of pizza and a deli meat sandwich (actual foods).	Industry-friendly sources emphasize diversity in sodium sensitivity and treat "too little" sodium as a major problem. Following the guideline would mean reduced demand for processed food and restaurant food.

(Continued)

Table 8.3 Continued

Advisory committee	Official guidelines report	Policy significance
Recommends "reducing" consumption of saturated fat and "substituting saturated fats with polyunsaturated alternatives."	"Limit calories from" saturated fat. Also: "[R]eplacing saturated fats with polyunsaturated fats" is associated with a reduced risk of heart attacks and deaths from heart disease. The recommendation about saturated fat (a nutrient) is accompanied by an illustration of a cheeseburger and an ice cream sundae (actual foods).	Recent editions now take more care to avoid encouraging carbohydrates (including sugar) as a substitute for saturated fats. Following the guideline could mean reduced demand for meat, butter, cheese and mixed foods, and more demand for vegetable oils.
Recommends reducing consumption of red meat and processed meat.	Omitted. No direct recommendation to reduce. Instead, encouragement for "lean meats."	The red and processed meat industries are powerful. A strong guideline could mean reduced demand not only for meat but also for inputs such as grains and oilseeds.
Sustainability: "[A] diet higher in plant-based foods . . . and lower in calories and animal-based foods is more health promoting and is associated with less environmental impact than is the current U.S. diet."	Omitted.	After heated discussion and national media coverage, including vigorous opposition from meat and dairy producers, this distinctive conclusion of the advisory committee was omitted from the official report for 2015–2020 (see Chapter 3).

Source: Dietary Guidelines Advisory Committee (2015) and US DHHS and USDA (2015).

There are vociferous dissents to the recommendations in the *Dietary Guidelines* on important questions, such as the appropriate role of meat and dairy in the diet. On the one hand, advocates for low-carbohydrate diets encourage heavy consumption of meat and dairy products, and they dispute the federal government's recommendation to limit solid fats (Taubes, 2011). On the other hand, vegetarian-friendly public interest groups say the guidelines should have explicitly recommended reduced consumption of meat and dairy products. The Physicians Committee for Responsible Medicine, a nonprofit health research and advocacy group, filed a lawsuit in February 2011 complaining that the 2010 guidelines used "deliberately obscure language regarding foods consumers should avoid" (Physicians Committee for Responsible Medicine, 2011). The *Dietary Guidelines for Americans, 2015–2020* reflects an intermediate position on these issues.

Box 8.2 Interest Group Influence on Dietary Guidance

The food industry is far from united in its advice to the government about dietary guidance. Each industry sector's judgment of the scientific facts is colored by its economic interests. As just two examples from many that could have been chosen, the *Dietary Guidelines for Americans, 2010* received diverse written comments from industry associations about limiting added sugars and promoting fruits and vegetables.

Limiting Added Sugars

The DGAC had recommended that most Americans reduce their intake of added sugars, such as the sugar in desserts and sodas. The committee was gentler on naturally occurring sugars in fruit because increased fruit intake is encouraged. This emphasis suited many juice manufacturers just fine. The Juice Products Association wrote in July 2010 "to reinforce the many positive benefits that consumption of 100 percent fruit juice contributes to the diets of Americans" (Juice Products Association, 2010).

However, cranberry juice manufacturers disagreed, because cranberry juice nearly always includes added sugars to offset the natural acidity of the product. Ocean Spray Cranberries, Inc., wrote "that the focus for consumers should be on total sugar consumption. . . . Placing the focus on added sugar, as opposed to total sugar, puts the cranberry at a disadvantage compared to other naturally sweet fruits" (Ocean Spray Cranberries, Inc., 2010).

The American Beverage Association (ABA), whose members include major sweetened beverage companies, even more completely exonerated added sugars and criticized other nutrients instead:

> ABA believes the report's focus on added sugars from beverages is misplaced since added sugars themselves are not uniquely associated with higher energy intake or obesity, have played only a minor role in increased Calorie consumption patterns over time (unlike added fats and oils and flour and cereal products), and are not directly associated with negative health effects (unlike solid fats, cholesterol, sodium and alcohol). (American Beverage Association, 2010).

Of course, many comments from other industry associations disputed whether solid fats, cholesterol, sodium and alcohol are really so bad.

Promoting Fruits and Vegetables

The Dietary Guidelines Advisory Committee report recommended increased intake of fruits and vegetables. The fresh produce industry wanted the guidelines more explicitly to favor fresh rather than processed fruits and vegetables. The United Fresh Produce Association wrote in July 2010 to support "increased access to more fresh fruits and vegetables, for all Americans."

By contrast, the Grocery Manufacturers Association (GMA), which represents leading processed food manufacturers (see Chapter 5), advised against emphasizing fresh produce and preparation from scratch, which "may be unrealistic and unachievable for many Americans." Instead, GMA favored "positive and non-judgmental total diet recommendations that encourage incremental changes that will help Americans build healthier diets" (Grocery Manufacturers Association, 2010).

8.4.5 Translating Dietary Guidance for the Public

For the general public, the federal government seeks to communicate principles of dietary guidance through high-profile graphics such as MyPyramid and, more recently, MyPlate (Figure 8.3). At a more individual level, the government also seeks to reach interested individual consumers through federal nutrition education programs.

Balancing Calories

* Enjoy your food, but eat less.
* Avoid oversized portions.

Foods to Increase

* Make half your plate fruits and vegetables.
* Make at least half your grains whole grains.
* Switch to fat-free or low-fat (1 percent) milk.

Foods to Reduce

* Compare sodium in foods like soup, bread and frozen meals—and choose the foods with lower numbers.
* Drink water instead of sugary drinks.

Figure 8.3 USDA's MyPlate graphic and selected messages for consumers (2011)

USDA's dietary guidance graphics are inevitably controversial. To communicate to a broad public, with diverse educational backgrounds and levels of literacy, the graphic must pare down the essence of the *Dietary Guidelines* into a simple image and very brief accompanying text. This distillation means that the final product reflects the judgment of nutrition educators and not just hard scientific evidence alone.

When USDA released the first Food Guide Pyramid in the early 1990s, it provoked sharp opposition from meat producers, who objected to the meat group's comparatively small role in the graphical portrayal of a balanced diet (Nestle, 2003). In 2005, the Food Guide Pyramid was replaced by MyPyramid. Because the main version of the graphic no longer included food images within sections of the MyPyramid, it became more difficult to discern the broad food groups from which one should consume more or less in order to achieve the recommended diet. In 2011, USDA replaced the pyramid shape with the MyPlate graphic (Figure 8.3), using a plate image. An accompanying website (www.choosemyplate.gov) provides more detail about tailoring food choices to individual nutrition needs and choosing healthy foods on a budget.

The MyPlate graphic returns to the first Food Guide Pyramid's more explicit message of proportionality. Fruits and vegetables make up half of the plate. The protein group, relegated to one quarter of the plate, encompasses meat, poultry, fish, eggs and legumes. Dairy is depicted by a glass of milk. Selected messages for consumers, in the accompanying text, advise reasonable portion sizes, promote whole grains and low-fat milk and recommend alternatives to high-sodium processed foods and high-sugar beverages.

8.5 Comparing Current Consumption to Guidelines

Federal dietary guidance recognizes that there are many ways to seek a healthy diet. The official report provides estimates of usual food intake for adults (adjusted to a 2,000-calorie level). For example, compared to the **USDA Food Pattern**, the 2010 *Dietary Guidelines* report showed that Americans' usual food intake includes far too much of solid fats and added sugars, a little too much of meat and far too little of vegetable oils, vegetables, beans and peas, dairy and fruit (Figure 8.4).

These excesses and shortfalls may provoke the question: what changes in U.S. agricultural trade and production would be required if consumers started to follow the *Dietary Guidelines* more closely? A decrease in consumption of meat and solid fats would free up substantial resources in meat production and animal feed production, making these resources available for producing other crops. Similarly, a decrease in consumption of added sugars could induce reduced sugar imports or reduced domestic corn sweetener production. By contrast, an increase in fruit and vegetable consumption would require some combination of increased imports and increased domestic production. USDA researchers estimated in 2006 that meeting the fruit recommendation through domestic production alone would require an additional 4.1 million acres for fruit production (compared to production in the 2000s on 3.5 million acres). Meeting the vegetable recommendation would require an additional 8.9 million acres for vegetable production (compared to production in the 2000s on 6.5 million acres) (Buzby et al., 2006). In total, these changes in fruit and vegetable production would require a reallocation of just 1.7 percent of U.S. agricultural land. The reallocation would be even smaller if part of the increased demand for fruits and vegetables were supplied by imports.

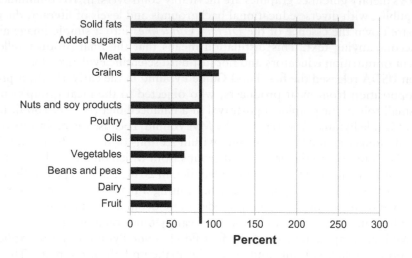

Figure 8.4 Eating pattern comparison: usual U.S. intake for adults (adjusted to a 2,000-calorie level) as a percentage of the corresponding recommendation in the USDA Food Pattern

Source: *Dietary Guidelines for Americans, 2010.*

How could such a reallocation of resources be coordinated? It would be folly to imagine a government commission reassigning land in this manner. Instead, as consumer preferences shifted in the direction of the *Dietary Guidelines*, the increased demand for some foods and reduced demand for others would induce price adjustments that would motivate the necessary changes in both U.S. production and international agricultural trade. In particular, it would be essential for fruit and vegetable prices to increase. Although such changes cannot happen in a single year, the U.S. food and agricultural economy has demonstrated its capacity for such changes within a span of several years. To take one recent example, biofuels mandates and higher petroleum prices raised the market price of corn (maize), motivating a dramatic reallocation of U.S. corn land and production resources from food uses to biofuels in less than a decade (Chapter 3). The changes required to achieve the *Dietary Guidelines* would be smaller. Although such a change in consumer demand is entirely hypothetical at this point, there is no long-term production barrier standing in the way.

8.6 Policy Instruments

Proposals to reconcile food consumption with the *Dietary Guidelines* intersect with a wide range of U.S. food policy topics covered throughout this book. Some have proposed that farm policy should be redesigned to promote fruits and vegetables in place of commodity crops, but we noted earlier that the effects of U.S. farm programs are commonly misunderstood in such proposals (Chapter 2). Likewise, some have proposed that nutrition assistance programs should be reformed to promote healthier food, but it is helpful also to understand the multiple anti-hunger and nutrition objectives of these programs (Chapters 10 and 11). This section explores two types of more direct policy instruments to guide consumers toward healthful food choices: (1) taxes and subsidies and (2) nudges and behavioral economics.

8.6.1 Taxes and Subsidies

Consumer choices are strongly influenced by economic variables, especially income and prices. Some public health advocates, researchers and policy-makers suggest that the government should tax less healthy foods and beverages and subsidize their more healthy counterparts. The success of such policy instruments depends on the size of the consumer response to a change in the price of food.

These consumer responses are expressed in terms of elasticities. Recall from Chapter 2 that a price elasticity shows the percentage change in a product's quantity consumed in response to a 1 percent increase in a price. The own-price elasticity shows the demand response to a change in the good's own price. A cross-price elasticity shows the demand response to a change in the price of a substitute or complement. The income elasticity shows the demand response to a change in income.

Is it better to tax a food that has a large price elasticity or a small one? Perhaps surprisingly, the answer is not obvious, but depends on a tradeoff between economic efficiency and health impact.

- Economists who study taxation policy tend to prefer that taxes be placed on goods whose demand is inelastic (not responsive to a change in price), because these taxes do not distort the market equilibrium as much (Deaton, 1997). Also, a tax on a good whose demand is inelastic raises more revenue.
- By contrast, health policy advocates tend to prefer that taxes be placed on unhealthy foods whose demand is elastic (responsive to a change in prices), because these taxes have the biggest impact on food choices. It is true that such taxes raise less revenue, because the tax itself reduces the volume of sales on which the tax can be collected, but health policy advocates may be more interested in the consumer response than in revenue generation.

Some proposals seek the best of both worlds by taxing an unhealthy food and earmarking the resulting revenue for health promotion programs. Thus, if the demand turns out to be elastic, one could say, "Good, this policy will reduce consumption of an unhealthy product." And if the demand turns out to be inelastic, one could say, "Good, this tax is economically efficient, avoids market distortion and raises plenty of revenue for the health promotion program."

It is useful to learn to read tables of elasticity estimates to understand own-price and cross-price effects. For example, USDA economists considered a tax on caloric sweetened beverages and found the estimated response to be surprisingly elastic (Smith et al., 2010) (Table 8.4). This research helps in assessing a policy proposal from the former director of the Centers for Disease Control and Prevention, Thomas Frieden, and two CDC colleagues: "A tax of 1 cent an ounce on sugar-sweetened beverages—about a 10 percent price increase on a 12-ounce can—would be likely to be the single most effective measure to reverse the obesity epidemic" (Frieden et al., 2010). Such a table shows two types of results:

- The first important result is that a 1 percent increase in the price of caloric sweetened beverages would lead to a 1.26 percent decrease in the quantity consumed

Table 8.4 Elasticities show how beverage quantities respond to changes in prices and total beverage spending

Outcome (% change)	In response to a 1% change in . . .				
	Price of caloric sweetened beverages	Price of diet beverages	Price of juices	Price of bottled water	Total beverage spending
Caloric sweet'd beverages	**–1.26**	–0.19	0.23	0.13	1.05
Diet beverages	–0.46	**–0.75**	0.10	–0.04	1.24
Juices	0.56	0.16	**–1.01**	–0.09	0.88
Bottled water	0.75	–0.09	–0.26	**–0.97**	1.03

Note: Own-price elasticities are in bold.

Source: adapted from Smith et al. (2010), Appendix Table 4.

(top left cell of Table 8.4, in bold). If one assumes that this price effect stays constant even for larger price changes, the 10 percent sales tax proposed by Frieden and colleagues would lead to a dramatic 12.6 percent decrease in soda consumption.

* The second important result in the table is the cross-price effects, showing how the price change in caloric sweetened beverages affects consumption of other beverages. These cross-price effects shed light on the possible concern that a soda tax would encourage people to shift their consumption to juice, which naturally also has sugar. The study did find that a 1 percent increase in the price of soda leads to a 0.56 percent increase in the quantity of juices, but this increase was not nearly enough to offset the beneficial effect from reduced consumption of caloric sweetened beverages.

Overall, the USDA researchers concluded that the tax could have a large benefit for average body weight in the population.

Nutrition taxes face several sources of opposition. First, they generally are regressive; that is, they have a higher relative budget impact for low-income populations than for higher-income populations. Second, as noted throughout the chapter, there may be disputes over the nutrition science basis for singling out particular foods, although one possible exception with comparatively broad scientific support is a tax on caloric sweetened beverages. Third, political support is fragile, because taxes are unpopular.

Despite the challenges, policy-makers' interest in sugar-sweetened beverage (SSB) taxes has been growing at the local level. The city of Berkeley, CA, implemented a 1 penny-per-ounce excise tax on SSB purchases in March, 2015. Researchers compared changes over time, from before implementation to after implementation, in Berkeley and in nearby comparison cities (Oakland and San Francisco). They found that consumption of SSBs fell by 21 percent in Berkeley, while increasing in Oakland and San Francisco. To make sure they had not just picked up an unrelated or coincidental trend in beverage consumption in Oakland, they also measured water consumption, finding a larger increase for Berkeley than for the comparison cities. The results suggested that the tax quite strongly influenced beverage consumption in a healthful direction (Falbe et al., 2016).

The following year, in 2016, SSB taxes were passed in San Francisco, Oakland, Boulder, Chicago and elsewhere. In the journal *Food Policy*, political scientist Robert Paarlberg and colleagues noted some patterns in the jurisdictions where beverage tax proposals were successful. They found that such proposals were more likely to pass if the municipal leadership was Democratic and if there was external financial support for pro-tax advocates. They also suggested that public health arguments in favor of the tax did better for ballot initiatives, while budget revenue arguments for the tax did better for city council votes (Paarlberg, Mozaffarian and Micha, 2017). Although the U.S. Congress has shown little interest so far in a national tax, such proposals may spread further at the municipal level.

8.6.2 Nudges and Behavioral Economics

Some policy innovators are exploring gentler options for "nudging" consumers toward more healthful choices. These proposals draw insight from both psychology and economics. A key insight is that consumers may not always adhere to the assumptions of rational choice but instead may use **heuristics**, or rules of thumb, to make decisions.

For example, at an all-you-can-eat pizza restaurant, the traditional economic assumptions suggest that rational consumers will base their decision about how much to eat on marginal costs (the free cost of an additional slice) rather than fixed costs (the price of admission for the meal). By contrast, new behavioral economics research finds that the price of admission is surprisingly influential. The authors hypothesized that consumers may be following a heuristic that they should eat enough to get their money's worth (Just and Wansink, 2011).

Various heuristics of this type have been proposed as explanations for consumer decisions about food (Just et al., 2007):

- Consumers may be strongly influenced by default offerings, even when given the opportunity to select a different option. For example, it may make a difference whether a children's meal from a quick-service restaurant chain includes milk or soda as the default option for customers who do not volunteer a preference.
- Consumers may be affected by distractions because of the cognitive burden of making healthful choices. One study found that subjects were more likely to choose cake over fruit salad if they were required to make other decisions at the same time (Just et al., 2007). Similarly, people may make less-healthful decisions when hungry or under time stress.

Policy-makers might exploit these heuristics to influence consumer choices. Perhaps students in school meals programs would make better decisions if the location of the salad bar were altered or if a different tender (cash or school meals program card) were required for different products. On the other hand, one must recognize that "nudges" do not come free. For example, some proponents of behavioral economics might doubt the effectiveness of food service decisions to limit the sale of ice cream;

instead, they may hope it is sufficient to alter the location of the ice cream freezer so that this dessert is chosen less frequently. Yet for a school food service director who must balance a budget, it makes little difference if a certain loss of ice cream revenue comes from limiting sales to certain days of the week or from relocating the ice cream freezer. In either case, there is no magic wand that generates large public health improvements for small economic costs. It remains to be seen whether the potential for "nudges" turns out to be a comparatively small niche opportunity or a major new tool in social policy.

8.7 Conclusion

Using scientific evidence in nutrition policy involves two important steps. For any particular claim about diet and health, one must (1) characterize the strength of scientific evidence for the claim and (2) decide what strength of evidence is appropriate for a proposed policy application. Commonly, scientists and public health experts address the first step precisely but are not explicit about the second step.

Strength of evidence can be described on a spectrum. At one end of the spectrum, weak evidence can be found for myriad scientific statements about diet and health, many of which are mutually contradictory. At the other end of the spectrum, very few claims about diet and health enjoy evidence sufficiently strong to be described as certain proof. For most statements that matter for nutrition policy, the strength of evidence falls in between.

Wise nutrition policy depends on assigning the burden of proof as well as possible, balancing the risk of harm from two types of error. Drawing an analogy from statistics, one could say Type I error happens when an ineffective policy is mistakenly adopted by policy-makers. Type II error happens when an effective policy is mistakenly rejected by policy-makers as insufficiently promising. In policy arguments, opponents of a policy will attempt to shift the burden of proof onto the policy's supporters, calling on them to offer strong evidence that their supporting claims are true. Conversely, supporters of a policy will attempt to shift the burden of proof onto opponents, calling on the opponents to offer strong evidence that the claims are false.

For dietary guidance, a midlevel burden of proof seems appropriate. Consumer-oriented guidance should be based on the balance of the scientific evidence, even though this evidence may be revised in the future. Consumers remain free to believe or disbelieve this dietary guidance, and they are free to choose their own preferred diet. For other policy purposes, the burden of proof on a policy's supporters is much higher. When the federal government intervenes directly to raise market prices (discussed in Section 8.6) or to regulate diet/health claims in food labeling and advertising (discussed in Chapter 9), an error in the government's scientific judgment would be costly and disruptive.

Food choices have major consequences for the food economy and for public health. It is natural for the government to take great interest in the nutrition science basis for dietary guidance. Food choices also are intensely personal, and the United States is divided by profound regional and cultural differences in food preferences and practices. Policy-makers face a difficult challenge in responding to the most important public health issues of the day while at the same time avoiding the hazards of policy overreach.

Summary List of Key Terms (identified in bold in the text)

- Body Mass Index
- cross-sectional designs
- experimental designs
- filtering
- health equity

- heuristics
- prospective cohort designs
- representativeness
- response rate
- USDA Food Pattern

9 Food Labeling and Advertising

9.1 Introduction

Food labeling and advertising can provide valuable information for consumers, but they also can serve up a loud muddle of false, misleading and true-but-trivial marketing claims. The challenge for consumers is to distinguish the informative signal from the noise. The challenge for policy-makers is to strengthen the signal-to-noise ratio.

To organize the discussion of these issues, food safety and advertising policies may be classified on a spectrum (Figure 9.1). Some information provision is mandatory; some marketing claims are voluntary and weakly regulated; some marketing claims are strongly regulated; and some claims are prohibited outright. Drawing on examples from across this spectrum, this chapter:

- introduces economic principles for analyzing food and nutrition information policy (Section 9.2);
- introduces legal principles for the regulation of commercial speech (Section 9.3);
- considers the merits of mandatory information provision through the Nutrition Facts Panel and menu labeling in restaurants (Section 9.4);
- sorts through the tangle of U.S. rules covering health claims in food labeling and advertising (Section 9.5);
- reviews the policy dilemma surrounding food and beverage advertising targeting children (Section 9.6); and
- describes the federal government's generic commodity advertising or "checkoff" programs (Section 9.7).

9.2 Economics of Food Labeling and Advertising

In the economics of food labeling, as in food safety (Chapter 7) and dietary guidance (Chapter 8), the performance of private-sector markets varies with the quality of information that these markets provide to consumers. The public policy prescription that best addresses a particular concern about food labeling or advertising depends in part on the nature of the information failure in private-sector markets. In both theory and practice, there are a variety of public- and private-sector approaches to information disclosure, each of which has strengths and weaknesses in particular applications.

Consumers can get information about food product attributes in several different ways (Caswell and Mojduszka, 1996):

- For **search attributes**, the consumer can determine a product's quality by visual inspection in the store. There is little need for government regulation to encourage disclosure.

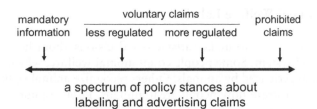

Figure 9.1 A spectrum of food labeling and advertising policy stances, ranging from mandatory information to prohibition against false and misleading claims

- For **experience attributes**, the consumer can determine a product's quality after purchasing it, learning lessons that can be used in future purchases. An example of an experience attribute is a product's taste. For products that are purchased repeatedly, such as grocery products, there is again not much need for government regulation.
- For **credence attributes**, the consumer cannot confirm a product's quality and must trust the information provided by the seller, by the government or by a third party.

A single good may have some attributes that fall into one category and other attributes that fall into a different category.

Government may have an important role in claims about credence attributes, such as organic production (Chapter 3), country of origin (Chapter 4), nutrition and health qualities (Chapter 8) or humane treatment of animals (Box 9.1). False and misleading claims about credence attributes may fool consumers. To make things worse, false and misleading claims may crowd out true information as consumers become jaded and skeptical. As a USDA report on the economics of food labeling observed, "Widespread deception makes consumers less responsive to messages, even those that provide truthful information" (Golan et al., 2001).

However, even for credence attributes, markets could in theory function well on their own. Some manufactured food products carried Nutrition Facts Panels voluntarily even before these panels became mandatory in the 1990 Nutrition Labeling and Education Act (NLEA). One might at first suspect that only the healthiest products would provide nutrition information, but competitive pressure may in principle force a wider range of products to disclose such information (Ippolito, 1999).

The economic theory that explains competitive incentives for disclosure is sometimes called the **unfolding theory**. Suppose that, in the absence of government regulation, four food companies offer four snack food products with, respectively, 5 percent, 10 percent, 20 percent and 40 percent of the daily reference value for sodium. The first snack food company has a strong incentive to voluntarily disclose that its product "contains only 5 percent of the daily maximum for sodium." The manager of the second company may think, "The consumer already can guess that my product has more than 5 percent of the maximum for sodium, so it would be better to disclose my 10 percent level than to have the consumer think the sodium level is higher." Once the second company discloses, a manager at the third company may decide to disclose, following the same logic. In this theory, only the worst product might remain unlabeled, and the consumer could be well informed even without mandatory disclosure.

Box 9.1   Animal Welfare Labels

It is difficult for society to make satisfactory decisions about how to treat animals in the food system. Some people count **animal welfare**, which is the happiness and pain experienced by animals. Others recognize **animal rights**, which are principles that constrain how people treat animals. Public opinion—at least the human public's opinion—is divided.

One leading policy approach is voluntary labels. However, existing labels are confusing. Few consumers likely understand the distinctions between a certified label with strict rules and on-farm inspections (such as "Animal Welfare Improved" or "Global Animal Partnership, Step 5") and a more permissive label that allows continuous confinement in crowded cages (such as "United Egg Producers Certified") (Consumer Reports Greener Choices, 2017). Consumers may overestimate how much animal welfare is protected by labels that are mostly about other production qualities (such as "Certified Organic" or "Grassfed") or whose definitions have nothing to do with animal welfare (such as "Natural"). Moreover, there may be a more fundamental conceptual problem with using voluntary labels to address animal welfare concerns (Lusk, 2011). Consider three groups of consumers with different views about meat: (1) regular carnivores, (2) compassionate carnivores and (3) vegetarians/vegans. Groups (1) and (2) purchase and consume meat. Groups (2) and (3) care about animal welfare. Even if voluntary animal labels were clear and meaningful, the only group likely to be influenced by them is (2) compassionate carnivores. This middle group may be too small to motivate major changes to industry production methods.

There have been many efforts to use policy levers more directly. In 2008, California voters approved a policy to regulate confinement practices for various farm animals, including egg-laying hens. With deep divisions between the United Egg Producers (UEP) on the one hand and the Humane Society of the United States (HSUS) on the other, many observers expected a long and bitter public disagreement. Instead, as the Congressional Research Service explained, "In July 2011, the animal agriculture community was stunned when the UEP and HSUS announced that they had agreed to work together to push for federal legislation to regulate how U.S. table eggs are produced" (Greene and Cowan, 2012). After a phase-in period, all producers would use enhanced cages allowing more space for movement and follow stricter definitions for animal welfare terms on food labels. Yet despite having support from the American Veterinary Medical Association (AVMA) and sponsors from both parties in the House and Senate, the bill never passed.

In the 2016 election, Massachusetts voters approved a ballot measure that prohibited the sale of pigs, calves and hens that are confined to the extent that they cannot turn around, extend their limbs or lie down in their pen. Scheduled for implementation in 2020, the measure covers not just Massachusetts producers but applies to food produced in other states. The initiative will trigger major national food policy arguments in both the courts and the U.S. Congress about federalism and the power of states to regulate interstate trade.

In practice, such incentives are only partly effective. For example, while some food manufacturers disclosed nutrition facts earlier, many other manufacturers began to provide Nutrition Facts Panels only after they became mandatory in the 1990 NLEA. Consumers are not always sufficiently well informed to notice and interpret the absence of certain information disclosures, as the unfolding theory requires.

The pressure for voluntary disclosure would be more intense if food manufacturers vigorously criticized each other through comparative advertising. For example, in 2008, Campbell's Soup released an advertisement for its health-oriented "Select Harvest" line of canned soups, with reduced amounts of monosodium glutamate (MSG), a flavor enhancer. The advertisement noted that a competing brand, Progresso Soup, contained MSG. In response, Progresso released a counterattack reminding consumers that many other Campbell's Soups (presumably not part of the Select Harvest line) also contained MSG. This type of negative advertising is quite rare and may do companies more harm than good. For companies with a large portfolio of food brands with diverse health profiles, the market incentive for comparative advertising may be quite weak.

Even when companies do not voluntarily provide consumers with complete information, there may be other public- and private-sector sources of information. The for-profit media frequently cover food issues, describing recent research in nutrition science and food safety. Private not-for-profit organizations also can serve as independent watchdogs. The Center for Science in the Public Interest (CSPI) reaches 900,000 member/subscribers with its *Nutrition Action Healthletter*, which warmly praises or tartly criticizes the nutrition qualities of new food product introductions. Not-for-profit organizations or for-profit businesses may offer **third-party certification** of nutrition labeling claims made by food companies (Caswell and Anders, 2011). For example, in return for a fee paid by food companies, the American Heart Association (AHA) allows food manufacturers to label products with an AHA heart-check symbol if they meet the association's standards.

To summarize, economic analysis suggests an important role for both government policy and private-sector incentives to provide consumers with sound information about food and beverage products. The traditional economic perspective does not rule out government regulation, but it does pose some questions about how well a proposed government policy compares to market-based alternatives:

- How well would private-sector markets provide information to the consumer in the absence of government intervention?
- Is a proposed government intervention well matched to the nature of the information failure?
- Taking into account the strengths and shortcomings both of private-sector markets and government agencies, will the proposed policy be better than the alternative of not intervening?

9.3 Legal Principles

Food labeling is regulated by FDA and USDA's FSIS. Advertising is regulated principally by three other institutions. First, FTC has a lead role in overseeing food advertising. Second, the Federal Communications Commission (FCC) shares in oversight responsibilities for broadcast media, such as radio and television. Third, the National

Advertising Division (NAD) of the Council of Better Business Bureaus (BBB) is the advertising industry's own self-regulatory initiative.

Laws constrain the federal government's ability to regulate food labeling and advertising. The First Amendment to the U.S. Constitution prevents Congress from abridging freedom of speech. For most of the twentieth century, this freedom was thought to apply to **political speech** but not necessarily to **commercial speech** such as food labeling and advertising. Beginning in the 1970s, courts began to interpret the First Amendment more broadly to provide some protections for commercial speech. For example, in the mid-2000s, as FTC discussed policies regarding food advertising to children, an agency workshop report dismissed the possibility of government restrictions: "[T]ailoring such restrictions to conform to First Amendment constraints could present significant challenges" (Federal Trade Commission and Department of Health and Human Services, 2006).

First Amendment concerns place limits on the government's decisions about whether to prohibit certain types of marketing (see Figure 9.1, right side). However, these constitutional constraints should not be exaggerated. The courts do permit the government to restrict speech for products that are illegal. This means there is no First Amendment right to advertise alcohol to children, for example. Moreover, the courts permit the government to restrict speech that is outright false or misleading. So there is no First Amendment right to lie to customers.

In particular, it is clearly permitted for the government to ban commercial speech that is **inherently misleading**, in a sense that can be proven. It is more difficult for the government to prohibit speech that is merely **potentially misleading**. Examples arise frequently in U.S. food policy where a marketer seeks to make a claim that has some evidence for support, but the evidence is not very strong. In 1976, the Supreme Court ruled in *Virginia State Board of Pharmacy v. Virginia Citizens Council* that the government may require additional warnings or disclaimers in such cases, but the court interpreted the First Amendment to hinder the government from banning "potentially misleading" marketing outright (Pomeranz, 2016).

To decide more difficult cases about restricting commercial speech that is truthful, an influential doctrine used by the Supreme Court is called the **Central Hudson test**, which takes its name from the 1980 Supreme Court decision in *Central Hudson Gas & Electric Corp. v. Public Service Commission*. According to this standard, the government is permitted to restrict commercial speech if the restriction passes the four "prongs" of the test:

- As noted previously, a restriction is permitted if the product is unlawful or the claims are deceptive (prong 1).
- If the product is legal and the claims are not deceptive, restrictions are permitted if they meet all three of the following criteria:

  - they advance a governmental interest (prong 2),
  - the governmental interest is substantial (prong 3) and
  - the restrictions are no more extensive than necessary to serve that governmental interest (prong 4).

The current legal frontier is defining exactly how rigorously the government must prove that a proposed restriction is "no more extensive than necessary." Supporters of a laissez-faire (free-market) approach to food marketing describe the Central Hudson test as a strict restraint on the types of regulations the government may impose. Supporters of a more activist government role suggest instead that the Central Hudson test can be treated "not as an elaborate ruse for the erection of uncrossable barriers to the regulation of commercial speech, but as a template for carefully reviewing the rationale and appropriateness of commercial speech regulations" (Parmet and Smith, 2006).

The First Amendment protections for commercial speech have been strengthened over the course of several legal decisions in recent years, although they remain less stringent than the constitutional protections for political speech (Institute of Medicine, 2006). The Supreme Court has struck down government attempts to regulate truthful advertising because the regulations failed to meet the last standard of the Central Hudson test (Pomeranz, 2016). The courts have permitted restrictions on commercial speech that is misleading, but they have made it difficult for the government to restrict commercial speech on other public interest grounds.

To summarize, First Amendment scrutiny raises a series of legal questions that can be answered well by some, but not all, proposed policy responses to public health nutrition concerns. In this sense, the legal principles in this section are similar to the economic principles described earlier in Section 9.2, which ends with a series of economic questions that a proposed policy may be expected to answer.

9.4 Mandatory Labeling

Some food policy debates address potential policies to compel certain types of information disclosure (see Figure 9.1, left side). Until the start of the twentieth century, food labeling was voluntary and nearly unregulated. Beginning with the Federal Pure Food and Drugs Act of 1906 (Table 9.1), requirements were added over the years for labeling features that Americans now take for granted, including formal standards of identity that define the names of foods used on food labels, the net weight statement for a package's contents, the manufacturer's name and address and the ingredients list.

The Nutrition Facts Panel is more recent. From the 1970s until the early 1990s, a Nutrition Facts Panel was voluntary except for foods with certain types of fortification or nutrient content claims. The 1990 NLEA made the Nutrition Facts Panel mandatory on nearly all packaged manufactured foods. In the most notable overhaul of the panel for many years, FDA in 2016 published a final rule making several changes designed to make the label easier to read, give greater emphasis to information related to maintaining a healthy weight and provide new information about added sugars. In 2017, the incoming Trump administration postponed implementation of the new rule, noting concerns about the added sugars requirement in particular.

The Nutrition Facts Panel (Figure 9.2) has the sober demeanor of a data table in an academic journal. The word "Facts" in the panel's title stakes its claim to impartiality. Yet every square centimeter of this panel carries some policy significance, frequently reflecting the long history of controversy and policy argument:

1. The serving size is, in principle, based on the **Reference Amount Customarily Consumed (RACC)**, an official estimate based on nationally representative survey data. Serving size determination is complex. For a single serving container,

Table 9.1 Selected milestones in food labeling law, 1906–2010

Date	Law, regulation or court decision
1906	The Federal Pure Food and Drugs Act outlawed interstate trade in adulterated and misbranded foods. Courts later ruled that a misleading or deceptive claim may be prohibited even if technically true.
1938	The Federal Food, Drug and Cosmetic Act required the label of packaged manufactured foods to contain the manufacturer's name and address and the product's name, net weight and (in some cases) the list of ingredients.
1957	The Poultry Products Inspection Act applied food labeling rules to poultry products under USDA jurisdiction.
1967	The Fair Packaging and Labeling Act expanded requirements for labeling of contents, weight and name of foods.
1973	FDA issued regulations requiring mandatory nutrition facts for manufactured foods containing added nutrients and health claims.
1990	The Organic Food Production Act defined what foods may carry the "organic" label.
1990	The Nutrition Labeling and Education Act established a mandatory Nutrition Facts Panel for most manufactured foods under FDA jurisdiction and formally defined many nutrient content claims and health claims (USDA regulations applied similar rules to meat and poultry products under USDA jurisdiction).
1994	The Dietary Supplement Health and Education Act relaxed requirements for dietary supplements, making the manufacturer responsible for determining that labeling claims are true and not misleading, with no prior approval from FDA. In practice, this law is applied to foods as well as supplements.
1997	The Food and Drug Administration Modernization Act made it easier for manufacturers to use health claims that have significant scientific agreement.
2001	The Supreme Court ruled in *Pearson v. Shalala* that FDA must allow supplement health claims with merely partial evidence if the label carries an appropriate disclaimer (FDA applied the new more relaxed rules to foods as well).
2002	The 2002 Farm Bill required country-of-origin labeling (COOL) for many food products. Some regulations were delayed until after the 2008 Farm Bill.
2004	The Food Allergen Labeling and Consumer Protection Act required labeling of foods that contain certain allergens.
2006	FDA added *trans* fats to the list of nutrients required on the Nutrition Facts Panel.
2010	The Patient Protection and Affordable Health Care Act required calorie labeling for restaurants with 20 or more outlets.
2016	FDA publishes a final rule, for the first time requiring "added sugars" disclosure, and makes several other changes to the Nutrition Facts Panel. In 2017, implementation of the changes is postponed.

Source: Golan et al. (2001); Food and Drug Administration (2009, 2017).

the Nutrition Facts Panel must reflect the contents of the whole container. For many other foods and beverages, consumers may choose actual serving sizes that differ greatly from the RACC. For many years, consumer organizations noted that the reference amounts commonly understated the amounts that consumers typically eat (Center for Science in the Public Interest, 2011), so FDA updated these reference amounts for many food categories as part of the 2016 rule.

2. Because of the high level of policy concern about overweight and obesity, the most prominent nutrition number is food energy (calories). Of course, the calories per serving vary systematically with the serving size. Daily food energy intake is closely related to risk of overweight and obesity, but that does not necessarily mean most consumers can track calories over time using the

Nutrition Facts	
Serving Size 2/3 cup (55g)	
Servings Per Container About 8	

Amount Per Serving	
Calories 230	Calories from Fat 72

	% Daily Value*
Total Fat 8g	**12%**
Saturated Fat 1g	**5%**
Trans Fat 0g	
Cholesterol 0mg	**0%**
Sodium 160mg	**7%**
Total Carbohydrate 37g	**12%**
Dietary Fiber 4g	**16%**
Sugars 1g	
Protein 3g	

Vitamin A	10%
Vitamin C	8%
Calcium	20%
Iron	45%

* Percent Daily Values are based on a 2,000 calorie diet. Your daily value may be higher or lower depending on your calorie needs.

	Calories:	2,000	2,500
Total Fat	Less than	65g	80g
Sat Fat	Less than	20g	25g
Cholesterol	Less than	300mg	300mg
Sodium	Less than	2,400mg	2,400mg
Total Carbohydrate		300g	375g
Dietary Fiber		25g	30g

Nutrition Facts	
8 servings per container	
Serving size	**2/3 cup (55g)**

Amount per serving	
Calories	**230**

	% Daily Value*
Total Fat 8g	**10%**
Saturated Fat 1g	**5%**
Trans Fat 0g	
Cholesterol 0mg	**0%**
Sodium 160mg	**7%**
Total Carbohydrate 37g	**13%**
Dietary Fiber 4g	**14%**
Total Sugars 12g	
Includes 10g Added Sugars	**20%**
Protein 3g	

Vitamin D 2mcg	10%
Calcium 260mg	20%
Iron 8mg	45%
Potassium 235mg	6%

* The % Daily Value (DV) tells you how much a nutrient in a serving of food contributes to a daily diet. 2,000 calories a day is used for general nutrition advice.

Figure 9.2 FDA illustration describing 2016 changes to the Nutrition Facts Panel for a hypothetical packaged food product

Source: Based on Food and Drug Administration (2017).

Nutrition Facts Panel. In the 2016 rule, the FDA made the calorie information more prominent.

3. In recent years, dietary guidance about fat has evolved (see Chapter 8). While older guidance emphasized both total fats and saturated fats, more recent guidance focuses specifically on limiting solid fats (including saturated fats and *trans* fats). The Nutrition Facts Panel includes both total fat and saturated fat in a section that may be interpreted as nutrients to limit.

4. The Nutrition Facts Panel still has a significant section encouraging consumers to get enough of nutrients such as Vitamin D, calcium, iron and potassium, even though specific micronutrient deficiencies are no longer a principal focus of federal dietary guidance for most consumers.

5. The recommended level for some food components varies systematically with a person's total energy needs. An adult male who exercises five times per week might need 2,500 calories per day, while an adult female who exercises three times per week might need only 2,000 calories per day. When the regulations to

implement NLEA were being written in the early 1990s, USDA suggested that the panel assume a 2,500 calorie diet, while DHHS recommended assuming a 2,000 calorie diet. The footnote to the current Nutrition Facts Panel contains a political compromise, showing both diets (Sims, 1998, p. 197). The corresponding footnote in the 2016 FDA rule has just the 2,000 calorie diet.

6. The percent Daily Value (DV) column shows how one serving's supply of a food component compares to recommended levels. The percent DV column assumes a 2,000 calorie diet. If the regulations had instead used the USDA assumption of a 2,500 calorie diet, the percent DV column would have made each serving appear to contain less of some components that are expressed in proportion to calories (i.e., fat, saturated fat, fiber and carbohydrates).

7. Most importantly, after years of debate, FDA's 2016 rule for the first time required disclosure of "added sugar" content, in keeping with changes in the focus of federal dietary guidance over the years.

Debates over the Nutrition Facts Panel are just one example of a policy choice between mandatory and voluntary labeling (Figure 9.1). Similar examples include the policy debates over mandatory country of origin labeling (Chapter 4) and over mandatory calorie labeling for chain restaurant menu boards (later in this chapter). The food industry seldom favors mandatory food labeling rules in principle but has sometimes agreed to such rules as part of a political compromise that offers the industry something of great value: national uniformity in regulation (see Box 9.1). For example, in the years preceding the 1990 NLEA, food manufacturers were concerned about increasingly activist regulation of food labeling by state governments in Texas, California and other states (Sims, 1998). Industry trade associations relaxed their opposition to some provisions in the final stages of Congressional debate in return for some compromises on the content of the rules plus federal preemption of state and local ordinances. This preemption was carefully worded to exclude labeling requirements related to food safety; so, for example, California is still allowed to have special mandatory warning labels for particular food chemicals that concern regulators in that state, but there is no variation in the Nutrition Facts Panel requirements across states (Pomeranz, 2016).

In practice, of course, consumers may simply overlook the Nutrition Facts Panel. USDA research found that about 62 percent of consumers reported sometimes or always using the Nutrition Facts Panel in 2005–2006, down just slightly from 65 percent a decade earlier (Todd and Variyam, 2008). Food and beverage manufacturers have been experimenting with a variety of **front-of-pack** labeling approaches, which would provide a smaller amount of key nutrition information in a more visible location on the package. These strategies hold some promise for increasing consumer awareness about nutrition content, but there is serious concern about potential misuse in marketing. Some existing voluntary front-of-pack systems give nutrition facts out of context, without providing a full picture of a product's healthfulness. The Institute of Medicine in 2011 recommended a new standard front-of-pack labeling system that is simple, clear and conveys meaning without relying on written information. The system would ignore less important food components and instead would focus especially on saturated and *trans* fats, sodium and sugar. The Institute of Medicine (IOM) advised FDA to test and implement this new system, replacing the alternatives currently being used (Institute of Medicine, 2011a). However, there have been no new requirements to make front-of-pack nutrition labeling mandatory.

9.5 Claims About Nutrients and Health

9.5.1 Claims on Food Labels

Manufacturers' health claims on food labels present another difficult policy conundrum. On the one hand, the government forbids false and misleading statements. On the other hand, the government allows most factual statements, which the consumer can confirm by reading the Nutrition Facts Panel. The problem is that many claims fall in between, neither surely true nor obviously false.

Consider a hypothetical cereal that is high in fiber and low in saturated fat. The manufacturer may consider the following label statements:

- "Eating this cereal prevents heart disease."
- "Eating this cereal daily as part of a complete breakfast may reduce your risk of heart disease."
- "The *Dietary Guidelines for Americans* suggest that a diet high in fiber and low in saturated fat may reduce your risk of heart disease."

The first claim is a misleading exaggeration for a product that is after all an ordinary food, not a miracle drug. The last claim correctly describes the mainstream scientific view in the *Dietary Guidelines*, but it is boring and technocratic. The middle claim would win the support of some, but not all, nutrition policy experts. Some would say that comparatively healthy products should be allowed to make strong claims in plain English in order to have a real impact on the healthfulness of American diets. Others would say that—even with the verb "may"—this middle claim overstates the scientific evidence. It is difficult to identify the exact point that divides a misleading claim from a true claim.

Because different responses to this conundrum have been attempted by different policy actors at different times, federal policy toward label claims about nutrients and health has become a tangle of conflicting rules. To navigate this tangle, one must learn to distinguish at least four types of statements that are found on food labels (Lytton, 2010; Pomeranz, 2016).

First, a **nutrient content claim** describes the level of a nutrient or food component (for example, "low fat" or "high in oat bran"). Under the NLEA, there are clear rules saying exactly what amount of a nutrient is the limit for making a nutrient content claim. There are also some rules forbidding true-but-misleading claims. For example, it is illegal to label a head of broccoli as "low fat," even though it really is low in fat, because all broccoli has this quality. As another example, if a high-fiber product also happens to be high in fat, then a "high-fiber" claim on the label must be accompanied by a disclaimer pointing out the fat content, so the consumer may correctly understand the health profile of the product as a whole. Such rules focused on total fat may be out of step with the current focus of the *Dietary Guidelines for Americans 2015–2020*, which emphasizes reductions in saturated fat but not necessarily total fat.

Second, a **health claim**—which may be called a *real* health claim to distinguish it from a *qualified* health claim, see next—connects a food product to a disease or health condition (for example, a statement ending with the words "may reduce the risk of heart disease"). The NLEA put FDA in the driver's seat, assigning the agency to review the evidence for health claims submitted by food companies. NLEA told FDA to approve only claims that have "significant scientific agreement," a fairly high standard. The 1997 Food and Drug Administration Modernization Act (FDAMA) made it easier for food manufacturers to use claims that reflected statements in the *Dietary Guidelines* or other highly authoritative documents as evidence of significant scientific agreement, even if the claims had not yet been approved by FDA.

Third, a **qualified health claim** is a claim that lacks significant scientific agreement. In a 2001 reversal of federal rules for health claims, the Supreme Court decided in *Pearson v. Shalala* that a supplement manufacturer should be allowed to make health claims that had some scientific evidence, even if there was not enough evidence to count as significant scientific agreement. In this decision, the Supreme Court argued that a blanket prohibition against claims that might be true was a violation of the right to free speech. As a consequence, FDA now must allow qualified health claims. Although the adjective "qualified" sounds similar to "well-qualified," really these health claims are backed by less strong evidence. For qualified health claims that pass FDA's review, the agency issues a "letter of enforcement discretion" to the manufacturer, acknowledging that the manufacturer may make the claim, so long as the package label includes an appropriate disclaimer. For example, after mentioning evidence of a health benefit, a disclaimer may say, "FDA has determined that this evidence is limited and not conclusive." These cumbersome rules are a byproduct of the tension between Congressional intent in the NLEA and the Supreme Court's vigorous defense of First Amendment rights for commercial speech. Research suggests that consumers are confused by qualified health claims, and manufacturers have not heavily used them (Hooker and Teratanavat, 2008; U.S. Government Accountability Office, 2011a).

Fourth, a **structure/function claim** connects a food product to the structure or function of the human body. For example, a claim that a dairy product "prevents osteoporosis" is a health claim, which must meet a high standard of evidence; a claim that the product "builds strong bones" is a structure/function claim, which the manufacturer is allowed to make even without FDA approval. Structure/function claims allow manufacturers to hint at health benefits. These claims were established by the Dietary Supplement Health and Education Act (DSHEA) of 1994, which partially repealed the earlier authority given to FDA by the 1990 NLEA. Despite its name, the DSHEA, in practice, guides federal policy for both supplements and foods. In principle, manufacturers are only supposed to use structure/function claims for which they have good evidence, but FDA lacks the authority to require manufacturers to supply the evidence that justifies the claims (U.S. Government Accountability Office, 2011a).

9.5.2 *Claims in Food Advertising*

In contrast with FDA's regulation of nutrient content claims and health claims on food labels, FTC's approach to claims in food advertising is more permissive in some respects. Congress gave different authority to FDA and FTC. In the NLEA,

Congress gave FDA responsibility (a) for ensuring that food labels are truthful and not misleading and (b) for using food labels to educate the public about nutrition and health. In the Federal Trade Commission Act, by contrast, Congress gave FTC authority only to ensure that advertising claims are truthful and not misleading. FTC has no education mandate. Following the implementation of the NLEA, FTC issued a policy statement to establish partial uniformity between FDA regulation of food labels and FTC regulation of food advertising. The statement says, for example, that FTC will follow FDA's lead in deciding what health claims are considered misleading. Yet, although FDA sometimes requires disclaimers that provide the full nutrition context for a nutrient content claim on a food label, FTC will not require anything comparable for food advertising. FTC considered these disclaimers to be an "educational" function, beyond the scope of FTC's authority to prevent false or misleading advertising.

FTC's enforcement effort tends to focus only on outrageously misleading claims, such as those sometimes found in nutrition supplement advertisements. For example, in August 2010, FTC announced a court order against Internet marketers of acai berry weight-loss pills and colon cleansers. The disputed advertising copy proclaimed, "WARNING! AcaiPure is fast weight loss that works. It was not created for those people who only want to lose a few measly pounds. USE WITH CAUTION! Major weight loss in short periods of time may occur." In addition to the advertising claims, FTC said the marketers had falsely claimed endorsements by trusted media figures such as Rachael Ray and Oprah Winfrey and had deceived customers using misleading online credit card billing options (Federal Trade Commission, 2010). Similarly, in 2015, FTC settled charges with "Nourish Life," whose ads for the "Speak" line of nutrition supplement ads included heart-wrenching testimonials from parents who said their autistic children started speaking after taking the supplement. The company agreed to pay $200,000 and to disclose its financial arrangements with endorsers.

For many less extreme cases of misleading advertising, FTC lacks the resources it would need to monitor the industry systematically. To a large extent, FTC relies on the advertising industry to regulate itself. NAD, the industry's self-regulatory body, reviews selected advertising campaigns, usually based on complaints by a competitor but sometimes at NAD's own initiative. Compared with FTC or FDA, NAD uses an easier-to-meet standard for evaluating the scientific evidence. NAD does not require evidence that has "significant scientific agreement" (as required for FDA health claims), nor does it require manufacturers to "consider all relevant research relating to the claimed benefit" (as FTC requires). If a company disagrees with a decision by NAD, compliance with the decision is voluntary. NAD has no enforcement authority, but may refer the case to FTC for consideration.

While defending their advertising in cases before FTC and NAD, companies frequently argue that a particular claim is **puffery**, which is a legal term for exaggerated advertising copy (see Box 9.2). In reading NAD case reports (www.narcpartners. org), it might seem strange that companies often describe their own advertising with such disparaging language, but there is a logic to this self-deprecation. Neither FTC nor NAD requires companies to provide scientific evidence for puffery, because most adult consumers recognize its nonfactual nature and persuasive intent. In contrast with claims about scientific facts, outright puffery is a form of commercial speech that enjoys a high degree of constitutional protection.

Box 9.2   An Example of Voluntary Regulation From the Files of the National Advertising Division

NAD, the advertising industry's self-regulatory body, reviews health-related claims made by food and supplement manufacturers, but NAD's standards are not always difficult to meet. For example, the supplement manufacturer Pharmavite, LLC, in 2010 introduced a product called Nature Made GreatMind, with six vitamin and nutraceutical ingredients. The accompanying advertising copy included powerful claims:

- "Keep your mind great with Nature Made GreatMind!"
- "Helps guard against normal cognitive decline associated with aging."
- "Nature Made GreatMind has a unique, patent-pending formula that enhances mental performance, clarity and short-term memory with daily use."

The claim to "guard against normal cognitive decline" is designed to qualify merely as a structure/function claim, which does not require FDA approval or significant scientific agreement. If the manufacturer had instead sought to make a health claim, it would have to show evidence of significant scientific agreement, such as corroboration by the *Dietary Guidelines for Americans* or by a leading medical association. If the manufacturer claimed to treat a disease, such as Alzheimer's, it might have to file a new drug application.

Even for structure/function claims, a manufacturer must have some basis for believing the claims to be true and not misleading. In this case, NAD initiated an investigation to determine if there was sufficient evidence for the Pharmavite claim. NAD reviewed evidence submitted by Pharmavite, mainly studies by a research team led by Professor Thomas Shea, Ph.D., one of the authors of the patent application mentioned in the advertising copy. Based on the intellectual property in the patent application, Pharmavite licensed the supplement formula from Shea's employer, the University of Massachusetts. Pharmavite had consulted Shea in developing its advertising claims. The research by Shea's team recruited adult individuals aged 18 to 86 years old without dementia and randomly assigned them either to receive the supplement or a placebo, for a period of either two weeks or three months (Chan et al., 2010). In an analysis of just 105 of these subjects, all under 74 years old, from both time periods, those who received the supplement scored better on just one of three parts of a cognitive test used in the study. Supplement takers who were 74 years or older showed no improvement relative to placebo. Yet, NAD agreed with the claim that the supplement will "guard against normal cognitive decline associated with aging." According to NAD, the manufacturer said the first claim was "not an objective claim, but mere puffery, because the term 'great' is highly subjective and not capable of measurement." In conclusion, NAD upheld all claims, and the advertiser issued a statement praising the "rigorous standards employed by NAD" and expressing appreciation for "the opportunity to participate in the self-regulatory process."

9.6 Food Advertising Directed at Children

Advertising that targets children is especially controversial (Wilde, 2009). Adults need little help from the government for protection from food advertising, so long as the advertising is nondeceptive. Children are more vulnerable. The American Psychological Association says that children younger than 7 or 8 years old cannot understand an advertiser's persuasive intent, so advertising to young children should be restricted (Kunkel et al., 2004). Opponents of such restrictions say that parents, not governments, should protect children from advertisers. Yet, advertisers reach children in a variety of settings that parents cannot monitor, including marketing messages that reach children at school.

Whether voluntary or mandatory, guidelines to restrict advertising apply to advertising on children's television shows, such as a Nickelodeon or Disney cartoon, but choices about other marketing channels are more difficult. For example, if family television shows (such as *American Idol*) are excluded, then the guidelines would overlook many of the ads that children actually see. If these family shows are included, then the guidelines necessarily affect some adult audiences as well as child audiences.

The current debate in the United States over food marketing to children has roots dating back 30 years. In 1978, in what became known as the "Kid-Vid" proposal, FTC requested public comment on several possible options for rules to remedy the widespread marketing of high-sugar food to children (at the time, the concern was dental cavities caused by sugar). Congress removed FTC's authority to use one of the main regulatory tools at its disposal: the legal argument that advertising to children is "unfair." After three years of heated controversy, FTC terminated the proposed rule-making without taking any action. FTC's retreat in the Kid-Vid controversy for many years left federal agencies and many U.S. policy-makers reluctant to pursue any effort to limit food marketing to children.

The matter was left to rest until it was revived by increasing concerns about childhood obesity in the 2000s. The Institute of Medicine's report *Food Marketing to Children and Youth: Threat or Opportunity?* marked a turning point in the public debate when it was published in 2006. Summarizing evidence from 123 research studies of the effect of advertising on children's food choices and health outcomes, the report concluded that "Food and beverage marketing practices geared to children and youth are out of balance with healthful diets and contribute to an environment that puts their health at risk" (Institute of Medicine, 2006).

Subsequently, FTC issued two reports that have influenced the policy discussion. The first report used proprietary Nielsen data collected from electronic boxes on televisions in the homes of a nationally representative sample of households (Holt et al., 2007). The study found that, in a 1-year period, children aged 2 to 11 years watched 25,600 advertisements, 5,500 of which were for food and beverages. The greatest number of food advertisements seen by children were for restaurants and fast food, followed by cereals (mostly sweetened cereals) and desserts and sweets. During the year, children saw on average 1,400 advertisements for fast food and restaurants, 16 advertisements for vegetables and legumes and no advertisements for fresh fruit.

The second FTC report used marketing expenditure data collected directly from food manufacturers and advertising firms using federal powers of subpoena (Federal Trade Commission, 2008). The study reported that food and beverage companies spent $1.6 billion in 2006 on food marketing and promotion directed at children and adolescents, of which $745 million was for television advertising. Carbonated beverages, quick-service restaurants and breakfast cereals (predominantly sweetened cereals) accounted for 63 percent of the spending.

As with advertising targeting adults, most oversight of advertising targeting children is left to industry self-regulation, through a fragmented collection of initiatives. Two of these initiatives are managed by BBB, the same industry organization that hosts NAD. First, since 1974, the Children's Advertising Review Unit has promulgated voluntary guidelines that address *how* foods are advertised to children. These guidelines ask advertisers not to disparage healthy foods or to blur advertising with programming content (for example, by using characters from a children's program in advertising that is broadcast during the same time slot). The guidelines also ask advertisers to encourage "responsible use" of food and beverages, by showing, for example, cereal as part of a complete breakfast. Second, since 2006, the Children's Food and Beverage Advertising Initiative has overseen voluntary commitments that address *what* foods are advertised to children. The initiative asks participating companies to devote at least 50 percent of their advertising dollars aimed at children under 12 years of age to promoting healthy dietary choices and healthy lifestyles. Within broad guidelines, the participant companies get to write their own standards, which vary considerably from company to company. In addition to the two BBB initiatives, separate initiatives led by snack food and soft drink companies maintain voluntary standards that apply specifically to marketing in school settings.

Although these self-regulatory efforts leave unscathed most of the advertising to children that causes greatest concern, these efforts play a big role in the rhetoric of policy debates about advertising to children. Under the Central Hudson test (Section 9.3), a government agency may have to demonstrate that a proposed policy is no more burdensome than necessary to achieve an important public objective. To satisfy this legal principle, it is significant that policy-makers pursued only less-burdensome self-regulatory efforts during the years after the 2006 Institute of Medicine (IOM) report. Participants in policy debates in the mid-2000s thought that stronger government action might be necessary if self-regulation proved too weak. "If industry fails to demonstrate a good faith commitment to this issue and take positive steps," FTC chairman Deborah Platt Majoras warned in 2005, "others may step in and act in its stead" (Federal Trade Commission and Department of Health and Human Services, 2006).

In 2009, Congress passed bipartisan legislation proposed by Sen. Tom Harkin (D-IA) and Sen. Sam Brownback (R-KS), requesting that FTC, FDA, CDC and USDA form an Interagency Working Group (IWG) to issue a progress report and make recommendations for improvements to the system of voluntary rules on advertising. At the time, FTC Chairman Jon Leibowitz said, "We are calling on the food industry to tackle this threat and boldly reinvent the food marketplace" (Wilson and Roberts, 2012). In 2011, the IWG released draft voluntary nutrition guidelines for foods advertised to children. The guidelines included limits on sugar, salt and fat for food advertised to children age 17 and younger. Through the next several months, the IWG received strongly worded objections from food and beverage manufacturers, members of Congress and a large number of public comments. FTC considered some steps to address the objections, such as removing adolescents aged 12–17 years from the population covered by the guidelines. Yet, the damage had already been done. In late

2011, Congress made its displeasure clear by requiring FTC to conduct a cost-benefit analysis of the guidelines. FTC announced that the guidelines would be postponed indefinitely. An FTC spokesman said, "Congress has clearly changed its mind about what it would like the Interagency Working Group to do with regard to the report on food marketed to children." The Reuters news service quoted FTC Chairman Leibowitz saying, "It's probably time to move on" (Wilson and Roberts, 2012).

The current state of food policy regarding advertising to children leaves almost nobody happy. In the midst of an epidemic of childhood obesity, public health constituencies argue strongly that such advertising should be restrained somehow. Yet self-regulatory efforts have been exceedingly gentle, and proposed government-led initiatives have been successfully thwarted by a mix of industry opposition and public concern about excessive regulation.

9.7 Generic Commodity Checkoff Programs

The federal government's generic **commodity checkoff** advertising programs were discussed briefly in Chapter 2, as examples of government policies that benefit agricultural producers by expanding consumer demand. The largest checkoff programs are for meat and dairy products (Figure 9.3). Total annual collections for the leading checkoff programs exceed $650 million, overshadowing other federally sponsored consumer communications about food. In contrast with branded advertising that is funded by a particular producer, "generic advertising is designed to increase overall market demand" (Kaiser, 2011).

The advertising campaigns from the checkoff programs include "Beef. It's What's for Dinner"; "Ahh, the Power of Cheese"; "Pork. The Other White Meat"; "Got Milk?"; and the "Milk Mustache" campaign. These campaigns are so familiar that

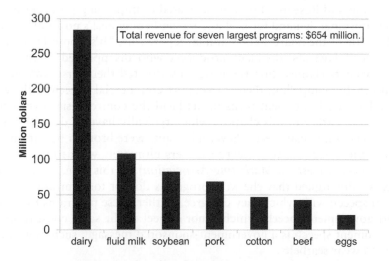

Figure 9.3 Annual revenue from mandatory assessments for the federal government's seven largest commodity checkoff programs, 2010

Note: Dairy and fluid milk revenue are for 2009 (the most recent released by USDA). Programs with annual revenue less than $20 million (not shown) include avocados, potatoes and peanuts.

Source: Annual reports from checkoff program websites.

many U.S. readers will recognize the slogans immediately and be surprised to hear that they come from the federal government. Checkoff programs are established by Congress and managed jointly by producer boards and USDA. The federal government enforces the collection of mandatory assessments on producers and approves each advertising and marketing program.

Taken as a whole, the checkoff advertising messages are in tension with the *Dietary Guidelines for Americans*, discussed in Chapter 8 (Wilde, 2006). There is no checkoff for poultry or fish or whole grains, and checkoff support for fruits and vegetables is tiny. It seems impossible to increase overall U.S. consumer demand for milk, cheese, butter, beef and pork while simultaneously achieving diets with less food energy and a smaller fraction of food energy from saturated fat.

A common economic justification given for checkoff boards is that a public goods problem hinders commodity producers who would like to advertise on their own. Economic theory maintains that government assistance is required for spending on public goods, such as roads and national defense, because private voluntary contributions will be insufficient (Kaiser, 2011). According the theory of industry structure reviewed in Chapter 6, a manufacturer of a branded product under monopolistic competition has a strong economic incentive to advertise, but a farmer who produces a commodity in a perfectly competitive market has only a weak incentive to advertise. Hence, checkoff proponents argue that public intervention is required for adequate commodity advertising. However, this public goods argument would make sense only if the increased advertising really were in the public interest—for example, because Americans ate too little hamburger and cheese for good nutrition or were exposed to too little advertising for their psychological health (Wilde, 2006).

Instead of providing a sound public goods rationale, Congress' objective is to support the private-sector interests of the dairy, beef and pork producers. For example, the beef checkoff program's mission statement is as follows: "The Cattlemen's Beef Promotion and Research Board is dedicated to improving producer profitability, expanding consumer demand for beef and strengthening beef's position in the marketplace." The title of the board's 2005 annual report was, "It's About Demand."

In a series of lawsuits, dissident producers who disapproved of the mandatory checkoff payments claimed that the programs violated their First Amendment right to free speech by compelling them to support commercial speech with which they disagreed. This legal argument turns on its head the controversies over commercial speech reviewed earlier in this chapter, which typically have to do with government restrictions on commercial speech. Several lawsuits were brought by various producer groups, and the one brought by beef producers ultimately went to the U.S. Supreme Court (*Johanns v. Livestock Marketing Association*). In this case, the federal government successfully argued that checkoff programs do not force producers to support commercial speech with which they disagree. Rather, these programs force producers to support **government speech**, which is not subject to the same constitutional objection. Government speech is a government-sponsored message, such as a campaign to get people to wear seatbelts.

The government speech argument identifies the checkoff messages as the government's own message (Crespi and McEowen, 2006). It may seem difficult to believe that most Americans recognize the checkoff programs as government programs or that all the advertisements for beef, pork and cheese could be attributed to the same federal government that published the *Dietary Guidelines*. Yet, in May 2005, by a six to three margin, the U.S. Supreme Court decided the case in favor of USDA and the beef checkoff board. In his majority opinion upholding the checkoff program, Justice Antonin Scalia wrote, "The message of the promotional campaigns is effectively controlled by the Federal Government itself. The message set out in the beef promotions is from beginning to end the message established by the Federal Government" (*Johanns v. Livestock Marketing Association*).

9.8 Conclusion

The U.S. system for regulating food labeling and advertising developed over time as first one approach and then another prevailed in a long history of political and legal struggles. At different times, and on different issues, U.S. labeling and advertising policy has taken many different positions on the spectrum illustrated earlier in Figure 9.1.

A good example is federal rules for label claims about nutrients and health. Until the 1980s, federal policy generally prevented most health claims on food products (a policy stance toward the right side of the figure). In 1990, the NLEA took a position that could be described as voluntary labeling with a high level of regulation (the center-right stance in the figure). Subsequent legislation and litigation have made the rules constraining voluntary labeling decisions more permissive (the center-left stance in the figure). The Nutrition Facts Panel itself is a mandatory label element (the leftmost policy stance in the figure).

There are several reasons to be dissatisfied with the mix of current policies. First, the collection of policies is cumbersome and inconsistent. One example is that FDA requires some disclosures on labels that FTC does not require in advertising. Even within the labeling jurisdiction of FDA alone, small wording differences in a labeling claim may lead to differences in how the claim is categorized for purposes of regulation. No policy-maker composed this mix of policies from scratch, intending them to be coherent. Instead, the inconsistencies are the detritus left behind after the ebb and flow of legal battles over the years. The resulting distinctions are surely lost on consumers.

Second, federal policies appear insufficient to address some serious public health concerns, including especially vigorous marketing of unhealthy food and beverages to children. Proposals to restrain such advertising have been beaten back on multiple occasions, as food manufacturers and advertisers successfully argue that such proposals intervene too much in the free operation of the market economy. Yet, even while refusing to intervene to restrain advertising to children, the federal government does intervene in the market economy to solve a perceived "public goods" problem in marketing and advertising for commodity food products, including most prominently dairy, pork and beef products (Section 9.7). Through checkoff programs for these commodities, the federal government intervenes not to restrain marketing and promote public health but instead to increase advertising for the purpose of raising consumer demand.

One avenue of policy reform is to regulate marketing messages more strictly. In U.S. food policy, this approach has substantial support in the public health community. From a public health perspective, food companies seek to establish "health halos" for manufactured food products, even if the products have offsetting nutritional disadvantages. If FDA or another federal agency were more fully empowered to forbid each misleading message, the agency could try to rein in the confusing private-sector market for information about diet and health. However, the scientific evidence on nutrition and health messaging is itself contested, and it changes over time, so policy-makers would face difficult choices in refereeing each class of message.

Another avenue of policy change would be to give up on strict regulation. In an unconventional 2011 commentary on restaurant menu labeling in the *International Journal of Obesity*, the nutrition scientist David Allison wrote:

> Proposals for policy-based approaches almost invariably meet resistance when the policies offend the moral or political sensibilities of some persons. This especially occurs when the proposed policy is seen as treading on the rights or autonomy of individuals in the interests of public health paternalism. Therefore, if we wish to minimize such resistance, we should aim to advance proposals that are freedom and choice promoting, rather than restricting.
>
> (Allison, 2011)

A similar argument could be made with regard to advertising rules, which also seem invariably to meet resistance and offend moral and political sensibilities.

Upon initial contemplation, a retreat from government oversight of food labeling and advertising would appear to be a victory for business and a disaster for public health and nutrition objectives. Certainly, one early consequence would be even greater proliferation of implausible marketing claims in every possible venue. On further reflection, however, how would consumers and companies respond to a fully unregulated marketing environment? Would consumers return to the principle of "buyer beware"? Would companies find the effectiveness of their nutrition-related marketing blunted? Food and beverage advertisers might come to miss the good old days when consumers believed—often mistakenly—that food and beverage marketing messages in the United States had passed some type of meaningful government scrutiny.

Summary List of Key Terms (identified in bold in the text)

- animal rights
- animal welfare
- Central Hudson test
- commercial speech
- commodity checkoff
- credence attributes
- experience attributes
- front-of-pack
- government speech
- health claim
- inherently misleading
- nutrient content claim
- political speech
- potentially misleading
- puffery
- qualified health claim
- Reference Amount Customarily Consumed
- search attributes
- structure/function claim
- third-party certification
- unfolding theory

10 Hunger and Food Insecurity

10.1 Introduction

A fundamental objective of any society is to provide enough food to feed its people. Policy discussions about poverty focus on society's success or failure in providing concrete basic needs such as shelter, health care and food. In the United States, SNAP and other food assistance programs seek to promote food security and reduce the prevalence of hunger.

To evaluate national progress toward these objectives, it is easy to find authoritative statistics about **hunger** and **food insecurity** in the United States, but it is difficult to discern what the statistics really mean. For example, this chapter will discuss in detail the following two nationally representative estimates for 2015 (Coleman-Jensen et al., 2016):

- 12.7 percent of U.S. households (containing 42 million persons) were food insecure at some point during the year;
- 4.2 percent of household respondents were hungry but couldn't afford to eat at some point during the year.

Feeding America, the umbrella organization for U.S. food banks, describes food insecurity as a condition of struggling with hunger: "42 million people struggle with hunger in the United States" (Feeding America, 2017a). By contrast, using similar numerical estimates, the Heritage Foundation finds little evidence of hunger:

> Political advocates proclaim that the USDA reports show there is widespread chronic hunger in the U.S. But the USDA clearly and specifically does not identify food insecurity with the more intense condition of "hunger". . . . As the USDA report explicitly states, most "food insecure" homes did not cut back their intake at all.
>
> (Rector, 2010)

Such disputes are connected with more specific questions. How severe are the household-level circumstances that are captured in the federal government's food insecurity statistics? What level of food spending is sufficient for an adequate diet? Is hunger an inevitable consequence of U.S. poverty, or should policy-makers tackle the two problems separately? This chapter:

- focuses on U.S. poverty as the context for hunger and food insecurity (Section 10.2);
- reviews the history and explains the methodology of food insecurity and hunger measurement (Section 10.3);

- explores the adequacy of the federal government's Thrifty Food Plan (TFP), which defines an adequate food bundle for federal policy purposes (Section 10.4);
- describes the history, structure and effectiveness of SNAP (Section 10.5); and
- describes the charitable emergency food system, including food banks, food pantries and meals programs (Section 10.6).

This chapter is closely linked with Chapter 11, which covers federal nutrition assistance programs especially for children. As the word "nutrition" in its name indicates, SNAP cultivates a strong identity as a nutrition program in addition to its service as the leading anti-hunger program. Other nutrition assistance programs in Chapter 11 include the Special Supplemental Nutrition Program for Women, Infants and Children (WIC) and the school meals programs. While this book divides these topics into two chapters for convenience, the programs in both chapters are motivated both by nutrition and anti-hunger objectives.

10.2 Poverty as the Context for Food Insecurity and Hunger

Food insecurity is closely related to poverty. Food insecurity measurement and poverty measurement have been intertwined for decades. U.S. statistics measure the poverty rate as the percentage of people in households with income below the federal poverty guideline (for example, $24,600 for a family of four in 2017). The federal poverty guideline is updated each year for inflation. The original federal poverty guideline, established in the 1960s, was based in large part on estimates of the income level required to afford enough food (Fisher, 1997).

The U.S. Census Bureau each year publishes both an official poverty measure and an alternative Supplemental Poverty Measure, with some differences in the specification of household income and in-kind benefits, which have some implications for how we think about food insecurity and hunger (Renwick and Fox, 2016).

- **Official poverty measure.** The poverty threshold is three times the cost of a minimum food diet in 1963, updated for inflation. Family resources are defined as pre-tax cash income. Cash assistance benefits from the government count as resources, but tax credits (such as the Earned Income Tax Credit, or EITC, which especially benefits low-income working parents with children) and in-kind benefits (such as SNAP) do not count as resources.
- **Supplemental Poverty Measure.** The poverty threshold is 1.2 times the cost of a larger bundle of basic needs including food, clothing, shelter and utilities. Family resources are defined as cash income plus in-kind benefits (such as SNAP) minus certain basic expenses (work, out-of-pocket medical expenses and child support payments) and minus net taxes (after accounting for tax credits such as the EITC).

The U.S. Census Bureau estimated a poverty rate in 2015 of 13.5 percent, just slightly higher than the prevalence estimate for household food insecurity. In 2015, the prevalence of food insecurity was 38.3 percent for poor households (with income below the poverty guideline) and only 5.8 percent for households with income above 185 percent of the poverty guideline. Both poverty and food insecurity are more prevalent for households with children and for non-Hispanic black and Hispanic households (Coleman-Jensen et al., 2016).

Over recent decades, the official poverty measure shows dramatic reductions in poverty from the 1950s to the early 1970s, followed by little further progress from the 1970s to the present. Because the Supplemental Poverty Measure counts the EITC and in-kind benefits, both of which have offered increased benefits to low-income Americans from the 1980s to the present, this measure shows somewhat more progress in poverty reduction during this period. Yet, it remains worrisome that market incomes for poor Americans have not increased enough from the 1980s to the present to contribute much to poverty reduction (Furman, 2017).

Average per capita gross domestic product (GDP)—a rough but commonly used measure of economic resources—is higher in the United States than in most industrialized countries. However, income inequality in the United States also is greater than in other industrialized countries, and the U.S. government's social safety net lifts a smaller fraction of the population out of poverty. Poverty estimates depend on whether one uses a fixed real income threshold for absolute poverty (as in U.S. poverty statistics) or a relative-income threshold that also reflects income inequality (as is common in European poverty statistics). When a consistent measurement approach is applied to data from multiple countries, the United States has either the highest poverty rate or (along with the United Kingdom) one of the two highest poverty rates among high-income industrialized nations (Smeeding, 2006).

To explain why so many Americans are poor, some analysts have traditionally emphasized factors that depend in part on individual responsibility, such as single parenthood and failures in educational attainment and labor market participation. Other analysts have traditionally emphasized factors that an individual cannot change, including discrimination by race and ethnicity, gender, disability and a long-term secular decline in wages for workers without a high school diploma. This difference in emphasis should not obscure points of consensus among researchers. For example, a 2015 consensus report from a collaboration between two leading Washington think tanks, one generally conservative and the other more liberal, focused evenly on (a) family composition, (b) work and wages and (c) education (AEI/Brookings Working Group on Poverty and Opportunity, 2015).

In recent decades, anti-poverty policies in the United States have been undermined by several circumstances: changes in public opinion about welfare programs; political rhetoric that is reluctant to mention domestic poverty; and the leading influence of comparatively high-income constituencies in the U.S. policy-making process (Bane, 2009). These trends help explain the shrinking role of general anti-poverty programs and the growing role of food assistance programs such as SNAP (Section 10.5) and child nutrition programs (Chapter 11) in the U.S. social safety net.

In-kind assistance does help in addressing poverty. Without SNAP, the poverty rate measured using the Supplemental Poverty Measure would have been 1.4 percentage points higher (Furman, 2017). Yet in-kind assistance is unlikely to be enough on its own to achieve strong reductions in U.S. poverty.

Future improvements in market incomes depend on three major factors (Furman, 2017): productivity growth, income inequality and labor force participation. Although technological change sometimes also has a downside, raising concern about labor displacement along with hopes for higher wages (see Box 2.3, for example), productivity growth remains a fundamental source of increased prosperity. To reduce U.S. food insecurity and hunger, one must think not just about food programs and safety nets but also about long-run poverty reduction through improved wages for low-income

Americans (see Section 6.5, for example). These economic themes have implications for policy debates about tying SNAP participation more closely to work in the labor force, so that the program can serve not just as short-term assistance but also as part of a broader road out of poverty (Section 10.5).

10.3 Food Insecurity and Hunger Measurement

10.3.1 History

From the end of the Great Depression of the 1930s through the early 1960s, domestic hunger was not a leading topic in U.S. food policy discussions. In 1967, Sen. Robert Kennedy and other members of a Senate subcommittee on employment and poverty visited the Mississippi Delta and witnessed for themselves the hard conditions in a part of the country that had been left out of the more general prosperity. The following year, a CBS television documentary, *Hunger in America*, popularized this concern. Hunger was a major focus for a "select" (or temporary) committee on nutrition and human needs in the Senate from 1968 through 1977 and for a select committee on hunger in the House of Representatives from 1984 through 1993.

Economic growth in the 1980s was accompanied by increasing homelessness and the early expansion of the private charitable emergency food system (Section 10.6), including food banks, pantries and soup kitchens (Eisinger, 1998). The growing number of people using emergency food sources was alarming, but food distribution statistics in part reflected growth in the supply of emergency food services. The number of U.S. children with symptoms of malnutrition such as stunting (low height-for-age) or wasting (low weight-for-height) was reassuringly low, but these anthropometric statistics fail to capture the effect of milder and more sporadic hardships.

In 1990, Congress passed the National Nutrition Monitoring and Research Act, which called for a standardized definition of hunger and a more systematic measurement approach. Drawing in part on work by researchers at Cornell University and a parallel measurement effort sponsored by the nonprofit Food Research and Action Center, USDA developed the survey-based approach that has been used on national surveys since 1995 (National Research Council, 2006).

10.3.2 Definitions

In its measurement approach, USDA adapted definitions proposed by the Life Sciences Research Office, a leading association in biology and nutrition science (National Research Council, 2006).

* **Food security** is "access at all times to enough food for an active, healthy life." It includes, at a minimum, (a) "the ready availability of nutritionally adequate and safe foods" and (b) "an assured ability to acquire acceptable foods in socially acceptable ways (e.g., without resorting to emergency food supplies, scavenging, stealing, or other coping strategies)."
* **Food insecurity** "exists whenever the availability of nutritionally adequate and safe foods or the ability to acquire acceptable foods in socially acceptable ways is limited or uncertain."

- **Hunger** was initially defined as (a) "the uneasy or painful sensation caused by a lack of food" and (b) "the recurrent and involuntary lack of food." These two descriptions of hunger were intended to be wholly consistent, but in recent years they have been recognized as distinct. The word "hunger" is used sometimes to describe an individual experience and sometimes to refer to a societal problem (National Research Council, 2006).

10.3.3 Survey Questions

The federal government's measurement approach uses a battery of 18 survey questions about particular symptoms of food insecurity on one or more occasions in the past 12 months. Ten questions are asked of respondents in households with and without children (Table 10.1). Another eight questions refer to the experiences of children and are asked only of respondents in households with children (Table 10.2). If respondents report no symptoms of food insecurity on earlier questions, some later questions about severe hardship are skipped to reduce respondent burden, and their response is presumed negative. The government includes the survey questions in an annual supplement to the Current Population Survey (CPS) and several other major federal surveys.

Table 10.1 Ten adult-referenced survey items used for all households in the 12-month U.S. Food Security Supplement

Survey items (responses that count as "affirming" the item)	Among all households, % affirming item in 2015
1. "We[1] worried whether our food would run out before we got money to buy more." (Often or sometimes true in the last 12 months)	17.0
2. "The food that we bought just didn't last, and we didn't have money to get more." (Often or sometimes true in the last 12 months)	14.1
3. "We couldn't afford to eat balanced meals." (Often or sometimes true in the last 12 months)	13.8
4. In the last 12 months, did you or other adults in the household ever cut the size of your meals or skip meals because there wasn't enough money for food? (Yes)	7.8
5. In the last 12 months, did you ever eat less than you felt you should because there wasn't enough money for food? (Yes)	7.9
6. (If yes to Question 4) How often did this happen? (3 or more months)[2]	6.0
7. In the last 12 months, were you ever hungry but didn't eat because there wasn't enough money for food? (Yes)	4.2
8. In the last 12 months, did you lose weight because there wasn't enough money for food? (Yes)	2.5
9. In the last 12 months, did you or other adults in your household ever not eat for a whole day because there wasn't enough money for food? (Yes)	1.6
10. (If yes to Question 9) How often did this happen? (3 or more months)	1.2

[1] The survey instrument says "(I/We)" throughout. [2] "Three or more months" is determined based on the survey instrument's response options, "almost every month, some months but not every month, or in only 1 or 2 months."
Source: Coleman-Jensen et al. (2016).

10.3.4 U.S. Food Insecurity and Hunger Statistics

USDA consolidates the survey responses into summary statistics, such as the estimate cited in the introduction that 12.7 percent of U.S. households were food insecure in 2015. If a household affirms three or more of the 18 survey items, USDA classifies the household as food insecure. Despite several complications, methodologists judged this three-item cutoff to be the best match with the official definition (National Research Council, 2006). The statistical tool used in such judgments, called item response theory (IRT), has both strengths and shortcomings for this task. Raising a number of empirical concerns about the most-used IRT model, the Center for National Statistics recommended that more flexible IRT models be explored (National Research Council, 2006). These more complex models also present problems of their own, and they have not yet been used in official food security statistics (Wilde, 2011).

The terminology for measuring hunger has become mired in controversy. Before 2005, if a household without children affirmed six or more items (or if a household with children affirmed eight or more items), USDA classified it as food insecure with hunger. Critics of this terminology objected that some households were classified as hungry even though they failed to affirm the survey items that specifically used the word "hungry," such as Question 7 in Table 10.1. After an expert panel of the Center for National Statistics questioned use of the word "hunger" in official statistics (National Research Council, 2006), USDA changed the term "food insecurity with hunger" to "very low food security." The federal government stopped using the word "hunger" in official statistics.

Currently, although they are seldom cited, the best nationally representative estimates of the extent of hunger in the United States are the simple response frequencies to the survey questions about hunger. For example, 4.2 percent of household respondents were hungry but couldn't afford to eat at some point during 2015 (Table 10.1). Among households with children, 0.9 percent contained children who were hungry at some point during 2015, due to the household's inability to afford food (Table 10.2).

Table 10.2 Eight child-referenced survey items used for households with children in the 12-month U.S. Food Security Supplement

Survey items (responses that count as "affirming" the item)	Among households with children, % affirming item in 2015
11. "We[1] relied on only a few kinds of low-cost food to feed our children because we were running out of money to buy food." (Often or sometimes true in the last 12 months)	13.6
12. "We couldn't feed our children a balanced meal, because we couldn't afford that." (Often or sometimes true in the last 12 months)	8.4
13. "The children were not eating enough because we just couldn't afford enough food." (Often or sometimes true in the last 12 months)	3.6
14. In the last 12 months, did you ever cut the size of any of the children's meals because there wasn't enough money for food? (Yes)	1.7

Survey items (responses that count as "affirming" the item)	Among households with children, % affirming item in 2015
15. In the last 12 months, were the children ever hungry but you just couldn't afford more food? (Yes)	0.9
16. In the last 12 months, did any of the children ever skip meals because there wasn't enough money for food? (Yes)	0.6
17. (If yes to question 16) How often did this happen—almost every month, some months but not every month, or in only 1 or 2 months? (3 or more months)[2]	0.5
18. In the last 12 months, did any of the children ever not eat for a whole day because there wasn't enough money for food? (Yes)	0.1

[1] The survey instrument says "(I/We)" throughout. [2] "Three or more months" is determined based on the survey instrument's response options, "almost every month, some months but not every month, or in only 1 or 2 months."
Source: Coleman-Jensen et al. (2016).

Official food security prevalence estimates are frequent subjects of political spin. One writer may select a narrow definition of hardship (very low food security) and a short reference time period (30 days) to describe a problem experienced by "only" 2.9 percent of U.S. households in 2015. Another writer may select a broader definition of hardship (food insecurity) and a longer reference period (12 months) to describe a problem experienced by 12.7 percent of U.S. households in 2015, a much higher prevalence. A writer seeking to be impartial therefore cannot quote a statistic on its own but must state the corresponding reference period and indicate the severity of hardship.

10.3.5 Trends

The prevalence of food insecurity fluctuates over time (Figure 10.1). Among U.S. households, 12 percent were food insecure in 1995. In 1996, the U.S. government adopted a national goal of reducing household food insecurity by half, from 12 percent to 6 percent by 2010. For the purpose of assessing the performance of food assistance programs, additional targets were adopted for very low food security among low-income Americans in particular (see Section 10.5.4). Based on data from the late 1990s, such goals appeared realistic (Nord and Andrews, 2002). However, the prevalence of food insecurity reversed course, deteriorated (increased) during the recession of the early 2000s, failed to improve during the economic expansion of the mid-2000s and surged again during the economic crisis and recession of 2008 and 2009, reaching the highest level since the current measurement effort began. The most recent data as of this writing, for 2015, show that food security was slow to begin recovering after the Great Recession and has not come close to meeting the U.S. target (Figure 10.1). There is some evidence that food insecurity is more common in the United States than in other developed countries (Wilde, 2011).

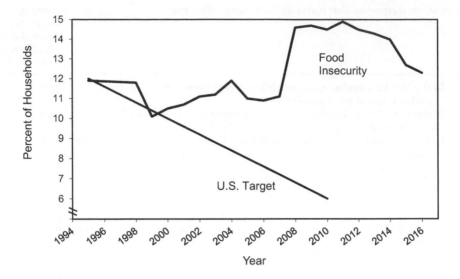

Figure 10.1 The prevalence of household food insecurity in the United States, 1995–2015, and the Healthy People 2010 target

Data note: USDA's Economic Research Service each year publishes summary statistics about food security (www.ers.usda.gov/topics/food-nutrition-assistance/food-security-in-the-us). The household-level micro-data are available from the Current Population Survey (www.ers.usda.gov/data-products/food-security-in-the-united-states). The Healthy People 2010 objectives and 2020 objectives, with accompanying progress statistics, are available from the CDC (www.healthypeople.gov).

Source: Jensen-Coleman et al. (2016) and earlier reports in the same series.

10.4 The Cost of an Adequate Diet

10.4.1 Different Assumptions

Food insecurity might seem like a simple problem of having an inadequate food budget. For example, the food insecurity survey items ask respondents about not having "enough money for food." However, deciding what amount is "enough money" turns out to be a challenge, requiring a careful definition and a systematic approach.

The economist George Stigler famously estimated that the minimum cost required to meet narrowly defined nutrition targets was only pennies per day (Stigler, 1945). By contrast, others commonly conclude that an adequate diet is quite expensive. For example, researchers at the Brigham and Women's Hospital estimated the monthly cost in 2003 of a heart-healthy and culturally appropriate diet in a low-income Boston neighborhood to far exceed maximum food stamp benefit at the time (Johnson et al., 2004). Following the publication of an Institute of Medicine report suggesting that cost estimates should take greater account of the time costs for food preparation (Yaktine and Caswell, 2014), the economist Jim Ziliak suggested that the SNAP benefit should be pegged to an amount 20 percent higher than the Thrifty Food Plan (Ziliak, 2016). Although Stigler knew that some nutritionists and economists of his day used higher cost estimates, he said that they imposed unnecessary "cultural requirements" regarding palatability, variety and prestige, which "should not be presented in the guise of being part of a scientifically-determined budget."

The estimated cost of an adequate diet depends on two things. First, it depends systematically on what food and nutrition standards are chosen. The more food that is deemed necessary and the more nutrition constraints that are imposed, the higher the estimated cost will be. Second, and less widely understood, the estimated cost of an adequate diet depends on how much one expects consumers to change their current eating habits. The cost is higher for a diet based on current eating habits than for a model diet that picks inexpensive alternatives.

10.4.2 The Thrifty Food Plan

The maximum SNAP benefit amount is related to the cost of the **Thrifty Food Plan**, a model spending plan appropriate for people on a tight budget. For people with higher income, the federal government also publishes three less well-known food plans, which are used in applications ranging from determining military food allowances to establishing alimony levels in divorce cases.

USDA formerly revised the food quantities in the TFP every several years to reflect current economic conditions and dietary guidance. However, following the most recent revision of the Thrifty Food Plan in 2006 (Carlson et al., 2007), USDA did not publish any further revisions through 2017. The TFP revision is widely thought to determine the maximum SNAP benefit amount, but this is mistaken. Really, when USDA revises the TFP, it just revises the food quantities and leaves the real inflation-adjusted cost level unchanged. In each revision, a team of economists and nutritionists uses a computer program to choose a food plan that differs as little as possible from current average consumption patterns for low-income Americans, but which does differ enough to meet several constraints.

- Cost constraint. The model food plan must not cost more than the inflation-updated cost of the preceding version of the TFP (for example, in 2001 dollars, $3.89 per day for an adult woman).
- Energy constraint. The model food plan must provide the recommended amount of food energy (for example, 2,200 calories per day for an adult woman).
- Nutrient constraints. The model food plan must provide adequate amounts of essential nutrients, such as calcium, while avoiding excessive amounts of other nutrients, such as saturated fat. The nutrient constraints are based on recommendations in the Recommended Dietary Allowances and the *Dietary Guidelines for Americans* (see Chapter 8).
- MyPyramid food constraints. The model food plan must provide amounts within specified ranges for major categories of foods, such as vegetables, and secondary categories of foods, such as dark green vegetables. In the 2006 TFP revision, these ranges were derived from recommendations for food categories in MyPyramid, the dietary guidance document in use at that time (see Chapter 8).
- Additional constraints. In each model food plan, USDA imposes a number of more idiosyncratic constraints, to make sure that the food plan does not have uncommonly high or low amounts of particular foods and food groups (Carlson et al., 2007). One consequence of these additional constraints is to bump up the amounts of some meat products.

Table 10.3 shows how a model food plan is selected, using the same 2001 data that USDA used for the 2006 revision of the TFP. This example uses spending data and

Table 10.3 The effect of different constraints on the most recent Thrifty Food Plan (TFP)

Characteristics of the diet	Target range[1]	Current average	Constraints imposed	
			Cost, energy, nutrients	Official TFP
	(1)	(2)	(3)	(4)
Cost ($/day, 1 person)[2]	$3.89	$5.34	$3.89	$3.89
Distance function		0.0000	0.0907	6.6538
MyPyramid Servings[3]				
Milk	> 3.00	1.38	1.78	3.15
Meat/beans	> 6.00	6.27	4.95	6.3
Grains	> 7.00	7.65	4.69	7.35
Fruits	> 2.00	0.97	0.69	2.10
Vegetables	> 3.00	1.53	6.00	3.37
Added fats/sugars (Cal)	< 290	806	698	290
Selected nutrients				
Fat (% Cal)	20–35%	33%	32%	31%
Saturated fat (% Cal)	< 10%	10%	9%	8%
Calcium (mg)	1,000–2,500	796	1,000	1,315
Iron (mg)	18 to 45	16	18	19
Sodium (mg)	< 2,300	2,774	2,693	2,808

[1] For some rows, the target range includes a minimum and a maximum. For other rows, the target range has just one boundary. [2] Costs are in 2001 dollars, not adjusted for inflation. [3] MyPyramid was a dietary guidance graphic that preceded the MyPlate graphic currently in use.
Data note: 2001 data for adult women, aged 20–50 years old, from the 2006 TFP (Carlson et al., 2007), which was the most recent edition of the TFP as of 2017.

Source: Wilde and Llobrera (2009).

dietary recommendations for adult women, just one of the several demographic groups used in the official TFP. Column (1) shows selected constraints that USDA imposes in choosing a food plan (for example, the foods must cost no more than $3.89 per day and must provide at least three servings of milk products and 1,000 mg of calcium). Column (2) describes the corresponding characteristics of the actual average food-spending pattern for a low-income population (for example, a total food cost of $5.34 per day, average milk product intake of 1.38 servings and average calcium intake of 796 mg). Column (3) describes a food plan that results from imposing only the cost constraint, food energy constraint and nutrient constraints (for example, costing $3.89 per day and providing 1,000 mg of calcium). Column (4) shows USDA's official TFP, which includes all of the previous constraints plus MyPyramid food group constraints and additional constraints. The **distance function** is a measure of how much a proposed model diet differs from current consumption.

Surprisingly, it is comparatively easy to satisfy the cost, energy and nutrient constraints. In the third column, using just these constraints, the distance function is quite small, indicating that the model diet is fairly similar to the current consumption pattern. For example, this model low-cost diet provides enough calcium even though it gets only 1.78 servings from the milk group, because some calcium comes from other food groups.

By contrast, it is comparatively difficult to satisfy the MyPyramid constraints and additional constraints. In the fourth column, using all the constraints together, the distance function is quite large, indicating that the model diet is different from the current consumption pattern. USDA's official TFP provides more servings from the milk group and the meat and beans group, but doing so at a sufficiently low cost requires a diet that differs greatly from current consumption (Wilde and Llobrera, 2009).

These results present a food policy dilemma. A diet high in plant foods and low in animal foods is both nutritious and inexpensive. The comparatively low-meat diet in column (3) of Table 10.3 meets all the RDAs for nutrients. On the other hand, for USDA and for many Americans, having a sufficient quantity of animal foods seems like an essential part of the definition of an adequate diet. Hence, USDA's official TFP provides for more meat and dairy products than the model would otherwise have chosen based on nutrient needs alone.

An important theme of this section is that the estimated cost of an adequate diet depends systematically on assumptions about nutrition needs and preferences for particular foods. To further explore such tradeoffs using the same data that USDA used, readers can try out the Thrifty Food Plan Calculator accompanying this chapter (Box 10.1). Or, for a more personal approach, readers may attempt their own **SNAP challenge**, learning about food costs and food needs by living for a certain time period on a constrained food budget (Box 10.2). Suggestions for improving the TFP have been discussed by the Institute of Medicine (Yaktine and Caswell, 2014) and the Brookings Institution (Ziliak, 2016), among others, but, as of this writing in 2017, these suggestions have not yet been converted into policy changes.

Box 10.1   The Thrifty Food Plan Calculator

The Thrifty Food Plan Calculator is an interactive Excel-based application, useful for exploring food cost and nutrition tradeoffs in a model diet of your own design (nutrition.tufts.edu/research/thrifty-food-plan-calculator).

In the spreadsheet, you enter hypothetical daily spending levels for 58 food groups. The calculator provides feedback showing how much your model diet costs, how far different it is from current average consumption, how many servings it provides for each MyPyramid food category and how well it meets each nutrient constraint. The calculator provides several suggested starting points, such as current average consumption or USDA's official TFP. Then, you can experiment with modifying the food group quantities to pursue whatever nutrition or policy goals you choose.

For example, if you are curious to know whether a low-meat diet is both nutritionally and economically adequate, you could begin with the official TFP and explore lowering the meat quantities and replacing them with other sources of protein and iron. Or, if you suspect that the current SNAP benefit is too low to support a palatable food budget, you could design a model food diet that seems more appealing to investigate how much more food spending would be required.

Box 10.2   The SNAP Challenge

A SNAP challenge is a short-term discipline—perhaps one week or one month long—living on the food budget that would be available to a low-income American. It offers a direct way to learn about the price of food and the cost of an adequate diet, using whatever definition of adequacy you personally find most compelling. At one time or another, members of Congress, governors, journalists and private individuals have undertaken this challenge. The Food Research and Action Center (FRAC) offers a toolkit for members of Congress, encouraging them to attempt this challenge as a way of learning more about SNAP and about hunger in the United States (Food Research and Action Center, 2016).

In pursuing a SNAP challenge, the first question is what budget to use. The FRAC toolkit suggests the average per-person SNAP benefit, approximately $4.18 per day. However, as explained in Section 10.5, the poorest SNAP participants receive substantially more benefits than this amount. A more realistic discipline is to seek to live on the current Thrifty Food Plan budget, approximately $40 per adult per week in 2017 ($5.75 per day). If you attempt a food stamp challenge yourself, you may find that you can meet some but not all of your own personal food goals.

10.5 Supplemental Nutrition Assistance Program

10.5.1 SNAP History

SNAP, the largest federal food assistance program, has roots in a Great Depression-era food stamp program that sought to dispose of agricultural surpluses by giving away paper vouchers that could be redeemed for food. This early program was discontinued when the surpluses ended during the Second World War. In its modern incarnation, the Food Stamp Program began as a pilot program in 1961 and was authorized by Congress as a permanent program in 1964 (Table 10.4). The caseload grew as the program spread across the country from the mid-1960s to the mid-1970s (Eisinger, 1998; Hoynes and Schanzenbach, 2009).

Initially, participants had to purchase their food stamps at a discounted rate using their own cash income. In the Food Stamp Act of 1977, Congress eliminated this purchase requirement, making the program more appealing to potential participants and kicking off another period of caseload expansion. Since that time, the caseload has risen and fallen in response to economic conditions and periodic changes in program rules. Beginning in the 1990s, benefits have been distributed through electronic benefit transfer (EBT) cards, much like debit cards. The FSP was renamed the Supplemental Nutrition Assistance Program in 2008 to acknowledge that EBT cards have replaced paper food stamp coupons and to strengthen the program's identity as a nutrition program.

10.5.2 SNAP Eligibility and Benefits

SNAP is a **mandatory**, or **entitlement**, program, which means that the federal government has committed to supplying whatever funds are required to provide benefits to all eligible applicants. This entitlement status influences the program's participation

Table 10.4 Program summary: Supplemental Nutrition Assistance Program (SNAP)

Overview: The largest U.S. nutrition assistance program and a cornerstone of the social safety net, formerly known as the Food Stamp Program.	
Year begun	*1961*
Scale of operation	
Participants, fiscal year 2016 (% of U.S. population)	13.6
Average monthly participation, 2016 (million persons)	44.2
Budget	
Total annual expenditure, 2016 ($ billion)	71.0
Eligibility	
Gross monthly income test for most households (% of poverty standard)	130
Net monthly income test after deductions (% of poverty standard)	100
Benefits: Monthly benefit equals a maximum benefit minus 30% of net income after deductions. Benefits are delivered through an electronic benefit transfer (EBT) card for use in authorized food retailers.	
Maximum monthly benefit, family of four, fiscal year 2016 ($)	649
Mean monthly benefit, per person, fiscal year 2016 ($)	126

Data note: SNAP national and state-level participation statistics are available from USDA's Food and Nutrition Service (www.fns.usda.gov/data-and-statistics).

Source: Oliveira (2017).

dynamics and its sources of political support. Entitlement status also means that one must pay attention to fairly arcane rules about eligibility and benefits in order to understand the big-picture issues of program budgets, trends and overall effectiveness. The first criterion for SNAP eligibility is low income. To be eligible, in most cases, a household generally must have **gross income** of less than 130 percent of the federal poverty standard. For example, gross income had to be less than $2,633 per month for a family of four people in 2017 (this benefit level is held constant through the end of the subsequent fiscal year, in this case through September 2017). In some states, households can satisfy this gross income requirement based on meeting the slightly different income threshold for another safety net program, such as Temporary Assistance for Needy Families. Gross income includes household members' cash income from almost any source, whether from labor market earnings, retirement benefits or government cash assistance programs. A household also must have **net income** less than 100 percent of the federal poverty standard (for example, net income less than $2,025 per month for a family of four people in 2017). Net income equals gross income minus certain deductions, including a fixed standard deduction and deductions for 20 percent of earned income, some housing expenses, some childcare expenses and other smaller deductions.

There are several secondary eligibility criteria. There is a limit on a household's financial assets, so a middle-class family that experiences a job loss may have to spend down its financial assets before it becomes eligible. The value of a home that a household owns does not count toward the asset limit, but automobiles above a certain value may count toward the limit. Undocumented immigrants have always been ineligible, while restrictions against legal immigrants have been added and removed over the years. In 2017, most otherwise-eligible adult immigrants could participate if they were refugees or had lived in the country for five years, and child immigrants could participate even if they arrived more recently.

The monthly benefit amount is based on the household's net income. If the household is nearly destitute, so net income after deductions is zero, the household receives the **maximum SNAP benefit** ($649 per month for a family of four in 2017). The maximum benefit is related to the cost of the TFP (see Section 10.4), which varies by household size and is adjusted each year for price inflation. The American Recovery and Reinvestment Act (ARRA) of 2009, a centerpiece of the federal government's response to the financial crisis and recession, provided an additional temporary 13 percent increase in the maximum SNAP benefit, but that boost has ended.

The **benefit reduction rate** is 30 percent, which means that the monthly benefit is reduced by 30 cents for every dollar of net income. For example, in 2017, a family of four with $1,000 per month in net income would receive a SNAP benefit of $349 per month ($649 – 0.30 × $1,000).

The SNAP benefit formula is progressive, giving a higher benefit to poorer participants. At the same time, this benefit structure could in principle reduce participants' financial incentive to seek work in the labor market (Huffman and Jensen, 2008). A household member who is offered $10 per hour for additional work might really gain only about $7.80 per hour in total household resources, after considering the reduction in SNAP benefits (this computation considers both the benefit reduction rate and the 20 percent earned income deduction).

To offset this concern about work disincentives, SNAP rules include some employment requirements. Able-bodied adults without dependents (ABAWDs, an acronym that only a bureaucrat could love) have a three-month time limit for participation in every 36-month time period unless they meet the work requirement. This requirement was waived in many locations and also was temporarily set aside during the economic crisis of 2008–2009, and then was reinstated in 2016.

The benefits credited to the SNAP EBT card each month may be used only for food and allowable beverages from authorized retailers. The benefits may be used for seeds for home gardening, but they may not be used for alcoholic beverages, tobacco, paper goods and other nonfood items. With some minor exceptions, benefits cannot be used for hot foods served ready to eat. The motivation for this latter restriction is consistency across different types of business, given that restaurants mostly may not be authorized retailers. Authorized retailers include almost any store that sells a range of grocery items for use at home, including traditional grocery stores, supermarkets, food warehouses, specialty food stores, corner stores and convenience stores.

The federal government pays the full cost of SNAP benefits, the full cost of federal oversight and administration by USDA and half the cost of program administration in the field by state government agencies. In addition to the program benefits delivered through EBT cards, SNAP supports a nutrition education program. As with other administrative costs incurred by state agencies, the federal government pays 50 percent of the nutrition education costs. To be eligible for this match, the state agency must develop an approved SNAP nutrition education plan focused on promoting energy balance, physical activity and increased consumption of fruits and vegetables, whole grains and low-fat milk products. In many cases, the state agency responsible for SNAP works with the state's Cooperative Extension System to carry out the plan. The SNAP nutrition education allocation was $408 million for fiscal year 2016. This sum is small relative to overall SNAP program costs ($70.9 billion in 2016) but large relative to other sources of nutrition education for low-income Americans.

10.5.3 SNAP Participation Trends and Costs

SNAP generally has been considered a uniform national program, with nationwide eligibility and benefit rules determined by Congress. However, even in SNAP, states do have discretion over some administrative details that turn out to be important. For example, states have authority over how frequently program participants must provide new documentation to recertify their continued eligibility (Hanratty, 2006; Klerman and Danielson, 2011). Because SNAP is an entitlement, the caseload and program cost can fluctuate from year to year in response to economic conditions, sometimes surprising and even distressing legislators and administrators. Caseload trends are closely scrutinized, and there is high-level interest in understanding factors that influence program participation.

Research has shown that economic conditions and policy changes are important determinants of SNAP participation levels (Hanratty, 2006; Ratcliffe et al., 2011; Klerman and Danielson, 2011). Participation fluctuates because of changes both in the number of eligible people and in the percentage of eligible people who choose to take up the benefit. Compared to eligible unemployed people, eligible working people are less likely to take the trouble to participate, because they may not have time to deal with the application process and also because their earned income makes them eligible for a smaller benefit. Overall, about 72 percent of eligible people participate in SNAP (Leftin, 2011).

Researchers use state-level data to investigate how the caseload responds to economic and policy variables that change over time and differ across states. For example, when the unemployment rate rises during recessions, workers lose earnings and more families become eligible for SNAP benefits. During economic recovery, the SNAP caseload falls back down again (Figure 10.2). Similarly, at a single point in time, states with higher unemployment rates tend to have a higher percentage of the population participating in SNAP (Figure 10.3).

When the caseload declined in the second half of the 1990s, one of the causes was the 1996 welfare reform, which intentionally reduced participation in cash assistance and may have affected food stamps as a side effect. During this period, some states also began using shorter recertification periods, requiring households with labor market earnings to prove their continued eligibility every three months as a way of avoiding errors in benefit determination. When the caseload increased beginning in the early 2000s, policy changes again were part of the explanation. Congress allowed states to relax some reporting and recertification requirements. The federal government provided funding for advertising to encourage eligible nonparticipants to apply (Dickert-Conlin et al., 2012). In the economic crisis of 2008–2009, Congress increased SNAP benefits as a way of quickly boosting aggregate economic demand. By 2011, SNAP participation had reached record levels, accounting for more than 10 percent of all U.S. food retail spending (Wilde, 2012). From 2013 to 2017, participation finally began to recede again, as one would expect during a period of macroeconomic growth (Figure 10.2).

10.5.4 SNAP Effects on Food Insecurity

To understand the potential effect of SNAP on food insecurity, we must first consider how the program affects food spending. The best-known economic theory of consumer

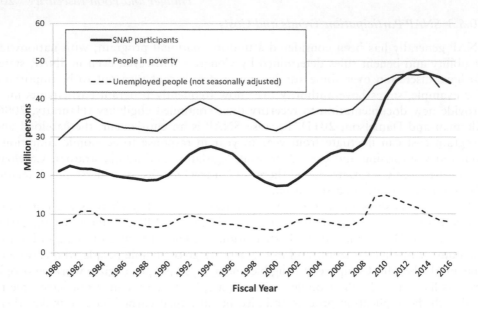

Figure 10.2 SNAP participants, people in poverty and unemployed people, 1980–2015

Data note: SNAP national statistics (www.fns.usda.gov/pd/snapmain.htm) and household characteristics (www.fns.usda.gov/ops/supplemental-nutrition-assistance-program-snap-research) are available from USDA's Food and Nutrition Service. More detailed household-level microdata are available in quality control data files (https://host76.mathematica-mpr.com/fns/). Unemployment data come from the Bureau of Labor Statistics (BLS) (www.bls.gov/bls/unemployment.htm).

Source: Gray et al. (2016); Economic Research Service.

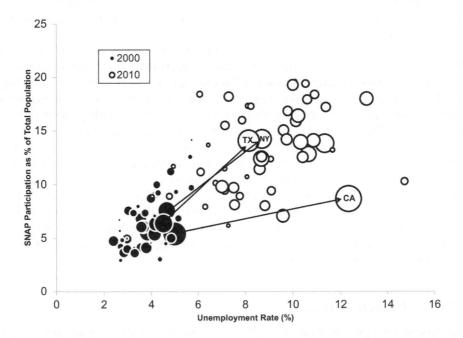

Figure 10.3 SNAP participants and unemployment rates across the states, 2000–2010

Note: Bubble size is proportional to state population.

Source: Author's computations using data from Census Bureau, BLS, USDA/FNS.

choice with a targeted food benefit, called the Southworth Hypothesis, offers insight into how SNAP benefits function within the household budget (Wilde et al., 2009). This theory distinguishes between the behaviors of two types of households:

- Unconstrained (or **inframarginal**) households contribute some of their own cash income toward their food budget, in addition to spending their SNAP benefits on food. Such households would not be motivated to sell their SNAP benefits illegally in return for cash benefits. Households with relatively high income, and therefore relatively low SNAP benefits, are more likely to be inframarginal. If they choose, such households legally can reduce their own cash spending on food, freeing up money for other purchases.
- Constrained (or **extramarginal**) households rely on their SNAP benefits alone for their monthly grocery spending. They do not contribute any of their own cash income toward their food budget. They would be better off if it were possible to convert some of their SNAP benefits to cash resources. Households that are destitute of cash income, and who therefore receive the maximum SNAP benefits, are more likely to be extramarginal. Such households cannot legally increase their nonfood purchases by reducing their food spending, because of the rule that SNAP benefits must be spent on food.

Box 10.3 provides a more formal illustration of how the Southworth Hypothesis works. Analysis of SNAP effects should keep in mind both inframarginal and extramarginal participant households. In practice, the division between these two types of households is not as sharp as the theory would have it. For several reasons, households with some cash spending on food may nevertheless be influenced by the form of the SNAP benefit (Wilde et al., 2009). Having a small amount of cash spending on food is not enough to make a household behave in a completely unconstrained (inframarginal) manner. Yet the main insight of the Southworth model remains sound: SNAP benefits are expected to have the biggest impact in very poor households, where the SNAP benefits account for a large fraction of all grocery spending.

Because households that face greater hardship are more likely to take the trouble and time to participate in SNAP, rates of household food insecurity are dramatically higher among SNAP participants than among low-income nonparticipants. In 2015, the prevalence of household food insecurity was 52.5 percent among low-income SNAP participants and 25.3 percent among low-income nonparticipants (Table 10.5). This pattern makes it difficult to use simple comparisons of participants and nonparticipants to estimate the real impact of a program (Box 10.4).

Table 10.5 (a) Food spending relative to the Thrifty Food Plan budget and (b) prevalence of household food insecurity, by income category and SNAP participation status, 2015

Income-to-poverty ratio	SNAP	(a) Median spending-to-TFP ratio	(b) Food insecure (%)
< 1.3	Participant	.94	52.5
	Nonparticipant	.94	25.3
< 1.85		.95	32.8
1.85 and higher		1.33	5.8
Income unknown		1.18	8.3

Source: Coleman-Jensen et al. (2016), Tables 10.2, 10.6 and 10.8.

Box 10.3   The Economics of a Targeted Food Benefit

The distinction between inframarginal and extramarginal households can be illustrated by continuing the example from Chapter 6, in Box 6.3, about the theory of consumer choice. The consumer has the same total resources as before ($12/day), but now she has $2/day in SNAP benefits and only $10/day in cash income (Figure 10.4). The price of other goods remains $1, and the price of food remains $2.40 for every thousand grams. A consumer with the same preferences as before would again choose $7.20 in nonfood spending and 2,000 g for food, just as in the earlier example from Chapter 6. The consumer in Figure 10.4 is unaffected by having some cash income converted to SNAP benefits because she is unconstrained (or inframarginal). The purchase of 2,000 g of food requires all $2 of the SNAP benefit plus $2.80 of cash income. SNAP rules introduce a "kink" in the budget constraint, limiting nonfood spending to no more than $10/day, but the kink does not influence this consumer's choice. She would have freely chosen much less than $10/day in nonfood spending anyway.

Things would be different if the SNAP benefit were higher. Now, suppose the consumer still has $12 per day in total resources, but $7 comes from SNAP benefits, leaving only $5 from cash income (Figure 10.5). The consumer in Figure 10.5 is constrained (or extramarginal), because all food (about, 2900 g) is purchased with the $7 in SNAP benefits. The kink in the budget constraint now influences the consumer's food-spending choice, allowing a comparatively generous food budget while leaving her nearly destitute of cash resources.

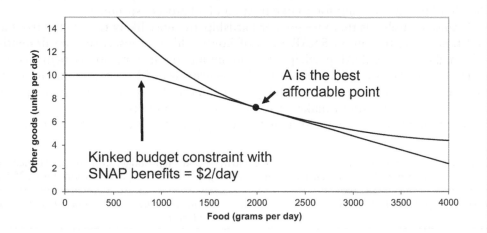

Figure 10.4 An inframarginal or unconstrained consumer

Note: The consumer who chooses bundle "A" is unaffected by the kink in the budget constraint.

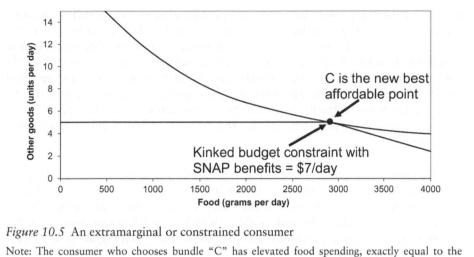

Figure 10.5 An extramarginal or constrained consumer

Note: The consumer who chooses bundle "C" has elevated food spending, exactly equal to the SNAP benefit amount.

Low food spending alone does not explain the extraordinarily high prevalence of household food insecurity among SNAP participants. As one would expect, higher-income households have much greater food spending than low-income households have (Table 10.5). Likewise, as one would expect, the prevalence of food insecurity is much higher (worse) in the low-income households. However, within the low income population, some surprises arise. SNAP participants and low-income nonparticipants have similar food-spending levels, but the SNAP participants have much higher rates of household food insecurity (Table 10.5). This pattern shows that SNAP receipt is no guarantee of household food security.

Because benefits are credited to the EBT card just once per month, many SNAP participants experience a sharp monthly cycle in food spending, with a large spike in food spending shortly after benefits are received, followed by a longer period of comparatively low food spending from SNAP benefits (Wilde and Ranney, 2000). It is likely that the SNAP spending cycle could be smoothed out if benefits were delivered twice monthly. Although twice monthly benefit delivery has been proposed at the state level, this policy has not yet been implemented even on a pilot basis.

Box 10.4   Research Design for Measuring Program Effects

Because food assistance programs have such a large role in the U.S. social safety net, there is intense policy interest in understanding program impacts. An important research goal is to compare what actually happened under a particular program to the relevant **counterfactual**, a measure of what would have happened in the absence of the program. Many studies compare participants to nonparticipants, sometimes using regression models to hold constant other factors such as income, race, ethnicity and geographical region of the country. The difficulty is that the participants may differ from the comparison group in unobservable ways because of **self-selection** into the program. Self-selection means that people who voluntarily choose to participate in a program may have lower food security or greater food needs or better information about social welfare programs, compared with apparently similar nonparticipants, leading to biased estimates of program effects.

There are several research designs that seek to address this self-selection problem:

- **Random assignment.** If individuals are randomly assigned to a participant group and a control group, one can interpret average differences between the two groups as the effect of the policy being studied. This approach was used in the Healthy Incentives Pilot, which tested financial incentives for fruit and vegetable purchases with the SNAP EBT card (Wilde et al., 2015; Olsho et al., 2016).

- **Pre/post comparison.** A simple research design compares outcomes before and after a change in participation status or program rules. The main drawback is that other changes in the economic or social environment may have happened at the same time. A pre/post design is used when a policy change is significant enough to have a big effect, and data can be collected from shortly before and shortly after the change.

- **Difference-in-difference comparison** (sometimes called a double-difference design). An important variation is to study program changes that differed across locations. For example, one could compute the change over time in food spending in (a) counties where a new program was introduced and (b) counties where the program was not yet introduced. Chapter 11 will discuss research that measures changes in dietary quality between summer months and school-year months in locations that do or do not have widespread participation in a school breakfast program during the school year.

- **Panel data models.** Panel data or longitudinal data contain repeated observations over time on each individual in the sample. One family of panel data models, called random effects models, is designed merely to get more precise estimates. Another family of panel data models, called fixed effects models, is designed to compensate for self-selection bias in certain circumstances. If the unobserved individual circumstances are constant over time, then fixed effects models can generate unbiased estimates of program effects.

- **Instrumental variables models.** Finally, still more complex statistical models can address self-selection concerns in some circumstances (Gundersen and Oliveira, 2001; Ratcliffe et al., 2011). An instrumental variable is an explanatory variable that is related to the program participation decision but which does not itself suffer from the self-selection problem. If an instrumental variable can be found, it can in principle be used to generate unbiased estimates of program effects. However, these statistical models require strong assumptions that cannot be proven empirically. If the assumptions are incorrect, then the instrumental variables model may be no better than simpler regression-based comparisons (Wooldridge, 2015).

10.6 The Charitable Emergency Food System

Although much smaller than SNAP, charitable emergency food programs are a prominent part of the American public's response to hunger. For example, when ABC News does a Thanksgiving report on hunger in the midst of plenty, it provides a donation link for Feeding America, the national food bank network. This network developed from smaller food banking and gleaning initiatives that began in the 1980s and now is one of the nation's largest charities. The emergency food system experienced particularly rapid growth during the economic crisis and recession of the late 2000s. According to Feeding America's *Map the Meal Gap 2017* report, the network provided food to 46 million people in 2015 (Feeding America, 2017b), which represents an 80 percent increase since 2006.

This charitable emergency food system includes several categories of nonprofit institutions, of which four categories are most central (Mabli et al., 2010):

- **Food banks** (numbering about 200) are the system's wholesale operations, taking in large volumes of food, providing warehouse and transportation services and distributing food to local charitable agencies. The food banks are predominantly secular nonprofit organizations, with paid management and labor force.
- Emergency **food pantries** (numbering about 33,500) provide groceries directly to clients, for preparation at the client's home. The pantries are predominantly faith-based organizations, relying heavily on volunteer labor and sometimes on volunteer management as well. About 75 percent of the food comes from food banks; the rest comes mostly from local food drives and direct purchases from cash donations.
- Emergency **soup kitchens** (numbering about 4,500) offer meals to clients who do not reside on the premises. They also may provide lighter meals and snacks or "kids cafe" meals for children. About 60 percent of kitchens have some paid staff. About 50 percent of the food comes from food banks.
- **Emergency shelters** (numbering about 3,600) include homeless shelters and transitional shelters that also offer meals. Management and staff for shelter programs are commonly paid employees, in contrast with food pantries. About 41 percent of the food comes from food banks.

The food bank network acquires its food supplies mainly from government programs and industry donations. The most important federal program is The Emergency Food Assistance Program (TEFAP). The budget for TEFAP is somewhat complex. In fiscal year 2015 Congress allocated $376 million in spending to TEFAP, plus approximately $300 million in surplus commodity foods that USDA purchases to support agricultural prices.

The industry donations are just one component of the extensive and mutually beneficial cooperation between food industry organizations and the food bank network. Feeding America's summer 2017 impact report credits partners such as Walmart, Campbell Soup, General Mills, Kellogg Company, Kraft Heinz Company, PepsiCo and Discover (Feeding America, 2017c). With support from the dairy checkoff programs (see Section 9.7), Feeding America promotes the Great American Milk Drive, which it says has delivered more than 1 million gallons of milk and "raised awareness of the ways that America's dairy farmers and milk producers are helping provide more milk to children in need." For the industry partners, the cooperation offers a good humanitarian outlet for donated food, a tax deduction for the value of donated food and valuable publicity for brand-linked campaigns. Such partnerships also draw concern—ranging from gentle nudges to fierce criticism—from advocates for anti-poverty strategies that focus more sharply on wage growth and reduced income inequality (Poppendieck, 1998; Fisher and Jayaraman, 2017).

The client base for the emergency food system is partly—but only partly—overlapping with the participant rolls for SNAP and other nutrition assistance programs. Of U.S. households that participated in SNAP in December 2015, USDA estimates that 31 percent had also obtained food from a food pantry, while of all low-income households that had obtained food from a food pantry, 55 percent participated in SNAP (Coleman-Jensen et al., 2016). The emergency food system offers clients an important resource for meeting unanticipated food needs, typically without burdensome paperwork, while SNAP offers a larger and steadier resource for food purchases through normal retail channels.

10.7 Conclusion

In one perspective, hunger and food insecurity can be seen as a simple problem of insufficient food spending. For example, this chapter reviewed how the federal government constructs the Thrifty Food Plan, a model food-spending pattern. Through SNAP, the federal government seeks to provide sufficient resources for families to be able to afford the TFP cost. Feeding America publishes a national estimate of the additional money required to purchase the meals that food insecure households are missing. For 2015, Feeding America estimated that closing this "meal gap" would cost only $22.2 billion (far less than 1 percent of the federal budget). A food-centered approach has considerable appeal, offering solutions to hunger that seem comparatively inexpensive and politically feasible.

In another perspective, food insecurity can be seen as closely intertwined with the broader problem of poverty. In recent U.S. safety net policy, targeted programs that provide particular goods have had greater political success than general anti-poverty programs have had. This trend helps to explain the increasing role of SNAP in the national food economy, discussed in this chapter, and the growing importance of other nutrition assistance programs, discussed next in Chapter 11.

While recognizing the merit of a food-centered approach, some long-time observers of anti-hunger policy nonetheless recommend a poverty-centered approach to address these concerns (Poppendieck, 1998). For example, Mark Winne, who was a long-time community food security advocate and leader in the charitable emergency food system in Connecticut, writes,

> The risk is that the multibillion-dollar system of food banking has become such a pervasive force in the anti-hunger world, and so tied to its donors and its volunteers, that it cannot step back and ask if this is the best way to end hunger, food insecurity and their root cause, poverty.
>
> (Winne, 2008)

According to a poverty-centered perspective, food insecurity likely will remain widespread in the United States for as long as Americans accept unusually high rates of poverty as a normal condition.

Summary List of Key Terms (identified in bold in the text)

- benefit reduction rate
- counterfactual
- difference-in-difference comparison
- distance function
- emergency shelters
- entitlement
- extramarginal
- food banks
- food insecurity
- food pantries
- food security
- SNAP challenge
- gross income

- hunger
- inframarginal
- instrumental variables models
- mandatory
- maximum SNAP benefit
- net income
- official poverty measure
- panel data models
- pre/post comparison
- random assignment
- self-selection
- soup kitchens
- Supplemental Poverty Measure
- Thrifty Food Plan

11 Nutrition Assistance Programs for Children

11.1 Introduction

The nutrition status of children and youth is a public policy concern, not merely a private matter. In the traditional economic perspective on policy-making (Chapter 1), the role of government is different when children are involved. The discussion of advertising to children in Chapter 9 noted that children cannot defend their own economic interests in the marketplace as adults can. In other respects, as this chapter will explore, the federal government already is more heavily involved in nutrition decisions for children than for the adult population.

For example, just 14 percent of the U.S. population participates in SNAP, the nation's largest anti-hunger program (Chapter 10). By comparison, 48 percent of infants born in the United States are participants in WIC, a targeted nutrition program for women, infants and children (Section 11.4), and 59 percent of schoolchildren participate in the National School Lunch Program (NSLP) (Section 11.3). In addition to WIC and the school meals programs, the federal government also serves children through a variety of smaller programs. For low-income children who receive a school breakfast, a school lunch and food at an after-school program, federal nutrition assistance is involved in a large fraction of daily food intake.

Just as the Farm Bill reauthorizes agricultural programs (Chapter 2), conservation programs (Chapter 3) and anti-hunger programs (Chapter 10), Congress typically uses a different legislative vehicle—child nutrition reauthorization—to revise and modernize the school meals programs and WIC. For example, the 2010 Healthy Hunger-Free Kids Act reauthorized the child nutrition programs through September 2015. At the signing ceremony for this legislation, after describing the responsibility of parents for children's nutrition, First Lady Michelle Obama went on to say, "But when our kids spend so much of their time each day in school, and when many children get up to half their daily calories from school meals, it's clear that we as a nation have a responsibility to meet as well" (Obama, 2011b).

When it came time for the next child nutrition reauthorization in the summer of 2015, the legislation was caught up in broader partisan disputes, and Congress was unable to agree on a bill. The Senate finally passed its version of a reauthorization bill in January 2016, and the House passed its version in May 2016, but the two houses could not reconcile the differences, so the legislation expired. As of 2017, most major U.S. child nutrition programs continued under permanent authorization from years earlier. For some smaller programs, such as a small WIC farmers' market voucher program, Congress has simply continued appropriating funds one year at a time even without permanent authorization (Congressional Research Service, 2017).

The first goal of federal child nutrition programs is to enhance food security and prevent hunger. As Chapter 10 explained, food insecurity among households with children is a serious concern. In USDA's annual food security survey, respondents in 13.6 percent of households with children reported relying on only a few kinds of low-cost food to feed their children at some point during the year, because they were running out of money to buy food. Although outright hunger is less frequent, it is a more serious problem when it occurs. Respondents in 0.9 percent of households with children reported that the children were hungry at some point during the year (see Table 10.2).

The second goal of federal child nutrition programs is to promote nutrition and health. One can measure eating patterns, nutrient intake, physical fitness or rates of Type II diabetes, for example. On each of these measures, there is evidence that U.S. children are doing poorly (Institute of Medicine, 2012). The most visible outcome measure is the prevalence of childhood obesity. Obesity alone should not be taken as a full description of children's nutritional status, and indeed direct policy responses should be crafted to avoid weight bias, stigma and discrimination (Gearhardt et al., 2012). Nonetheless, national statistics on childhood obesity, defined using age-specific thresholds established by the Centers for Disease Control and Prevention (CDC), provide useful insight into nutritional changes over time and differences across income strata. Across all population subgroups and both sexes, the prevalence of obesity among children aged 2–19 years doubled or nearly doubled from 1988–1994 to 2007–2008 (Figure 11.1). In both time periods, obesity was more prevalent for children in

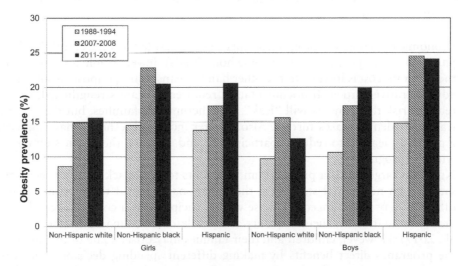

Figure 11.1 Prevalence of obesity among children aged 2–19 years, by race/ethnicity and sex, from 1988 to 2012

Note: In the data for 1988–1994, the Hispanic group represented just children of Mexican and Mexican-American origin. In the more recent years, NHANES data were representative for Hispanic Americans.

Data source: NHANES.

Source: Ogden et al. (2016); Fryar et al. (2014).

low-income households than in higher-income households and more prevalent for non-Hispanic black and Hispanic children than for non-Hispanic white children. Subsequently, from 2007–2008 to 2011–2012, the prevalence of childhood obesity leveled off, with modest increases for some population subgroups and modest decreases for others (Fryar et al., 2014; Ogden et al., 2016).

With attention to both food security and nutrition issues, this chapter:

- describes principles and tradeoffs in the design of nutrition assistance programs for children (Section 11.2);
- provides an overview of federal school lunch and school breakfast programs (Section 11.3);
- provides an overview of the WIC program (Section 11.4); and
- explores both the substance and politics of efforts to improve child nutrition programs (Section 11.5).

11.2 Principles and Tradeoffs

The design of child nutrition programs requires policy-makers to balance competing goals, such as improving dietary quality for children and supporting the larger educational mission of school systems, while limiting program costs. Influential policy constituencies include public health advocates; anti-hunger and anti-poverty advocates; school administrators; food and beverage manufacturers whose products are used by the programs; food service companies; associations of government employees and program administrators; and taxpayer advocates concerned principally about limiting the budgetary costs. No program design can satisfy all objectives and all stakeholders, so tradeoffs are required.

- Economic targeting. If a program adopts a means test (an income cutoff that limits participation to people in low-income households), fewer people are eligible and the program cost is lower. On the other hand, means testing imposes a substantial administrative burden. If documentation requirements are strengthened, there is reduced risk that benefits will "leak" to higher-income families, but the administrative burden increases further. Also, stricter income thresholds may stigmatize a program, leading to reduced participation and reducing the public's familiarity with the program.
- Nutrition targeting. If a program limits benefits to food packages and meals that satisfy high nutritional standards, the nutritional value of the program's direct offerings may be enhanced for those who participate. As a consequence, the program's reputation for dietary quality and wholesomeness may be higher (Basu et al., 2017). However, children and their families may offset some of the impact of the program's direct benefits by making different spending decisions with non-program resources such as cash income. Furthermore, strict nutrition standards raise concerns about **paternalism**, in which government authorities behave as parents and treat other people as children. Strict standards may lower the program's perceived value to participants, reducing program participation. The complexity of program rules may increase, and the administrative burden may be higher. As an alternative to limiting foods, nutrition assistance programs may provide

optional nutrition education programs while allowing participants to make their own choices (Box 11.1).

- Program budget. If budgets are increased, nutrition assistance programs may be able to serve more people and provide healthier offerings. However, when program budget constraints are relaxed, some fraction of the increased resources may be captured by constituencies involved in program delivery. This capture may sometimes be a good thing and sometimes not. For example, if school meal reimbursements are raised, food and beverage manufacturers might find they can charge higher prices, or school food service workers may be able to demand higher wages and improved working conditions. In all cases, the government's ability to increase nutrition assistance spending is constrained by competing budgetary priorities.

Box 11.1   Effectiveness of Nutrition Education Programs

The federal government funds public nutrition education through several programs, including the following: (a) the Expanded Food and Nutrition Education Program (EFNEP), which was originally an extension program (a type of USDA outreach and education program), and (b) the voluntary nutrition education component of SNAP. There is a modest literature in peer-reviewed journals that seeks to estimate the effectiveness of these approaches to nutrition education.

In an evaluation of EFNEP in New York State (Dollahite et al., 2008), researchers took a survey of nutrition education class participants, recording their adoption of an array of healthy eating practices. Based on assumptions about the link between food choices and the risk of particular chronic diseases, the authors used these self-reports to extrapolate the reduced risk of chronic disease. Then, by assuming particular fixed constants representing the health burden and economic cost per case of disease, they estimated the savings that can be attributed to the EFNEP classes.

The authors assumed that each respondent who reported adopting the recommended amount of dairy intake had substantially lower risk of osteoporosis, a disease involving loss of bone tissue. This lower risk in turn leads to a large economic benefit per student. The New York study's researchers estimated that participants on average saved $729 in health costs, of which 57 percent was attributed to reduced osteoporosis. Similarly, in older EFNEP research in Virginia, results for osteoporosis drove the overall results. The Virginia study's researchers estimated that participants saved on average $5770 in health costs, of which 90 percent was attributed to reduced osteoporosis alone (Rajgopal et al., 2002).

This research on the effects of nutrition education depends on the accuracy of participant responses in an after-class survey. The results also depend on assumed parameters for particular diseases. Even though nutrition education programs focus on dietary practices that reduce risk of all the major chronic diseases, the results seem heavily dependent on estimates for osteoporosis. It

> may be easier to convince people to consume more calcium by increasing intake of dairy products than to reduce consumption of salt, sugar and solid fats. For now, the estimated effects of these nutrition education programs should be taken as fairly rough approximations.

11.3 Child Nutrition Programs

11.3.1 Child Nutrition History

Progressive reformers developed a diversity of local school lunch programs in the early twentieth century, accompanying the spread of universal access to public education. During the Great Depression of the 1930s, in response both to collapsing consumer demand for agricultural products and to widespread poverty, the federal government began to provide surplus agricultural commodities to local lunch programs. Although surpluses had disappeared by the end of the Second World War, legislators worried that undernourished school-age children would be unfit for eventual military service. Consolidating elements from several earlier efforts, Congress established the NSLP in 1946 (Poppendieck, 2010; Ralston et al., 2008) (Table 11.1).

Initially, the NSLP was highly decentralized, delegating important decisions to local governments. One reason was the long tradition in the United States of deferring to local authority on education policy. Another reason was that some legislators from Southern states opposed the extension of federal involvement in local education matters because the federal government might oppose Jim Crow laws and racial

Table 11.1 Program summary: National School Lunch Program (NSLP)

Overview: The oldest and largest federal school meals program.	
Year begun	*1946*
Scale of operation	
Participants, fiscal year 2016 (% of school-age population)	59
Mean daily participation, fiscal year 2016 (million lunches)	30.3
Budget	
Total annual expenditure, 2016 ($ billion)	13.5
Eligibility	
Free lunch, household income test (% of poverty standard)	130
Reduced-price lunch, household income test (% of poverty standard)	185
Benefits: Direct meal provision by school food authorities (SFAs).	
Federal reimbursement per "paid" lunch, 2016–2017, base, most states ($)	0.30
Federal reimbursement per reduced-price lunch, 2016–2017, base, most states ($)	2.76
Federal reimbursement per free lunch, 2016–2017, base, most states ($)	3.16
Additional per-lunch performance-based incentive, 2016–2017	0.06

Note: See also School Breakfast Program (online supplemental Table S11.1) and Child and Adult Care Food Program (online supplemental Table S11.2) (both on the online Companion Website).

Data note: NSLP national and state-level participation statistics are available from USDA's Food and Nutrition Service (www.fns.usda.gov/data-and-statistics).

Source: USDA FNS; Oliveira (2017).

segregation. From the 1950s through the 1970s, a long series of incremental policy changes increased the federal government's role, establishing more uniform eligibility criteria, financing and oversight.

The smaller School Breakfast Program (SBP) originated during the period of growing concern about U.S. hunger and undernutrition in the 1960s (Table S11.1; see online Companion Website). A pilot program was established in 1966, and the national program was permanently authorized in 1975. Expanding school breakfast was a priority for anti-hunger organizations in the 1990s and 2000s. The Child and Adult Care Food Program (CACFP) reimburses meals provided through childcare homes, daycare homes and adult daycare facilities (Table S11.2).

11.3.2 Child Nutrition Eligibility and Benefits

Unlike SNAP and WIC, which are only available to low-income Americans, all U.S. school-aged children may participate in the school meals programs. School meals are prepared and served by nonprofit food service entities called **School Food Authorities** (SFAs), which typically have the same boundaries as a school district and answer to the district's authority. Oversight is provided by a state agency and, at the federal level, by USDA's Food and Nutrition Service.

For the NSLP, the federal government funds the SFA through a per-meal reimbursement, which varies according to a child's household income as follows:

- **Free.** For a student whose household's income is below 130 percent of the federal poverty guideline, the lunch is free to the student, and the basic federal reimbursement to the SFA was $3.29 in the 2017–2018 school year.
- **Reduced price.** For a student whose household income is between 130 percent and 185 percent of the federal poverty guideline, the lunch costs $0.40 to the student, and the basic federal reimbursement to the SFA was $2.89 in the 2017–2018 school year.
- **Paid.** For a student whose household income is higher than 185 percent of the federal poverty guideline, the lunch price is set by the SFA, and the basic federal reimbursement to the SFA was $0.37 in the 2017–2018 school year.

The federal reimbursement for lunches is slightly higher in poor school districts (defined as districts where more than 60 percent of students are eligible for free or reduced-price lunches) and in Alaska and Hawaii. The federal breakfast program uses a parallel schedule of reimbursement rates, varying by household income. In addition to the financial reimbursement, the federal government provides **entitlement commodities**, worth about $0.23 per school lunch, and may provide **bonus commodities** that are in surplus in a particular year. In some school districts, commodities are used directly in school meals. In many districts, commodities are sent to a commercial vendor, which processes the commodities into ready-to-use meal components.

The detailed procedures for ascertaining household income are carefully negotiated by policy-makers. At the start of each school year, the SFA collects an application from the parent, including self-reported income. Under a procedure called **direct certification**, it is possible to certify some children for free lunch based on the household's participation in other means-tested programs such as SNAP or cash assistance. In November of each school year, the SFA must verify a small percentage of parents' applications to confirm the self-reported income. The federal government monitors the verification efforts of SFAs.

Similarly, the definition of a reimbursable meal is carefully negotiated. Originally, SFAs had to serve a meal that contained sufficient quantities from the major food groups. These rules became unsatisfactory because the food group quantities did not guarantee that a meal would meet dietary guidelines (see Chapter 8). Also, the rules seemed to encourage plate waste by requiring a food to be served even if a child knew that he or she would not eat a particular meal component. Currently, under a policy known as **offer versus serve**, the SFA must offer sufficient components for a reimbursable meal, but the child may decline to take some components.

Outside of the federal lunch and breakfast programs, most SFAs market a wide variety of other foods in the cafeteria and throughout the school environment. These **competitive foods** may include desserts, carbonated beverages, snacks and alternative meals that would not qualify as a reimbursable meal. The venues for competitive foods may include vending machines and *á la carte* cafeteria lines. SFAs can be seen as business firms, similar in some respects to businesses in other sectors of the food service and restaurant industry (Chapter 6). Although SFAs do not pay profits to shareholders, they typically are required by school districts to break even, paying all food service costs from food sales and program revenues. The multiple constraints faced by SFAs have been described as a "trilemma" involving: (a) nutrition quality, (b) affordability (limited cost) and (c) student participation (which is influenced by meal quality and taste) (Ralston et al., 2008). SFAs may find it feasible to satisfy one or two constraints but difficult to satisfy all three constraints together (Figure 11.2).

The late 2000s and early 2010s were a period of innovation and experimentation in school food service. In the 2004 reauthorization of child nutrition programs, Congress required school districts to develop school wellness policies, stating the district's rules for school food. Some districts found ways to improve the nutrition quality of school food without losing participants or going broke (Poppendieck, 2010). Many other districts felt compelled to compromise on nutrition quality, offering quick-service restaurant type food with considerable student appeal.

In the 2010 child nutrition reauthorization, Congress strengthened nutrition standards for reimbursable meals, increasing the amounts of fruits, vegetables, whole grains

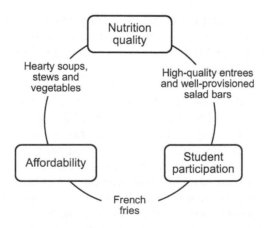

Figure 11.2 The school nutrition "trilemma"

and milk, while reducing the amounts of sodium, saturated fat and *trans* fat. Implementation proved controversial, and some school food programs objected to the cost of providing more nutritious meals and questioned the realism of some standards (see Section 11.5). In 2017, the incoming Trump administration announced plans to slow or reverse implementation of several provisions, including most notably the goals for sodium reduction (Severson, 2017).

11.3.3 Child Nutrition Participation Trends and Costs

Participation in the school meals programs responds to economic conditions, policy changes and the size of the population of school age. In the NSLP, participation grew from the 1980s until 2011 and then declined slightly from 2011 through 2016 (Figure 11.3). This decline was due to lower purchases of paid lunches, which raised questions about whether changing nutrition standards had reduced the program's appeal for students who had a choice about whether to participate. As a fraction of school-age children, participation is higher for elementary school students (and especially low-income students) than for high school students (at all income levels). The SBP is much smaller, but in recent years has increased more rapidly, as a growing fraction of school districts with lunch programs has begun to participate in the breakfast program as well. In 2016, 30.3 million lunches and 14.5 million breakfasts were served on average each school day. The NSLP was the second most expensive food assistance program (after SNAP), with an annual cost of $13.5 billion in 2016 (Table 11.1). The SBP cost $4.2 billion in 2016 (online supplemental Table S11.1).

Program costs at the national level depend on the average cost of providing a school meal. USDA conducts periodic analyses of school meals costs, including Bartlett et al.

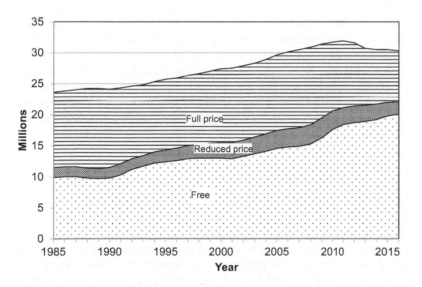

Figure 11.3 Mean school lunches served per school day, 1985–2016

Data note: NSLP national and state-level participation statistics are available from USDA's Food and Nutrition Service (www.fns.usda.gov/pd/cnpmain.htm).

Source: USDA ERS; USDA FNS.

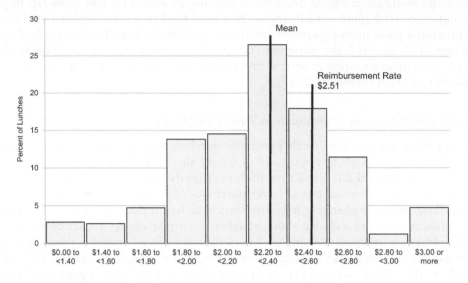

Figure 11.4 Distribution of lunches by reported cost per reimbursable lunch

Note: The online supplemental materials in the companion website will update this figure using new results from the School Meals Nutrition and Cost Study scheduled for publication in 2018.

Source: Bartlett et al. (2008).

(2008). An updated analysis of school meals' nutrition quality and costs jointly is scheduled for publication in 2018. Based on a national sample of SFAs, Bartlett et al. (2008) found that the mean cost per lunch was $2.25 in the 2005–2006 school year, somewhat less than the reimbursement rate of $2.51 that year. This average statistic obscures important variation across districts (Figure 11.4). About 24 percent of lunches were served in districts where the per-meal cost was less than $2.00, much less than the reimbursement rate. At the other end of the spectrum, 17 percent of lunches were served in districts where the per-meal cost exceeded $2.60, substantially more than the reimbursement rate. The widely varying costs depend on whether a district is urban or rural, whether it pays high wages or low wages, whether it prepares meals by cooking from scratch or reheating packaged commercial meals, and many other factors.

11.3.4 Child Nutrition Program Effects

Researchers have studied the effects of child nutrition programs on diverse outcomes (Ralston et al., 2017). For some outcomes, such as increased scores on standardized math tests in states with a school breakfast program mandate (Frisvold, 2015), it is clear that a positive finding reflects well on the program. For other important outcomes, the desired direction of change is ambiguous and differs from one child to another. For example, increased food energy intake represents a nutrition improvement for a hungry child but may be a mixed outcome for a child whose food energy needs are already met. Policy-makers must consider the risk both of not providing enough food and of providing too much food or at least too much highly palatable food containing excessive sugar, solid fats and salt.

As with the research about SNAP and household food security discussed in the previous chapter (Box 10.4), research on child nutrition programs is complicated by strong self-selection patterns. For instance, due to self-selection, the prevalence of household food insecurity among children in low-income households is comparatively high (16.2 percent in 2014–2015) for children who received SNAP and a free or reduced-price school meal in the preceding 30 days but lower (4.7 percent in 2014–2015) for children who did not receive benefits from these programs (Ralston et al., 2017). Nobody believes that getting a free or reduced-price school meal causes the increased risk of food insecurity. Instead, these findings show that free and reduced-price school meals are served to an especially vulnerable population of children.

Researchers have tried to develop methods that seek to account for self-selection patterns. Most of the methods introduced earlier in Chapter 10 have been applied to child nutrition programs at one time or another. One approach has been to compare outcomes in summer months and school-year months (Bhattacharya et al., 2006; Nord and Romig, 2006). The hope is that the outcomes in the summer months can provide a counterfactual for comparison to outcomes under the meals program. Although the federal government does support a summer food program, and some NSLP meals also are available to children during the summer, access to child nutrition programs is commonly far lower in the summer than during the school year. Evidence from longitudinal data suggested that a measure of food insufficiency rose in the summer for children who participated in the NSLP but stayed more steady (though lower) for students who did not participate (Huang et al., 2015; Ralston et al., 2017). In 2012–2014, an ambitious large-scale research study investigated alternative electronic benefit transfer (EBT) mechanisms for delivering additional support to low-income households with children during the summer (Box 11.2).

Other research has measured the quality of school meals. Once every several years, USDA sponsors a large study called the School Nutrition Dietary Assessment (SNDA). The fourth round, SNDA IV, found that lunches from the federal program do well at meeting some standards. Schools offered enough of selected nutrients (such as protein, vitamins and minerals) at lunch in 85 percent of all schools, and the lunches actually served had enough of these nutrients in 75 percent of all schools (Fox and Condon, 2012). Most schools came moderately close to meeting the standards for saturated fat. However, 99 percent of schools served lunches that exceeded upper limits on sodium, and most schools exceeded the standard by a margin of more than 50 percent. Sodium is the most serious challenge in meeting nutrition standards for federal school meals, and therefore remains a central focus of recent policy arguments. For the next study in the SNDA series, scheduled for publication in 2018, USDA plans to combine results on meal cost and nutrition quality.

In light of concern about both insufficient and excessive nutrients in school lunches, still other research has investigated the association between NSLP participation and risk of overweight and obesity, with a mix of positive, negative and neutral findings (Cawley and Datar, 2017). For example, Schanzenbach (2009) and Millimet et al. (2010) used panel data from the Early Childhood Longitudinal Survey to compare weight outcomes for elementary schoolchildren, holding constant the same children's weight in earlier grades while also using statistical methods to account for self-selection patterns. The authors were persuaded that NSLP participation appeared to increase

Box 11.2   Summer Electronic Benefit Transfer for Children (SEBTC)

To address poor nutrition among children and elevated risk of food insecurity in summer, when children are out of school, Congress instructed USDA to conduct demonstrations that would address both issues together. In 2012–2014, with USDA support, researchers carried out an ambitious pilot with a strong evaluation design (Collins et al., 2016; Gordon et al., 2017).

In sites around the country, households with children who were eligible for free and reduced-price meals received $60 in additional monthly support. Depending on the site, the participating households received either (a) a general food-related benefit similar to SNAP or (b) a more targeted nutritional benefit similar to WIC. Within each site, the households were randomly assigned to a treatment group that received support or a control group that did not.

The SEBTC benefits had a statistically significant impact in reducing food insecurity among children and increasing healthy food intake outcomes such as increased fruit and vegetable intake. The rate of food insecurity among children was 34.7 percent in households that received a benefit and 43.0 percent in households that did not (an 8.3 percentage point improvement). The children's daily fruit and vegetable intake was 3.3 cup equivalents in households that received the benefit and 2.9 cup equivalents in households that did not (a 0.4 cup equivalent improvement).

A critical food policy question is whether there is a tradeoff between pursuing nutrition and anti-hunger goals. The WIC-style EBT benefit was even more effective than the SNAP-style EBT benefit at increasing fruit and vegetable intake. Yet the two benefit delivery systems had similar impacts on food insecurity among children. This result suggested that the more targeted WIC-style benefit might be better at meeting nutrition and anti-hunger goals simultaneously, although both approaches were fairly effective.

Recognizing that Congress likely would skeptically scrutinize proposals for a substantial new national nutrition assistance support, USDA supported a third year of the study using a smaller $30 benefit, finding that a substantial portion of the beneficial outcomes could be achieved at reduced cost (Collins et al., 2016).

The strong random assignment research design of this evaluation enhances its credibility for policy purposes. Throughout Chapters 10 and 11, we have been wrestling with the difficulty of using other research designs when there is serious self-selection into safety net programs. It is sometimes argued that strong random assignment research designs cannot be used for nutrition assistance research, because it would be unethical to take away benefits to which children are entitled. In the case of the SEBTC study, low-income families already lacked access to some school meals supports during the summer, so no benefits were taken away. One might ask, now that the study has been conducted and published, demonstrating a method for increasing children's fruit and vegetable intake and reducing their risk of food insecurity, whether it is ethical *not* to implement such a program nationwide.

the risk of childhood obesity (Schanzenbach, 2009; Millimet et al., 2010), although the results depended in part on the assumptions of the statistical models used.

Overall, the evidence is uncertain that school meals programs cause harm, but clearly the nutrition quality of school meals could be upgraded. The research on child nutrition programs, food insecurity and risk of obesity puts considerable pressure on school nutrition policy-makers to consider further measures to improve the healthfulness of school meals programs, but without sacrificing participation levels and the programs' potential benefits for children's food security.

11.4 Special Supplemental Nutrition Program for Women, Infants and Children

11.4.1 WIC History

Policy-makers in the late 1960s increasingly worried about the nutrition status of low-income pregnant women and infants. In 1969, President Richard Nixon convened a White House Conference on Food, Nutrition and Health that was chaired by the nutrition scientist Jean Mayer, who later became president of Tufts University. The summary report from the conference described hunger and malnutrition among pregnant women and infants as a national emergency requiring immediate response. In part based on recommendations from that conference, Congress established the WIC program as a pilot in 1972, and WIC began operation as a permanent program in 1974 (Table 11.2). WIC provides nutrition services, referrals and a package of nutrient-dense foods to eligible women, infants and children.

Table 11.2 Program summary: Supplemental Nutrition Program for Women, Infants and Children (WIC)

Overview: Nutrition assistance for three selected populations with elevated risk of nutrient deficiency.	
Year begun	1975
Scale of operation	
Total, average monthly participation, fiscal year 2016 (million)	7.7
Women, average monthly participation, fiscal year 2016 (million)	1.8
Infants, average monthly participation, fiscal year 2016 (million)	1.9
Children, average monthly participation, fiscal year 2016 (million)	4.0
WIC infants, 2012 (as % of U.S. infants in 2012)	51
WIC children, 2012 (as % of U.S. children in 2012)	28
Budget	
Total annual expenditure, fiscal year 2016 ($ billion)	5.9
Eligibility	
Gross household income test (% of poverty standard)	185
Benefits: Nutrient-dense food packages, nutrition services and referrals.	
Monthly food cost per person, fiscal year 2016 ($)	42.62

Data note: WIC national and state-level participation statistics are available from USDA's Food and Nutrition Service (www.fns.usda.gov/data-and-statistics).

Source: USDA FNS; Oliveira, 2017; Oliveira and Frazao, 2015.

In the 1970s and early 1980s, USDA officials expressed doubt that the program would have large impacts on food intake. A national WIC evaluation in the 1980s, led by Dr. David Rush, reported health benefits and increased consumption of qualifying foods associated with WIC participation. USDA released an edited version of this evaluation in 1986, downplaying some favorable findings, but the authors independently published the complete findings in 1998 in the *American Journal of Clinical Nutrition* (Rush et al., 1988).

The WIC program expanded during the 1990s and 2000s, and its political support solidified. The principal policy controversies concerned funding levels and incremental policy changes, such as revisions to the WIC package (Institute of Medicine, 2005) or changes to the eligibility of higher-income participants (Besharov and Call, 2009).

11.4.2 WIC Eligibility and Benefits

WIC provides nutrition services and food packages to low-income pregnant and post-partum women, infants up to 1 year of age and children up to their fifth birthday. The income eligibility cutoff is less strict than SNAP's, allowing WIC participation if income is less than 185 percent of the federal poverty standard ($3,746 per month for a family of four in 2015) (Table 11.2). Under a procedure called **adjunctive eligibility**, participants in other programs, such as SNAP and Medicaid, may be certified as eligible for WIC. Because some states use an income cutoff for Medicaid eligibility that is higher than 185 percent of the poverty standard, some applicants with household income higher than this level may be adjunctively eligible for WIC.

WIC officially is a **discretionary** or **nonentitlement** program, which means that spending levels are determined in annual appropriations legislation. The appropriations committees in the House and Senate strongly influence WIC spending. In principle, if funding runs out in a given year, applicants are placed on a waiting list. In practice, in most recent years, the program has functioned nearly as an entitlement. The federal appropriations have been based on estimates of the funding level required to provide benefits to all eligible applicants.

In addition to the income eligibility rule, WIC participants must be at **nutritional risk**, based on any of several nutritional criteria specified in program rules. The nutritional risk criteria do not constrain eligibility very much in years when there is sufficient funding. Most applicants meet one risk criterion or another. For example, although only 12 percent of pregnant WIC participants were classified as having nutritional risk based on a biological marker such as low hemoglobin, 70 percent were at risk based on overweight and 31 percent based on "inappropriate nutrition practices" (Geller et al., 2012). Nutritional risk criteria will matter more if WIC budgets fall short in future years, as fiscal constraints tighten. If there is a waitlist, WIC uses a priority system that gives higher priority to pregnant and breastfeeding women, infants and then children whose nutritional risk is certified based on hematological or anthropometric measurements instead of eating patterns.

The WIC benefit package is defined in terms of specific food and beverages, with the goal of enhancing intake of particular nutrients and, more recently, fruits, vegetables and whole grains. In most states, WIC participants receive a voucher or electronic benefit transfer (EBT) benefits for the food packages, which the women can redeem from authorized food retailers. In some states, women pick up the packages directly from the WIC office. The federal government supports the full program cost, both for the WIC packages and for nutrition services and administration by state and local agencies.

An economically important component of the package is infant formula. New WIC mothers and their case workers must choose between three options:

- **full breastfeeding** (with no infant formula, but receiving an enhanced package of foods for the breastfeeding mother),
- **partial breastfeeding** (with some infant formula and an enhanced package of foods for the breastfeeding mother) or
- **full formula** (with infant formula and a smaller package of food for the nonbreast-feeding mother).

USDA in 2007 published revised rules to fit better with current nutrition concerns in low-income populations, including overnutrition and poor diets as well as nutrient deficiencies. For women, the packages may include carrots, cereal, fish, cheese and fruit juice (currently, less cheese and fruit juice than before the revision). For infants, the packages may include infant formula or infant cereal, depending on the infant's age. The policy revision reduced the maximum amount of formula that could be received under the partial breastfeeding package, essentially encouraging mothers to make a sharper choice between full breastfeeding or full formula options.

11.4.3 WIC Participation Trends and Costs

WIC participation grew steadily from 1980 through 2010, pausing only briefly during the favorable economy of the late 1990s (Figure 11.5). The number of participants in

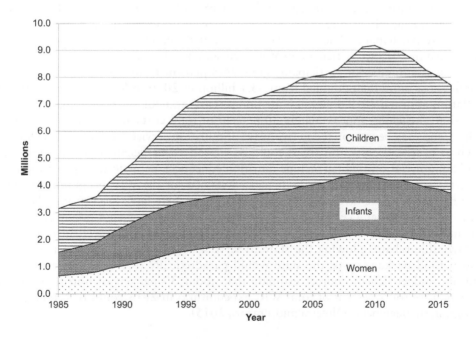

Figure 11.5 Mean monthly WIC participants, 1985–2016

Data note: WIC participation statistics are available from USDA's Food and Nutrition Service (www.fns. usda.gov/pd/wicmain.htm).

Source: USDA ERS; USDA FNS.

the largest category, children aged 1 to 4 years, grew from less than 2 million in the late 1980s to almost 5 million by 2010. After 2010, WIC participation declined for all three participant types, most likely because of demographic trends in the number of births.

WIC growth during the late 1980s and early 1990s was facilitated by a policy innovation, when states began requiring infant formula suppliers to bid competitively for the opportunity to become the sole supplier to state WIC programs. WIC makes up a large share of the U.S. infant formula market, so suppliers had a strong economic incentive to compete hard for the states' business. In return for sole-source contracts, the suppliers offered rebates of more than half of the face value of the formula. Infant formula rebates were worth almost $2 billion in recent years, essentially providing sufficient funding to serve one quarter of WIC participants (Oliveira and Frazao, 2015).

About half of all U.S. infants, and just over a quarter of all children aged 1 to 4 years, participate in WIC. There has been a lively debate for many years about how to estimate the participation rate as a percentage of the number of eligible people (Swann, 2010). This participation rate is closely watched, because it may indicate whether WIC funding was sufficient, or whether eligible people remained unserved. In early years, USDA compared the number of WIC participants based on administrative records to the number of people who appeared to be eligible based on income data from the Current Population Survey (CPS). In this computation, the number of WIC infants in the early 2000s was more than 20 percent larger than the estimated number of eligible infants, making it appear that the program must be serving some ineligible infants. In more recent years, USDA has used a revised statistical approach, adjusting for known measurement problems with the CPS and taking more careful account of adjunctive eligibility. Using the revised approach, it no longer appears that there are too many participants. For example, only about 83 percent of eligible infants were estimated in 2015 to participate in WIC (Oliveira and Frazao, 2015).

While the number of participants grew 26.8 percent from 2000 to 2010, the program's cost more than doubled from $3.1 billion in 2000 to $6.8 billion in 2010 (in inflation-adjusted 2010 dollars). Nutrition services and administration made up a rising share, reaching approximately 30 percent of total costs at the end of the 2000s. This trend may be interpreted in two ways. If nutrition services and administration are seen as overhead costs, this trend could be viewed as inefficient. If nutrition services and administration—which include nutrition education, breastfeeding promotion and referrals—are seen as part of the beneficial services of the WIC program, this trend can be viewed more favorably. From time to time, there have been proposals to cap nutrition services at a certain percentage of total costs, but such a policy could have an unintended side effect. With a cap, when state agencies succeed in negotiating a favorable rebate, allowing the state to serve a larger number of participants with lower food package costs, the state would paradoxically receive a smaller administration budget. USDA sources estimate that about 30 percent of nutrition services expenditure (or 9 percent of total WIC expenditure) in 2013 could be thought of as program management (Oliveira and Frazao, 2015).

11.4.4 WIC Program Effects

Because WIC includes nutrition services plus many different food packages for different groups of participants, researchers have studied a diversity of potential program outcomes. In contrast with SNAP, which lets participants choose any foods or nonalcoholic beverages, the specificity of the WIC food packages means that the program is likely to have a larger effect on consumption of particular foods. For example, a child's monthly WIC package may include, among other foods, a dozen eggs, 35 ounces of fortified breakfast cereal and 2 pounds of whole wheat bread. Even after considering that some of this food may be consumed by other members of the household, it is likely that the package will increase the child's consumption of these particular foods. Yet because the WIC package is explicitly designed to be supplemental, merely one part of the child's food supply, it is far from clear that the WIC package either does or should increase the child's overall food intake. Following the changes in the WIC package in 2009, research showed a shift in participants' food spending away from juice, whole milk and cheese and toward lower fat milk, whole grains and fruits and vegetables (Andreyeva and Luedicke, 2015; Oliveira and Frazao, 2015).

Some of the most influential WIC research has addressed the effect of participation during pregnancy on birth outcomes. Research in the 1980s and early 1990s suggested that pregnant women who participate in WIC had higher birthweights for their infants. For women at risk of undernutrition, higher birthweight is unambiguously a good outcome, although in populations at risk of both undernutrition and overweight the relationship between birthweight and health is more complex (Whitaker, 2004). By comparing birth outcomes in counties that were early or late adopters of the WIC program in the 1970s and early 1980s, Hoynes et al. (2011) concluded that WIC appears to have a positive effect on infant birthweights. Other research using statistical models that compare birth outcomes for WIC participants and nonparticipants has been more mixed (Colman et al., 2012). Key results appear to depend on the statistical modeling choices one makes, so even readers who care principally about practical policy issues may find it necessary to consider the merits of different statistical models (Box 11.3).

Another important research topic is WIC's potential effects on breastfeeding practices. Health and medical authorities recommend exclusive breastfeeding for infants throughout the first several months of life. The federal government's Healthy People 2020 objectives seek to achieve a breastfeeding initiation rate of 82 percent of U.S. infants (www.healthypeople.gov). Similarly, WIC policy strongly emphasizes the goal of promoting breastfeeding. Yet by providing free infant formula, WIC also could have the practical effect of encouraging formula feeding (Ryan and Zhou, 2006; Colman et al., 2012).

When the WIC package changes were designed in 2007 and implemented in 2009, one goal was to improve the program's effectiveness at promoting breastfeeding over formula feeding. The revisions reduced the amount of infant formula provided to mother-infant pairs in the partial breastfeeding category. After implementation, the results appeared mixed. Evaluation research in California, where the package change was accompanied by intensive training of frontline staff to encourage breastfeeding, found a shift from the full formula package toward the full breastfeeding package (Whaley et al., 2012; Oliveira and Frazao, 2015). In a national evaluation, fewer mother-infant pairs did indeed get the partial breastfeeding package after implementation, as expected. More mother-infant pairs received the full breastfeeding package after implementation, but more pairs also received the full formula package (Wilde et al., 2012). Taken together, these changes suggested that the package change was

Box 11.3   Specification Choices in WIC Research

In WIC evaluation research, as in many other fields, the results depend on statistical assumptions that researchers make. For example, a simple statistical model would look at the association between WIC participation and birthweight:

(1) $bw = \beta_0 + \beta_1 WIC + u$

In this model, *bw* is birthweight in grams, *WIC* is an indicator variable (= 1 if the mother participates in WIC and = 0 otherwise), β_0 is the mean birthweight if the mother is a nonparticipant, β_1 is the increase in mean birthweight if the mother is a participant and *u* is all the factors other than WIC that influence birthweight. Because such a model fails to control for self-selection, apparent differences in mean birthweight outcomes could be caused by omitted variables, including income and education, rather than by WIC participation.

As a partial remedy, a second statistical model might include household income and mother's education as explanatory variables:

(2) $bw = \beta_0 + \beta_1 WIC + \beta_2 inc + \beta_3 educ + u$

For mothers who share a particular household income and education level, β_1 shows the approximate difference in mean birthweight outcomes that is associated with WIC participation.

Some researchers would go further, taking account of gestational age at the time of birth (the number of weeks the pregnancy had lasted), because a birth after a full pregnancy of 36–40 weeks is likely to be healthier than an earlier birth.

(3) $bw = \beta_0 + \beta_1 WIC + \beta_2 inc + \beta_3 educ + \beta_4 gestational\ age + u$

Now, for mothers whose pregnancies lasted the same length (and who also share the same income and education), β_1 shows the approximate difference in mean birthweight outcomes that is associated with WIC participation.

Researchers who think that WIC influences gestational age by keeping mothers healthier during pregnancy prefer models similar to (2). These researchers tend to estimate that WIC strongly raises birthweights (Bitler and Currie, 2005). In a review from the Center on Budget and Policy Priorities, a nonpartisan liberal advocate for safety net programs, "[C]orrecting for gestational age at birth may understate WIC's positive impact on birth outcomes because it effectively eliminates any positive effect WIC has on extending the duration of healthy pregnancies" (Carlson and Neuberger, 2017).

Researchers who think of gestational age largely as an independent variable instead of a program outcome prefer models similar to (3). Failing to control for gestational age would be a mistake, they say, because it gives WIC credit for favorable birth outcomes that really had other causes. These researchers tend to estimate that WIC has smaller effects on birthweight (Colman et al., 2012; Carlson and Neuberger, 2017).

In the competing studies on this issue, the researchers mostly agree on the empirical facts. Yet, in the polite and subdued tones of scholarly research, they sharply disagree about the best specification and hence about the conclusions for WIC policy.

not enough on its own to significantly improve breastfeeding practices for WIC mothers. Future initiatives could consider reducing the economic value of the full formula package, increasing outreach to pregnant women during pregnancy (when they may be making the most important decisions about breastfeeding intentions) and making further improvements in state and local administration of the new food packages.

Discussion of research design is itself part of the WIC policy debate. At a 2010 meeting to discuss USDA's WIC research agenda, one participant suggested a pilot study where women would be randomly assigned either to the standard WIC package options or to an alternative that did not include infant formula (Institute of Medicine, 2011b). A random assignment research design offers the strongest possible evidence of true WIC impacts on breastfeeding, because it is less susceptible to the self-selection problem. Such a design is ethical only if scientists do not know which group of participants will fare better; it is unethical to randomly assign some participants to receive a package that is thought to be inferior to the current standard of care. In the case of WIC food packages, it is truly unknown whether providing free infant formula is beneficial for infant health. Congress would have to authorize such a pilot study, which likely could not be undertaken by USDA on its own initiative alone.

11.5 Improving Child Nutrition Programs

To support food security for children and address the problem of childhood obesity and poor nutrition, there is intense policy interest in improving child nutrition programs. High-profile public efforts include Michelle Obama's Let's Move Campaign, the Partnership for a Healthier America, ChildObesity180 and many other initiatives in national, state and local policy. Yet, as this section will discuss, it turns out to be difficult to craft school nutrition reforms that have both substantive merit and political and economic viability.

One objection to some reform proposals is that they could be economically infeasible, raising the cost of reimbursable meals and damaging the other revenue streams that SFAs need to make ends meet. Yet, this objection may misunderstand the internal economics of federal school meals programs. Providing free lunches at the reimbursable rate is comparatively feasible, while the other income streams are not always as helpful to SFA finances as one might expect. For example, as discussed earlier (Section 11.3.3), far from making higher revenue from *a la carte* sales, some school districts implicitly cross-subsidize *a la carte sales* using revenue from the NSLP reimbursable meals. Similarly, the revenue from paid lunch sales may not be as high as the reimbursement from serving free lunches. On average, SFAs set the prices for paid lunches at approximately $2.21 (in the most recent year of data available, for 2012–2013). For SFAs, the per-meal revenue from paid lunches (approximately $2.58 after including the $0.37 reimbursement) typically is lower than the per-meal revenue from the federal reimbursement for free lunches ($3.29). This means that, surprisingly, the federal free lunch program for low-income children has been implicitly cross-subsidizing the sale of paid lunches to higher-income children. Congress passed a provision to discourage this economically regressive cross-subsidization in 2011, which appears to have reduced but not eliminated the practice (Standing et al., 2016).

In her 2010 book *Free For All*, the sociologist Janet Poppendieck discusses ambitious proposals to increase the per-lunch reimbursement by 50 cents or to replace the three-tier pricing system of the NSLP and SBP with a universal free program (Poppendieck, 2010). She argues that a universal program would benefit both poor children, "who would no longer have to eat a meal seasoned by shame," and middle-income children, "for whom healthy school meals would become the norm." Poppendieck notes that some European countries have successful universal free lunch programs. In the 2010 Healthy Hunger-Free Kids Act, a Community Eligibility Provision (CEP) extended a more limited universal free program to just selected school districts or parts of districts with particularly high rates of low-income students (Ralston et al., 2017).

Given the high estimated cost of universal free lunch in a tight budgetary environment, it is not surprising that legislative proposals were more modest as Congress took up child nutrition reauthorization in the 2010 Healthy Hunger-Free Kids Act. The Food Research and Action Center floated a universal school breakfast proposal (leaving the larger school lunch program with tiered pricing), but it was not adopted. President Barack Obama proposed to increase the per-lunch reimbursement for the NSLP by 20 cents, at a cost of approximately $1 billion per year. In the Senate, legislators proposed a budget increase of a little less than half this amount, and some of the additional funding would have been subtracted from the SNAP program. In the final legislation, as passed by both Houses of Congress and signed by the president in December 2010, the per-lunch reimbursement was increased by only 6 cents (less than a 3 percent increase) and only for districts that comply with new meal requirements.

These nutrition requirements were based on two reports from the Institute of Medicine (IOM). A 2007 IOM report proposed standards for competitive foods outside of the federal meals programs, seeking to promote healthier options and restrain the sale of less healthy snack foods and sugar-sweetened beverages. A 2010 IOM report proposed standards for the federal meals programs themselves (Institute of Medicine, 2010). FNS published a slightly revised version of these new meal standards in the *Federal Register* in early 2011. The proposed changes would promote fruits, vegetables, whole grains and low-fat dairy, while reducing sodium, saturated fat and *trans* fat. More than 133,000 public comments were submitted, of which approximately 123,000 came from organized letter-writing campaigns (Table 11.3). It is not possible to treat tabulations of public comments as if they came from a representative public opinion survey, because clearly there is great variation in people's motivation to submit comments. Yet, in general, the submitted comments were mostly favorable to USDA's proposed changes. Some farm organizations and food manufacturers (including American Frozen Food Institute, a national trade association), organized opposition to particular provisions. Disputed provisions included a limit on the frequency with which starchy vegetables such as potatoes could be served at lunch and a limit on the amount of vegetable servings that would be credited for tomato sauce, which amounted to a restraint on serving pizza in school lunch (Mercier, 2012).

Subsequently, the nutrition standards have been partly rolled back. Senate appropriations legislation in 2011 included a rider barring USDA from restricting the use of potatoes as vegetables. Then, in November 2011, the House/Senate conference committee for fiscal year 2012 appropriations also acted to reverse the provision regarding tomato sauce on pizza. USDA's final rule, published in January 2012, backed down on both provisions. The Congressional intervention was a victory for potato growers

Table 11.3 Summary of public comments on selected issues in USDA's proposed new school meals standards, 2011

Type of comment	860	Unique submissions with substantive comments
	6,247	Other unique submissions
	122,715	Form letters from 172 mass mailing campaigns
	3,446	Duplicates and nongermane comments
	133,268	Total
Overall	41,595	Generally supportive
	430	Generally opposed
Starchy vegetables	73,950	Support limit on weekly starchy vegetables in school lunch
	4,170	Oppose limit on starchy vegetables
Saturated fat	20,265	Support limiting saturated fat
	5	Oppose limiting saturated fat
Sodium	46,420	Support new limits on sodium
	325	Oppose new limits on sodium (940 favored milder limits)
Offer versus serve	40	Support requiring student to accept at least one fruit or one vegetable
	1,540	Oppose requirement (3,550 concerned about plate waste)
Tomato paste	110	Support limiting credit for tomato paste (e.g., on pizza)
	390	Oppose limiting credit for tomato paste

Source: USDA FNS.

and frozen pizza manufacturers, but of course that means it was a loss for other farmers and other manufacturers who compete with potatoes and pizza. Extensive media coverage slammed Congress for "treating pizza as a vegetable." The controversy increased public awareness of the food industry's substantial political power in child nutrition program design and delivery, even during a time of high-profile public campaigns to promote improved school nutrition (Mercier, 2012).

An influential player in these debates is the School Nutrition Association (SNA), a national nonprofit association with 56,000 members in the school food service industry. Over time, the SNA leadership soured on the proposed nutrition standards. In 2014, the association replaced its lobbyist Marshall Matz, an attorney with a decades-long history as a moderate power-broker in school meals policy, with representation that would protect SFAs more vigorously from what they perceived as burdensome regulation (Confessore, 2014). For the next several years, argument over child nutrition program reform remained so fiercely divided that Congress never passed a subsequent round of child nutrition reauthorization legislation. Instead, through 2017, the child nutrition programs mostly continued as they were under previous legislative authority (see Section 11.1). Even from the older 2010 Healthy Hunger-Free Kids Act, not all changes to nutrition standards have been carried out, and schedules for finalizing implementation of the new sodium standards and several other provisions remain in dispute.

11.6 Conclusion

Nutrition assistance programs for children provide a good example of important policy dilemmas that have been discussed throughout this book. First, policy choices require real tradeoffs between competing priorities. Notwithstanding the passion that participants bring to the argument, it is difficult to discern which policies are most beneficial. Second, policy outcomes depend on a struggle between advocacy coalitions representing diverse public goals and private interests. In this struggle, beneficial policies may win or lose.

The nutrition assistance programs discussed in Chapters 10 and 11 address both anti-hunger and nutrition objectives. Anti-hunger objectives motivate support for increasing program resources and avoiding excessive paternalism. Nutrition objectives motivate proposals to define program benefits more narrowly, as in proposals to restrict SNAP benefits to healthier products or to strengthen nutrition standards for school meals (Section 11.5).

A recurring theme in public policy is the tension between rules and discretion (Chapter 1). Many policy decisions discussed in this book involve the assignment of social choices either to markets or to government action, each of which has strengths and weaknesses in particular circumstances. More than almost any other area of U.S. food policy, some significant choices about children's nutrition are assigned to government programs. The importance of this particular assignment helps explain the intensity of policy debates about such seemingly arcane topics as the design of WIC packages for breastfeeding and formula feeding infants or the classification of potatoes and tomato paste in vegetable serving counts for the NSLP. Under the pressures of limited resources—and the challenges of coherent governance in the face of divided public input—these nutrition assistance programs bear a weighty responsibility for the nourishment of the next generation of Americans.

Summary List of Key Terms (identified in bold in the text)

- adjunctive eligibility
- bonus commodities
- competitive foods
- direct certification
- discretionary
- entitlement commodities
- free
- full breastfeeding
- full formula
- nonentitlement
- nutritional risk
- offer versus serve
- paid
- partial breastfeeding
- paternalism
- reduced price
- School Food Authority

12 Looking Forward

12.1 Introduction

Food policy will not be the same throughout readers' careers as it is today. Although every chapter of this book has described facts and institutions that offer insight into the current state of food policy in the United States, the book also seeks to present an approach to interpreting data, weighing perspectives, assessing options and understanding policy formulation that may be useful looking forward into the future.

This chapter:

- describes federal government forecasts for key variables in the food system, based on social, economic and environmental trends (Section 12.2);
- reviews the policy responses that these food system trends may trigger (Section 12.3); and
- contemplates the wide diversity of approaches that reasonable people may take in seeking to improve the future performance of the food system (Section 12.4).

12.2 Food System Forecasts

Government agencies and nongovernmental organizations seek to forecast how the food system will change and develop in the future. As with weather forecasts, these prognostications are fairly accurate in the short term and highly speculative over a longer time horizon. We might be tempted to condemn the creators of longer-term forecasts for vanity, but these analysts already recognize that their forecasts may be wrong. They generate these forecasts simply because they must. Some essential government policy-making processes require forecasts. For example, to set the premium rates for federal crop insurance programs, one must make a guess about future planting decisions, weather, yields and crop losses. To weigh the budgetary tradeoffs in a Farm Bill or other major food policy legislation, one must make a guess about future economic trends, tax revenues, commodity prices and program expenditures. When the forecasts prove incorrect, nobody is surprised or shocked. The policy process relies on a system of forecasts that are continually updated in response to new information.

For the broader federal budget process in the United States, the most important forecasts are generated by the Congressional Budget Office (CBO) for a five-year and a 10-year time horizon (Congressional Budget Office, 2016), offering projections for government revenues, expenditures and budget deficits. For U.S. food policy more narrowly, forecasts are generated by a USDA interagency committee (USDA Interagency

Agricultural Projections Committee, 2016), offering projections for farm income, farm program expenditures, commodity prices for major commodities, imports and exports. For both CBO and USDA, new reports in the same series will be published in years to come.

These food system forecasts are related to nearly all of the previous chapters in this book. For example, here are forecasts related to just four of the most important external influences on the U.S. food system:

- Economic growth. USDA assumes global real economic growth of 3.1 percent annually in 2016–2025, which is "slightly below the long-term trend prior to the 2008 financial crisis" (USDA Interagency Agricultural Projections Committee, 2016). Economic growth in the United States affects the consumer demand for agricultural products (Chapter 2), food manufacturing (Chapter 5) and retail and restaurants (Chapter 6). It affects the number of people in poverty, and hence the numbers of people who require food assistance (Chapter 10). U.S. food policy also is affected by economic growth in developing countries, which USDA expects to remain strong, but not as high it has been in recent years (Chapter 4).
- Population. The growth in the world's total number of people to feed is not some independent fact of nature, but rather it responds to the short-run business cycle and long-run economic development. USDA projects that economic growth "contributes to the continued slowing of population gains around the world as birth rates decline." National and global population forecasts are useful for understanding topics ranging from the likely number of U.S. schoolchildren in future years (Chapter 11) to the prospects for having enough food to feed the world (Chapter 3).
- Trade. The U.S. dollar was comparatively weak from 2002–2011, meaning that a dollar could be exchanged for comparatively few units of other countries' currencies. A weak dollar caused U.S. agricultural exports to be comparatively attractive to overseas buyers (see Chapter 4). The dollar strengthened in 2015, and USDA projects further appreciation, which will tend to limit U.S. agricultural exports and increase imports.
- Energy prices. Crude oil prices began falling in mid-2014, in response to heavy production in traditional oil-exporting regions (such as the Persian Gulf) and newer sources (such as oil sands in Canada). From their low levels, USDA assumes that oil prices will rise faster than inflation, but not fast enough to return to the high prices of the early 2010s. Comparatively low oil prices reduce the cost of key agricultural inputs, such as nitrogen fertilizer and the fuel used in agricultural machinery (Chapter 2). Low oil prices may lower the incentive to convert food stocks into biofuels, and they also may reduce the economic feasibility of adopting alternative renewable energy sources such as wind and solar, with implications for all of the world's major environmental challenges (Chapter 3).

Based on these factors, USDA forecasts the production and prices for each major category of agricultural commodity. For example, in 2016–2025, USDA expects prices for major row crops such as corn, wheat and soybeans to be much lower than they were during the price spikes of the late 2000s and early 2010s, though still higher than they were during the low-price period of the 1990s and early 2000s (Figure 12.1). These prices in turn affect other major food system outcomes. For starters, these prices

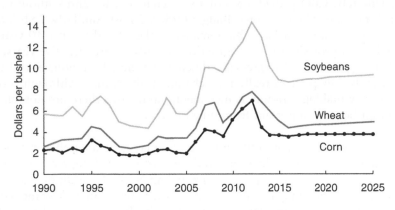

Figure 12.1 U.S. farm-level price forecasts: corn, wheat and soybeans

Data note: Each year, in February, the USDA Interagency Agricultural Projections Committee offers forecasts for food system variables over the next 10-year period (www.usda.gov/oce/commodity/projections/).

Source: USDA Interagency Agricultural Projections Committee, 2016.

directly affect farm household incomes and the cost of government subsidies for agriculture. Because corn and soybeans are major sources of animal feed, these prices also influence the prices for meat, dairy and eggs. Because these crops are major sources of biofuel stock, they are part of a feedback loop that simultaneously is influenced by and influences energy prices. Finally, the prices of crops, animal products and energy all influence the prices of foods in grocery stores and restaurants, which affect consumer well-being, food insecurity and the cost of government nutrition assistance programs.

Of course, alternative assumptions about inputs to these forecasts (such as crop yields or energy prices) would generate different food system outcomes (such as prices for crops and animal foods). The analysts who produced the USDA forecast (Figure 12.1) have treated the price spikes of the late 2000s and early 2010s as an exception, unlikely to return. That expectation makes sense if one views these price spikes as a product merely of temporary causes such as bad weather, commodity speculation or supply glitches in the energy market. On the other hand, if we believe the high prices were a response to long-term trends, including a slowdown in agricultural productivity growth, increasingly severe environmental constraints and rising long-term energy costs during a time of climate change (Bourne, 2015), then we may expect higher food prices in the future.

12.3 Policy Responses to Food System Trends

In making forecasts, one of the greatest challenges is deciding what assumptions to make about future policy responses. For example, the CBO is required by law to generate baseline forecasts on the assumption that current laws remain in place. You might think it is easy to hold policy constant, but this requirement leaves considerable ambiguity. For example, current laws may include a "temporary" tax cut, which is officially scheduled to expire after a couple years, but which Congress most likely will extend indefinitely. CBO provides alternative scenarios with and without the exten-sion of such tax cuts (Congressional Budget Office, 2016). Similarly, USDA forecasts assume that the most recent Farm Bill remains in place for the entire 10-year period, even though most provisions of the legislation actually expire after five years, because it is widely recognized that Congress is unlikely to let these farm policies end abruptly.

More broadly, key policies really may change in the future. Although progress in U.S. food policy-making typically is incremental and slow, there are notable sources of change that become important from time to time:

- *New information.* New scientific information may generate policy change on top-ics ranging from food production and the environment (Chapter 3) to food safety policy (Chapter 7) to dietary guidance (Chapter 8). In addition, new ways of sharing information may influence food policy, as when an environmental organi-zation publishes an online database of farm subsidy payments (Chapter 2), when new food labeling elements are invented or when a Freedom of Information Act request leads a government agency to share information that previously had not been in the public domain. The agricultural and food industries are constantly changing as technological advances generate novel business opportunities.
- *New advocacy coalitions.* Although some advocacy coalitions in U.S. food policy do appear stable, policy innovations sometimes generate realignments, eroding political support for some policies and building support for others. Long-standing cooperation between public health advocates and anti-hunger advocates seemed to weaken in the early 2010s, frayed by debates over policy proposals such as restrictions on SNAP benefits (Chapters 10 and 11). From the 1980s through the 2010s, farm policy reformers sought to pick apart the political coalition that had long backed traditional subsidy programs, proposing an alternative bundle of farm policies including stronger conservation programs, reduced support for large farms, continued support for small farmers and budgetary savings for taxpayers. In response, at least during the 2000s, traditional farm policy constituencies suc-ceeded in compiling their own bundle of counterproposals, combining continued grain and oilseed subsidies with modest support for organic and sustainable agri-culture initiatives and for fruit and vegetable growers.
- *External events.* Finally, food policy evolves or changes in response to external circumstances. Some external events may be sudden, such as a foodborne illness outbreak, a hurricane or a financial crisis. Other changes may be slower, such as demographic changes that increase consumer preferences for convenience and restaurant food (Chapter 6) or that alter the mix of immigrant and U.S.-born workers in the labor force for agriculture and food processing (Chapter 4). World population growth, increased globalization and trade and climate change all influ-ence the context in which U.S. food policies are determined.

United Nations member countries in fall 2015 adopted the Sustainable Develop-ment Goals as a global action agenda, with specific targets for the years 2016–2030. Several of these goals involve food and agriculture. For example, Goal 1 (no poverty), Goal 2 (zero hunger), Goal 3 (good health and well-being) and Goal 13 (climate action) all imply major policy responses to food system challenges. In our expectations for the future, should we treat Sustainable Development Goals as mere wishful think-ing? Or should we treat them as real plans for a plausible policy response that may actually affect global outcomes? There are good reasons why official baseline forecasts usually assume "no policy change," but, for actually predicting the future, we should recognize that governments and nongovernmental institutions will want to try to alter the trends that have been forecast.

12.4 A Shared Sense of Purpose

This book uses U.S. food policy debates to motivate the reader's study of policy fundamentals, economic principles, scientific research and institutional details. Without policy debates, studying these topics may seem academic. Without study, the policy debates descend into pointless stone-throwing.

Sometimes food policy arguments seem like a battle between well-entrenched armies, endlessly lobbing the same attacks across a barren and stagnant front. Just as the two dominant U.S. political parties have divided the citizenry, reducing politics to a ferocious struggle over a small territory of undecided voters in the middle, food policy debates may initially seem like a war of attrition between pro-business interests and progressive activists. When I encourage readers to engage with policy debates, I certainly do not suggest that they line up in the trenches on one side or the other, hoping that new attacks today will dislodge the enemy even though similar attacks failed yesterday and the day before. On the contrary, this book is for readers who seek some nearby hill behind the lines from which to observe, reflect and plan a more fruitful course of action.

From this vantage point, the first thing to notice is that the opposing trenches are more fragmented than they seem up close. A recurring theme of this book is that the food industry is divided in politically significant ways. There are broad divisions between agriculture (Chapter 2), food and beverage manufacturing (Chapter 5) and the food retail and restaurant industries (Chapter 6). Within each of these industries, there are divisions across products and geographic regions and distinctions from one policy debate to the next. The companies within a particular industry sometimes cooperate and sometimes compete intensely with each other in the public policy arena, just as they do in economic markets. Even a single company may oppose government regulations most of the time and then actively seek out government involvement when faced with a particular problem, such as a food safety crisis that provokes a costly loss of consumer confidence (Chapter 7).

Similarly, public interest organizations work together on many environmental issues (Chapter 3), nutrition and public health issues (Chapter 8) and food security issues (Chapter 10) and yet sometimes find themselves on opposite sides of food policy debates that require difficult choices between competing social objectives. Even though they generally are organized as nonprofit organizations, which do not earn profits for shareholders, public interest and advocacy organizations have their own business models, drawing economic support variously from government agencies, foundations, public membership, charitable donations and business operations such as sales of publications or other goods and services. Public interest organizations make diverse decisions about building or not building alliances with industry organizations in the same areas of policy debate.

The second thing to notice is that policy perspectives are not as doctrinaire as they may at first appear. The economic perspective on food policy controversies is correctly reputed to favor market-oriented solutions to social problems and to be instinctively skeptical of proposals for new government programs and regulations. Yet the economic perspective also offers fine material to work with in pursuit of public interest goals. The mainstream economic perspective acknowledges a variety of market failures (see Chapter 1), such as environmental externalities (Chapter 3), imperfectly competitive markets (Chapters 5 and 6) and imperfect information (Chapters 7, 8 and 9), which lead to constructive and illuminating debates about how best to employ the comparative strengths of market institutions and government institutions to solve social problems.

Similarly, leading U.S. public interest organizations are ideologically diverse, practical and far more balanced about the role of governments and markets than they are given credit for. It is true that activist organizations sometimes broadly characterize the agricultural and food industries as a united opponent, while dismissing the economic perspective on food policy controversies as mere rhetorical cover for this opponent, but that stance is only part of the story. In a book chapter on "strategies for changing the food system," G.W. Stevenson and colleagues describe the diversity of public interest perspectives using the three-part metaphor of warrior, builder and weaver work (Stevenson et al., 2008).

1. Warrior work "consciously contests . . . corporate trajectories and operates primarily, but not exclusively, in the political sector."
2. Builder work "seeks to create alternative food initiatives and models and operates primarily (and often less contentiously) in the economic sector."
3. Weaver work "focuses on developing strategic and conceptual linkages within and between warrior and builder activities. . . . This is the work of connection."

For readers who thoughtfully consider multiple perspectives on food policy controversies, the contrasts in writing style between market-oriented economists and public interest advocates are ultimately secondary. Economists may chuckle at the food system reformers' colorful metaphors, and food system reformers may object to the formality of diagnosing market failures. Yet, despite these contrasts, what stands out is a widely shared sense of purpose in harnessing both markets and governments to improve the performance of the food system.

References

Aduddell, R. M. and Cain, L. P. (1981) "Public policy toward 'the greatest trust in the world'," *The Business History Review*, 55(2), 217–242.

AEI/Brookings Working Group on Poverty and Opportunity (2015) *Opportunity, Responsibility, and Security: A Consensus Plan for Reducing Poverty and Restoring the American Dream*, American Enterprise Institute and Brookings Institution, Washington, DC.

Aguilar, J., Gramig, G. G., Hendrickson, J. R., Archer, D. W., Forcella, F. and Liebig, M. A. (2015) "Crop species diversity changes in the United States: 1978–2012," *PloS One*, 10(8), e0136580.

Allcott, H., Diamond, R. and Dube, J. P. (2015) *The Geography of Poverty and Nutrition: Food Deserts and Food Choices Across the U.S.*, New York University Working Paper, New York, NY.

Allison, D. B. (2011), "Evidence, discourse and values in obesity-oriented policy: Menu labeling as a conversation starter," *International Journal of Obesity*, 35(4), 464–472.

Alston, J. M., Beddow, J. M. and Pardey, P. G. (2009) "Agricultural research, productivity, and food prices in the long run," *Science*, 325(5945), 1209–1210.

American Beverage Association (2010) "Written public comments," *Dietary Guidelines for Americans, 2010,* July 15, health.gov/dietaryguidelines/2010/, accessed November 22, 2017.

Amundson, R., Berhe, A. A., Hopmans, J. W., Olson, C., Sztein, A. E. and Sparks, D. L. (2015) "Soil and human security in the 21st century," *Science*, 348(6235), 1261071.

An R. (2016) "Fast-food and full-service restaurant consumption and daily energy and nutrient intakes in US adults," *European Journal of Clinical Nutrition*, 70(1):97–103. doi:10.1038/ejcn.2015.104.

Andreyeva, T. and Luedicke, J. (2015), "Incentivizing fruit and vegetable purchases among participants in the special supplemental nutrition program for women, infants, and children," *Public Health Nutrition*, 18(1), 33–41.

Artz, G. M. (2012) "Immigration and meatpacking in the Midwest," *Choices Magazine*, 27(2), 1–5.

Atkinson, R. L. (2005) "Editor's note," *International Journal of Obesity and Related Metabolic Disorders*, 29(11), 1392.

Azzam, A. M. and Anderson, D. G. (1996) *Assessing Competition in Meatpacking: Economic History*, USDA Grain Inspection, Packers and Stockyards Administration, Washington, DC.

Baffes, J. and Haniotis, T. (2016) "What explains agricultural price movements?," *Journal of Agricultural Economics*, 67(3), 706–721.

Bailey, M. (2010) *Livestock Production and Water Quality: Interest Groups, Investments, and Implementation of USDA's Environmental Quality Incentives Program*, Ph.D. thesis, Tufts University, Boston, MA.

Bailey, R. (2011) *Growing a Better Future: Food Justice in a Resource-Constrained World*, Oxfam, Oxford, UK.

Balagtas, J. V., Krissoff, B., Lei, L. and Rickard, B. J. (2013) "How has US farm policy influenced fruit and vegetable production?," *Applied Economic Perspectives and Policy*, 36(2), 265–286.

Bane, M. J. (2009) "Poverty politics and policy," *Focus*, 26(2), 75–80.

Barrett, C. B. and Maxwell, D. G. (2005) *Food Aid After Fifty Years: Recasting Its Role*, Routledge, New York, NY.

Bartlett, S., Glantz, F. and Logan, C. (2008) *School Lunch and Breakfast Cost Study—II*, USDA Food and Nutrition Service, Alexandria, VA.

Basu, S., Seligman, H. K., Gardner, C. and Bhattacharya, J. (2014) "Ending SNAP subsidies for sugar-sweetened beverages could reduce obesity and type 2 diabetes," *Health Affairs*, 33(6), 1032–1039.

Beghin, J. C. and Jensen, H. H. (2008) "Farm policies and added sugars in US diets," *Food Policy*, 33(6), 480–488.

Bentley, J. (2014) "Trends in US per capita consumption of dairy products, 1970–2012," *Amber Waves*, 1.

Berry, W. (1990) *What Are People For?* North Point Press, New York, NY.

Besharov, D. and Call, D. (2009) *The Expansion of WIC Eligibility and Enrollment, Good Intentions, Uncontrolled Local Discretion and Compliant Federal Officials*, American Enterprise Institute Working Paper, www.aei.org/publication/the-expansion-of-wic-eligibility-and-enrollment/, accessed September 17, 2017.

Bhattacharya, J. and Bundorf, M. K. (2009) "The incidence of the healthcare costs of obesity," *Journal of Health Economics*, 28(3), 649–658.

Bhattacharya, J., Currie, J. and Haider, S. J. (2006) "Breakfast of champions? The school breakfast program and the nutrition of children and families," *Journal of Human Resources*, 41, 445–466.

Bitler, M. P. and Currie, J. (2005) "Does WIC work? The effects of WIC on pregnancy and birth outcomes," *Journal of Policy Analysis and Management*, 24, 73–91.

Bollinger, B., Leslie, P. and Sorensen, A. T. (2010) *Calorie Posting in Chain Restaurants*, National Bureau of Economic Research, Cambridge, MA.

Bourne, J. K. (2015) *The End of Plenty: The Race to Feed a Crowded World*, WW Norton & Company, New York, NY.

Buchanan, R. and Suhre, B. (2005) "Chemical and microbial risk assessment," in S. A. Hoffman and M. R. Taylor (eds) *Toward Safer Food: Perspectives on Risk and Priority Setting*, Resources for the Future Press, Washington, DC.

Buzby, J. C., Farah-Wells, H. and Hyman, J. (2014) *The Estimated Amount, Value, and Calories of Postharvest Food Losses at the Retail and Consumer Levels in the United States*, USDA Economic Research Service, Washington, DC.

Buzby, J. C., Wells, H. F. and Vocke, G. (2006) *Possible Implications for U.S. Agriculture from Adoption of Select Dietary Guidelines*, USDA Economic Research Service, Washington, DC.

California Center for Public Health Advocacy (2007) *The Food Landscape in California Cities and Counties*, www.publichealthadvocacy.org/wp-content/uploads/2016/09/Searchfor HealthyFood_study-and-policyrecs.pdf, accessed November 22, 2017.

Campbell, T. C. and Campbell, T. M. (2007) *The China Study: Startling Implications for Diet, Weight Loss and Long-Term Health*, Wakefield Press, Cambridge, MA.

Canning, P., Rehkamp, S., Waters, A. and Etemadnia, H. (2017) *The Role of Fossil Fuels in the US Food System and the American Diet*, USDA Economic Research Service, Washington, DC.

Carbon Pricing Leadership Coalition (2017) *Report of the High-Level Commission on Carbon Prices* (Stiglitz, J. and Stern, N., chairs), World Bank, Washington, DC.

Card, D. (2009) "Immigration and inequality," *American Economic Association Ely Lecture*, National Bureau of Economic Research Working Paper Series, no. 14683, Cambridge, MA.

Card, D. and Krueger, A. B. (1994) "Minimum wages and employment: A case study of the fast food industry in New Jersey and Pennsylvania," *The American Economic Review*, 84(4), 772–793.

Carlson, A. and Jaenicke, E. (2016) *Changes in Retail Organic Price Premiums from 2004 to 2010*, USDA Economic Research Service (ERR 209), Washington, DC.

Carlson, A., Lino, M., Juan, W.Y., Hanson, K. and Basiotis, P.P. (2007) *Thrifty Food Plan, 2006*, USDA Center for Nutrition Policy and Promotion, Alexandria, VA.

Carlson, S. and Neuberger, Z. (2017) *WIC Works: Addressing the Nutrition and Health Needs of Low-Income Families for 40 Years*, Center on Budget and Policy Promotion, Washington, DC.

Carney, T. P. (2012) "Political cash sweetens federal sugar boondoggle," *The Washington Examiner*, washingtonexaminer.com/article/1354956, accessed September 17, 2017.

Carstensen, P. (2016) "The mixed record of the Obama administration in food competition policy leaves many unresolved issues: 'Talking the talk, but not walking the walk'" *Concurrences*, 2016(1), 15–21.

Cash, S. (2011) "Policy evaluation and benefit-cost analysis," in J. Lusk, J. Roosen and J. Shogren (eds) *The Oxford Handbook of Food Policy and Consumption*, Oxford University Press, Oxford.

Caswell, J. A. and Anders, S. M. (2011) "Private versus third party versus government labeling," in J. Lusk, J. Roosen and J. Shogren (eds) *The Oxford Handbook of Food Policy and Consumption*, Oxford University Press, Oxford.

Caswell, J. A. and Mojduszka, E. M. (1996) "Using informational labeling to influence the market for quality in food products," *American Journal of Agricultural Economics*, 78(5), 1248–1253.

Cawley, J. and Datar, A. (2017) "Economic considerations in childhood obesity," in Goran, M. I. (ed) *Childhood Obesity: Causes, Consequences and Intervention Approaches*, CRC Press, Boca Raton, FL.

Center for Science in the Public Interest (2011) *Letter to Dr. Margaret Hamburg, FDA Commissioner*, http://cspinet.org/new/pdf/serving-size-comment-062811.pdf, accessed September 17, 2017.

Chakravorty, U., Hubert, M. H., Moreaux, M. and Nøstbakken, L. (2017) "Long-run impact of biofuels on food prices," *The Scandinavian Journal of Economics*, 119(3), 733–767.

Chan, A., Remington, R., Kotyla, E., Lepore, A., Zemianek, J. and Shea, T. B. (2010) "A vitamin/nutriceutical formulation improves memory and cognitive performance in community-dwelling adults without dementia," *The Journal of Nutrition, Health and Aging*, 14(3), 224–230.

Chase, L. and Grubinger, V. (2014) *Food, Farms, and Community: Exploring Food Systems*, University of New Hampshire Press, Lebanon.

Chite, R. M. (2016) *The 2014 Farm Bill (P.L. 113–79): Summary and Side-by-Side*, Congressional Research Service (R43076), Washington, DC.

Claassen, R., Cattaneo, A. and Johansson, R. (2008) "Cost-effective design of agri-environmental payment programs: US experience in theory and practice," *Ecological Economics*, 65(4), 737–752.

Coase, R. H. (1960) "The problem of social cost," *Journal of Law and Economics*, 3, 1–44.

Coleman-Jensen, A., Rabbitt, M. P., Gregory, C. A. and Singh, A. (2016) *Household Food Security in the United States in 2015*, USDA Economic Research Service, Washington, DC.

Collins, A. M., Briefel, R., Klerman, J. A., Wolf, A., Row, G., Logan, C., Enver, A., Fatima, S., Gordon, A. and Lyskawa, J. (2016) *Summer Electronic Benefit Transfer for Children (SEBTC) Demonstration: Summary Report*, Abt Associates, Inc., and Mathematica Policy Research, Inc., for USDA Food and Nutrition Service, Alexandria, VA.

Colman, S., Nichols-Barrer, I. P., Redline, J. E., Devaney, B. L., Ansell, S. V. and Joyce, T. (2012) *Effects of the Special Supplemental Nutrition Program for Women, Infants and Children (WIC): A Review of Recent Research*, Mathematica Policy Research, Inc., for USDA Food and Nutrition Service, Alexandria, VA.

Confessore, N. (2014) "How school lunch became the latest political battleground," *The New York Times Magazine* (October 7).

Congressional Budget Office (2016) *The Budget and Economic Outlook: 2016–2026*, Washington, DC.

Congressional Research Service (2016) *Agricultural Conservation: A Guide to Programs*, Washington DC (June).

Congressional Research Service (2017) *Tracking the Next Child Nutrition Reauthorization: An Overview*, Washington DC (May).

Consumer Reports Greener Choices (2017) "'Humanely raised': What it means," http://greenerchoices.org/2017/06/21/humanely-raised/, accessed September 16, 2017.

Cope, M. B. and Allison, D. B. (2010) "White hat bias: A threat to the integrity of scientific reporting," *Acta Paediatrica*, 99(11), 1615–1617.

Costello, C., Gaines, S. D. and Lynham, J. (2008) "Can catch shares prevent fisheries collapse?," *Science*, 321, 1678–1681.

Courtemanche, C. and Carden, A. (2011) "Supersizing supercenters? The impact of Walmart Supercenters on body mass index and obesity," *Journal of Urban Economics*, 69(2),165–181.

Cowan, T. and Feder, J. (2008) *The Pigford Case: USDA Settlement of a Discrimination Suit by Black Farmers*, Congressional Research Service, Library of Congress.

Crespi, J. M. and McEowen, R. A. (2006) "The constitutionality of generic advertising checkoff programs," *Choices Magazine*, 21(2).

Cummins, S., Flint, E. and Matthews, S. A. (2014) "New neighborhood store increased awareness of food access but did not alter dietary habits or obesity," *Health Affairs*, 33, 283–291.

Das, R., Steege, A., Baron, S., Beckman, J. and Harrison, R. (2001) "Pesticide-related illness among migrant farm workers in the United States," *International Journal of Occupational and Environmental Health*, 7(4), 303–312.

Davison, J. (2010) "GM plants: Science, politics and EC regulations," *Plant Science*, 178(2), 94–98.

Deaton, A. (1997) *The Analysis of Household Surveys: A Microeconometric Approach to Development Policy*, World Bank, Washington, DC.

Diaz, R. J. and Rosenberg, R. (2008) "Spreading dead zones and consequences for marine ecosystems," *Science*, 321(5891), 926–929.

Dickert-Conlin, S., Fitzpatrick, K. and Tiehen, L. (2012) *The Role of Advertising in the Growth of the SNAP Caseload*, National Poverty Center Working Paper Series, no 12–07, Ann Arbor, MI.

Dietary Guidelines Advisory Committee (2015) *Scientific Report of the 2015 Dietary Guidelines Advisory Committee*, USDA Center for Nutrition Policy and Promotion, Washington, DC.

Diffenbaugh, N. S., Swain, D. L. and Touma, D. (2015) "Anthropogenic warming has increased drought risk in California," *Proceedings of the National Academy of Sciences*, 112(13), 3931–3936.

Dollahite, J., Kenkel, D. and Thompson, C. S. (2008) "An economic evaluation of the Expanded Food and Nutrition Education Program," *Journal of Nutrition Education and Behavior*, 40(3), 134–143.

Drewnowski, A. (2010) "The cost of US foods as related to their nutritive value," *American Journal of Clinical Nutrition*, 92(5), 1181–1188.

Du, X., Feng, H. and Hennessy, D. A. (2016), "Rationality of choices in subsidized crop insurance markets," *American Journal of Agricultural Economics*, 99(3), 732–756.

Dubowitz, T., Ghosh-Dastidar, M., Cohen, D. A., Beckman, R., Steiner, E. D., Hunter, G. P., Florez, K. R., Huang, C., Vaughan, C. A. and Sloan, J. C. (2015) "Diet and perceptions change with supermarket introduction in food desert, but not because of supermarket use," *Health Affairs*, 34, 1858–68.

Dyckman, L. J. (2004) "Federal food safety and security system: fundamental restructuring is needed to address fragmentation and overlap," *Government Accountability Office*, Washington, DC, www.gao.gov/products/GAO-04-588T, accessed November 21, 2017.

Eisinger, P. K. (1998) *Toward an End to Hunger in America*, Brookings Institution Press, Washington, DC.

Elbel, B., Kersh, R., Brescoll, V. L. and Dixon L. B. (2009) "Calorie labeling and food choices: a first look at the effects on low-income people in New York City," *Health Affairs*, 28(6), w1110-w1121.

Elbel, B., Moran, A., Dixon, L. B., Kiszko, K., Cantor, J., Abrams, C. and Mijanovich, T. (2015) "Assessment of a government-subsidized supermarket in a high-need area on household food availability and children's dietary intakes," *Public Health Nutrition*, 18(15), 2881–2890.

Escalante, C. L. and Luo, T. (2017) "Sustaining a healthy farm labor force: Issues for policy consideration," *Choices Magazine*, 32(1), 1–9.

Falbe, J., Thompson, H. R., Becker, C. M., Rojas, N., McCulloch, C. E. and Madsen, K. A. (2016) "Impact of the Berkeley excise tax on sugar-sweetened beverage consumption," *American Journal of Public Health*, 106(10), 1865–1871.

Federal Trade Commission (2008) *Marketing Food to Children and Adolescents: A Review of Industry Expenditures, Activities and Self-Regulation,* Federal Trade Commission, Washington, DC.

Federal Trade Commission (2010) *Court Orders Internet Marketers of acai Berry Weight-Loss Pills and 'Colon Cleansers' to Stop Deceptive Advertising and Unfair Billing Practices*, www.ftc.gov/opa/2010/08/acaicolon.shtm, accessed September 17, 2017.

Federal Trade Commission and Department of Health and Human Services (2006) *Perspectives on Marketing, Self-Regulation & Childhood Obesity*, www.ftc.gov/reports/perspectives-marketing-self-regulation-childhood-obesity-report-joint-workshop-federal-trade, accessed November 21, 2017.

Feeding America (2017a) *Hunger and Poverty Facts*, www.feedingamerica.org/hunger-in-america/hunger-and-poverty-facts.html, accessed September 3, 2017.

Feeding America (2017b) *Map the Meal Gap 2017*, http://map.feedingamerica.org/, accessed September 4, 2017.

Feeding America (2017c) *Impact Report*, www.feedingamerica.org/about-us/donor-impact-report.html, accessed September 4, 2017.

Finkelstein, E. A. and Strombotne, K. L. (2010) "The economics of obesity," *The American Journal of Clinical Nutrition*, 91(5), 1520S–1524S.

Fisher, A. and Jayaraman, S. (2017) *Big Hunger: The Unholy Alliance Between Corporate America and Anti-Hunger Groups*, MIT Press, Cambridge MA.

Fisher, G. M. (1997) *From Hunter to Orshansky: An Overview of (unofficial) Poverty Lines in the United States from 1904 to 1965*, U.S. Census Bureau, www.census.gov/content/dam/Census/library/working-papers/1997/demo/fisher4.pdf, accessed September 17, 2017.

Food and Drug Administration (2009) *Milestones in Food and Drug Law History*, www.fda.gov/AboutFDA/WhatWeDo/History/Milestones/default.htm, accessed September 17, 2017.

Food and Drug Administration (2010) *Briefing Packet: AquAdvantage Salmon*, www.fda.gov/AnimalVeterinary/DevelopmentApprovalProcess/GeneticEngineering/GeneticallyEngineered-Animals/ucm280853.htm, accessed September 17, 2017.

Food and Drug Administration (2017) *Changes to the Nutrition Facts Label*, www.fda.gov/Food/GuidanceRegulation/GuidanceDocumentsRegulatoryInformation/LabelingNutrition/ucm385663.htm, accessed August 27, 2017.

Food and Agriculture Organization (2014) *Building a Common Vision for Sustainable Food and Agriculture: Principles and Approaches*, Rome, Italy.

Food Chain Workers Alliance and Solidarity Research Cooperative (2016) *No Piece of the Pie: U.S. Food Workers in 2016*, Food Chain Workers Alliance, Los Angeles, CA.

Food Research and Action Center (2015) *National School Lunch Program: Trends and Factors Affecting Student Participation*, http://frac.org/wp-content/uploads/national_school_lunch_report_2015.pdf, accessed September 11, 2017.

Food Research and Action Center (2016) *Take Action: SNAP Challenge Toolkit*, http://frac.org/wp-content/uploads/take-action-snap-challenge-toolkit.pdf, accessed September 4, 2017.

Fortin, N. D. (2009) *Food Regulation: Law, Science, Policy, and Practice*, Wiley, Hoboken, NJ.

Fox, M. K. and Condon, E. (2012) *School Nutrition Dietary Assessment Study-IV: Summary of Findings*, Mathematica Policy Research for USDA Food and Nutrition Service, Alexandria, VA.

Frieden, T. R., Dietz, W. and Collins, J. (2010) "Reducing childhood obesity through policy change: acting now to prevent obesity," *Health Affairs*, 29(3), 357.

Frisvold, D. (2015) "Nutrition and cognitive achievement: An evaluation of the School Breakfast Program," *Journal of Public Economics*, 124, 91–104.

Fryar, C. D., Carroll, M. D. and Ogden, C. L. (2014), *Prevalence of Overweight and Obesity among Children and Adolescents: United States, 1963–1965 through 2011–2012*, Division of Health and Nutrition Examination Surveys, National Center for Health Statistics.

Furman, J. (2017) *Reducing Poverty: The Progress We Have Made and the Path Forward*, Center on Budget and Policy Priorities, Washington, DC.

Garcia Martinez, M., Fearne, A., Caswell, J. A. and Henson, S. (2007) "Co-regulation as a possible model for food safety governance: Opportunities for public-private partnerships," *Food Policy*, 32(3), 299–314.

Gearhardt, A. N., Bragg, M. A., Pearl, R. L., Schvey, N. A., Roberto, C. A. and Brownell, K. D. (2012) "Obesity and public policy," *Annual Review of Clinical Psychology*, 8, 405–430.

Geller, D. M., Harrington, M. and Vinokurov, A. (2012) *National Survey of WIC Participants II, Volume 2: State and Local Agencies*, USDA Food and Nutrition Service, Alexandria, VA.

Gilbert, J., Sharp, G. and Felin, M.S. (2002) "The loss and persistence of black-owned farms and farmland: A review of the research literature and its implications," *Southern Rural Sociology*, 18(2), 1–30.

Gillespie, N. (1995) "Cereal killers," *Reason*, http://reason.com/archives/1995/05/01/cereal-killers, accessed November 21, 2017.

Giskes, K., van Lenthe, F., Avendano-Pabon, M. and Brug, J. (2011) "A systematic review of environmental factors and obesogenic dietary intakes among adults: Are we getting closer to understanding obesogenic environments?," *Obesity Reviews*, 12(5), e95–e106.

Gittelsohn, J., Rowan, M. and Gadhoke, P. (2012) "Interventions in small food stores to change the food environment, improve diet and reduce risk of chronic disease," *Preventing Chronic Disease*, 9, E59.

Glauber, J. W. and Effland, A. (2016) *United States Agricultural Policy: Its Evolution and Impact*, International Food Policy Research Institute (Discussion Paper 1543), Washington, DC.

Glauber, J. W., Sumner, D. A. and Wilde, P. E. (2017) *Poverty, Hunger, and U.S. Agricultural Policy: Do Farm Programs Affect the Nutrition of Poor Americans?*, American Enterprise Institute, Washington, DC.

Golan, E., Kuchler, F., Mitchell, L., Greene, C. and Jessup, A. (2001) *Economics of Food Labeling*, USDA Economic Research Service, Washington, DC, www.ers.usda.gov/publications/pub-details/?pubid=41204, accessed November 21, 2017.

Gordon, A. R., Briefel, R. R., Collins, A. M., Rowe, G. M. and Klerman, J. A. (2017) "Delivering summer electronic benefit transfers for children through the Supplemental Nutrition Assistance Program or the Special Supplemental Nutrition Program for Women, Infants, and Children: Benefit use and impacts on food security and foods consumed," *Journal of the Academy of Nutrition and Dietetics*, 117(3), 367–375.

Gray, K. F., Fisher, S. and Lauffer, S. (2016) *Characteristics of Supplemental Nutrition Assistance Program Households: Fiscal Year 2015*, Mathematica Policy Research, Inc., for USDA Food and Nutrition Service, Alexandria, VA.

Greene, C. R., Dimitri, C., Lin, B. H., McBride, W. D., Oberholtzer, L. and Smith, T. A. (2009) *Emerging Issues in the US Organic Industry*, USDA Economic Research Service, Washington, DC.

Greene, J. L. and Cowan, T. (2012) *Table Egg Production and Hen Welfare: The UEP-HSUS Agreement and H.R. 3798*, Congressional Research Service, Washington DC.

Grocery Manufacturers Association (2010) "Written public comments," *Dietary Guidelines for Americans, 2010,* July 15, http://health.gov/dietaryguidelines/2010/, accessed November 22, 2017.

Gundersen, C. and Oliveira, V. (2001) "The food stamp program and food insufficiency," *American Journal of Agricultural Economics,* 83(4), 875–887.

Hamrick, K. S., Andrews, M., Guthrie, J., Hopkins, D. and McClelland, K. (2011) *How Much Time Do Americans Spend on Food?,* Economic Information Bulletin (EIB 86), USDA Economic Research Service, Washington, DC.

Hamrick, K. S. and Okrent, A. (2014) *The Role of Time in Fast-Food Purchasing Behavior in the United States,* USDA Economic Research Service (ERR-178), Washington, DC.

Hanak, E., Lund, J., Arnold, B., Escriva-Bou, A. Gray, B., Green, S., Harter, T. Howitt, R., Mac-Ewan, D., Medellin-Azuara, J., Moyle, P. and Seavy, N. (2017) *Water Stress and a Changing San Joaquin Valley,* Public Policy Institute of California, San Francisco, CA.

Handbury, J., Rahkovsky, I. and Schnell, M. (2016) *Is the Focus on Food Deserts Fruitless? Retail Access and Food Purchases Across the Socioeconomic Spectrum,* Wharton School Research Paper (91), University of Pennsylvania.

Hanratty, M. J. (2006) "Has the food stamp program become more accessible? Impacts of recent changes in reporting requirements and asset eligibility limits," *Journal of Policy Analysis and Management,* 25, 603–621.

Hansen, M. (2010) "Comments of Consumers Union on genetically engineered salmon," *Consumers Union,* Washington, DC, www.consumersunion.org/pdf/CU-comments-GE-salmon-0910.pdf, accessed September 17, 2017.

Haspel, T. (2015) "If the GMO salmon is as good as its maker says, why not label it?," *Washington Post Online,* November 19, www.washingtonpost.com/lifestyle/food/fda-approves-gmo-salmon-a-first-for-the-us-food-supply/2015/11/19/d5d1b60e-8ec3–11e5-acff-673ae92ddd2b_story.html?hpid=hp_hp-more-top-stories_gmo-950am, accessed August 19, 2017.

Hausman, J. and Leibtag E. (2007) "Consumer benefits from increased competition in shopping outlets: measuring the effect of Wal-Mart," *Journal of Applied Econometrics,* 22(7), 1157–1177.

Heller, M. C. and Keoleian, G. A. (2015) "Greenhouse gas emission estimates of US dietary choices and food loss," *Journal of Industrial Ecology,* 19(3), 391–401.

Hendrix, C. and Kotschwar, B. (2016) "Agriculture," *Assessing the Trans-Pacific Partnership,* Peterson Institute for International Economics, Washington, DC.

Hijmans, R. J., Choe, H. and Perlman, J. (2016) "Spatiotemporal patterns of field crop diversity in the United States, 1870–2012," *Agricultural & Environmental Letters,* 1(1).

Hoffmann, S., Maculloch, B. and Batz, M. (2015) *Economic Burden of Major Foodborne Illnesses Acquired in the United States,* Economic Information Bulletin No. 140, USDA Economic Research Service, Washington, DC.

Holt, D. J., Ippolito, P. M., Desrochers, D. M. and Kelly, C. R. (2007) *Children's Exposure to TV Advertising in 1977 and 2004: Information for the Obesity Debate,* Federal Trade Commission, Washington, DC.

Hooker, N. H. and Teratanavat, R. (2008) "Dissecting qualified health claims: Evidence from experimental studies," *Critical Reviews in Food Science and Nutrition,* 48(2), 160–176.

Hoppe, R. and Macdonald, J. M. (2016). *America's Diverse Family Farms, 2016 Edition.* Economic Information Bulletin No. (EIB-164). USDA Economic Research Service Washington, DC.

Horowitz, R. (2006) "Meat packing industry," in C. Geisst (ed.) *Encyclopedia of American Business History,* Facts On File, Inc., New York.

Howlett, M., Ramesh, M. and Perl, A. (1995) *Studying Public Policy: Policy Cycles and Policy Subsystems,* Oxford University Press, Oxford, UK.

Hoynes, H., Page, M. and Stevens, A. H. (2011) "Can targeted transfers improve birth outcomes?: Evidence from the introduction of the WIC program," *Journal of Public Economics*, 95, 813–827.

Hoynes, H. W. and Schanzenbach, D. W. (2009) "Consumption responses to in-kind transfers: evidence from the introduction of the food stamp program," *American Economic Journal: Applied Economics*, 1, 109–139.

Huang, J., Barnidge, E. and Kim, Y. (2015) "Children receiving free or reduced-price school lunch have higher food insufficiency rates in summer," *Journal of Nutrition*, 145(9), 2161–2168.

Huffman, S. K. and Jensen, H. H. (2008) "Food assistance programs and outcomes in the context of welfare reform," *Social Science Quarterly*, 89, 95–115.

Huffman, W. E. (2014) "Agricultural labor: Demand for labor," *Encyclopedia of Agriculture and Food Systems*, 105–122.

Institute of Medicine (2005) *WIC Food Packages: Time for a Change*, National Academies Press, Washington, DC.

Institute of Medicine (2006) *Food Marketing to Children and Youth: Threat or Opportunity?* National Academies Press, Washington, DC.

Institute of Medicine (2010) *School Meals: Building Blocks for Healthy Children*, National Academies Press, Washington, DC.

Institute of Medicine (2011a) *Front-of-Package Nutrition Rating Systems and Symbols: Promoting Healthier Choices*, National Academies Press, Washington, DC.

Institute of Medicine (2011b) *Planning a WIC Research Agenda: Workshop Summary*, National Academies Press, Washington, DC.

Institute of Medicine (2012) *Accelerating Progress in Obesity Prevention: Solving the Weight of the Nation*, National Academies Press, Washington, DC.

Ippolito, P. M. (1999) "How government policies shape the food and nutrition information environment," *Food Policy*, 24(2–3), 295–306.

Jardim, E., Long, M. C., Plotnick, R., van Inwegen, E., Vigdor, J. and Wething, H. (2017) *Minimum Wage Increases, Wages, and Low-Wage Employment: Evidence from Seattle*, National Bureau of Economic Research (No. w23532).

Jin, G. Z. and Leslie, P. (2005) "The case in support of restaurant hygiene grade cards," *Choices Magazine*, 20(2).

Johnecheck, W. A. (2010) *Consumer Information, Marks of Origin and WTO Law: A Case Study of the United States—Certain Country of Origin Labeling Requirements Dispute*, Tufts University Friedman School of Nutrition Science and Policy Working Paper Series, no 43, Boston, MA.

Johnecheck, W., Wilde, P. and Caswell, J. (2011) "Market and welfare impacts of COOL on the U.S.-Mexican tomato trade," *Journal of Agricultural and Resource Economics*, 35(3), 503–521.

Johnson, P., Wilson, R., Fulp, R., Schuetz, B. and Orton, P. (2004) *The Healthy Heart Initiative: Barriers to Eating a Heart Healthy Diet in a Low Income African American Community*, Brigham and Women's Hospital, Boston, MA.

Johnson, R. (2016) *Federal Food Safety System: A Primer*, Congressional Research Service (RS22600), Washington, DC.

Juice Products Association (2010) "Written public comments," *Dietary Guidelines for Americans, 2010,* July 15, http://health.gov/dietaryguidelines/2010/, accessed November 22, 2017.

Just, D. R., Mancino, L. and Wansink, B. (2007) *Could Behavioral Economics Help Improve Diet Quality for Nutrition Assistance Program Participants?* USDA Economic Research Service, Washington, DC.

Just, D. R. and Wansink, B. (2011) "The flat-rate pricing paradox: conflicting effects of 'allyou-can-eat' buffet pricing," *Review of Economics and Statistics*, 93, 193–200.

Kaiser, H. (2011) "Effects of generic advertising on food demand," in J. Lusk, J. Roosen and J. Shogren (eds) *The Oxford Handbook of Food Policy and Consumption*, Oxford University Press, Oxford.

Kessler, D. A. (2009) *The End of Overeating: Taking Control of the Insatiable American Appetite*, Rodale Books, Emmaus, PA.

Key, N. D. and McBride, W. D. (2007) *The Changing Economics of US Hog Production*, USDA Economic Research Service, Washington, DC.

Klerman, J. A. and Danielson, C. (2011) "The transformation of the Supplemental Nutrition Assistance Program," *Journal of Policy Analysis and Management*, 30, 863–888.

Koo, W. W. and Kennedy, P. L. (2005) *International Trade and Agriculture*, Wiley-Blackwell, Hoboken, NJ.

Krebs-Smith, S. M., Reedy, J. and Bosire, C. (2010) "Healthfulness of the US food supply: little improvement despite decades of dietary guidance," *American Journal of Preventive Medicine*, 38(5), 472–477.

Kuchler, F. and Stewart, H. (2008) *Price Trends Are Similar for Fruits, Vegetables and Snack Foods*, USDA Economic Research Service, Washington, DC.

Kumanyika, S. K. (2016) "Health equity is the issue we have been waiting for," *Journal of Public Health Management and Practice*, 22, S8–S10.

Kunkel, D., Wilcox, B., Cantor, J., Palmer, E., Linn, S. and Dowrick, P. (2004) *Psychological Issues in the Increasing Commercialization of Childhood*, American Psychological Association, Washington, DC, www.apa.org/pi/families/resources/advertising-children.pdf, accessed September 17, 2017.

Lakdawalla, D., Philipson, T. and Bhattacharya, J. (2005) "Welfare-enhancing technological change and the growth of obesity," *American Economic Review*, 95(2), 253–257.

Lang B., Harries C., Manon M., Tucker J., Kim E., Ansell S. and Smith P. (2013) *Healthy Food Financing Handbook*. Philadelphia, PA: The Food Trust.

Lappé, A. (2010) *Diet for a Hot Planet: The Climate Crisis at the End of Your Fork and What You Can Do About It*, Bloomsbury, New York, NY.

Larson, N., Story, M. and Nelson, M. (2009) "Neighborhood environments: Disparities in access to healthy foods in the U.S.," *American Journal of Preventive Medicine*, 36(1), 74–81.

Layne, N. (2015) "Wal-Mart to impose charges on suppliers as its costs mount," *Reuters*, June 23, www.reuters.com/article/us-wal-mart-stores-suppliers-idUSKBN0P400K20150624, accessed July 28, 2017.

Leftin, J. (2011) *Trends in Supplemental Nutrition Assistance Program Participation Rates: 2002–2009*, Mathematica Policy Research, Inc., for USDA Food and Nutrition Service, Alexandria, VA.

Lesser, L. I., Ebbeling, C. B., Goozner, M., Wypij, D. and Ludwig, D. S. (2007) "Relationship between funding source and conclusion among nutrition-related scientific articles," *PLoS Medicine*, 4(1), 41–45.

Levenstein, H. A. (2003) *Paradox of Plenty: A Social History of Eating in Modern America*, University of California Press, Berkeley.

Lin, B. H. and Guthrie, J. (2012) *Nutritional Quality of Food Prepared at Home and Away From Home*, USDA Economic Research Service, Washington, DC

Linnekin, B. J. (2016) *Biting the Hands that Feed Us: How Fewer, Smarter Laws Would Make Our Food System More Sustainable*, Island Press, Washington, DC.

Low, S. A., Adalja, A., Beaulieu, E., Key, N., Martinez, S., Melton, A., Perez A., Ralston K., Stewart, H., Suttles, S. and Vogel, S. (2015), *Trends in US Local and Regional Food Systems: Report to Congress*, USDA Economic Research Service, Washington, DC.

Lowell, K., Langholz, J. and Stuart, D. (2010) *Safe and Sustainable: Co-Managing for Food Safety and Ecological Health in California's Central Coast Region*, The Nature Conservancy of California and the Georgetown University Produce Safety Project, San Francisco, CA, and Washington, DC.

Ludwig, D. S. and Nestle, M. (2008) "Can the food industry play a constructive role in the obesity epidemic?" *Journal of the American Medical Association*, 300(15), 1808–1811.

Ludwig, J., Sanbonmatsu, L., Gennetian, L., Duncan, G. J., Katz, L. F., Kessler, R. C., Kling, J. R., Lindau, S. T., Whitaker, R. C. and McDade, T. W. (2011) "Neighborhoods, obesity and diabetes—a randomized social experiment," *New England Journal of Medicine*, 365(16), 1509–1519.

Lusk, J. L. (2011) "The market for animal welfare," *Agriculture and Human Values*, 28(4), 561–575.

Lusk, J. L. and Norwood, F. B. (2009) "Some economic benefits and costs of vegetarianism," *Agricultural and Resource Economics Review*, 38(2), 109–124.

Lytton, T. D. (2010) "Banning front-of-package food labels: First amendment constraints on public health policy," *Public Health Nutrition*, 14(6), 1123–1126.

Mabli, J., Cohen, R., Potter, F. and Zhao, Z. (2010) *Hunger in America 2010: National Report Prepared for Feeding America: Final Report*, Mathematica Policy Research, Inc., and Feeding America, Princeton, NJ.

MacDonald, J. M. (2016) "Concentration, contracting, and competition policy in U.S. agribusiness: Competition law and policy and the food value chain," *Concurrences*, 2016(1), 22–35.

MacDonald, J. M., Perry, J., Ahearn, M., Banker, D., Chambers, W., Dimitri, C., Key, N., Nelson, K. E. and Southard, L. W. (2004) *Contracts, Markets, and Prices: Organizing the Production and Use of Agricultural Commodities*, USDA Economic Research Service, Washington, DC.

Martin, P. (2013) "Immigration and farm labor: Policy options and consequences," *American Journal of Agricultural Economics*, 95(2), 470–475.

Martin, P. (2017) "Trump, immigration, and agriculture," *Choices Magazine*, 32(1), 1–5.

Martinez, S. (2007) *The US Food Marketing System: Recent Developments, 1997–2006*, USDA Economic Research Service, Washington, DC.

Martinez, S., Hand, M., Da Pra, M., Pollack, S., Ralston, K., Smith, T. and Vogel, S. (2010) *Local Food Systems: Concepts, Impacts, and Issues, United States Department of Agriculture*, USDA Economic Research Service, Washington, DC.

Masters, W. A. (2011) "Economic development, government policies and food consumption," in J. L. Lusk, J. Roosen and J. Shogren (eds) *The Oxford Handbook of the Economics of Food Consumption and Policy*, Oxford University Press, New York, NY.

McFadden, J. R. and Huffman, W. E. (2017) "Willingness-to-pay for natural, organic, and conventional foods: The effects of information and meaningful labels," *Food Policy*, 68, 214–232.

McMinimy, M. A. (2016) *U.S. Sugar Program Fundamentals*, Congressional Research Service, Washington, DC.

Melina, V., Craig, W. and Levin, S. (2016) "Position of the Academy of Nutrition and Dietetics: vegetarian diets," *Journal of the Academy of Nutrition and Dietetics*, 116(12), 1970–1980.

Menus of Change (2017) "Fruit and Vegetable Consumption and Production" (by Wilde, P.), *2017 Annual Report*, Culinary Institute of America and Harvard T. H. Chan School of Public Health, Boston, MA.

Mercier, S. (2012) *Review of U.S. Nutrition Assistance Policy: Programs and Issues*, AGree: Transforming Food & Ag Policy, http://foodandagpolicy.org/sites/default/files/AGree%20Review%20 of%20US%20Nutrition%20Assistance%20Policy.pdf, accessed September 17, 2017.

Merrigan, K., Griffin, T., Wilde, P., Robien, K., Goldberg, J. and Dietz, W. (2015) "Designing a sustainable diet," *Science*, 350(6257), 165–166.

Miller, J. C. and Coble, K. H. (2007) "Cheap food policy: fact or rhetoric?," *Food Policy*, 32(1), 98–111.

Millimet, D. L., Tchernis, R. and Husain, M. (2010) "School nutrition programs and the incidence of childhood obesity," *Journal of Human Resources*, 45, 640–654.

Monke, J. (2017) *Agriculture and Related Agencies: FY 2017 Appropriations*, Congressional Research Service (R44588), Washington, DC.

Monsivais, P., Aggarwal, A. and Drewnowski, A. (2010) "Are socio-economic disparities in diet quality explained by diet cost?," *Journal of Epidemiology and Community Health*, 66(6), 530–535.

Moschini, G. C. (2010) "Competition issues in the seed industry and the role of intellectual property," *Choices Magazine*, 25(2).

Moss, M. (2009) "Woman's shattered life shows ground beef inspection flaws," *The New York Times*, 3 October, p A1.

Moss, M. (2013) *Salt, Sugar, Fat: How the Food Giants Hooked Us*. Random House, New York, NY.

Mueller, M. (2017) *Healthy Menu Changes and Healthy Meal Promotions in Restaurants: Evaluating Consumer Responses and Industry Trends over the Past Decade*, Ph.D. dissertation, Friedman School of Nutrition Science and Policy, Tufts University.

National Academies of Sciences, Engineering, and Medicine (2016) *Genetically Engineered Crops: Experiences and Prospects*, National Academies Press, Washington, DC.

National Center for Health Statistics (2016) *Health, United States*, Hyattsville, MD.

National Academies of Sciences, Engineering, and Medicine (2017) *The Economic and Fiscal Consequences of Immigration*, in Blau, F. and Mackie (Eds), National Academies Press, Washington, DC.

National Research Council (2002) *At What Price?: Conceptualizing and Measuring Cost-of-Living and Price Indexes*, National Academies Press, Washington, DC.

National Research Council (2006) *Food Insecurity and Hunger in the United States: an Assessment of the Measure*, National Academies Press, Washington, DC.

National Research Council (2009) *Science and Decisions: Advancing Risk Assessment*, National Academies Press, Washington, DC.

National Research Council, Committee on Twenty-First Century Systems Agriculture (2010) *Toward Sustainable Agricultural Systems in the 21st Century*, National Academies Press, Washington, DC.

Neff, R.A., Palmer, A. M., McKenzie, S. E. and Lawrence, R. S. (2009) "Food systems and public health disparities," *Journal of Hunger & Environmental Nutrition*, 4(3), 282–314.

Neff, R. A., Kanter, R. and Vandevijvere, S. (2015) "Reducing food loss and waste while improving the public's health," *Health Affairs*, 34(11), 1821–1829.

Nestle, M. (2003) *Food Politics: How the Food Industry Influences Nutrition and Health*, University of California Press, Berkeley, CA.

Nevo, A. (2001) "Measuring market power in the ready-to-eat cereal industry," *Econometrica*, 69(2), 307–342.

Noonan, R. (undated) "Made in America: Food, Beverages, and Tobacco Products," *Economics and Statistics Administration*, U.S. Department of Commerce, Washington, DC.

Nord, M. and Andrews, M. (2002) *Reducing Food Insecurity in the United States: Assessing Progress Toward a National Objective*, USDA Economic Research Service, Washington, DC.

Nord, M. and Romig, K. (2006) "Hunger in the summer," *Journal of Children and Poverty*, 12, 141–158.

Obama, M. (2011a) "First Lady Michelle Obama on Making a Difference in Cities with Food Deserts," https://obamawhitehouse.archives.gov/blog/2011/10/25/first-lady-michelle-obama-making-difference-cities-food-deserts, accessed November 22, 2017.

Obama, M. (2011b) "Remarks by the President and First Lady at the Signing of the Healthy Hunger-Free Kids Act," http://obamawhitehouse.archives.gov/the-press-office/2010/12/13/remarks-president-and-first-lady-signing-healthy-hunger-free-kids-act, accessed November 21, 2017.

Ocean Spray Cranberries, Inc. (2010) "Written public comments," *Dietary Guidelines for Americans, 2010*, July 14, health.gov/dietaryguidelines/2010/, accessed November 22, 2017.

O'Donoghue, E. J., Hungerford, A. E., Cooper, J. C., Worth, T. and Ash, M. (2016) *The 2014 Farm Act Agriculture Risk Coverage, Price Loss Coverage, and Supplemental Coverage Option Programs' Effects on Crop Revenue*, USDA Economic Research Service, Washington, DC.

Ogden, C. L., Carroll, M. D., Lawman, H. G., Fryar, C. D., Kruszon-Moran, D., Kit, B. K. and Flegal, K. M. (2016) "Trends in obesity prevalence among children and adolescents in the United States, 1988–1994 through 2013–2014," *JAMA*, 315(21), 2292–2299.

Oliveira, V. (2017) *The Food Assistance Landscape: Fiscal Year 2016 Annual Report*, USDA Economic Research Service, Washington, DC.

Oliveira, V. and Frazao, E. (2015) *The WIC Program: Background, Trends and Economic Issues, 2015 Edition*, USDA Economic Research Service (EIB 134), Washington, DC.

Ollinger, M., Wilkus, J., Hrdlicka, M., and Bovay, J. (2017) *Public Disclosure of Tests for Salmonella: The Effects on Food Safety Performance in Chicken Slaughter Establishments*, USDA Economic Research Service, Washington, DC.

Olsho, L. E., Klerman, J. A., Wilde, P. and Bartlett, S. (2016) "Financial incentives increase fruit and vegetable intake among Supplemental Nutrition Assistance Program participants: A randomized controlled trial of the USDA Healthy Incentives Pilot," *American Journal of Clinical Nutrition*, 104(2), 423–435.

Olson, M. (1965) "The logic of collective action: public goods and the theory of groups," reprinted in S. Kernall and S. Smith (eds) *Principles and Practice of American Politics: Classic and Contemporary Readings* (3rd edn, 2007), CQ Press, Washington, DC.

Organisation for Economic Co-operation and Development (2016) *Agricultural Policy Monitoring and Evaluation 2016*, OECD Publishing, Paris.

Ostrom, E. (1990) *Governing the Commons: The Evolution of Institutions for Collective Action*, Cambridge University Press, New York, NY.

Otten, J., Diedrich, S., Getts, K. and Benson, C. (2016) *Food Waste Prevention and Recovery Assessment Report*, University of Washington Center for Public Health Nutrition, Seattle, WA.

Oxfam America (2017) *Trade*, policy-practice.oxfamamerica.org/work/trade/, accessed July 18, 2017.

Paarlberg, R., Mozaffarian, D. and Micha, R. (2017) "Can US local soda taxes continue to spread?," *Food Policy*, 71, 1–7.

Park, T., Ahearn, M., Covey, T., Erickson, K., Harris, J. M., Kuethe, T. and McGath, C. (2010) *Agricultural Income and Finance Outlook*, USDA Economic Research Service, Washington, DC.

Parmet, W. E. and Smith, J. A. (2006) "Free speech and public health: A population-based approach to the First Amendment," *Loyola of Los Angeles Law Review*, 39, 363–446.

Pasour, E. C. and Rucker, R. R. (2005) *Plowshares and Pork Barrels: The Political Economy of Agriculture*, Independent Institute, Oakland, CA.

Patel, R. (2009) "Food sovereignty," *Journal of Peasant Studies*, 36(3), 663–706.

Petri, P. A. and Plummer, M. G. (2016) "The economic effects of the TPP: New estimates," *Assessing the Trans-Pacific Partnership*, Peterson Institute for International Economics, Washington, DC.

Pew Center for Global Climate Change (2011) *Climate Change 101: Understanding and Responding to Global Climate Change*, Pew Charitable Trusts, Arlington, VA.

Physicians Committee for Responsible Medicine (2011) *Doctors Sue Federal Government for Deceptive Language on Meat, Dairy in New Dietary Guidelines* (press release).

Pollan, M. (2006) *The Omnivore's Dilemma: A Natural History of Four Meals*, Penguin Group, New York, NY.

Pomeranz, J. L. (2016) *Food Law for Public Health*, Oxford University Press, New York, NY.

Poppendieck, J. (1998) *Sweet Charity? Emergency Food and the End of Entitlement*, Penguin Group, New York, NY.

Poppendieck, J. (2010) *Free for All: Fixing School Food in America*, University of California Press, Berkeley, CA.

Rajgopal, R., Cox, R. H., Lambur, M. and Lewis, E. C. (2002) "Cost-benefit analysis indicates the positive economic benefits of the Expanded Food and Nutrition Education Program related to chronic disease prevention," *Journal of Nutrition Education and Behavior*, 34(1), 26–37.

Ralston, K., Newman, C., Clauson, A., Guthrie, J. and Buzby, J. (2008) *The National School Lunch Program: Background, Trends, and Issues*, USDA Economic Research Service, Washington, DC.

Ralston, K., Treen, K., Coleman-Jensen, A. and Guthrie, J. (2017) *Children's Food Security and USDA Child Nutrition Programs*, USDA Economic Research Service (EIB-174), Washington, DC.

Ratcliffe, C., McKernan, S. M. and Zhang, S. (2011) "How much does the supplemental nutrition assistance program reduce food insecurity?," *American Journal of Agricultural Economics*, 93, 1082–1098.

Rector, R. (2010) "Significant food shortages rare in America," *The Washington Times*, 24 November 2010.

Reinvestment Fund, The (2015) *2014 Analysis of Limited Supermarket Access: Summary Brief*, www.reinvestment.com/wp-content/uploads/2015/12/2014_Limited_Supermarket_Access_Analysis-Brief_2015.pdf, accessed July 29, 2017.

Renwick, T. and Fox, L. (2016) *The Supplemental Poverty Measure: 2015*, U.S. Census Bureau, Washington, DC.

Reuben, S. H. (2010) *Reducing Environmental Cancer Risk: What We Can Do Now*, The President's Cancer Panel, National Institutes of Health, Washington, DC.

Ribaudo, M., Hansen, L. R., Hellerstein, D. and Greene, C. (2008) *Use of Markets to Increase Private Investment in Environmental Stewardship*, USDA Economic Research Service, Washington, DC.

Rose, D. (2007) "Food stamps, the thrifty food plan and meal preparation: The importance of the time dimension for US nutrition policy," *Journal of Nutrition Education and Behavior*, 39(4), 226–232.

Rosegrant, M. W, Zhu, T., Msangi, S. and Sulser, T. (2008) "Global scenarios for biofuels: Impacts and implications," *Review of Agricultural Economics*, 30, 495–505.

Rowe, S., Alexander, N., Clydesdale, F. M., Applebaum, R. S., Atkinson, S., Black, R. M. and Dwyer, J. T. (2009) "Funding food science and nutrition research: Financial conflicts and scientific integrity," *American Journal of Clinical Nutrition*, 89, 1285–1291.

Rubenstein, K., Heisey, D. K., Shoemaker, R., Sullivan, J. and Frisd, G. (2005) *Crop Genetic Resources: An Economic Appraisal*, USDA Economic Research Service, Washington, DC.

Rush, D., Horvitz, D. G., Seaver, W. B., Alvir, J. M., Garbowski, G. C., Leighton, J., Sloan, N. L., Johnson, S. S., Kulka, R. A. and Shanklin, D. S. (1988) "The national WIC evaluation: Evaluation of the Special Supplemental Food Program for Women, Infants and Children: I background and introduction," *American Journal of Clinical Nutrition*, 48, 389–393.

Ryan, A. S. and Zhou, W. (2006) "Lower breastfeeding rates persist among the Special Supplemental Nutrition Program for Women, Infants and Children participants, 1978–2003," *Pediatrics*, 117, 1136–1146.

Saitone, T. L. and Sexton, R. J. (2012) *Market Structure and Competition in the US Food Industries*, American Enterprise Institute, Washington, DC.

Scallan, E., Hoekstra, R. M., Angulo, F. J., Tauxe, R. V., Widdowson, M. A., Roy, S. L., Jones, J. L. and Griffin, P. M. (2011) "Foodborne illness acquired in the United States—major pathogens," *Emerging Infectious Diseases*, 17(1), 7–15.

Schanzenbach, D. W. (2009) "Do school lunches contribute to childhood obesity?" *Journal of Human Resources*, 44, 684–709.

Schechinger, A. W. and Cox, C. (2017) *Is Federal Crop Insurance Policy Leading to Another Dust Bowl?*, Environmental Working Group, Washington, DC.

Schlosser, E. (2002) *Fast Food Nation: The Dark Side of the All-American Meal*, Houghton Mifflin, New York, 2002.

Schmitz, A. and Moss, C. B. (2016) "Mechanized agriculture: Machine adoption, farm size, and labor displacement," *AgBioForum*, 18(3).

Schnepf, R. (2016) *US International Food Aid Programs: Background and Issues*, Congressional Research Service, Washington, DC.

Schnitkey, G. and Zulauf, C. (2016) "The farm safety net for field crops," *Choices Magazine*, 31(4), 1–8.

Severson, K. (2017) "Will the Trump era transform the school lunch?," *New York Times*, September 5.

Sexton, R. (2013) "Market power, misconceptions and modern agricultural markets" (AAEA presidential address), *American Journal of Agricultural Economics*, 95(2), 209–219.

Sheldon, I. (2011) "Food standards and international trade," in J. Lusk, J. Roosen and J. Shogren (eds) *The Oxford Handbook of Food Policy and Consumption*, Oxford University Press, Oxford.

Sheldon, I. M. (2017) "The competitiveness of agricultural product and input markets: a review and synthesis of recent research," *Journal of Agricultural and Applied Economics*, 49(1), 1–44.

Sims, L. S. (1998) *The Politics of Fat: Food and Nutrition Policy in America*, ME Sharpe, Armonk, NY.

Smeeding, T. (2006) "Poor people in rich nations: the United States in comparative perspective," *The Journal of Economic Perspectives*, 20, 69–90.

Smith, T., Lin, B.-H. and Lee, J.-Y. (2010) *Taxing Caloric Sweetened Beverages Potential Effects on Beverage Consumption, Calorie Intake, and Obesity*, USDA Economic Research Service, Washington, DC.

Standing, K.,Gasper, J, Riley, J., May, L., Bennici, F., Chu, A. and Dixit-Joshi, S. (2016) *Special Nutrition Program Operations Study: State and School Food Authority Policies and Practices for School Meals Programs School Year 2012–13*, Endahl, J. (Project officer), prepared by Westat for USDA Food and Nutrition Service, Alexandria, VA.

Stevenson, G. W., Ruhf, K., Lezberg, S. and Clancy, K. (2008) "Warrior, builder and weaver work: strategies for changing the food system," in C. C. Hinrichs and T. A. Lyson (eds) *Remaking the North American Food System: Strategies for Sustainability*, University of Nebraska Press, Lincoln, NE.

Stewart, H. (2011) "Food away from home," in J. Lusk, J. Roosen and J. Shogren (eds) *The Oxford Handbook of Food Policy and Consumption*, Oxford University Press, Oxford.

Stigler, G. J. (1945) "The cost of subsistence," *Journal of Farm Economics*, 27, 303–314.

Stone, D. A. (1997) *Policy Paradox: The Art of Political Decision Making*, WW Norton, New York, NY.

Sumner, D. (2011) *Picking on the Poor*, American Enterprise Institute, Washington, DC.

Sumner, D. A., Alston, J. M. and Glauber, J. W. (2010) "Evolution of the economics of agricultural policy," *American Journal of Agricultural Economics*, 92(2), 403–423.

Swann, C. A. (2010) "WIC eligibility and participation: the roles of changing policies, economic conditions and demographics," *The BE Journal of Economic Analysis & Policy*, 10(1), 1–37.

Taubes, G. (2007) *Good Calories, Bad Calories: Challenging the Conventional Wisdom on Diet, Weight Control, and Disease*, Random House of Canada, Toronto, Ontario, Canada.

Taubes, G. (2011) *Why We Get Fat: And What to Do About It*, Anchor Books, New York, NY.

Teicholz, N. (2015) "The scientific report guiding the US dietary guidelines: is it scientific?," *BMJ*, 351, h4962.

Teisl, M. (2011) "Environmental concerns in food consumption," in J.L. Lusk, J. Roosen and J. Shogren (eds) *The Oxford Handbook of the Economics of Food Consumption and Policy*, Oxford University Press, New York, NY.

Tester, M. and Langridge, P. (2010) "Breeding technologies to increase crop production in a changing world," *Science*, 327(5967), 818–822.

Todd, J. E., Mancino, L. and Lin, B. H. (2010) *The Impact of Food Away from Home on Adult Diet Quality*, USDA Economic Research Service, Washington, DC.

Todd, J. E. and Variyam, J.N. (2008) *The Decline in Consumer Use of Food Nutrition Labels, 1995–2006*, USDA Economic Research Service, Washington, DC.

Trichopoulou, A., Martínez-González, M. A., Tong, T. Y., Forouhi, N. G., Khandelwal, S., Prabhakaran, D., Mozaffarian, D. and de Lorgeril, M. (2014) "Definitions and potential health benefits of the Mediterranean diet: Views from experts around the world," *BMC Medicine*, 12(1), 112.

Trostle, R., Marti, D., Rosen, S. and Wescott, P. (2011) *Why Have Food Commodity Prices Risen Again?*, USDA Economic Research Service, Washington, DC.

U.S. Agency for International Development (2012) Fact Sheet: Food for Peace, *FY 2011 Programs*, Washington, DC.

U.S. Department of Health and Human Services, Office of Community Services (2016) *Healthy Food Financing Initiative*, www.acf.hhs.gov/ocs/programs/community-economic-development/healthy-food-financing, accessed June 15, 2017.

U.S. Department of Health and Human Services, Office of Community Services (2016) *Healthy Food Financing Initiative*, www.acf.hhs.gov/ocs/programs/community-economic-development/healthy-food-financing, accessed June 15, 2017.

U.S. Environmental Protection Agency (2017) *Inventory of U.S. Greenhouse Gas Emissions and Sinks, 1990–2015* (EPA 430-P-17–001). Washington, DC.

U.S. Government Accountability Office (2009) *U.S. Agriculture: Retail Food Prices Grew Faster Than the Prices Farmers Received for Agricultural Commodities, but Economic Research Has Not Established That Concentration Has Affected These Trends*, www.gao.gov/products/GAO-09-746R. pdf, accessed November 21, 2017.

U.S. Government Accountability Office (2010) *Food Safety: FDA Should Strengthen Its Oversight of Food Ingredients Determined to Be Generally Recognized as Safe (GRAS)*, www.gao.gov/products/GAO-10-246, accessed November 21, 2017.

U.S. Government Accountability Office (2011a) *Food Labeling: FDA Needs to Reassess Its Approach to Protecting Consumers from False or Misleading Claims*, www.gao.gov/products/GAO-11-102, accessed November 21, 2017.

U.S. Government Accountability Office (2011b) *International Food Assistance: Funding Development Projects through the Purchase, Shipment and Sale of U.S. Commodities Is Inefficient and Can Cause Adverse Market Impacts*, Washington, DC.

U.S. Government Accountability Office (2014) *Food Safety: FDA and USDA Should Strengthen Pesticide Residue Monitoring Programs and Further Disclose Monitoring Limitations*, Washington, DC.

U.S. Government Accountability Office (2017) *Food Safety: A National Strategy is Needed to Address Fragmentation in Federal Oversight*, Washington, DC.

United Nations, Department of Economic and Social Affairs, Population Division (2017) *World Population Prospects: The 2017 Revision, Key Findings and Advance Tables*, Working Paper No. ESA/P/WP/248.

Unnevehr, L. J. and Jensen, H. H. (2005) "Industry costs to make food safe: now and under a risk-based system," in S. A. Hoffman and M. R. Taylor (eds) *Toward Safer Food: Perspectives on Risk and Priority Setting*, Resources for the Future Press, Washington, DC.

U.S. Department of Health and Human Services and US Department of Agriculture (2015) *2015–2020 Dietary Guidelines for Americans. 8th ed.*, Washington, DC, December.

USDA (2012) *FY 2013: Budget Summary and Annual Performance Plan*, USDA, Washington, DC.

USDA Economic Research Service (2012b) *U.S. Sugar Production*, www.ers.usda.gov/topics/crops/sugar-sweeteners/background.aspx, accessed November 13, 2012.

USDA Economic Research Service (2017) *Food Expenditures by Families and Individuals as a Share of Disposable Personal Income*, www.ers.usda.gov/data-products/food-expenditures.aspx, accessed July 30, 2017.

USDA Food Safety Inspection Service (1999) *Generic HACCP Model for Poultry Slaughter*, Washington, DC.

USDA Food and Nutrition Service (2016) "The Emergency Food Assistance Program (TEFAP)," *Nutrition Program Fact Sheet* (June), www.fns.usda.gov/sites/default/files/tefap/pfs-tefap.pdf, accessed June 14, 2017.

USDA Interagency Agricultural Projections Committee (2016) *USDA Agricultural Projections to 2025*, USDA, Washington, DC.

Ver Ploeg, M., Breneman, V., Farrigan, T., Hamrick, K., Hopkins, D., Kaufman, P., Lin, B.H., Nord, M., Smith, T. and Williams, R. (2009) Access to Affordable and Nutritious Food: Measuring and Understanding Food Deserts and Their Consequences. *Report to Congress*, USDA Economic Research Service, Washington, DC, www.ers.usda.gov/publications/pub-details/?pubid=42729, accessed June 26, 2012.

Ver Ploeg, M., Mancino, L., Todd, J. E., Clay, D. M. and Scharadin, B. (2015) *Where Do Americans Usually Shop for Food and how Do They Travel to Get There?: Initial Findings from the National Household Food Acquisition and Purchase Survey*, USDA Economic Research Service, Washington, DC.

Vina, S. (2006) *The Private Testing of Mad Cow Disease: Legal Issues*, Congressional Research Service, Washington, DC.

Volpe, R., Kuhns, A. and Jaenicke, T. (2017) *Store Formats and Patterns in Household Grocery Purchases*, USDA Economic Research Service, Washington, DC.

Vos, N. (2017). "Agricultural drainage and the Des Moines water works Lawsuit," *Drake Journal of Agricultural Law*, 22, 109–403.

Walthall, C. L., J. Hatfield, P. Backlund, L. Lengnick, E. Marshall, M. Walsh, S. Adkins, M. Aillery, E. A. Ainsworth, C. Ammann, C. J. Anderson, I. Bartomeus, L. H. Baumgard, F. Booker, B. Bradley, D. M. Blumenthal, J. Bunce, K. Burkey, S. M. Dabney, J. A. Delgado, J. Dukes, A. Funk, K. Garrett, M. Glenn, D. A. Grantz, D. Goodrich, S. Hu, R. C. Izaurralde, R. A. C. Jones, S-H. Kim, A. D. B. Leaky, K. Lewers, T. L. Mader, A. McClung, J. Morgan, D. J. Muth, M. Nearing, D. M. Oosterhuis, D. Ort, C. Parmesan, W. T. Pettigrew, W. Polley, R. Rader, C. Rice, M. Rivington, E. Rosskopf, W. A. Salas, L. E. Sollenberger, R. Srygley, C. Stöckle, E. S. Takle, D. Timlin, J. W. White, R. Winfree, L. Wright-Morton and L. H. Ziska (2013) *Climate Change and Agriculture in the United States: Effects and Adaptation*, USDA Technical Bulletin 1935, Washington, DC.

Whaley, S. E., Koleilat, M., Whaley, M., Gomez, J., Meehan, K. and Saluja, K. (2012) "Impact of policy changes on infant feeding decisions among low-income women participating in the Special Supplemental Nutrition Program for Women, Infants, and Children," *American Journal of Public Health*, 102(12), 2269–2273.

Whitaker, R. C. (2004) "Predicting preschooler obesity at birth: the role of maternal obesity in early pregnancy," *Pediatrics*, 114, e29–e36.

Wiebe, K. D. and Gollehon, N. R. (2006) *Agricultural Resources and Environmental Indicators*, USDA Economic Research Service, Washington, DC.

Wilde, P. (2006) "Federal communication about obesity in the dietary guidelines and checkoff programs," *Obesity*, 14(6), 967–973.

Wilde, P. (2009) "Self-regulation and the response to concerns about food and beverage marketing to children in the United States," *Nutrition Reviews*, 67(3), 155–166.

Wilde, P. E. (2011) "Food security policy in developed countries," in J. Lusk, J. Roosen and J. Shogren (eds) *The Oxford Handbook of the Economics of Food Consumption and Policy*, Oxford University Press, New York, NY.

Wilde, P. E. (2012) "The new normal: The Supplemental Nutrition Assistance Program (SNAP)," *American Journal of Agricultural Economics*, 94 (advance publication online).

Wilde, P. E. and Llobrera, J. (2009) "Using the Thrifty Food Plan to assess the cost of a nutritious diet," *Journal of Consumer Affairs*, 43, 274–304.

Wilde, P. E. and Ranney, C. K. (2000) "The monthly food stamp cycle: Shopping frequency and food intake decisions in an endogenous switching regression framework," *American Journal of Agricultural Economics*, 82, 200–213.

Wilde, P. E., Troy, L. and Rogers, B. (2009) "Food stamps and food spending: An Engel function approach," *American Journal of Agricultural Economics*, 91(2), 416–430.

Wilde, P., Klerman, J., Olsho, L. and Bartlett, S. (2015) "Explaining the impact of USDA's Healthy Incentives Pilot on different spending outcomes," *Applied Economic Perspectives & Policy* (published online, Nov 30: 10.1093/aepp/ppv028).

Wilde, P., Llobrera, J. and Ver Ploeg, M. (2014) "Population density, poverty, and food retail access in the United States: An empirical approach," *International Food and Agribusiness Management Review*, 17, 171–187.

Wilde, P. E., Wolf, A., Fernandes, M. and Collins, A. (2012) "Food-package assignments and breastfeeding initiation before and after a change in the Special Supplemental Nutrition Program for Women, Infants and Children," *American Journal of Clinical Nutrition*, 96(3), 560–566.

Wilson, D. and Roberts, J. (2012) "Special report: How Washington went soft on childhood obesity," *Reuters*, www.reuters.com/article/2012/04/27/us-usa-foodlobby-idUS-BRE83Q0ED20120427, accessed November 22, 2017.

Willett, W., Skerrett, P. J., Giovannucci, E. L. and Callahan, M. (2005) *Eat, Drink, and Be Healthy: the Harvard Medical School Guide to Healthy Eating*, Free Press, New York, NY.

Wilson, J. Q. (1989) *Bureaucracy: What Government Agencies Do and Why They Do It*, Basic Books, New York, NY.

Winne, M. (2008) *Closing the Food Gap: Resetting the Table in the Land of Plenty*, Beacon Press, Boston, MA.

Wohlgenant, M. K. (2011) *Sweets for the Sweet: The Costly Benefits of the US Sugar Program*, American Enterprise Institute, Washington, DC.

Wooldridge, J. M. (2015) *Introductory Econometrics: A Modern Approach (Sixth Edition)*, South-Western Cengage Learning, Mason, OH.

World Bank (2007) *World Development Report, 2008: Agriculture for Development*, World Bank, Washington, DC.

World Bank (2009) *World Development Report, 2010: Development and Climate Change*, World Bank, Washington, DC.

World Bank (2017) *Atlas of Sustainable Development Goals 2017: World Development Indicators*, World Bank, Washington, DC.

World Cancer Research Fund and American Institute for Cancer Research (2007) *Food, Nutrition, Physical Activity, and the Prevention of Cancer: A Global Perspective*, American Institute for Cancer Research, Washington, DC.

Yaktine, A. L. and Caswell, J. A. (2014) "SNAP benefits: Can an adequate benefit be defined?," *Advances in Nutrition: An International Review Journal*, 5(1), 21–26.

Zemel, M. B., Richards, J., Mathis, S., Milstead, A., Gebhardt, L. and Silva, E. (2005) "Dairy augmentation of total and central fat loss in obese subjects," *International Journal of Obesity*, 29(4), 391–397.

Ziliak, J. P. (2016) *Modernizing SNAP Benefits*, Brookings Institution (Policy Proposal 2016–06), Washington, DC.

Index